This
Fine
Place
So Far
From
Home

**Voices of
Academics
from the
Working
Class**

edited by
**C. L.
Barney
Dews**

and

**Carolyn
Leste
Law**

 Temple
University
Press
Philadelphia

This
Fine
Place
So Far
From
Home

Temple University Press, Philadelphia 19122
Copyright © 1995 by Temple University, except Chapter 14, which is © Wilson J. Moses
All rights reserved
Published 1995
Printed in the United States of America

☉ The paper used in this book meets the requirements of the American National
Standard for Information Sciences—Permanence of Paper for Printed Library Materials,
ANSI Z39.48-1984

Text design by Adrianne Onderdonk Dudden

Library of Congress Cataloging-in-Publication Data
This fine place so far from home : voices of academics from the
    working class / edited by C. L. Barney Dews and Carolyn Leste Law.
        p.   cm.
    Includes bibliographical references.
    ISBN 1-56639-290-X (alk. paper). — ISBN 1-56639-291-8 (pbk. :
alk. paper)
    1. Working class—Education (Higher)—United States.   2. College
teachers—United States—Social conditions.   3. Social mobility—
United States.   I. Dews, C. L. Barney (Carlos Lee Barney), 1963–
II. Law, Carolyn Leste, 1961–
LC5051.T45   1995
378.1'2—dc20   94-28730

ISBN 13: 978-1-56639-291-4 (paper : alk. paper)

111507P

Contents

Acknowledgments   **viii**

Introduction   1
CAROLYN LESTE LAW

Part One   Lives Are Not Essays

1   Stupid Rich Bastards   13
LAUREL JOHNSON BLACK

2   A Real Class Act: Searching for Identity in the "Classless" Society   26
JULIE A. CHARLIP

3   Bronx Syndrome   41
STEPHEN GARGER

4   The Screenwriter's Tale   54
JENNIFER LAWLER

5   You Were Raised Better Than That   66
NATON LESLIE

6   In the Shadow of My Old Kentucky Home   75
GEORGE T. MARTIN, JR.

7   *Todos Vuelven:* From Potrero Hill to UCLA   87
ROSA MARÍA PEGUEROS

8   Another Day's Journey: An African American in Higher Education   106
GLORIA D. WARREN

Part Two Border States

9 Useful Knowledge **127**
MARY CAPPELLO

10 A Carpenter's Daughter **137**
RENNY CHRISTOPHER

11 Paper Mills **151**
HEATHER J. HICKS

12 The Social Construction of a Working-Class
Academic **159**
DWIGHT LANG

13 Working-Class Women as Academics: Seeing
in Two Directions, Awkwardly **177**
NANCY LAPAGLIA

14 Ambivalent Maybe **187**
WILSON J. MOSES

15 Class Matters: Symbolic Boundaries and
Cultural Exclusion **200**
SHARON O'DAIR

16 Nowhere at Home: Toward a Phenomenology
of Working-Class Consciousness **209**
CHRISTINE OVERALL

17 Past Voices, Present Speakers **221**
DONNA BURNS PHILLIPS

Part Three The Intellectual Worker/
The Academic Workplace

18 Workin' at the U. **233**
MILAN KOVACOVIC

19 Class, Composition, and Reform in
Departments of English: A Personal
Account **249**
RAYMOND A. MAZUREK

20   Complicity in Class Codes: The Exclusionary
Function of Education   **263**
IRVIN PECKHAM

21   Is There a Working-Class History?   **277**
WILLIAM A. PELZ

22   Psychology's Class Blindness: Investment in
the Status Quo   **286**
DEBORAH PIPER

23   Working It Out: Values, Perspectives, and
Autobiography   **297**
JOHN SUMSER

Part Four   Awayward Mobility

24   The Work of Professing (A Letter to
Home)   **309**
MICHAEL SCHWALBE

Afterword   **332**
C. L. BARNEY DEWS

About the Contributors   **337**

Acknowledgments

Any project of this sort is indebted, directly and indirectly, to many people. We thank all the faculty and graduate students in the English Department at the University of Minnesota who encouraged us with their enthusiasm and helpful insights. Thanks to Kent Bales, Robin Brown, Karen Frederickson, Phil Furia, Rose Hendrickson, and Laureen Norby for invaluable assistance in every category. We would especially like to acknowledge Shirley Nelson Garner, a most conscientious mentor, for her advice at the critical early stages of this project.

We extend thanks to Meg Brissenden, Mary Lymer, Geri Malandra, Susan Noakes, and Cheryl Noble at the University of Minnesota for their generous encouragement. We also appreciate the interest shown throughout the editing of this volume by numerous colleagues around the country, especially Jake Ryan at Ithaca College. At Temple University Press, we are grateful to Michael Ames and Micah Kleit for their fine work and faith in the book.

We owe special thanks to Bret Pearson for his constant support, patience, and good humor. We would also like to extend thanks to Jill Braithwaite, Rachelle Turner, and Craig Anderson for special help along the way. Finally, we wish to thank all those who entrusted us with their stories but whose essays we were not able to include in the book. The knowledge that this book speaks to and for so many of us was our greatest inspiration.

This
Fine
Place
So Far
From
Home

Introduction

Carolyn Leste Law

I

When I mentioned to my mother that I was leaving my teaching job (after the third year of a three-year, untenurable lectureship) at a regional state university in a small town in Missouri to pursue a Ph.D. in literature in Minnesota, she said to me, "Education destroys something." I was stunned. Despite all the reactions and objections I had anticipated and for which I had rehearsed convincing rebuttals, I had not foreseen this one. Had she complained that my master's degree wasn't paid for yet or that she'd miss me if I moved so far from home, I could have argued with her. But never had my mother spoken so eloquently before. In that statement, so absolute, so definite, so dazzlingly honest, is expressed the cruel duality of the working-class student in higher education, some of whom go on to become working-class academics like me and the others represented in this book.

While I have committed my life to an academic career in the belief that, in the words of Donna Burns Phillips in her chapter "Past Voices, Present Speakers," "Education is addition," I had that day to acknowledge that my mother was right. In my trajectory from working-class family of origin to the threshold of middle-class professional status, I have suffered a loss my present context doesn't even recognize as a loss; my education *has* destroyed something even while it has been re-creating me in its own image. The pride I feel in my academic and professional achievements, generously applauded by the institutions of higher education that believe they have served me, believe that I am their success story, is always tempered by the guilt I feel in having chosen a life path that has made me virtually unrecognizable to my kin. This book is about the ambivalence inherent in trajectories such as mine. Ambivalence, more than any other theme, is the common denominator in the stories of "awayward mobility," as Michael Schwalbe terms it in "The Work of Professing (A Letter to Home)," that are collected here.

What my co-editor and I hope to do in this volume is to open a space where we can finally say out loud what we have been saying clandestinely to one another for some time: that where we come from (the South, the working class) matters absolutely in how we interact with the academy now, with our colleagues, with our students, with the faceless mechanism that is the institution. We invited other academics from working-class families of origin to volunteer their own stories and experiences of academia, to fill this space with voices flavored with the accents, dialects, and colors of diverse working-class backgrounds. They responded in numbers we never dreamed of. Collectively, the voices of these scholars and teachers from New England to the Northwest, from Canada to southern California, began to blend in a shared story of class consciousness and class ambiguity peculiar to the working class in higher education.

II

I began college in the last months of the Carter administration. I attribute my college education solely to the death of my father when I was eight years old. At eighteen I would have forfeited Social Security payments had I chosen not to go to college. I thought my brother was simply foolish to quit after one year at a community college, foolish to turn down a tidy stipend. Now when I look back at the circumstances under which I went to college, a modest state school, a former normal school, I feel numb. The trade-off, my father's life in exchange for my bachelor's degree, is a transaction I can hardly ponder without feeling physically ill.

My ambition then was to become an English teacher. I admired my high school teachers; I liked their lives (what I could see of them). My mother, I know, was proud of me and glad that I was doing well in a world she had never known. What she could not have guessed, though, was that in the course of my teacher training, I learned, through myriad covert (and some not so covert) pressures and practices, to feel increasingly ashamed of my home, of my family. Again and again, I heard that children who do not read, whose parents work too hard and who have little time or skills to read to them, whose homes are not "literate" but oral and often pretty nonverbal as well, children who have never been taken to an art museum or who do not have library cards, these are the ones at risk, the ones most likely to fail (be failed by?) the traditional academic setting, in practical terms, the ones who make a teacher's job so daily frustrating. Never once did any of my professors entertain the thought that I or any of my classmates could possibly have been one of those children. That those children are also most often children of the working class seemed unremarkable at the time. It never occurred to me to question the implicit classism and institutional biases that view the child as the problem, not the system or the curriculum. I wanted then only to ask, "But what about me? How do you explain me?" but, of course, I did not dare.

It becomes the university's job to help children of the working class, when by some fluke or flash of good fortune they become undergraduates, to overcome their backgrounds. As Laurel Johnson Black writes in "Stupid Rich Bastards," "It's about every child's nightmare of losing her family and the ways in which the [academy] tries to make that nightmare come true, to make it not a nightmare but a dream, a goal." I eventually made that dream my own and day by day betrayed my self in order to gain acceptance in the academic community; my strategy was silence and lies. I never confessed that I recognized my own home in the patronizing, contemptuous examples of my well-intentioned professors, which every day increased my resolve to erase my past and elude the humiliation of being found an imposter. I had never seen my mother or my brother read a book. There were no books displayed in my home, except a 1955 edition of the *World Book Encyclopedia* (I was born in 1961). The few books my family owned were stored in a cupboard. One was *The Torch Is Passed,* about the assassination of John F. Kennedy, and another was a souvenir copy of *The Shepherd of the Hills* by Harold Bell Wright, a novel sold by the millions in the Ozarks and a book that I love more than I can say. While I knew that my mother was (and is still) the most competent person I have ever known and that my brother has skills and common sense that have made him equally successful in a stock car and in an executive meeting, and while I knew that my father could construct buildings from the ground up just like the ones my professors' cluttered offices were in, I was bombarded with messages discounting their competencies and, by extension, discounting their lives.

What I learned in teacher training was that I could not explain my own existence. What my mother doesn't know is that I learned, in my education curriculum and less directly in my humanities curriculum, to shift my allegiance, to complain about parents *just like mine!* To shake my head at students *just like me.* To undervalue and criticize high school graduates exactly like I was, who were in fact me. I learned to join conversations about the collapse of standards and the dilution of higher education across the country where open-admissions policies let any riff-raff in. But only my mother could teach me much later about the toll such relentless cognitive dissonance extracted from me. Even as early as my freshman year, I was learning to become a double agent, learning to lie with conviction in two contexts at once and fearing expulsion from both.

It seems I became a literary scholar against all odds. But my success in academia has been possible only through years of silence. Until recently, I never spoke about my family at school, and I never spoke about school with my family. As a student I knew that if I were to identify myself as working class in the English Department, I might be congratulated as an interesting exception but that their estimation of my working-class home would never really rise. And the effort required to defend my family in what I knew was a hostile environment was just too great. As an undergraduate, I wanted only to be accepted into the club, the university, not to champion the working class. So you better believe I kept my mouth shut.

At home, I could not bring myself to talk about books or ideas that never intersected with the lives of my mother and brother, my cousins and extended family. To talk about my studies seemed ridiculous and stuck-up at best in a context that appeared to be as mistrustful of academia as academia was condescending to it. No one in my family ever wrote a college paper, no one ever tried to enroll in classes that were closed, no one ever put together a degree program, and, more to the point, no one ever cared about such things. So you better believe I kept my mouth shut there too.

When I told my mother that Barney and I were preparing this book, she was torn between pride and anger. She bristled with fear that I might embarrass her, make fun of her, sound ungrateful or disrespectful. I want to tell her now that this book is our attempt finally to *stop* being embarrassed after a very long time of consciously hiding our pasts from the view of our colleagues and students, to reveal our working-class roots not in the terms of the academy that would seek to degrade them, but to reclaim our past lives, as well as the present lives of our families, through autobiography and to make those lives relevant in critically important ways to the work we do and will do as professors.

When I was teaching at that regional state university in Missouri, I worked with students very much like I had been, typically first-generation college students underprepared for college studies. They were mostly white rural and suburban and African American urban high school graduates whose parents had sent them off to school in the fall, much as my mother had, hoping for them the realization of the American Dream, but also hoping against hope that they'd be able to recognize their sons and daughters when the university was done with them. Go to college, they said, learn to do less back-breaking, soul-breaking work than we have had to suffer, learn to wear white collars. Be better off than your drop-out cousins, live easier lives overall, but come home to us essentially the same. In their heart of hearts, these parents wanted their children to return home to them virtually unchanged by their sojourn in the academy, so mysterious and impenetrable a place they might as well have sent their kids up the Amazon. These parents gave their children mixed messages about school and learning (do well but don't get too smart; succeed but don't make us look stupid; pursue your lofty goals with enthusiasm but don't become one of "them") that reflected their own mixed feelings. Working-class families, whether they are able to articulate it or not, know that a college degree has everything to do with class, unlike professional or managerial-class families, who believe it has to do with merit and entitlement. They know that somehow the very existence of a college degree undermines and actually threatens their children's and, consequently, their own working-class identity. In the end, they do not want what they would wish for.

III

The divisions of this book are intended only to group themes and to make the book more readable and coherent, not to pigeonhole or define the essays or the authors. In fact, certain themes (ambivalence, for instance) and specific rhetorical strategies (autobiography and narrative) wind through all the parts and the individual pieces. The "Lives Are Not Essays" part of this book argues that only autobiography is a sensitive enough instrument to register the subtle activity of social class in a milieu in which class is supposedly a nonfactor. Autobiography, or any other subjective trope, has traditionally been suspect in "serious" works of scholarship. To introduce one's childhood into a piece of writing intended for an academic audience feels inappropriate, "soft," or decidedly unprofessional to many of us trained in objectivist disciplines or academic conventions. Many of the contributors to this book, not just in this section, mentioned that they had never written in this style before and that the experience was both scary and exhilarating.

The soil for this work in the academy has obviously been prepared by the efforts of feminists, persons of color, and gays and lesbians, and by the development of fields of inquiry intent on making difference visible and relevant to the university and society at large. These pursuits, which have always recognized class as a distinct marker but have often seemed unable genuinely to engage it, teach us that when one has no voice one is as good as invisible, and invisibility is, in the long run, intolerable. The autobiographies in "Lives Are Not Essays" explode the crucial illusion upon which the self-congratulatory institution of higher education depends, that we are all middle-class here because we are indeed "here."

Several significant themes recur in this part: the centrality of language as a marker of difference (both in the university and at home); the importance of reading in childhood to the possibility of a life as an academic and the factor of voracious reading in childhood in contributing to a sense of separateness from one's family; and the importance of mentoring in the face of extreme naïveté. Stephen Garger's essay, "Bronx Syndrome," for instance, recounts the ongoing struggles to reconcile the ways of communicating in two different worlds. In essay after essay, we learn that many working-class academics begin as working-class readers and suffer for it in both worlds—feeling conspicuous for reading at home, feeling shamed at school for reading the "wrong" things. Ultimately, all these narratives acknowledge the influence of caring teachers, some in high school, others in colleges and universities. Unfortunately, these stories also make plain the stunting influence of a lack of mentoring or hateful, discouraging teachers and professors.

It is remarkable that certain events and experiences emerge consistently in the anecdotes, reconstructions, and life stories of otherwise very different people. Never would I have imagined, for example, that a white boy growing up in Appalachia (George T. Martin, Jr.) might share a common estrangement from family or have motives, ambitions, and frustrations similar to those of a young Latina in San Francisco (Rosa María Pegueros). Class poses different dilemmas than those posed by either race or gender in the academy. We do not cease being men and women, for instance, when we become doctors of philosophy. But, most of us do cease being working class when we become professors. (Thus the oxymoronic puzzle in the phrase "working-class academic.")

While our gender and race identities, comparatively stable and usually marked by readily visible signs, always send messages whether we intend them or not, our class identity is a good deal less stable and marked by signs more easily concealed. In order to claim working-class identity in a context that presumes middle-class homogeneity, we must *do* something. I, like the authors in "Lives Are Not Essays," had to choose to disclose myself, a politically charged gesture for which the university offers few opportunities; it in fact actively discourages such disclosure. In terms of self-disclosure, working-class autobiography is like gay and lesbian identity politics, which is also threatening to the "standards" and "discipline" of the essentially conservative institution.

The accounts in Part Two, "Border States," are full of images of the journey. These stories emphasize the position of working-class academics in the terrain of society. What is most characteristic about these essays is the uncomfortably ambiguous stance of the border crosser. Crossing from one world to another is never fully achieved for the working-class academic;

the transformation is never complete. In "The Social Construction of a Working-Class Academic," Dwight Lang writes:

> Many years ago I began an expedition and am still making my way. Having traveled across class lines, I am conscious of the realities and meanings of social class in America, perhaps more than others who remain in their class of origin. In many ways, I am carrying on a strong family tradition of geographical and social mobility that dates to the waves of European immigration to North America and to earlier decades when family members in Europe and Russia were mobile by choice and lifestyle as well as because of dramatic political and economic changes.

While one can appear to be a native in an adopted land, one is always haunted by voices from the other side of the border. These are narratives of profound conflict, of persons feeling out of place in both worlds and compelled as Nancy LaPaglia is to see "in two directions, awkwardly." These are stories of an ongoing search for community, a sense of being pushed and pulled between fear of alienation and the desire for camaraderie. Again and again, the stories vacillate between escape and arrival, perhaps most dramatically in Christine Overall's essay. She writes in "Nowhere at Home": "The presence in the university of faculty from the working class appears to confirm the myth of upward mobility. We must buy into academia in order to get out of the working class, but in doing so we also buy into the denigration of our origins and the preservation of class inequities. In the end, it seems the price of successful escape is to be intellectually and socially 'nowhere at home.'" These are stories about finding strength in numbers, about searching for colleagues but fearing that, like an imposter, one will always be the outsider.

Part Three, "The Intellectual Worker/The Academic Workplace," critiques disciplinarity and class-bound definitions of work and success. These accounts analyze the assumptions the university makes about the lives academics lead and the ways these assumptions trickle down to undergraduates in our classrooms. They compare our professional lives (research, teaching, campus politics) to other ways of working, experienced first hand. These essays examine the "exclusionary function," as Irvin Peckham puts it, and practices of our disciplines and the subtle ways with which the "classless" institution perpetuates itself. In this section the authors also concede their ambivalence. However much we might complain about and perhaps resent the university as an institution that has caused us pain and loss, if you press any one of us from the working class who knows what work is really about, we have to admit that this is a pretty fine place to be. Milan Kovacovic writes, "personal complaints seem unbecoming at this point. Tenure . . . gives me the option of determining my activities freely and thus maintaining my self-esteem and integrity. . . . My working conditions are truly incomparable!" Still, good working conditions cannot lull working-class academics into ignoring the shaming that the institution exerts on working-class faculty and students. The academy can't buy our silence with relatively good working conditions.

Part Four, "Awayward Mobility," is an open letter to the working-class parents who have unwittingly done so much to contribute to the loss of their children. In "The Work of Professing (A Letter to Home)," Michael Schwalbe attempts to explain to his parents what his life is like in the academy. While the other essays and divisions in the book address the academy about where we're from, Schwalbe explains where we are to the people we've left behind. By writing to his parents, literally because they participated in the production of his essay, he brings the book full circle. His closing, "Love, Mike," echoes our own goodbyes to people from home as we have returned to our academic lives.

IV

Neither Barney nor I is a sociologist. We have not attempted to define the admittedly troublesome term "working-class academic." Many who heard about our project asked what we had in mind, questioning the contradiction implicit in the term. Is income a viable marker of class? Should we define "working class" by level of parents' education (see Irvin Peckham's essay) or by how dirty or dangerous one's job is? Can a small business owner, such as Julie Charlip's father, be considered working class? Charlip records in "A Real Class Act" the definition of one sociology professor: "If you earn thirty thousand dollars a year working in an assembly plant, come home from work, open a beer and watch the game, you are working class; if you earn twenty thousand dollars a year as a school teacher, come home from work to a glass of white wine and PBS, you are middle class." We felt it was more important for contributors to define themselves than to impose any definition that would only hinder the process of individuals making sense of their lived experience. Our intent was never to pathologize or limit a group of people. Academics in this book, for our purely descriptive purposes and to our qualitative satisfaction, are working class if they say they are. While several of the contributors speak of working-class "credentials," more helpful I think is not pondering legitimacy but speaking with sincerity; those who identify with the "working class" for whatever reasons know the sense of displacement this book is about and the complex, ambivalent feelings it represents.

With this open attitude in mind, we posted a national call for papers. We offered no definition and expressed no preference for style or point of view. The project was driven all along by a desire to identify and connect. But it is important to acknowledge that not all possible voices or kinds of experiences are represented. We cast our net wide and landed an interestingly varied group of contributors. We were surprised, for instance, by a large number of essays from gay men and lesbians. Contributions were nearly evenly split between men and women. Every academic rank and every kind of college and university were represented. We received essays from professors in dozens of different academic arts and sciences. They came from administrators as well as from some who had left the profession for good. Probably a third of the contributors were graduate students at various stages in their work. This diversity, however, does not disguise two truths of equal opportunity in higher education: that only a tiny fraction of professionals in higher education are nonwhite and that, further, persons of color on university and college faculties are unbelievably overburdened because academia is more interested in the appearance of diversity than in the actual work of developing programs less discouraging to nonwhite students and faculty.

V

I paint walls for relaxation. The concreteness of it appeals to me. I bowl on a league every Sunday night. Only recently, though, have I been able to confess to university colleagues that I am an avid bowler and only recently have I described in detail to my teammates what I do for money. The prejudice against bowling alleys in departments of English is daunting; among my bowling pals the apparent cushiness of my academic life is embarrassing. Still, I find the immediate gratification of physical work and sport irresistible. When I gut my friends' kitchen during remodeling, something tangible, measurable, undeniably obvious happens. Like Renny Christopher in her enjoyment of carpentry or John Sumser's appreciation for Japanese joinery, I respect the solidity and certainty of labor. To make a crashing strike in the tenth frame is absolutely refreshing and unambiguous. Compared to the atmosphere of abstraction I spend most of my day breathing, these activities are small breaks of clarity and precision.

In the course of editing this book, in reading and rereading these rich and vibrant essays, I recognize in it parts of my own history. Through these essays I have come to believe that I might yet regain what I had feared I'd lost forever, my working-class origin, and reconcile it to the (in many ways enviable) life I live now. With this book perhaps I can convince my mother that education indeed builds something.

Deborah Piper, in "Psychology's Class Blindness: Investment in the Status Quo," recounts working with nontraditional students in an alternative baccalaureate program. What she found might have been predicted, that her students, mostly minority women, suffered greatly at the hands of formal education. Their struggle was obviously overdetermined, effected by the racist, sexist, and ageist, in addition to classist, biases of the institution. She writes: "It became clear to me . . . that the place to begin helping these students with reading and writing skills was by building on their own narratives, their own life experiences. . . . to illuminate the incredible talents and strengths of these women as they wrote of finding ways to advocate for themselves and their communities. . . . All became empowered by their own stories." Piper, in describing her students' experiences, might very well be describing her own life in the academy. Her essay does for her what she recognizes as most helpful for her students. By creating an academic self-text for publication in this book, she is "building on her own narrative, her own life experiences" to overcome the institutional oppression of working-class students, herself included. This book offers its contributors the space to do that work for themselves, the work Piper encourages her working-class students to perform—to find power in their own life stories. And I would add, to become empowered by the life stories of others as well. What working-class academics' autobiographies do best is to develop community and aver that the emperor has no clothes. We are finding that the working-class academic is not so rare as we often feel ourselves to be in the tense isolation of academic departments. While the illusion of class homogeneity in academia persists, partly because until fairly recently assimilation was the only prudent route open to us, that illusion, we contend, is wearing thin.

Part One | Lives Are Not Essays

1

Stupid Rich Bastards

Laurel Johnson Black

Sunday morning, six o'clock. Dad knocks on my door and in a stage whisper tells me to get up and get going. Trying not to wake up my sister, I crawl out of bed into the chilly Massachusetts air and pull on jeans, a T-shirt, a sweatshirt, and sneakers. Nothing that can't get dirty. This isn't church, but it might as well be, an education full of rituals, its own language, its mystery and rewards, its punishments for falling away.

Every Sunday, each child in turn went with Dad to the flea markets, the yard sales, the junk yards, the little stores with names like "Bob's Salvage," "Junk n Stuff," or "The Treasure House." Even in winter, when the outdoor flea markets closed down and leaves spun with litter in circles in the yards, the salvage stores stood waiting for us, bleak and weathered, paint hanging in little flaps from the concrete-block walls, and our breath hanging in the still, frigid air surrounding the old desks and radio tubes, the file cabinets and chandeliers. In each place the man behind the counter would grab the lapels of his old wool coat and pull them tighter around him, saying how one day he'd like to heat the joint. Dad would tell him about the great buy we just saw at the last place but had to pass up this time and then ask him what was new. And each time the answer was, "In heayah? Nothin's evah new! But I got some stuff I didn't have befoah!" They'd laugh with one another, and I would trace my initials next to someone else's in the dust on the display cabinet.

In summer, we passed by the vendors who hawked T-shirts, socks, perfume, or cheap jewelry and walked to the tables covered with stuff from home, tables full of things that someone had wanted and needed for a long time until they needed money more, to pay their rent, fix their car, or feed the next child. Wall hangings, little plaques, beverage glasses with superheroes on them, ashtrays, bedspreads, tricycles, lawn mowers, table lamps, kitchen pots and pans, picture frames, shoes, a spice rack. Always behind one of these tables stood an older man, deeply tanned and showing muscles from long years of hard work, gray-haired and with a cigarette and a hopeful smile, always willing to come down a little on an item, even though it meant a lot to him. Sometimes his wife would also be there, heavy, quiet, holding a styrofoam cup of coffee, sitting in a webbed lawn chair set back a little from the table, judging those who would judge the things she had loved and used for so long.

We touched these items carefully, with respect, because we were that child who needed to be fed, because we knew what it felt like to have your things laid on such a table, touched by many hands and turned over and over while the dew burned off and the pavement heated up and people began to move as though through water, their legs lost in the shimmering heat that slipped sticky arms around buyers, sellers, lookers, and dreamers. And the language of these people behind the tables, and those who re-spected them and understood why they were there, filled the air like the smell of French fries from the dirty little restaurant next door and hung in my mind and sifted down into my heart.

This is not an essay. This is a story. My life is not an essay. We don't live essays or tell them to each other on the front steps on hot nights with beer or iced coffee and pretzels or pass them on to our children or dream them. This is a story, one about love and fear. It's about every child's nightmare of losing her family and the ways in which the world I now tentatively live in tries to make that nightmare come true, to make it not a nightmare but a dream, a goal.

There are a lot of holes in this story that get filled in, as with all stories, differently depending upon who's listening, depending on how I need to fill them in. There's a plot, a very simple one: a young woman goes from poverty to the middle class using education to move closer and closer to the stupid rich bastards she has heard about all her life. She finds ever larger contexts into which she can place everything, can get perspective. ("Perspective"—a word her father used to describe why he kept driving away, a word her mother told her meant to make things seem small and unimportant.) Until someone says "Fuck you!" and it all collapses. Then she pulls it back to-gether like a quilt she had as a child, one she hid under rather than take her medicine, one she gasped under in the stifling heat rather than run through her room with the hornet circling in it. This is a story about war and injury, about stuffing the holes blown in hearts and brains and tongues with words, with the batting of anger and desire. It's about language.

Language for me has always been inseparable from what I am, from what and who people are. My house was filled with the language I associate with the working class and the poor, people who haven't the means to physically keep all the "dirty" parts of life at bay and who see no reason to do so with words. Shouting to each other across the yards in the old mill town where I grew up, my mother and her friends Pat and Barbara kept up their friendship and shared gossip and complaints about their lives. They wove their voices into the fabric of words and life I knew. As we played after school in the stand of woods along the river down behind the factory, we heard our names called for supper. The more time we took to get home to the table, the sharper the tone became and the longer the wonderful string of curses stretched out, echoing off the brick walls.

We talked about whatever touched us as we sat down to eat—who had stopped up the upstairs toilet, who had fought in the hallway at school, the girl who was stabbed in the head with a fork in the lunchroom, name calling on the bus, whether the home economics teacher was having an affair with the phys. ed. teacher, what my father saw in the house he'd just put a tub in, who we knew who'd been arrested. Bodily functions, secretions, garbage, crimes and delinquency, who got away with what were as much a part of our language as they were of our lives. They were part of the humor that filled my home. My father rising up from his chair to fart, shouting out in mock seriousness, " 'Repoaht from the reah!' the sahgent replied," set us off in hysterics, imitations, and stories of passed gas and the contexts that made them so funny. Swearing was also a part of our lives—among adults, among kids away from their parents, and in the bad kids' homes, everyone swore fluently before they were eighteen or out of school. "Damn" and "shit" were every other word and so became like "and" and "well" to us as we talked with each other.

I lived in a web of narrative, something I've missed in graduate school. My father was a storyteller and a traveler, a man who would go away for a week or two at a time on "business" of an undetermined nature. When he came back, he didn't bring presents but stories. Only a few years ago did I realize why the tale of Odysseus had seemed so familiar to me in the eighth grade and again as an undergraduate. He was a relative, or a friend, not just a character in an old story. In the tales told by my father and the men he bartered with, the "stupid rich bastards" almost always "got it" in the end, outwitted by the poor little guy. I learned that the stupid rich bastards always underestimated us, always thought we were as dumb as we were poor, always mistook our silence for ignorance, our shabby clothes and rusted cars for lack of ambition or enterprise. And so they got taken, and sharing stories about winning these small battles made us feel better about losing the war.

My father knew all the regular merchants at the flea markets. As we wandered along the aisles he'd yell over to Tony, a heavy man with thinning black hair patted into an ugly, oily arc across his head, "Hey! Ya fat Guinea! Ya still sellin' the same old junk? Huh? I've seen stuff move fasta in the toilets I unplug!" Tony would wave him off, turning a little away from him and throwing back over his shoulder, "What would you know about merchandise, ya stupid Swede? Huh? Shit for brains!" He'd touch his forehead with his middle finger, grin maliciously, and so would my father. As we worked our way closer to Tony, past the booth with old tools, past the book booth, Dad would ask, "So why haven't the cops bustid ya yet for alla this, Tony? What, you got a captain on ya payroll? This stuff is hot enough to burn ya hands off!" He'd blow on his fingers and wave them in the air, grinning. Tony grinned back at the compliment. "Naah, I buy this legit." He'd widen his eyes and look cherubic. "Really." They'd both laugh.

During the week, during my life, my father was a sometimes plumber, sometimes car salesman, sometimes junkman, sometimes something. My mother worked as a cook, a school crossing guard, at a McDonald's counter for a while. It was never enough. I remember one Saturday afternoon in August, my father was melting down old lead pipes. All afternoon he cut the soft pipes into small pieces and fed them into the heat of the kettle, then poured the liquid metal out into the little cupcake-shaped molds he'd set in the dirt of the driveway. Late in the afternoon, the heavy clouds broke and rain began spattering down on his back and shoulders. While I watched from the kitchen he kept working, the rain hissing and turning into steam as it struck the melting lead. Over and over, he reached forward to drop chunks of pipe in to melt, and his arms, then shoulders, then head disappeared in the fog of metal and mist. He became that man to me, the half-man in steam. He was the back I saw sometimes wearily climbing the stairs to sleep for a few hours. He was the chains rattling in the truck as it bounced down the pitted driveway and whined back up late at night as he came home. It wasn't enough. There was a stack of dunnings and notices that covered the end of the old stereo.

I remember when the man from the bank came to repossess our car. I had just broken my foot, and I hung onto the car door handle while my mother stood next to me talking to the man who wanted to take the car. Her voice was high, and with one hand she opened and closed the metal clasp on her purse. Finally she opened the car door, pushing me in and sliding in next to me. The man from the bank stepped back as she started the engine, and she rolled up the window as he leaned over to say something to us. She gunned it, careening wildly backward across the yard out into the street, crying. "So this is what we've got," she said. "This is it."

We were working poor and so we were alternately afraid and ashamed and bold and angry. We prayed to nothing in particular that no one would notice our clothes or that the police wouldn't notice the car didn't have a valid inspection sticker. My mother had to decide between a tank of gas and an insurance payment. She had to decide whether or not we really needed a doctor. We shopped as a group so that if my new dress for the year cost two dollars less than we had thought it would, my sister could get one that cost two dollars more. We didn't say such things out loud, though we thought them all the time. Words are ideas, ways of believing, connected to desire and fear. If I ate seconds, maybe I was eating my sister's dress. If Susan was really sick, then maybe I couldn't get new shoes. But if anyone ever said those things, it would all come crashing in. All of it—the idea that working hard would get you some place better, that we were just as good as anyone else—would crash to the floor like some heirloom dish that would never be the same again, even if we could find all the shards.

At some point in my life, when I was very young, it had been decided that I would be the one who went on to college, who earned a lot of money, who pulled my family away from the edge of the pit, and who gave the stupid rich bastards what they had coming to them. I would speak like them but wouldn't be one of them. I would move among them, would spy on them, learn their ways, and explain them to my own people—a guerrilla fighter for the poor. My father had visions of litigation dancing in his head, his daughter in a suit, verbally slapping the hell out of some rich asshole in a courtroom.

As I was growing up, the most important people I knew, the ones I most respected, were my teachers. I wanted to be like them. They had made the supreme sacrifice, had gone away and succeeded, but had chosen to come back to help us. They drove cars I could imagine appearing occasionally in my father's lot. They wore scuffed shoes and shopped at K-Mart. They didn't belong to a country club, didn't refuse to teach us because we were poor, didn't treat us with pity or condescension. They often worked year round, teaching summer school or even, as with my history teacher, driving a beer truck from June through August.

They were the only people I knew and trusted who might be able to teach me to speak like and understand the stupid rich bastards who held our lives in their hands and squeezed us until we couldn't breathe: doctors who refused to treat us without money up front; lawyers who wrote short, thick, nasty letters for credit companies who, in turn, spoke for someone else; insurance agents who talked in circles and held up payment; loan officers who disappeared into the backs of banks and didn't look at us when they told us we were too much of a risk; police and town selectmen who told us to get rid of our cars and clean up our disgraceful yards and lives—all the people who seemed always to be angry that they had to deal with us in any way. My teachers moved, I thought, with ease between my world and this other world. I hoped they would help me do the same.

My teachers tried to bridge the gap with speech. "In other words," they said, looking from the text to us, "what they're saying is . . ." They tried to bridge the gap with their bodies, one hand pointing to the board, the other hand stretched out palm up, fingers trying to tug words from mouths contorted with the effort to find the right speech. We were their college-bound students, the ones who might leave, might be them again, might even do better. They were like our parents in their desire to have us succeed, but they had skills and knowledge that counted to the white-shirted men who sat behind the glass windows at the savings and loan, to the woman who handled forms for free butter, cheese, and rice.

I wanted to be like my teachers, but I was afraid of standing up before a classroom filled with students like the ones who laughed in the back of the classroom. The only writing these students did was carving names and sexual slurs or boasts on their desks, and their dreams, I imagined, were of lives like they already knew. I was afraid, too, that when I had become like these teachers I admired so much, I would still drive down the main street of a rotting industrial town and go into the 7-Eleven and somehow I would be no different than I was now. The very ones I admired most I also most suspected: if my teachers were such successes, why were they back here? Why did they make so little money? Drive those cars? I was afraid I would have nothing to say or show to the students who sat in the back, afraid that if they actually asked what I only thought—"So what?"—I would have no answer.

I worked summers at a resort in Maine, making beds and scrubbing toilets, earning tips and room and board. During the school year, I worked as a cook in a nursing home and as a maid for rich women who made me change sheets, crawl out on window ledges to clean glass, and scrub their kitchen floors on my knees. I had saved about five hundred dollars. I sent in cards to request material from any college that would send it to me. Every day, stacks of brochures and catalogues and letters awaited me when I came home from school. One or two that looked good—smiling students on the cover—I brought with me to work at the nursing home, and I read the captions while I ate my supper. The others I looked through at night for the cost to attend and the amount of aid usually awarded. When I filled out the financial aid forms, my father told me to put a zero on every line. I told him that no one would believe it. "Yah? So what? Think they'd believe thirteen dollahs eitha? Put it down." I did.

I decided on three colleges, all small, private ones because I was afraid of the throngs of students in the brochures for the state schools. Some of the schools had said they were "teaching institutions"; I avoided those too, believing that I would have to become a teacher if I went there. I was going to be a lawyer, was going to fulfill my father's vision. I was going to go where the kids of lawyers went. I filled out forms largely on my own, knowing that my parents didn't understand the questions and would be embarrassed at not being able to help me. I took all the standardized tests and did only okay, confused by analogies of bulls and bears (I thought they referred to constellations, not the stock market) and questions about kinds of sailing boats.

When my first-choice college sent me a letter telling me I was on their waiting list, my mother hugged me and told me how proud she was. My father asked me how long I'd have to wait and if I'd work in the meantime. My mother thought that merely making the waiting list was an achievement, something she could brag about to Pat and Barbara and the mailman, while my father thought that there was only a limited number of spaces in colleges all over the country and each student waited in turn to get in. I went upstairs and cried for hours. When I came back down for supper, my mother had fixed a cake in celebration.

I was in my first English class at my second-choice school, never having made it off the waiting list at my first-choice school. I'd never visited this college and knew little about it. I hadn't gone to orientation, begging off because of work. That was only partially true. Actually, I had begun to look at those smiling catalogue faces and bodies and then to look at myself. I had crooked teeth. I wore makeup. I wasn't tanned and lithe from summers of tennis and sailing. I wore old jeans patched at the thighs and ragged around the cuffs. I wore T-shirts and work boots, not clothing from L. L. Bean's. I read statements from the happy students, moving my lips and trying to make the words sound like they could be mine, but I realized that it was wrong, that I was wrong. What could I say to all these people? What could they say to me? And what people did I belong to?

My mother had also seen the pictures. She tried to buy me some clothes that matched theirs, and she watched as I packed, anxious that I not be made fun of. My grandfather, who had completed grade school, told me gruffly, "Now that youah goin' to college, you'll be too good t' talk to us anymoah." I protested but he shook his head; it was the last thing he ever said to me. I felt like my family wanted me so badly to be something other than what I was. And suddenly, all I wanted to be was "Lau-doop," as my father had called me when I was younger. It was enough to have been accepted at a college, to have been a high school valedictorian. That was bragging rights forever for my mother. Why did I need more? What was wrong with what I had and was?

Now I was here, dropped off by my sister and brother, who had turned the car around and headed for home after dumping off my box and bag. My roommate was crying because she couldn't fit all her Pendleton wools in her closet and drawers and had taken over some of mine. Her father, a successful lawyer, sized up the situation, watching me sit in silence in my flannel shirt and unfashionable jeans. "What should we call you?" he asked politely. I thought for a moment. "Johnson." He laughed delightedly. "Johnson? That's great! Sue, this'll be good for you," he chortled as he led his sniffling daughter and perfectly coiffed wife out to get lunch.

Now I was being asked to write editorials, but I didn't know what one was. My family had always bought the newspaper with the big photos in it, and the little local weekly had columns about who'd been arrested and what stores had gone out of business. I didn't understand the articles I had to read in order to write my editorials. I summarized what I'd read in two major paragraphs and turned it in, over and over, week after week. I got a B each time, no comments.

In French government class, students talked excitedly about their travels abroad. I felt the chip on my shoulder getting heavier and heavier. I'd been through all of New England; they'd been to France. Big fucking deal. Lions, Lee-ons, Lyons, it's all the same. Unless someone laughs at you for not knowing how to say what everyone else can not only say but describe from personal experience.

Poetry class. I describe in a long narrative poem what things I see around my neighborhood. The teacher gushes over it. It reminds him of T. S. Eliot, he says, and when I say, "Who's that?" he is astounded. He decides he has a diamond in the rough; he calls me a lump of coal with lots of potential. (Later, he asks me if I want to sleep with him.)

I understand my students where I now teach. I understand their fear of poverty, of sliding backwards, of not being as successful as their very successful parents. They recoil in disgust and loathing from the poor, from the working class, and that, too, is familiar to me. They insist that if we all just try hard enough, everyone can succeed. But until then, they don't want to live with those who haven't really made it, who haven't tried. I understand how deep and visceral that fear of failure is. It keeps them in college and it keeps them from thinking about possibilities. They are in love with the status quo and terrified of idealism, of a vision and words charged with change.

I was terrified of success. By Thanksgiving of my first year in college, I wanted to go home and stay there. What was I doing at this place for rich kids? What was I accomplishing? How was I helping my family? I was a mute, a heavy drinker, a class skipper. My sister was in a nursing program and was paying rent to my mother; another sister was also working and helping out. What was I doing? I was going to college on grants and loans, and while I was not sucking money from my family, I wasn't contributing to it either. I knew I could go home and each day I had stayed in college would count as part of my success. I could have failed by my fellow students' standards and still not have failed by my own. I would have been part of that story where the system beats down the good ones who try to make it out, where you try and try and try and still the stupid rich bastards squish you just when you might succeed. I could have come home and said, "Hey, they were a bunch of rich assholes. What do you want?" No further explanation would have been demanded or necessary.

In the dormitories at night the girls gathered into groups in the lounges or the hallway floors and told stories about their lives. I was silent, stricken dumb with fear. What would I tell them when my turn came? The truth? A lie? But I needn't have worried. My turn never came. I don't know whether it was out of compassion or snobbishness, but no one ever asked me about my family, my home, my friends, even my major or my hoped-for career. And as much as I hated myself for being ashamed of my life, I hated the girls more for knowing it.

In my conferences with teachers I sat mute, nodding weakly when it seemed called for, when their voices rose as if in a question. Whatever they suggested was right. In lectures, I took notes furiously, narrative notes, full sentences, trying to get the exact words spoken by the teacher. I knew if I took down just a word here and there I would have to fill in the gaps with my own words, and those words were horribly wrong. I was horribly wrong.

Maybe my mother knew. She's dead now and I never asked her. But she wrote me letters every now and then, and not once did she say she'd like me back. Not once did she explicitly give me the option of returning. After one letter in which I came close to admitting my despair, she wrote back, "We love you and we're proud of you. Don't show your face in the door until you're supposed to."

I had gotten an F+ on an English paper. On the bottom of the last page, Dr. B. had written, "Come and see me about this." I was now a second-semester sophomore and still had not gotten an A in my major, English; in fact, I had barely survived the drinking and class cutting of my first year. My parents had never seen my grade report, only knew that I was allowed to come back a second year, more reason for pride. I had learned to buy my classmates' thrown-away clothes at the local thrift store, and if I kept my mouth shut I could pass as one of them in most of my classes. I stopped wearing makeup, even stopped sitting in the groups in the dorms. Instead, I worked in the library on Friday nights and Saturday mornings, which gave me an excuse (I imagined one day I would need one) for never going out and spending money with anyone on weekends. Now, though, I had to hide from teachers, the people I had once wanted so much to be like.

I went to Dr. B.'s office about one minute before his office hours were over. I made sure the secretary saw me and that I had a piece of paper to write a note like: "Stopped by to talk about my paper. I'll catch you some other time." I inched my way down the hall toward his door, reading the numbers so I could pretend I had missed him because I had gotten lost.

Dr. B was still in his office. He welcomed me in, appearing surprised. He pulled his chair over next to mine, took my paper, and began to go over it, line by line, word by word. He peered over his little glasses, sometimes giving his head a violent nod so they would drop down on his chest and he could sit back and watch my reactions to his statements. I couldn't breathe. My chest felt like it was full, but I had no air. I didn't dare blink because my eyes were full of tears. I kept my head bent, my chin in my hand, and stared at my paper.

He sighed. Finally, he said something like, "Look. See this paragraph? This is a good one. There's a good idea in here. That's your idea. But it's not phrased well. Listen to it phrased this way." And he reread my idea in words that sounded like all my professors. Words that could have kept a stupid rich bastard listening. My idea. His words. But they were connected then. For the first time, I felt like I might make it through. I choked out a thank you, and he looked up, surprised. The conference wasn't over, but I was standing up. I thanked him again, stuffing the paper into my bookbag, and left before the tears came pouring down my face. I didn't know why I was crying, whether it was because I was so stupid that I got an F+ and had to sit there and make a nice man frustrated or because I felt that I could take that one paragraph and begin again, begin learning how to speak about what I thought and felt to people who weren't like me. Stupidity and relief. They've dogged me ever since.

The phone rang at two in the morning. It was my little sister, sobbing and nearly hysterical. Her boyfriend, drunk or high on something, had leaped from a closet and attacked her. She had beaten him off, clubbing him with a brass statue that my mother had given her. Now, while two friends tried to stop her bleeding—she had a broken nose, broken ribs, a broken foot—she choked out why she had called.

"He said the apahtment was in his name an' I gotta be outta heyah tomorrow mohnin' or he's takin' all the stuff heyah an' sellin' it an' he'll keep the dog too! An' I OWN this stuff, I paid fuh it an' *I* pay the rent but I don't got anywayah to go. You know legal stuff, right? Laurel, ya gotta help me!"

I searched my brain for what little I remembered from my pre-law days at college, a decade earlier. Now in a Ph.D. program in composition and rhetoric, far away from the gritty New England town where my sister lived and near which we grew up, I felt useless. Again. I began to ask her about her lease, to tell her about the Legal Aid Society; I even began to think out loud through cases from a textbook I remembered. Suddenly she interrupted me, screaming over the line, "Fuck you! Fuck you! Don't talk to me like college, talk to me like a sista!"

I remember clearly the first time I chose to say to a professor, "Really!" instead of the more natural (to me), and what others might think of as more colorful, "Get outta heyah!" I remember when I began to believe that I might go into English and not law. It was a course on realism and naturalism. I began to tremble when I read *McTeague* (which I've been told many times since is not great literature but is useful as a demonstration of certain ideas in limited courses). Here were people I recognized! Here were characters who spoke like I did, who swore and hoped and dreamed for so damn little, for a place to stay that was clean, for respect, for something of their own that would last. Here were novels that showed that the poor weren't poor because they wanted to be, because they were lazy, but because of sweeping faceless economic forces that smashed them down and kept them down, and here were stupid rich bastards shown as they were in my own life. Here were writers who had words that spoke to me, that invited me not to join in some fantasy world but to confront and describe my own *real* world.

My parents (and in some ways, my whole family) never got over my defection from law. I tried to soften the blow by going into archeology; while it paid little, it was at least exotic and held out the hope of discovering some kind of lost treasure—imagine, money without working! But it was reconstructing lives and words, not ancient cultures but my own culture, that I kept being drawn to. I have come through poetry, sales, admissions, and finally composition, where first-year students begin to learn how their words hurt and heal, probe and hide, reshape, connect, embrace, and gag. It is a field that feels like work, where the texts are of a home and life so close to the world that the arguments mean something. They are like "sista," not "college."

Here, on paper, I can be in two worlds and control them both. But on the phone, my father asks me how that "school thing" is going, and what I still need to do, and what kind of salary I expect next year when I finally get a job. And I find it easier to slip into his world than to bring him into mine, to listen to his odysseys and believe in him as my mother did when she first married him. While a brother and sister are now doing well, two others are still living in poverty, and when I speak to my siblings my world slips around until I am dizzy.

I can bring their world into my own only in narratives, only distantly. No one in my family has ever read what I write. No one has visited my office or my classroom, at least not physically. I tell my students about my family, though; I talk to them in my language to show them there are many ways to say things. When we share our writing, I share a letter to home, full of swear words, little jokes, scatological humor, assertions that will be accepted without evidence solely because my sister and I "know" what stupid rich bastards are like and what they will say and do. And then we look at an essay I've written and then a poem, all dealing with my life, with words. They begin to feel their own words working in different ways, different contexts, begin to value the phrases and words that make them one thing and understand that these same words make it hard to be another thing. For most of my students, these exercises are often just an interesting diversion from reading literature. Some of them write in their journals of their relief. They, too, are first-generation college students, working class, afraid and silent. They appear at my door, ready to talk, knowing that I have been there and do not entirely want to leave.

When I work with my colleagues, with "real" faculty, I say little. I rehearse what I will say if I can predict the course of a meeting, and I miss some of what is going on while I hold my speech in my head, waiting for the opening in which I will speak like them long enough to fool them into thinking I *am* one of them. I am and I am not. My father's dream of how I would live and move between two worlds, two ways of speaking and knowing, haunts me.

I used to sit on the school bus on the way home from high school and look around at my classmates and wonder who would still be in my town in twenty years, who would go on, get out, succeed in ways that no one dreamed of. I used to think I would be one of those. Now I sometimes sit in meetings and classrooms and wonder who else would like to cut the shit and say what they feel. I feel suspended, dangling. If I put my toe down at any point, I might root there. I cannot move among the rich, the condescending, the ones who can turn me into an object of study with a glance or word, cannot speak like them, live in a house like them, learn their ways, and share them with my family without being disloyal to someone. I thought learning would make it easier for me to protect and defend my family, myself, but the more I learn the harder it is to passionately defend anything.

I am seeking a way to keep the language of the working class in academia, not just in my office with my working-class office mate, to nurture its own kind of vitality and rawness and directness, its tendency to ask "Why?" even as it says "Ah, what the fuck." I would like my colleagues to listen for the narratives embedded in their own writing, to feel the power of that movement forward just as they feel the power of the turning concept, the academic idea. And I would like my colleagues to turn my language over in their mouths with the same respect that my father and I turned over the items on those flea market tables.

2

A Real Class Act: Searching for Identity in the "Classless" Society

Julie A. Charlip

Marx and Engels wrote, "Society as a whole is more and more splitting up into two great hostile camps, into two great classes directly facing each other—bourgeoisie and proletariat" (10). If only that were true, things might be more simple. But in late twentieth-century America, it seems that society is splitting more and more into a plethora of class factions—the working class, the working poor, lower-middle class, upper-middle class, lower uppers, and upper uppers. I find myself not knowing what class I'm from.

In my days as a newspaper reporter, I once asked a sociology professor what he thought about the reported shrinking of the middle class. Oh, it's not the middle class that's disappearing, he said, but the working class. His definition: if you earn thirty thousand dollars a year working in an assembly plant, come home from work, open a beer and watch the game, you are working class; if you earn twenty thousand dollars a year as a school teacher, come home from work to a glass of white wine and PBS, you are middle class.

How do we define class? Is it a matter of values, lifestyles, taste? Is it the kind of work you do, your relationship to the means of production? Is it a matter of how much money you earn? Are we allowed to choose? In this land of supposed class-lessness, where we don't have the tradition of English society to keep us in our places, how do we know where we really belong? The average American will tell you he or she is "middle class." I'm sure that's what my father would tell you. But I always felt that we were in some no man's land, suspended between the classes, sharing similarities with some and recognizing sharp, exclusionary differences from others. What class do I come from? What class am I in now? As an historian, I seek the answers to these questions in the specificity of my past.

A FAMILY HERITAGE

All of us are the products not just of our immediate upbringing but also of the past that our parents and grandparents transmit. This is why class is never a matter of money alone. (Just ask the people with old money about the nouveau riche.)

My mother was the daughter of Russian Jewish immigrants who came to Lawrence, Massachusetts, in the early 1900s, before the revolution and during the pogroms. Her father died of pneumonia when she was a little girl, leaving her mother to raise five children during the Depression. Her mother ran a corner grocery, and she was too kind-hearted to deny her neighbors credit. The result was little for her own family, and my mother grew up in poverty. She was loath to talk about it, but when pressed she converted what must have been a nightmarish existence into the stuff of a warm-hearted B movie. "Oh, we were poor but happy," she would say. She finally revealed more when a high school history teacher assigned me to interview my parents about the Great Depression. My mother had two strong memories: the sight of families with all their belongings on the street, evicted from repossessed homes, and her sisters chasing the ragman to sell old cloth to get money for food. (It was a lasting legacy. Years later, when she died, I found an entire drawer filled with scraps of fabric cut from clothes she had hemmed.)

Mom's older brother moved to Trenton, New Jersey, and it was there that she met my father. Dad's grandparents had emigrated from Poland and Russia, settling in New York. His father moved to Trenton to seek his fortune, and he found it. They say every family has a story of a fortune made and lost; in mine, it's the story of Grandpa the bootlegger. Grandpa was one of the wealthiest men in Trenton. He had the Trenton police force and high-ranking officials on his payroll. Dad grew up knowing he didn't have to worry about money, yet his father, fearful of the federal authorities, was reluctant to display wealth. He bought old cars, and the family lived in apartments over the stores that were a front for his business. Dad tells colorful stories about working for his father, soaking corks to put in the bottles of "alky," putting liquor labels on bottles. But the only real comforts the wealth provided were the sumptuous meals that Grandpa hosted as patriarch. "He always set a good table," Dad recalled, a legacy Dad continued, along with his love for opera. Eventually, an angry cohort reported Grandpa to the feds, and he lost everything.

While Grandpa's wealth gave Dad a sense of financial security, he knew these ill-gotten gains did not provide him entry into the upper classes. In a touching memoir, Dad recalls that by error he was allowed to attend a junior high school in a rich neighborhood and how he hoped some of the "class" from the other students, the ones from the other side of the tracks, would rub off on him.

THE SMALL BUSINESS BLUES

Grandpa's talent for illegal business didn't carry over into legitimate enterprises, and when he died Harry's Supply Co. was nearly bankrupt, but Grandma begged Dad to take it over. Harry's Supply was a bar, restaurant, and party supply store located in an old downtown building: a long, narrow, high-ceilinged rowhouse that I remember as dusty and grimy, very different from the modern glass-and-chrome stores in the suburbs. The building itself was rented, a fact that puzzled me as a child; just what, I wondered, did my father own?

The staff consisted of Dad, Grandma, the part-time bookkeeper, the truck driver, and the warehouse kid. And, of course, my sister and me—a family business that was quite literally a *family* business.

Dad worked at the store from nine to five, Monday through Saturday. After dinner and a brief rest, he'd head down to his basement workshop. Dad had hit on the idea of imprinting matches, napkins, and ribbons as novelty items for parties and weddings. The printing process, hot stamping, combined enormous pressure and heat to impress loose type or lines of type through colored foil. I have a chilling childhood memory of Dad crushing his finger in the machine. For him, there was no employer to sue, no workmen's compensation or union benefits; there wasn't even much time to recuperate.

Dad would print until late at night, then get up to face another day at the store. Sunday, his "day off," would be spent mostly printing in that workshop. As a kid, I never really understood the supposed freedom of "being your own boss." It seemed to me that Dad was the prisoner, not the warden, of Harry's Supply. Because Dad couldn't leave the store unattended, there were no vacations. Instead, we went to New York for dinner and a Broadway show twice a year. We really couldn't afford vacations, anyway. As Dad put it, first you paid the employees and the bills; then if there was something left, it was yours. As a result, our resources varied drastically from week to week. Years later, after Dad lost the store to tax problems, he became manager for a former competitor. For the first time, he said, he looked forward to payday.

In Marxian terms, Dad's position as shopkeeper made him petit bourgeois, but what does that mean in actuality? Did that role make him an exploiter profiting from the work of his employees, a conservative force in society? That hardly seems accurate. He worked alongside his employees, for far longer hours and frequently for less money, while championing the liberal causes of change. Simultaneously, in Marxian terms, Dad was an artisan who owned his own tools. But again, what does this mean? That he was a skilled craftsman, an owner of small capital but threatened by the competition of big capital and mass production? In popular stereotypes, the petit bourgeois should have rising prosperity, a comfortable lifestyle imitating the upper classes and disdaining the lower. The artisan should be a worker with greasy hands, more skilled than the assembly-line worker but not in the same league as the middle class. But both Marxian and popular concepts seem simplistic when compared with reality.

Whether in Marxian or popular terms, my own role was clear: I was Dad's employee, owning only my labor power. This was no middle-class set of household chores, make-work designed to teach a sense of responsibility. I didn't receive an allowance; I earned wages. This was my job, a serious and essential part of Dad's business. When I grew up, he had to hire someone else.

I don't remember how old I was when I started work. Before I could count, I sorted matchbooks and paper napkins by color. Later, I packed the printed matches, cut imprinted ribbons, glued ribbons into glasses as novelty items, made car decorations for weddings, and printed on a small machine. I was paid for my work at less than the legal wage. Still, by the time I was twelve I earned enough to buy my own clothes. I also had hand-me-downs from my sister, Lindsey, and my parents would buy the more expensive items, such as winter coats, boots, or a fancy dress for a wedding, but essentially I was on my own. If there were no orders for me to work on, then I couldn't earn money.

Dad paid by the unit for the work I did at home and by the hour during summers when I worked in the store and punched the time clock. At times, Lindsey and I felt exploited. I was probably eight and Lindsey twelve when she convened the first labor negotiations. We sat Dad down and she declared that he either upped our wages or we'd go on strike. He laughed, amused at our youthful savvy. And he gave in. After all, Lindsey was right: if we quit, he'd have to hire "real" employees and pay at least the minimum wage.

Working for a parent, however, is not like working for any other employer; no other boss can forge such bonds of obligation. While the typical employer-employee relationship is impersonal, the family business relationship is patriarchal in the most literal and theoretical sense. Dad and I clashed as I grew up and wanted a social life. I insisted that Dad give me at least forty-eight hours' notice on orders for my work, as he usually did with his own work and that of his nonfamily suppliers. But on more than one Friday night he arrived home with orders due the next day. Already dressed for a party or a dance, waiting for my ride, I would complain bitterly of his unfairness, initially refusing to do the work. With a mixture of Jewish guilt and theater, Dad would blame the late order on my grandmother, whom I could not challenge. He would muse that he would have to do my work after finishing his own at midnight, and finally he would pledge to take me to the dance or party as soon as I finished. I always gave in, and Dad always saw that I made it, however belatedly, to parties and dances. But the responsibility of the work was always there; I could negotiate, but I couldn't quit.

LIFE IN THE 'BURBS

Harry's Supply was in Trenton, but my parents moved to a suburb, Hamilton Township, in 1955. This, however, was no case of white flight or upward mobility to the more affluent suburbs. Unlike the more prosperous communities that ringed Trenton—Ewing Township, Lawrence Township—Hamilton was a largely undeveloped, and therefore inexpensive, area. My father's first choice was to stay in Trenton, but he couldn't afford the housing prices. Instead he bought a small split-level tract home in a brand-new suburb designed for the veterans using their GI loan benefits.

Lindsey and I shared a bedroom and a bed. The small third bedroom was converted into a study for the two of us. A friend of Dad's built unvarnished shelves with a stand for the huge dictionary; two hinged panels pulled down to become our desks. The room was lined with books, mostly Book-of-the-Month Club selections and *Reader's Digest* condensed books, a few classics but no encyclopedias. The book collection was evidence to me that Dad must have been an avid reader in his youth, but I never saw him read a book. He devoured the local newspapers and an assortment of news magazines, but work left no time for leisure reading.

I read ravenously and uncritically; my parents were happy to see me reading but provided no guidance on my choices. I never knew whether they were allowing me my freedom—Dad wasn't allowed to have comic books as a child—or whether they were unprepared to judge. As a result, I still wince when people mention childhood classics that were not a part of my reading, and I have a deep aversion to the trashy novels that some of my colleagues delight in as respite from the serious, grad-student load.

In my childhood neighborhood, the fathers' occupations—most mothers stayed home—ranged from policeman to pharmacist, from working class to rising middle class. My best friend's father owned a pharmacy. Carol had music lessons, which I envied, and each summer visited her grandmother's beach house in tony Medford Lakes. When I went to the beach with Mom's family, eight aunts, uncles, and cousins piled into a rented apartment or bungalow.

Carol's family moved away to Princeton, following the expected pattern for neighborhoods like ours. These were supposed to be starter homes, where the middle class starts families and careers. Theoretically, there would be promotions and raises, or businesses would succeed and families would move to bigger and better homes. My father would still be in our little split-level had it not been for Interstate 295 cutting a swath directly through our house. After a protracted battle led by my father, we accepted a paltry settlement and moved to a new home in 1969. The new house cost more than the government settlement, and of course interest rates were higher and Dad was older, meaning a twenty-year instead of a thirty-year mortgage. What little savings the family had were wiped out.

The new house was bigger (at fifteen I finally had my own room), a three-bedroom ranch in another planned neighborhood with every house one of three models. Outside, it looked like the American Dream. But inside, the front room was virtually empty—there was one chair and my grandmother's cast-off table—and the den in the back was furnished with two rather shabby couches. We finally got a couch for the front room when my uncle gave us his old one.

Ends never met, the furniture was well worn, new clothes were limited, and yet my parents spent enormous amounts of money on food. They bought steak, veal, lamb—the legacy, I'm sure, of Mom's chasing the ragman and Grandpa's admonition always to set a good table. I found these contra-dictions confusing and viewed them as a middle-class façade pasted over a working-class income, not realizing that working-class incomes often were higher than ours. Nowhere was this contradiction sharper than at the res-taurants. Because of Dad's business, we spent many Sundays dining out, patronizing the businesses that patronized Harry's Supply. The meal was a business expense, and Dad usually came away with an order for merchan-dise. Many of the restaurants were casual, but others were ones we could never have afforded if not for the business connection. My favorite was Princeton's elegant Lahiere's. We dressed in our best clothes and learned to casually order escargots. But Lindsey and I marveled at the other pa-trons, whose wealth gave them a graceful ease while we carefully, nervously watched our manners.

On the other hand, I once went out to dinner with a group of friends, among them the daughters of a chiropractor. They seemed comfortably middle class to me. They had an above-ground pool, the kids didn't have to work, and their dad didn't work on weekends. But with five children, the family rarely went out to eat. I remember my friends freezing at the array of silverware. I couldn't understand how they could have more money than my family yet not know the social graces. I began to see that there was a complex interconnection between money and lifestyle, between social skills and acceptance. I didn't see then, however, that the obsession with manners is a middle-class phenomenon, as Paul Fussell notes in his book *Class*. The uppers feel entitled to do as they please—just think of the photo by Weegee of the gowned and jeweled dowager with her leg hiked unceremoniously on the table. And for whom did Lahiere's keep loaner ties at the front desk? Certainly not for those who wouldn't dare show up at such a restaurant without one.

I saw more contradictions with a new set of friends across town. We lived in a largely gentile area, and my parents, concerned about my social life, joined the Jewish Community Center and enrolled me in the youth group, B'nai B'rith Girls, which had a brother chapter of "nice Jewish boys," Aleph Zadik Aleph. I had always been amused by the stereotype of rich Jews, so foreign to my life. But at the community center, I thought I was the anomaly among these solidly middle- and upper-middle-class kids. Only three of my friends lived in Hamilton Township; the rest lived in Ewing or Lawrence, the high-income suburbs, or in the one "good" neighborhood left in Trenton. The Trenton girls, of course, did not attend Trenton High School. They were usually enrolled in Villa Victoria Academy, an excellent private Catholic girls' school with so many Jewish students that it closed for the High Holy Days.

Through the community center I became close friends with the daughter of Dad's attorney, a local judge. Her well-appointed home always had a quiet formality about it. In my home the TV was usually on, and we had a tendency to yell across the house. My friend's family was in another league: they had a cleaning woman, they had a boat, and they had enough money for private schools.

THE EDUCATIONAL DIVIDE

Eileen and I started out attending the same high school, but her parents quickly transferred her to the Hun School in Princeton. She read authors that I was not exposed to until college, and the curriculum included a class for girls called "How To Be a Gracious Member of Society," focusing on such important points as the care and storage of your furs and hosting a dinner party.

I, of course, continued at the local high school, Hamilton High West. The school was declared to be in a "depressed area" because of the adjacent African American neighborhood. There were at least thirty-five students to a class, and sometimes there were not enough books to go around. New college graduates taught there because the federal government reduced their college loans for each year of work in a "depressed area." Certainly no one ever thought of teaching us to be gracious; teachers routinely referred to the students as "animals" and called our parents ignorant. Some of our graduates were college bound, others functionally illiterate.

It was determined from an early age that I would go to college. A teacher at Kisthardt Elementary School, where two grades routinely shared a room and a teacher, told my parents that I was "college material." I was lucky that this was decided in my earliest school years, because students were tracked by perceived ability, and those who were not seen as college material didn't have access to preparatory classes. Many a bright but economically disadvantaged student whose home life was not conducive to studying could be passed over by the tests.

As we entered junior high school, college-bound students were separated from those in business or commercial curricula. I confounded the administration, however, when I insisted on a mix: algebra, junior business training, Spanish, and typing. I had been raised to be practical, and I wanted some tangible skills.

My career goals were vague; all I was sure of was that I loved to write. The only junior high teacher to take an interest in me was an English teacher who encouraged my writing. It was during a typing class in high school that I made my decision. If I spent the rest of my life behind a typewriter, it would be to record *my* words, not someone else's. I decided on journalism largely because I was influenced by my father, who had been founder and editor of his base paper in the Navy and who had longed to be a journalist, but he put those dreams aside to take over the family business. My decision was also a practical one, though. How else could I possibly support myself as a writer?

My family was intent on my attending college, but we understood none of the complexities of preparing for and choosing a school. I relied on my high school guidance counselor, a woman of great enthusiasm but little competence. I dreamed of going away to school and she encouraged me, guiding me to apply to Bates and Colby Colleges in Maine, Wesleyan University in Connecticut, and Ithaca College in New York. I had never heard of them, but I didn't want to go to the local schools, Trenton State College or Rider College. I never even daydreamed about schools like Princeton University, fifteen miles and fifteen light years away. Such schools were for other people, those who came out of the college preparatory academies.

I assumed, however, that I would be accepted and given financial aid at the schools we selected because everyone told me that I was smart enough to do it. I didn't understand that it was a rare student from my high school who could make it beyond Trenton State College because our training was so inadequate. And my grades were erratic. While I excelled in English, history, Spanish, anything that captured my interest and involved writing, I failed miserably at math and science. School administrators informed me that if I could excel in the social sciences and humanities, then I must be struggling in math and the physical sciences out of pure perversity. My parents tried to help, but they had never studied algebra, geometry, chemistry. There were no tutors, and the teachers facing crowded classrooms didn't worry about those of us who fell behind. I was lost and there were no guides. I gave up and huddled in the back of the room with author-philosopher Ayn Rand's *The Fountainhead* hidden inside my algebra book. Further, I tended to neglect my studies in favor of editing an award-winning newspaper for B'nai B'rith Girls and editing the high school newspaper before quitting in a censorship battle.

I also consulted a cousin with a doctorate in psychology, the only person in my family to have an advanced degree and whom I'd met only once. (Although many of my cousins started college, most dropped out.) His advice was to visit every campus for a personal interview to impress them with my enthusiasm and interest. I vividly remember visiting Bates with my mother. It was winter, and it was cold in Maine. She wore her good wool coat, the one to which she had sewn a small mink collar, the one she had had all my life. The dean of students greeted us in his plush office and looked my mother up and down with a sniff of disdain. Clearly he thought we were so far beneath him that he didn't need to mask his scorn. I felt small and inadequate and terribly sorry for Mom.

I was, as expected, rejected by Bates and by Wesleyan, wait-listed by Colby, which meant no financial aid, and accepted to Ithaca with no funding. I was stunned, but I had also learned by then that nothing comes easy. Mom and Dad raised me on a steady diet of such clichés as "Money doesn't grow on trees" and "Nothing comes without hard work." I dreaded what seemed to be my only option, Mercer County Community College, little more than an extension of high school. My sister and her husband lived in Bucks County, Pennsylvania, and he studied at Bucks County Community College, a much better school. High school quality depends on the local tax base, and because Bucks County was affluent, it had a higher caliber of students at the community college and attracted better faculty. I decided to use their address and go to Bucks.

I remember going into the cellar where Dad was working to tell him my plans: go to Bucks, transfer later to another school, and work my way through college. For the first time in my life, I saw my father cry. "It wasn't supposed to be like this," he said. "I've let you down; I was supposed to pay for your education." I was touched but also stunned; I had been raised to make my own way. I didn't feel let down in the least.

THE NEWSPAPER GAME

I landed a newspaper job the same week that I started college and worked twenty-five to thirty hours a week during the semester, full time summers. I earned high grades, and I still dreamed of going away to a big-name, four-year college, but my co-workers dissuaded me. After all, they said, you want to be a journalist and you've already got a job. Go to school in Trenton and keep working here. So I transferred to Rider College, the only local campus offering journalism. It was the easy way out: journalism classes were a snap after two years in the business. I felt that I had my career launched; college meant merely that piece of paper.

Rider was known mostly as a business school, and its journalism department was small. It wasn't until I left for a job in Kansas that I heard about the big journalism programs at midwestern universities. And when I moved on to California, I met reporters who majored in "serious" subjects—political science, economics—and brought that knowledge to journalism. It seemed that I'd learned a trade rather than received an education.

That feeling had been forged at *The Trentonian*. Journalism today may earn some respect, but when I started in 1972, Watergate was just developing and journalism was very suspect. Our old-fashioned tabloid newsroom, where we squashed our cigarette butts on the floor, was more akin to *The Front Page* than *All the President's Men*. Most reporters didn't have college degrees; they joked that journalism graduates had to be retaught everything. Starting there at eighteen, I grew up in a rough-and-tumble newsroom where reporters were skilled workers, perhaps, but certainly not professionals. We had a union, we bargained collectively, we threatened strikes.

As I moved on to other newspapers and journalism became more popular, I saw a trend toward better-educated reporters, self-identified professionals. While the scrappy self-trained reporters could still go far, the ones who ended up covering Washington, working as foreign correspondents, or writing books were often children of the elite. I filled my gaps with avid reading and lots of attitude. (A woman in journalism in the 1970s needed a lot of brass.) I was tough and smart, and since journalism takes you from the gutter to mansions, I learned to function in vastly different situations.

But my attitude, formed in Trenton, was fundamentally working class, and I brought that to Kansas, where I helped organize a union and ended up unofficially blacklisted. When I finally found a job—a union one—in Fresno, California, I jumped at the chance. But in a few years, I was dissatisfied with journalism. It wasn't just Trenton or Wichita or Fresno, I discovered. Partly I was disillusioned, a watchdog for justice fighting with editors who were ambitious climbers and publishers just out to make money. And despite journalism's seemingly endless variety, I began to find that the names changed while the stories remained the same. So I took a leave of absence and went to Central America to find myself.

FROM MANAGUA TO LOS ANGELES

I had first become interested in Central America when I wrote about a Latin America solidarity group in Fresno. They showed films and sponsored lectures, and their information clashed dramatically with the news stories that came across the wires. I decided to see for myself, satisfying my curiosity and my restlessness. I intended to travel throughout Central America, starting in Nicaragua at a school that would help me brush up my Spanish, place me in a private home, and give me guided tours. I fell in love with the country and stayed till my money ran out.

Nicaragua impressed me because the 1979 revolution had brought rapid change, seeming to compress the usual slow movement of history. Coming from a country where most people believe that voting makes no difference and "you can't fight city hall," I found Nicaragua refreshing. Despite dire poverty and US-waged aggression, Nicaraguans believed they held their future in their hands, and they were involved and excited by the prospects.

At thirty years old, twelve years after I began in journalism, I walked into a research institute in Nicaragua and asked how one got a job there. They admired my interest, my writing and editing experience, but wondered what I knew about Latin America and Third World problems. I decided on the spot; I was going back to school.

This time, I had a little more savvy than in my high school days. Deciding to get a master's degree in Latin American studies, I researched the schools and applied to the best, UCLA and the University of Texas at Austin. When I was accepted and UCLA recruited me with a fellowship, I was amazed. Would I really be able to fulfill my dream of attending a major university?

My parents, however, were shocked. Dad couldn't understand why I would leave an award-winning career. The idea of changing careers was alien to him; where I grew up, people kept their jobs for life. In Trenton, the ultimate job was to work for the state, with civil-service security. My mother couldn't understand what I'd do with a master's degree. "Now you're a journalist," she'd say. "When you get this degree, what will you be?"

I thought *they* were naive until I got to UCLA. When I told an adviser that I wanted to use my M.A. to do research, she laughed at me. She said that

I would need a Ph.D. and I would have to choose another field because I couldn't get a Ph.D. in Latin American studies. This, I thought, was my big chance. A high-ranking student at UCLA could be accepted at Princeton, Harvard, Yale—a working-class kid from Trenton in the Ivy League! Then my naïveté became clearer. Dr. E. Bradford Burns explained to me that I should consider not just universities but specific departments, indeed, specific fields within departments. The Ivy League schools offered at best one or two historians specializing in Latin America compared to UCLA's four, who included leaders in the field. The important thing, he said, was to find a professor who wanted to work with me; he encouraged me to stay at UCLA, which I didn't even realize has one of the country's top ten history departments. I had never imagined that I would study for a Ph.D., much less that a renowned professor would want to work with me.

I don't think Dr. Burns, who became my chair and mentor, ever realized just how uninformed I was about the machinations of academe. All those years as a journalist had made me adept at soliciting information in a way that sometimes masked my limited knowledge, a skill that prepared me well for graduate school and the often brutal games played by graduate students in seminars.

I needed that ability to pose when I arrived at UCLA because I was terrified. I remember one of my first classes, "The Political Economy of Latin America," taught by the brilliant Dr. Jeffry Frieden. During the first week, a student in the class casually asked a question about the Porfiriato, the period when Porfirio Díaz ruled Mexico. I had never heard the term, and I thought in dismay that I was clearly in over my head. Everyone seemed to know more than I did, to have better educations, to have read works that were never part of my curriculum. By the end of the quarter, however, the other student had dropped out, and I was still there, being encouraged to go on for a Ph.D. That support was crucial. Without mentors to reassure me, answer my questions, help guide me through the system, I would have been lost.

The master's degree confused my parents, but the Ph.D. is something else. They are very proud of their daughter the doctor, the future professor, and so am I. Students who come from privileged backgrounds, and there are many at UCLA, can never understand what it means to me. Graduates of fine colleges, they affect a jaded pose, a grad-school chic, about UCLA. I find UCLA to be a wonderland of knowledge and resources. They have no idea what it is like to go to unknown, inferior schools with limited resources. They are mostly children of the upper class, and they have a sense of entitlement that I will never know and that I will always envy. They have always known they belong at UCLA. I feel grateful that I was allowed in. Despite my accomplishments—awards, fellowships, teaching assistantships—I still have the sneaking suspicion that someone will shout "Fraud!" and send me away. A part of me doesn't believe that I can really know as much as they do or that I will ever fit in. Surely, this is all a mistake, and they will find me out someday. That's why they can take time out to read a bodice ripper while I feel I must read Dostoyevsky. After all, Dostoyevsky has nothing to do with Latin American history but everything to do with a well-read background; the problem isn't knowing the material in class but knowing the references made over cappuccino.

Those graduate students who are to the manor born have been groomed; everything in their backgrounds has prepared them for this life. To me, they are the diners at Lahiere's with their easy grace. They studied Russian in high school, read the classics as undergraduates, traveled extensively. And while I have bested many of them with ease, I will always feel that I have to work harder simply because my background has not entitled me.

Perhaps that is the greatest tragedy of a working-class background, if that is what mine is. The nagging feeling of inferiority intimidates many of us, sometimes to such an extent that fine minds never turn to academe. Some start and don't finish because the environment is so alien and because they can no longer tolerate worrying that they are frauds as they compete with those who are entitled. Graduate school is about more than what you know; it is an elite system designed to maintain the status quo. Social training and attitude matter here. Graduate students are expected to adapt to a system that is arcane and virtually medieval in its form. This is no stretch for the students who dined in eating clubs on the gothic Princeton campus. Ah, but the distance for the student who was just down the road at Rider College!

WHERE DO I BELONG?

What class am I from? How do you reconcile the definition of the bourgeois who owns his own business with the reality of the small businessman and his pile of debts? An employer's outlook with my Dad's labor-leaning, staunchly Democratic views? The opera buff who loves Broadway shows with the supposedly uncultured artisan working with his hands in the cellar? Even Marx and Engels, who defined the dual-class system, recognized the complexities. In part three of *Capital,* Marx notes that even in classically industrialized England, "intermediate and transitional strata obscure the class boundaries" (Bottomore 75). But Marx saw those strata as transitional, disappearing with the march of capitalism and its dualistic structure.

The great Flo Kennedy, the attorney who represented Black Panthers and the prostitutes' organization COYOTE, maintains that there are only those who work and those who don't. If you have to work for a living, Kennedy says, no matter how much money you make you are working class. On some level, she is right. The belief that we are different obscures the socioeconomic truth that a tiny percentage of the elite in this country owns the real wealth and the rest of us are dependent on them. In Kennedy's purely theoretical terms, there is no difference between a blue-collar union worker, my father the small businessman, and a corporate executive making a hundred thousand dollars a year. However, we all know that money does matter. The difference in income buys the wealthier among us opportunities for education, travel, upward mobility, entrance into groups with their own private signs and signals of inclusion and exclusion. It is possible, perhaps, for all of these groups to reach the same political conclusions. But there are differences in our psyches, in our expectations, our sense of entitlement, and the ways we move through the world. Those differences are rarely addressed by political theorists, but they are important.

The reality of class in America is more complex than dualistic models allow. On the surface, my father's small business and our home in the suburbs are the visage of the petit bourgeoisie, the middle class, the American Dream. Beyond that facile categorization is the reality of hard work, little money, limited opportunities, and far more insecurity than that of the blue-collar worker who has a steady paycheck and job benefits.

In *Class,* Paul Fussell notes that even our definition of the term is conditioned by our class standing: "At the bottom, people tend to believe that class is defined by the amount of money you have. In the middle, people grant that money has something to do with it, but think education and the kind of work you do almost equally important. Nearer the top, people perceive that taste, values, ideas, style and behavior are indispensable criteria of class, regardless of money or occupation or education" (3). Fussell comes up with nine classes—top out-of-sight, upper, upper middle, middle, high proletarian, mid-proletarian, low proletarian, destitute, and bottom out-of-sight. It's a tricky business, and I guess my background falls somewhere in the high proletarian to middle range. The middle class, according to Fussell, suffers from psychic insecurity, is concerned about manners and appearances, and includes salesmen and managers; the high proles are the former lower-middle class, skilled workers and craftsmen, who pride themselves on independence.

To what class do I belong now, as I head from grad-school poverty to the rather ill-paid life of the mind? Marx and Engels placed intellectuals somewhat outside the class dialectic, perhaps rising from one of the classes but choosing to ally with one class or the other, the conservatives protecting the interests of the state and the progressives siding with the working class. Similarly, Fussell would call us "category X," not members of a class at all. Formerly called "bohemians," Fussell writes: "You are not born an X person, as you are born and reared a prole or a middle. You become an X person, or, to put it more bluntly, you earn X-personhood by a strenuous effort of discovery in which curiosity and originality are indispensable. And in discovering that you can become an X person, you find the only escape from class" (212–13).

On the latter, of course, Fussell is dead wrong. Scratch an X-person's bohemian, even eccentric, façade, and you'll find attitudes and a sense of self molded by membership in a particular class. I can never escape from my class background, and there's nothing quite like the hallowed, upper-class halls of academe to remind me of it. As a journalist, I was a professional outsider, observing and criticizing. As an academic, however, I must now be an insider, functioning within a system designed by and for the elite. I know all too well the system's effect on me; the question is whether I can affect the system.

WORKS CITED

Bottomore, Tom, ed. *A Dictionary of Marxist Thought*. Oxford: Basil Blackwell, 1985.

Fussell, Paul. *Class*. New York: Ballantine, 1983.

Marx, Karl, and Friedrich Engels. *The Communist Manifesto*. Ed. Samuel H. Beer. New York: Meredith Corp., 1955.

3

Bronx Syndrome

for Herb

Stephen Garger

I was leading a faculty luncheon discussion in 1987 at Central College, a liberal arts school in Iowa. Fourteen of us were sitting around a table in a little room with a fireplace set aside for faculty in the student commons. We had finished eating and were fifteen minutes into the session when I found myself seriously considering strangling a fellow professor.

It was my second year of full-time college teaching. That fall the college had awarded me and a colleague from the psychology department a research grant to attend a seminar concerning the Meyers-Briggs Type Indicator, a personality inventory. As part of the grant we made a formal presentation to the faculty that was well enough received that many requested we run a luncheon discussion. This provided me and my psychologist friend the opportunity to meet with faculty six consecutive Tuesdays in order to present and discuss the Meyers-Briggs material in more depth.

I was taken aback by the argumentative tone of the first two meetings. It seemed most of the faculty ended what could have been questions with periods: "This sounds like astrology." "I think the data here is soft." "I don't think this is reliable." Counting the formal presentation, this was only the fourth time I had been in front of a group of professors, and nothing in my years of teaching had prepared me for an audience as cantankerous as they seemed. I felt I was being attacked and forced to defend myself from people I thought were on my side. Now it was the third session and my partner was away; my anxiety had reached extreme proportions.

About halfway through the discussion, one of

the professors raised an objection to the material, asserting that it set up a simplistic series of dualities in defining personality. I responded that there was more depth to the Meyers-Briggs concepts and instrument than could be presented in our current format, and more rigorous study revealed to me the dualities had more flexibility than is readily apparent. They were certainly not simplistic. Again he objected that he could not accept such a simplistic model of personality, where something is either one way or the other. Once more I responded that the concepts were not simple and further reading and discussion would bear this out. I, too, had some intellectual reservations about the model, but in general I found the concepts sound. Again he pressed that the concepts and the research were overly simple and in his view life was not a question of either/or. This time I did not reply, and an uncomfortable silence descended around the table. Finally, my friend William jumped in with a discussion of yin and yang and quieted the thrice-raised objection with a fine display of verbal and intellectual aggression.

After the session ended, I thanked Will for coming to my rescue. He asked what had happened to me, and I explained, "When he made the same point for the third time, I felt attacked and got defensive and angry. The only response I could conjure up was 'Fuck you' followed by a leap across the table to throttle him. I decided to withhold my response."

This response is part of what I have taken to calling the "Bronx Syndrome." It is composed of roughly equal parts mispronunciation, bad language, and the urge to punch. We're not talking here about the northern Bronx of Riverdale, populated largely by white-collar people. We're talking blue-collar Bronx near Yankee Stadium, the way it was when I grew up there in the 1950s and 1960s. I was by no means a violent street kid—far from it. My parents were working-class people, both immigrants. We had a clean apartment, food on the table, and plenty of old-fashioned discipline.

I was in the seventh grade in 1961 when my dad, over the strenuous objections of my mom, bought a ten-stool, eight-booth restaurant. In order to make ends meet, my mom and I went to work with him. My dad did the cooking and buying, and he yelled at the help, which unfortunately included my mother and myself. He had come over from Hungary when he was eighteen, and restaurant work was the only job he knew. My mom waitressed, the job she took when she first came to New York City. She was fourteen at the time and just out of a coal-mining town in southwestern Pennsylvania. Her dad died in a mining accident when she was very young, and she was pretty much on her own from then on. I took cash, occasionally waited on tables or washed dishes, and spent my free time across the street in Bloomingdale's department store. (These were the years before Bloomingdale's was Bloomie's.) I worked every Monday and Thursday after school until 9:30 P.M. and every Saturday and every summer until the restaurant was sold in 1966.

The adage about husbands and wives not working together was proven true in our experience, with the added fact that a kid shouldn't enter into the situation either. But we had to work. My father couldn't afford to pay another waitress. I certainly couldn't stay home by myself and neither could my younger sister, although for the first couple of years a family friend in the neighborhood looked after her. Work eliminated any form of extracurricular activity. Two days a week I had to take the subway downtown after school. School activities on Saturdays were simply out of the question. No coach or activity moderator would make such allowances. My parents dismissed sports and extracurriculars with the statement, "Work and your studies are more important."

Education ("studies") was a value in our house, at least with regard to me. My sister, currently a sports marketing executive, surprised me just a few years ago when she said our parents would not let her go to college because they believed women get married and have kids and that college would only be a waste of money. I have always been dismayed and angered about the number of women I meet who received this message, but I had no idea my own sister was one of them. I do not know to what degree this is a class issue or simply a gender issue or exactly how the two intersect, but in our house the message my sister got was very different from the one I received: "Go to school. You're smart. Be something so you don't have to work hard all your life."

I appreciate that message now, but I didn't then. Practically all my friends skipped school on a regular basis. They smoked, hung out, didn't study much, failed, or simply decided not to learn. Their parents apparently left them alone, and it looked good to me. But my father, raised in the Old World, enforced his demands physically. I was always more afraid of him than I was of anybody or anything else. I stayed in school, never cut a class (let alone a whole day), and occasionally studied—almost always against my will and generally to avoid my father's wrath.

My peers on the street were great, though. We were all from similar backgrounds. Their parents sold jewelry and used cars, drove cabs and subway trains, worked in grocery stores, restaurants, or for the post office. One or two of my friends had parents who were building superintendents. Some were from single-parent families due to death, divorce, or desertion. We spent hours playing stickball, pick-up basketball, touch football, and pool or smoking and drinking beer. My work schedule never interfered since hanging out had no particular timetable. Most of us were as smart as we needed to be and certainly clever enough. We measured talent by how fast one ran and how well one could hit or throw. We seldom talked about school, used a lot of bad language, and argued splendidly until one or the other would back down. Occasionally, if somebody didn't show enough sense to give in, you fought, but never with anybody you hung with. That would have been traitorous. Fights were with kids from another block or another group on the same block. We seldom left the neighborhood. Everything we needed was there and, much like in a small town, everybody knew everybody and about everybody. Twenty years later, when I was researching and working with school dropouts, I discovered that today most of my friends would be classified "at risk." Not many finished high school, and just a few of those made it through college.

What saved my butt was reading. I loved it. One of my earliest memories was being taught to read by my mother at the kitchen table. If I was propelled from behind by a fear of my dad, I was pulled ahead by the written word. On a third-grade field trip I was introduced to the New York Public Library system and got my first library card. When I began working downtown at the restaurant I discovered bookstores. I read a lot but never discussed what I read with anybody. Most of my pals never read anything, and it didn't carry much weight either in school or in the neighborhood to let on that I did. I discovered this in the fifth or sixth grade when I revealed I had read *The Anger of Achilles* by Robert Graves and thought it was just great. "Oh. Garger read a book." "Get bent, Garger." "Have a smoke." All of this said in that good-natured-with-an-edge way guys have of making fun of other guys. I was called the "little professor" for a while, until the gang found out I could throw a football forty yards. Accurately. Now here was something useful we could all relate to. Achilles be damned.

My reading on the sly and not talking about it has had interesting and sometimes funny consequences. For example, in a college philosophy class during my freshman year I volunteered that this person Descartes sounded like he got an awful lot of his material from a philosopher I had read called "Des-car-tease." Oh. The teacher got more excited over the mispronunciation than the fact that somebody had actually read something by a philosopher. After this episode, I became reticent to volunteer anything in class remotely related to my reading. Mispronunciation went on all the time at home and is part of the Bronx Syndrome. When my mother and I get together to gossip, I find myself listening to her with some nostalgia. She still asks me if I ever learned anything in all those years I studied "the-olokee." Of the three Bronx Syndrome characteristics, mispronunciation is probably the clearest indication of my background. I can keep myself from cursing and from punching people, but words just come out for the world to hear and to prove that there is a wide gulf between a reading and a speaking vocabulary.

My parents had a pragmatic view of a college education. One went to college to become a doctor, businessman, lawyer, or engineer. That was it. You most certainly did not spend time and money "finding yourself." I majored in accounting primarily out of respect for my parents' wishes but also because, although it was extremely boring, it was the best path I could find to graduate, make lots of money, and never have to attend school again. What my parents could not and would not figure into their plans for me, especially since neither of them had even finished high school, was that on any college campus a student is going to encounter ideas.

A theology professor, Zeke Esposito, opened up the world of ideas to me and changed my life forever. He was the most dynamic person I had ever met. He drove a white T-Bird, was tough, played and composed jazz, and danced professionally. He taught me it was possible to be smart and cool. He introduced me to a world I didn't know existed, populated by the likes of Kierkegaard, Margaret Mead, Martin Buber, and Harry Stack Sullivan. While my parents would never understand, I like to think they opened the door to college for me and pushed me through it. They had no idea what was on the other side of that door, and what waited there for me would have little or nothing to do with their own dreams and fantasies. For them education had nothing to do with ideas, but for me ideas became everything. When I tried to share this discovery with them, they simply reiterated that going to college was to learn a profession so "you won't have to work with your hands and you'll make a lot of money." Much of my anger, frustration, and sadness in those years came from not feeling supported or understood at home.

The actual choice of a college was simple. One went near home so one could commute and not have to pay room and board. In our house, it also had to be a Catholic college. That criterion eliminated the excellent state and city universities in New York and it added high tuition, which meant I had to work a lot. At one point I was carrying eighteen semester credits, doing fifteen hours of work-study a week, driving a truck from four to seven each night for a bank, and occasionally working weekends in a deli. I didn't study much and didn't get many As. It wasn't until years later that I stopped beating myself up over my academic performance, when a friend pointed out I had been working close to forty hours a week while carrying a full load, whereas she did not work at all in college and sometimes studied because there was nothing else to do.

The college, located in the upper reaches of the Bronx, was small and at best mediocre. The majority of its students were local, and they brought a lot of good, if perhaps raw, intellectual potential to the campus. Yet it seemed many of the professors resented having to teach us. One of them once described in class the mission of the school as "teaching the first generation of immigrant children how to eat with a knife and fork." We knew we were being insulted, but in order to get as far as college we had learned that school was the one place in our experience where we couldn't get in somebody's face, specifically the teacher's. So we took it. A lot of my friends who did not make it to college were those who would not stand for that kind of treatment; they insulted back, skipped classes or school altogether, and then they got in trouble. They dropped out or were kicked out. Not surprisingly, I do not recall a parent in the neighborhood who could have been a role model for us in the academic world. Those of us who ventured past high school were breaking new ground.

I graduated with a so-so education, a middling grade point average, a lot of metaphysical questions, a job with a "Big Eight" accounting firm, and a high salary. I left the firm after ten months of auditing. I found the work, at least at the first-year level, as dull as the courses had been, and the money did not provide enough of an inducement for me to stay. In addition, despite what I thought when I graduated from college, I wanted to learn more. I applied to graduate school to study theology and took a job as a high school teacher. It brought a substantial decrease in salary, but teaching would allow me to earn a living and attend graduate school part-time until I could establish some credentials and move into full-time studies for my doctorate. I also had a sense of mission. Zeke had died at thirty-two in a skindiving accident the year before I graduated, and I thought that perhaps just as he had turned me on to learning and ideas I could do something similar for kids like me coming through the system.

My parents wouldn't talk to me. This change was one of the major disappointments in their lives. It embarrassed them to tell people their son had gone to college and was now studying religion and teaching high school. Explaining my decision to them was out of the question; I never recall having an intellectual conversation with my parents. About all I can remember us talking about was the Depression, baseball, and the restaurant.

Still, we had a set of encyclopedias in the house, and my father sometimes came home with books for me that he found on sale with titles like *Dictionary of Classical Terms* and *Introduction to Music: A Guide to Good Listening*. I still have those two volumes as a reminder of this touching and complicated gesture. Yet, I never saw my father or mother read anything themselves except the newspaper. About four years ago I met the parents of a faculty colleague and was amazed and a little jealous that they could engage us in conversation ranging from gourmet food to our jobs to politics to music. This is not to say that my parents were stupid. They were workers and they were working for a better life for me. From them I learned how to work hard, treat everybody fairly (especially to watch out for the "little guy"), say what I mean, and do what I say I am going to do. I learned to tell the truth and value friendship.

At any rate, I survived my undergraduate education, proved I could succeed on the graduate level, and then left New York City to earn an M.A. in religious studies and the psychology of religion at Ottawa University in Canada, the same school Zeke had attended. I taught high school around the country until I got my Ed.D. degree from Seattle University. I spent a couple of years in school administration and discovered I had less than a flair for dealing with politics and bureaucracy. Thanks in large part to my doctoral work and my fellow students, my vocabulary expanded and my pronunciation improved. The Bronx accent stayed. I had taught as adjunct professor at a number of universities in the Seattle area and felt the time had come to make the move to full-time college teaching. This was my ultimate goal in pursuing the doctorate. I seemed to have a gift for teaching, and inspiring beginning instructors would hopefully help more K-12 kids who needed great teaching to open the world of ideas to them.

When I entered college teaching I did not consider my social back-ground much of an issue. I had been out of New York for thirteen years and had no intention of returning. Urban blight had rolled over the old neigh-borhood, and nobody I knew lived there anymore. My dad died of cancer at fifty, and two years later my mother moved back to the coal-mining town where she was raised. In a very real sense, my past had disappeared; even if I had wanted to go back I couldn't. Although I had some anxiety about being a professor, I held three degrees, took pride in my teaching and administra-tive abilities, had published a couple of things, and was looking forward to the new challenge of working full time with undergraduates. Anyway, in a pinch, I could always open a restaurant! I was a little concerned about having to move to the Midwest, but it was the only region I would consider that was hiring at the college level. Getting a position in the Pacific North-west was practically impossible.

Iowa has a lot of fine private liberal arts colleges, and for me there could not have been a better situation to begin a college teaching career. At Central College I found myself surrounded by the most intelligent and articulate group of individuals I had ever worked with. At any one table in the student center or faculty dining room could be found poets, political scientists, philosophers, economists, psychologists, and musicians. The conversations were great, especially when two of the verbal masters took to arguing about modern music or deconstruction. For me it was like being the proverbial kid in a candy shop.

Some of my anxiety was lifting and I felt sure I could fit in. Growing up, I had learned plenty about masking doubts with aggression. I was confident enough to talk to anyone about philosophy, religious studies, literature, or education. And although I am normally introverted, I simply could not keep my mouth shut most of the time—I was too excited. I wanted to get my ideas out there.

Unfortunately, my first year I was so busy learning the area and the system that there was hardly time to think, and I was seldom on campus. An education school or department, especially one that prepares teachers, is responsible to state as well as outside accrediting agencies. Together these organizations mandate what has to be taught, and they perform periodic audits to monitor compliance. These regulations seem to change every three years as state legislators continue to grapple with intractable educational problems.

I was assigned three course preparations and the title "director of secondary education." Practically every education course today has a field experience, which requires placement and supervision of students at various school sites. My most difficult task was placing students, exacerbated by being new to the region and without personal school contacts.

I found a pecking order on campus, which didn't come as a complete surprise. Although a negative stereotype of education exists in the world I grew up in, I didn't find the system as a whole operating much differently than the world outside academia. Rookie professors had to prove themselves, and education professors had to prove a little more. I went directly at the stereotype, generally with humor. At one of my first curriculum committee meetings, the chair asked "to hear from our esteemed colleague from the Education Department." "I'm not sure I can talk without my puppets," I replied. "Once we educators get away from puppet making we get confused." There was a moment of silence followed by a lot of laughter. I also worked to establish myself intellectually. I would drop by faculty offices to b.s. about poetry and philosophy, and once I even engaged a biologist in a discussion about neurophysiology. I found after several humorous routines and office visits, I was accorded a fair amount of respect. More importantly, I had no problem once it got around campus I was a good teacher. A competent professor is an asset to a school no matter what the area of expertise. It was no concern of mine if some faculty chose to quibble over whether a Ph.D. is "better" than an Ed.D. I was there to teach students and do some research and writing and had little interest in comparing disciplines and biased and subjective rankings. I was, however, dismayed to find a class system clearly existing among the various subject areas, a discovery that surprised me at a liberal arts school.

Later on, through discussions with education faculty at other schools, I discovered the chauvinism regarding education as a discipline is widespread. Of all the disciplines, education has the most first-generation college graduates and the largest proportion of faculty with working-class backgrounds. Further, since most education professors began as elementary or secondary school teachers, they are often perceived to be more "practical," less theoretical, or intellectually less rigorous than their colleagues in other fields, especially in the liberal arts. While overemphasis on the practical concerns of the classroom can lead some education professors to anti-intellectualism, I think we could go a long way toward modeling intellectual flexibility for our students if we acted on the premise that the search for truth also moves laterally across disciplines. A diversity of opinion from the practical to the purely theoretical can provide a good stimulus to intellectual growth without need to rank disciplines or degrees on campus.

My own undergraduate education did little to prepare me for intellectual discourse, but the roots of the problem were in my early home and street environment. We did not argue politely either at home or in the street. Might made right. Neither my mother nor my father felt they had to justify anything they told my sister and me. Backed up against the wall verbally, all further discussion would end with "because I said so." Although this was an efficient way to win debates, it did very little to enhance listening skills. My parents never listened, and after a while neither did I. The important thing was to get my way.

On the street or playground, arguments generally ended in "do-overs" (when an impasse seemed to be reached, in the interest of time and avoiding bloodshed, the whole play was simply repeated as though the first one hadn't occurred) or fights, both following often lengthy, loud, crude, and insulting yelling matches. Not to engage in these verbal and physical battles was to be a wimp and could exclude one from any sort of street game or activity. We were all adept at colorful and aggressive shouting. I remember the kitchen scene in Martin Scorsese's *Raging Bull* where the Robert DeNiro and Joe Pesci characters are arguing at the table. They shouted so much and used the word *fuck* so many times I thought I was back in the old neighborhood. Bronx Syndrome at its best.

Where I came from, the immediate and practically the only response to a fellow ignoring or contradicting an explanation three times is to yell and go for the throat—literally and figuratively. Early in my college career silence was the only way to override that response, and this is exactly what happened in the faculty luncheon with which I began this essay. All the verbal cues I was receiving indicated the questioner was insulting me and pushing for a fight. However, his physical demeanor most certainly contradicted that impression. The mixed message I was getting was further clouded by the fact that we were close to violating the unwritten rule that you don't fight with the people you hang with. I might have expected to be attacked by a faculty person from Luther College, but not by somebody from my own campus.

I gained some insight into the rules of this new neighborhood, academia, from my friend and colleague William. Once we were walking across campus to a faculty meeting, and he said he was looking forward to the gathering because there were sure to be good arguments this time. I was surprised and asked, "You're actually looking forward to arguing?" His reply surprised me even more: "I like arguing. It's a good way to compete intellectually and have fun. The issue doesn't have to matter." He held the door open for me as we entered the meeting room, gave me one of his rare smiles, and said, "Academics like to argue."

This blew me away. Faculty were not necessarily searching for truth or the "right" answer. By challenging me about the either/or nature of the Meyers-Briggs research I was presenting, John, the questioner, just may have been opening the door for fun. When I did not respond according to protocol, he tried again and then again. Undoubtedly *he* was receiving mixed messages, too. It was as if we were engaged in different and separate rituals in which neither of us understood the rules the other was playing by.

I remembered how we argued about baseball back in the old days. When not much was going on and the prospects for anything happening were dim, somebody would say something like, "Mays is better than Mantle." Off we'd go, sometimes for hours. From the outset, the argument was never to be resolved. It gave us a chance to yell, jump up and down, but mostly to demonstrate what we knew about the game. How many records could we cite? How did the statistics compare? How many irrelevant players (e.g., Duke Snider) could we bring in to bolster our positions? Nobody took this type of argument personally enough to get the other guy in a headlock. It was just fun. Once I had this insight, I decided to approach academic squabbles like Mays/Mantle arguments.

Just how much academics like to argue received some objective validation when a friend in the communications department and I began timing debates at faculty meetings. We discovered the longer the argument ran, sometimes over an hour on a relatively minor issue, the more likely it was that when the motion was called it would pass unanimously. Viewed from my background, this represents a considerable waste of time and talent.

When I would talk with faculty as we filed out of the room, I discovered many of them were also frustrated with the length of the meeting, yet they were sometimes the most active participants in the discussion. On the other hand, I am sure my need for closure and to "get it done" amuses my colleagues. Many of these professors have ego needs rivaling the best of athletes. In the nonacademic environment of the lower Bronx, boys and young men were rated largely by their physical ability or lack thereof. In academia, men and women are rated by their knowledge and how they demonstrate it. Since professors can't get out and throw a pass or race a thought, one way we *can* test each other and discover some things about our own intellectual prowess is by discussing and arguing ideas. Once I hooked into this notion, I began to relax a little and work at learning this new game. Maybe I could get good at it too?

Of course, as with departments, I found there is a hierarchical ranking of academic players, too, much like there is in baseball. Metaphorically, some academics can't hit the curve, some are utility players. Some strike out a lot, and others are singles hitters. A few are good glove but no bat. Superstars share the field with some who don't belong on it. In addition, the academic game has silly uniforms (academic regalia), complex rules (tenure), standings (rank), different leagues (Ivy, Big Ten), and colorful history. The former baseball star Ralph Kiner once said, "That's the great thing about baseball— you never know exactly what's going on." No wonder so many academics have taken to writing about it.

For me all of this meant that what was originally threatening and aggravating had become fun. Coming out of a visiting author's reading, one of my colleagues said, "I can't see how she can write. She's a boring reader."

"Her writing is great. Have you read her?" I asked.

He responded, "I don't have to to know."

"Well, maybe if I had studied religion a little longer," I offered, "I would be omniscient by now, too." He didn't curse or get me in a headlock. He laughed. I laughed. And we went for a beer.

The good nature, intelligence, respect, and care of many of my colleagues at Central College went a long way to develop my confidence and to help me grow. I owe them a lot and feel especially lucky to have begun my career at a liberal arts college where disciplines are integrated rather than separated into schools. Near the end of my fourth year at Central a position opened in the School of Education at the University of Portland in Oregon. I realized the eleven years I spent in the Pacific Northwest made the place home. I missed the friends I had made there; I missed the landscape, the microbreweries, and the gourmet coffee. When I found myself missing the rain, I knew I had grown homesick and thought everything would be perfect if Central could be relocated to the Northwest. In one of the most difficult decisions I have made, I accepted the new position.

I found it easier to establish myself this time around. The biggest difference had little to do with my background and more to do with the structure of the university. The division of the university into separate schools made interdisciplinary discussion more difficult. I was talking about this with the dean, Verne Duncan, in his office one afternoon during a meeting relating to my professional goals. He told me a story: When he was very young his grandfather brought him to Salem, Oregon, where they visited the office of the state superintendent of public instruction. Verne recalled sitting behind the desk and thinking, "One day I want this to be mine." As it turned out, he went on to a successful career in education, including fifteen years as state superintendent before he took the deanship.

I couldn't help but think about the first time I visited my dad at work. Big stuff. I was six and my mother gave me a token to take the subway downtown to his restaurant on the upper east side of the city. It was a small, narrow place. There were no booths, just some stools and a counter. The kitchen was behind a swinging green door at the rear of the store. I met delivery men, police officers, mechanics, and workers from Rupert's brewery just across the street. I sat in the small back room with my dad and helped him peel potatoes. I was fascinated by how good he was at everything he did and at how many people he knew. They all seemed to like him, and they made a big deal over me. He sold the place five or six years later, and when we began working together in the new one the work was exposed as both unromantic and hard. But the first visit was a happy day and one of my best memories of my father.

Like the dean, most of the people I work with at college come from professional families. In many instances the parents of my colleagues are first-generation professionals, and I have often thought I would be more comfortable with them than with my peers. Their children take for granted a certain level of education and sophistication. If I had children, they would be comparable to my colleagues in terms of the intellectual opportunities available to them. These would not only encompass the people they would meet and know but also such basic things as family discussions and their choice of a university or college. It is as if I am a familial step behind in the academic world.

There is really nothing to be done for that. I have taught and counseled long enough to see in many colleagues and students the difference attending a great versus a good versus a mediocre college makes in a career. It is not only a question of being smart but also of who taught you and who is writing your references or making phone calls on your behalf. There is also much to be said for the quality of teachers and students you are surrounded by. Professors are certainly not announcing to classes at Stanford, Grinnell, or Brown that they are teaching table manners to first-generation kids. Regardless of what fosters that attitude, it is as rude and inappropriate as cursing and leaping across a table to choke somebody who disagrees with you.

The *dese, dose,* and *dems* that stream from my mouth when I am excited undoubtedly mark me. But as I grew more confident I began to take more pride in my background. I thought it gave me a chance to add a unique voice to the academic chorus. In some ways my accent has become symbolic, and I am reluctant to give it up even if I could. Zeke Esposito taught me I could be smart without being a nerd. Books and ideas are exciting, and looking back I think that discovery was probably what I was trying to share with my Bronx pals after I read *The Anger of Achilles.* My career could be viewed as ongoing attempts to model and explain this excitement to my students. To me this is an opportunity and a trust bordering on the sacred. It demands persistent effort to do the thing right. The tension inherent in being a working-class academic with Bronx Syndrome is part of that effort and a relatively small price to pay.

4

The Screenwriter's Tale

Jennifer Lawler

Everything I have been doing lately has been contaminated by Hollywood. As contaminations go, I'll take Hollywood every time. I'm pretty content with the idea of letting fame and fortune go to my head. I'm looking forward to becoming shallow and superficial.

What actually happened was, I wrote a novel and my agent showed it to a producer—this is the only useful thing my agent has ever done—and said producer asked if I would adapt the novel to a screenplay. I said, "Hell, yes." I'd like to know who wouldn't. So I've been sitting around waiting to get corrupted and stuff, and it can't happen fast enough to suit me.

The problem with adapting a novel to a screenplay is that you can't do anything else. For instance, I have spent four months rewriting plot outlines, since I am in charge of pleasing everyone at the studio. I have revised the plot outline seventeen times, and the outline they finally approved looks exactly like the first one I sent them. I am so busy pleasing the producer that I am incapable of doing anything else. I cannot finish the novel I am currently working on, I cannot write a scholarly research paper, I cannot even finish a letter to my sister, I am losing my mind. Susan says no one's noticed the difference, as far as she can see. Susan is my friend. She's a real scholar. I mean, you ask her a question like, "Who was Sir Walter Raleigh's son's tutor?" and she knows the answer. I mean, without having to look it up.

Anyway. Everywhere I look, all I see are possible movie scenes. I can't write a line without thinking, "I wonder how this would sound if Mel Gibson were saying it." I want Mel to star in my movie. Whenever I read anything, I sit there casting parts. I think Sean Connery would make a really good Green Knight. I wonder if Harrison Ford would be interested in doing *Beowulf*. I can't even go to the grocery store without making it a dramatic moment, fraught with significant silences and carefully crafted emotion: "You want *how* much for a grapefruit?" or I'm getting kissed by a guy and I'm wondering, Is this scene effectively conveyed to the audience?

Susan says it's unfortunate there was an audience to start with since kissing should be done in private.

So you see how this screenplay has affected me.

Susan says, "Don't blame the screenplay. You lacked decorum long before Hollywood ever got hold of you."

I keep waiting for all the sex scenes to happen, but unfortunately my life gets a G rating. It's really depressing when you can tell your mother every single intimate detail of your life and all she can say is, "That's nice, dear."

Do I look like I ever wanted to lead a NICE LIFE????

Ha.

I wanted to write mystery novels. Really incredibly good mysteries. I wanted to be moderately successful at this so that I wouldn't have to hold down a real job. I wanted to chain smoke Marlboro Reds and drink vodka straight from the bottle and stare moodily at the ceiling, just like all good mystery novelists do.

So that's what I set out to do, and, as you can see, Fate intervened. Fate is inevitable, according to most Anglo-Saxon poetry, and I've always thought that was a slightly redundant statement. But then, most Anglo-Saxon poetry is redundant. It's that oral-formulaic thing.

Anyway, Fate intervened and I ended up in graduate school, trying to be a scholar.

This is not as easy as it sounds. Neither the getting here nor the being here. It made sense at the time, you see; I wanted to write stories, but you have to eat somehow, and I got through college for that reason. Afterwards I held jobs where people criticized me for stupid things like keeping callers on hold too long, and so one day I gave it all up. (It's easy when you have nothing to lose.) I liked college the first time around and thought I'd give it another try. I could eat on a teacher's salary (that's what English majors become), but of course I never really had any say: it was all Fate.

And Fate is inevitable.

But graduate school has been nothing like college was the first time around, and trying to be a scholar is harder on me than I ever thought it would be, especially this year. Ever since I started the screenplay, I haven't been worth a damn as either a novelist or a scholar.

Susan says, "You weren't worth a damn as a novelist even before that producer got hold of you."

All I can say is, What does Susan know? She's never had to wring a 357-page novel from a six-word idea.

Susan says, "You weren't worth a damn as a scholar, either."

Susan is really a maternal person at heart, sort of like a mountain lion. She's been in charge of me for about a year now, and she takes her responsibilities very seriously, except when there's a football game on.

One of Susan's responsibilities involves making me act like a scholar. This consists of her saying, "You aren't wearing that to class, are you?" She reminds me, fairly constantly, that the English Department is very conservative and that I am not very conservative, and her conclusion is that one of us is going to lose. She also gives good advice like, "If you want to be taken seriously, you will never breathe the word *Hollywood* on campus. Never. And if I were you, thank God I'm not, I would never say anything about writing popular fiction. Maybe if you were capable of writing literature, that would be okay. But never say the words *mystery novel* around here."

Then she always says, "Look, do you want a tenure-track position or not?"

Susan is a practical person. It's one of her more annoying traits. I'm putting all this in so that you will realize that this essay is all Susan's fault. She didn't stop me in time. Her other responsibility is putting a stop to me. She feels that someone needs to, and maybe she's right.

Anyway, I'm going to talk about mysteries and Hollywood A LOT, see if I care. Just imagine I'm being my usual self, the way I am when Susan isn't making me be a scholar. Let me help you out here. Visualize a short brunette with delusions of grandeur who looks about ten years old but is really much older than that with an Irish temper and a sense of humor that no one has ever in the history of the world appreciated. I have a tiny scar on the left side of my face from falling out an apple tree when I was twelve, trying to climb too high. I inherited the Grecian nose from my father, who taught me how to think and tried also to teach me what to think, but this last failed. He doesn't mind. And the broad peasant cheekbones come from my mother, the merchant's daughter, who learned to be a lady and passed this on to me; the things I know, should I be in the presence of a king, I owe to her. I try not to forget them, and sometimes I practice when it is late at night. I balance the book on my head instead of reading it because the magazines showed my mother how this improved posture, but the things she wanted for me were things I did not understand. There is a whole history behind this face. It isn't just the twelve gray hairs and the wrinkles at the corners of my eyes or the fact that my skin got over being way too oily and now it's way too dry. It's the stories my aunts and uncles tell me when they look at me and say what I remind them of, and tangled up with the genealogy are memories of passion and love and hatred and leaving and "Ave Maria" and McCarthy and raising children and fixing cars and riding horses and prisoner-of-war camps and razor wire, things I make nightmares from. Things I make stories from, the stories that I tell, but I don't expect people to believe them, either.

If it were possible, I would describe myself, but I am far too tempted to lie. I would give myself a house and a lover or maybe a husband and three children or maybe a place in Manhattan and say that I can afford to park my car there. But really, if I were from New York, I would be from the Bronx. I try never to talk about myself in the English Department because I would be horrified if they found me out. They expect people to be truthful there; they don't appreciate artistic embellishments. When I hang out at the English Department, I try never to actually say anything about myself, but it happened that I was in the English Department one day, just schlepping around, talking to a professor, a medievalist. (I try only to talk to other medievalists.) So he says, "How's the reading list coming?" and I say it's not. I make the mistake of saying that I am having trouble with a scene I am trying to write, and it's taking all my time and effort.

"What scene?" he wants to know.

"I'm writing a screenplay," I say, trying not to wince. It sounds so awful when I say it out loud, especially in the middle of the English Department.

"You're doing WHAT?" he inquires.

"I've got a contract," I apologize.

"If I were you," he says, "I would never have done that."

"Oh," I say, or something like that.

He gives me a severe look and commences lecturing me on the duties and obligations of a graduate student. When he's done with that, he lectures me on the duties and obligations of a graduate teaching assistant. What it boils down to is, graduate students shouldn't write screenplays. If you want to be taken seriously as a scholar, you don't write movies, especially if any car-chase scenes are involved.

So I stand there, dumbfounded, staring across the chasm that separates us. What do you mean, I want to ask, what do you mean, not write? I do not think he understands about making things, about nails you put in boards and houses you make with your own hands. I think, you know, this is a guy who has to go to the gym to work up a sweat. I don't say this out loud.

I am a writer. He is a scholar. It's a distance between us. Sometimes it seems impossible. Sometimes it seems I do all the compromising.

All right. No one said the rules would change for me. The only writers welcome here are dead ones. The live ones are shunted into the creative writing program where they are never heard from again. They might as well be in another department for all the connection they have with literature. At some universities, they *are* in a different department.

A teacher I know says, "I get so irritated when my composition students think that's what English is." She explains to her students that composition classes are a service of the English Department and that composition is not what we do. What we do is Literature.

Oh. I see. Of course, any idiot knows that reading and writing have nothing to do with each other. Being a writer and being a student of literature are completely unrelated. A mere coincidence. An accident. You can be a writer and a scholar as long as your being a writer has no influence on your being a scholar.

I know of someone else who tried to do this, be a writer and a scholar, and, as Thomas Kirby remarked about him, "Surely there is at least something to be said for the writer who is sometimes brightly wrong rather than always dully right" (266). This, of course, after strongly cautioning that John Gardner was, after all, a popular novelist and therefore his biography of Chaucer was apt to be a little, oh . . . "abetted by imagination" (Kirby 265). Which I guess is a bad thing. I will have to ask Susan. She will surely know. That's one of the things Susan tells me. She says I sound like a writer, not a scholar. For instance, I refuse to use the words *tautological* and *belletristic* because I always forget we have them, and I use real words instead. This is WRONG of me, I know, and Susan has been trying to teach me to write like a scholar, which seems to consist mostly of obscuring ideas rather than communicating them. Susan has successfully failed to put any content into every paper she's ever written. That fact impresses the hell out of me. I wish I could do that. But no, I have spent my whole life developing this really great (okay, so *great* is a relative term) fiction style, and it just won't do for scholarship. No. You have to take really really long words and make them into really really long sentences, and then you take the really really long sentences and you make them into really really long paragraphs, and then you take the really really long paragraphs, and you arrange them in a closely argued way, using logic and reason. But none of the words are supposed to be yours, you have to borrow them from other people, because obviously your words aren't good enough, and then you have to tell the whole universe that you borrowed your words from other people, who presumably borrowed their words from yet someone else, referred to as a "scholar." And then there's this whole book on the proper way of borrowing words and also on how you admit to it, and then the whole thing has to follow a certain manuscript format, and all of it depends on what style manual you are told to use, there are about nine hundred of them, AND FRANKLY I DON'T NEED THAT KIND OF PRESSURE!!!

Life in academia is very hard on me.

I remember being absolutely horrified when I found out that scholars spent all this time borrowing other people's words and rearranging them into papers and then getting these papers published, and doing it for free. I mean, scholars don't get paid for publishing stuff. I think we need a union or something. I have never heard of this, you know; if my royalty checks are thirteen seconds late, I'm on the phone with my lawyer. But scholars, who are ladies and gentlemen, do these sorts of labors for love, not profit.

To which I always say, love is highly overrated.

Okay. Here's another true story. When I first spoke to my producer, she wanted to write a bio sheet, and she asked me what I did for a living. I told her I was a graduate student.

She said, "Oh, God. Not an academic. I can't tell them you're an academic."

You know how academics feel about people who make movies for a living? That's exactly the same way they feel about us.

So I said I also worked in a lumber yard, which was true at the time, and she was all excited. "I can tell them you are a blue-collar worker."

This, it seems, makes my writing real. Scholars don't know, of course, what the real world is like, the one that gives you callouses on your hands. I haven't had the nerve to tell her that I no longer work at the lumber yard. I'm not about to tell her I'm a teacher now. That would make everything worse. I'm not going to tell any of them. I may never own up. But I'm afraid someone's going to rat on me, do this big, startling exposé, and I'll never hear from my agent, editor, or producer again.

I am beginning to feel hunted.

I am in the middle of this war, you see, and when you are in the middle of a war, you declare your allegiance, you say to whom you are loyal. I'd do this, I would take a side, I would say, "I'm a writer" or "I am a scholar." I would do this, I would give one of them up, if I could find a way to do so without dying of the loss. I don't know. I guess scholars don't go around, bleating, "I would just die if I didn't read *Morte d'Arthur* once a year." Scholars—real scholars, I mean, like my friend Susan—approach literature differently from the way I do.

Lots of writers question the literacy of scholars because they so often get it wrong. Now, I study literature by reading it and saying, hey, that's pretty good.

This, also, is WRONG of me.

In the first place, I'm never entirely sure if it is appropriate for a scholar to actually like literature. For instance, I like medieval literature. No. I *love* medieval literature. Medieval literature is the only stuff I will read, unless I am forcibly made to look at Dickens or someone, which happens every now and then. Anyway, I read criticism on medieval literature because I am supposed to. You can't get a Ph.D. unless you do (there's something they don't tell you up front) and there's some guy, a Scholar, explicating (what the hell is wrong with the word *explaining?*), and he's helping me out by comparing hypermetric Type D2 oral-formulaic alliterative verse, or something, and I'm real thankful for that, you know, it really clarifies the whole thing for me.

This is what I know: If you recite *Beowulf* in Old English, it sounds just like the end of the world. You get some old Anglo-Saxon scholar to do it for you and I swear you will be on your knees, begging forgiveness. This appeals to me. You listen to *Beowulf* and you will hear doom. You are supposed to. That's what *Beowulf* is about. Doom.

I have another favorite. "The Wanderer." This is the first part:

Oft him anhaga   are gebideth
Metudes miltse   theah the he modcearig
geond lagulade   longe sceolde
hreran mid hondum   hrimcealde sae
Swa cwaeth eardstapa   earfetha gemyndig
wrathra waelsleahta   winemaega hryre
Oft ic sceolde ana   uhtna gehwylce
mine ceare cwithan   Nis nu cwicra nan
the ic him modsefan   minne durre
sweotule asecgan. . . .
(Cassidy and Ringler 324–25)

Isn't that the most beautiful poem in the whole world? Since my word processor has no wynn, ash, edh, thorn, or that weird-looking "z" letter that I can never remember the name of, I have transliterated them into their modern English equivalents. The really great thing about Old English is that if you don't know what the word means, it means "warrior."

All right, here's the translation into modern English:

Often, he who is the lone-dweller awaits grace,
the mercy of the Lord, even though for a long
time he, heart-anxious, over the waterway has
to stir up with his hands the ice-cold sea, to
journey the paths of exile: Fate is inevitable.

So spoke the earth-walker, mindful of hardship,
cruel slaughter, the fall of precious kinsmen:
"Often I must alone at each dawn my cares lament.
There is not now one living creature to whom I
dare openly tell my heart. . . ."[1]

If you know that a medieval warrior paid fealty to a lord and that if he showed cowardice or his lord died he became an exile, doomed to wander without protection, at the mercy of any old Geat or Dane, you'll appreciate "The Wanderer."

This is the kind of thing a scholar does know. A scholar knows about warriors and exile and the philosophy of the average Anglo-Saxon, and they (we, God forbid?) nod wisely and say, yes, that's the old wandering-the-paths-of-exile thing again.

The first time I read "The Wanderer," as a writer who liked the sounds of the words, I didn't know about exiles. And I found that you don't need to know about exiles to understand "The Wanderer." You need only have been lonely once.

Every time I read "The Wanderer," I forget that I am a scholar who knows about exiles. I forget, even, the long and arduous process of learning Old English. I forget about the oral-formulaic tradition, and the words "Fate is inevitable" sound profound to me.

I know exactly how the Wanderer feels. I knew before I ever studied literature in a systematic, scholarly way, and sometimes I am afraid that all I will eventually do is obscure the Wanderer from my sight. I worry about that. You'd think I'd have enough to worry about.

The Seafarer says, "Let us consider where we may have a home and then think how we may get there."

Why can I never say anything that well? I despair of ever saying anything that well. When I read, I think, if I could only say it that well. That's exactly right; if only I could say it like that.

My critical apparatus is pretty uncomplicated. If I envy it, it's good. If I envy it, it is profound and beautiful and true. If I don't envy it, somehow it's not literature.

I am constantly comparing myself to other writers. And when I think I am better than they, that should tell you something. It tells me something.

I have been reading the *Cursor Mundi*. That's the history of the world. The definitive edition, from Genesis to Doomsday. I picked it up to read it because I thought I might be in it and I have been wondering how all this turns out.

How can there be a history of the world till Doomsday? It's just the sort of thing a medieval scribe would do. It's just the sort of thing I would do. Remember Revelations? That's how the scribe knew what happens. Of course, the Vulgate version is different from what we have, but you remember, "And behold a pale horse and him that sat upon it was Death and Hell followed with him."

I love reading stuff like that.

They were storytellers, that's all. The need to tell stories has always been a human drive, ever since humans flopped out of the water and gasped on dry land. I imagine they looked around, those prehumans, and said, "This would make a really great story. Now if only we had hands to write it down with."

You know how the tribal storyteller would gather the people around and begin: This is the history of our people. There has never been a generation into which a storyteller was not born. It was a special position. Sometimes there were omens. This child will hold the memory of our people.

After a while, the storytellers began making their stories up, and this was usually okay with everyone because while only a few people are ever storytellers, all people have the need to hear stories.

To me, medieval literature is a group of stories. Just wonderful stories about some things. We have, I think, forgotten about storytelling. We have forgotten why we tell stories.

I study medieval writers so that I will never forget why I tell stories. We tell stories so that other people will hear them. I do, anyway. I don't worry about writing literature. Lit-ra-chur. I worry about telling stories.

Chaucer didn't worry about writing literature. Shakespeare didn't. Dickens didn't. They wrote stories for people, plain people, like the guys I used to work with at the lumber yard. They wrote because they had to, being storytellers. They wrote because they had to, and the rent was due. They managed to make literature out of their stories because they were geniuses.

Sometimes I am sad that we have become so snobbish and elitist. It's why I find Chaucer comforting. He told stories, just like a storyteller is supposed to.

Okay, okay. So maybe those stories aren't very realistic. Who cares? I've got "real" right outside my front door, you should see it. But you read stories with a willing suspension of disbelief. I hope you read my stories like that. I mean, in my screenplay, everyone lives happily ever after.

Oh, please. We all know about how likely that is. But I, like Chaucer's Knight, prefer happy endings. I always have happy endings when I am in charge of telling the stories.

This is how I read medieval literature. It is how I can read sexism and religious dogmas I don't believe in. I don't dismiss it. I don't go around saying, oh, that's so sexist. I read the damned story and I suspend my reality and I accept that Gawain is going to have an antifemale tirade. When he does, he is merely adding discourtesy to the long list of his flaws. (You think the Green Knight didn't know that?) I remember that these are just stories like the ones I tell, only better written.

I think I should probably be criticized for doing this. Probably a scholar isn't supposed to read this way. Probably scholars are supposed to use various interpretive approaches; but I imagine they have to use various interpretive approaches because they have never told stories. Only listened to them.

Sometimes I wonder why they think they should be allowed to get away with it, criticizing the storyteller. I think you should only be allowed to criticize the storyteller if you are a better storyteller. Anything else seems like armchair quarterbacking to me.

I know this is also WRONG of me. I know I don't sound like a serious scholar. Who cares? I know it sounds like I study medieval literature because it passes the time when I'm in the middle of writer's block. But that's not why I study literature. I study literature because I connect with it. Just not the same way a scholar does.

For instance, I'm reading Layamon's *Brut,* and I'm thinking, you know, I'm positive I am descended from the Picts. If I painted myself blue, I would look exactly like a Pict. I don't know that scholars are supposed to go around thinking things like that. I don't know how many scholars go, "Wouldn't it be cool if I were descended from the Picts?"

Sometimes I wonder what I am doing in academia. Sometimes I wonder what a scholar is good for. I know what storytellers are good for. I know Chaucer told stories because he had to. I'll bet you he even had writer's block a couple of times. I think that's how he ended up translating *La Roman de la Rose.* Imagine that, having writer's block and thereby changing the course of history. I am hoping to change the course of history sometimes when I have writer's block.

People keep assuring me I would understand medieval literature better if I approached it as a scholar, not as an envious writer, not as a kid from Kansas imagining how neat it would have been if only she could have been a Celtic warrior.

So I try. I try to understand what some scholars call the "peculiar character" of medieval literature. The "peculiar character" of the medieval mind.

Because, of course, you can't appreciate literature unless you understand all those things. I spend a lot of time visualizing myself as a medieval peasant. Trying to live on a GTA stipend, for instance, can give you some startling insights into the nature of poverty in the Middle Ages. I'd have killed the tax collector, too.

But most of the time, I am not exactly sure what I am supposed to do as a scholar. When I quit work at the lumber yard, I told the foreman I would be teaching part time and studying the rest of the time. He stared at me some and moved the wad of tobacco around in his mouth and finally said, "That ain't working." He gestured toward the loading dock where two semis were jockeying for position. It was our task to unload those trucks.

"Now that," he said slowly, patiently, so that I could grasp the concept, "*that's* workin'."

Sometimes I wonder if maybe that's why I am here, to get out of having to hold down a real job. I never much liked unloading those damned trucks. Sometimes I have the sneaking suspicion that that's why all of us are here. We just love to read, and if we call ourselves "scholars" we can fool everyone into thinking we are doing more than that, and we can get out of having to unload the semis.

I am here because the only two things I have ever loved—literature and writing—collided. I landed here writing creatively about Grendel, which, let it be said, was not exactly what anyone wanted. But it is exactly what I wanted because I labor under the assumption that, as a writer, I can share medieval literature with everyone in the world. I labor under the assumption that I can illuminate medieval literature, the way the monks once did.

This, I know, is WRONG of me.

I know that I put no less than twenty-three quotations from medieval literature into the screenplay, and the producer was "enchanted." Her word. The hero's nickname is Beowulf, not Rambo. The screenplay is a chivalric romance; the characters go on a crusade. The producer recognized that right off, even if she didn't have the right term for it. Well, it's not quite a chivalric romance. It's a chivalric romance the way Chaucer or the *Gawain* poet would write a chivalric romance. It's got satire and parody and irony and gallows humor. Chaucer would be proud of me. I like to think so, anyway. I am hoping to contaminate Hollywood the way Hollywood has contaminated me.

Sometimes after I have been studying all day, I indulge in a little fantasy. I'm at Yale or somewhere, I'm chair of the department, and I go stand in the middle of the campus and I shriek, "I write mystery novels! I write screenplays! And you can't stop me!"

Susan says a real scholar would never act like that.

I'm going to do it anyway.

NOTE

1. I am indebted to S.A.J. Bradley, whose modern English translation of "The Wanderer" (in *Anglo-Saxon Poetry,* trans. and ed. S.A.J. Bradley [London: J. M. Dent and Sons, 1982]) has greatly influenced my own.

WORKS CITED

Cassidy, Frederic, and Richard N. Ringler, eds. *Bright's Old English Grammar and Reader.* 3d ed. 2d corrected printing. New York: Holt, 1971.

Kirby, Thomas. "The General Prologue." In *Companion to Chaucer Studies,* ed. Beryl Rowland. Rev. ed. New York: Oxford University Press, 1979. 243–70.

5

You Were Raised Better Than That

Naton Leslie

We were drinking a beer. Driving and drinking a beer from a six-pack we'd bought at the corner drive-up beverage store. It was my father's idea. I had just bought this car, new.

"I was thinking," my father said, after we had opened the cans and taken a swallow. "Did I push you too hard to find work?" He paused and swallowed again to collect his thoughts. "I mean, I was always after you to get a good job, and you had all this college in mind. But you've done all right, the way you wanted to do it. I just hope I didn't push you too hard."

"No," I said. "It's like you used to say, finding a job is like being a ball in a roulette wheel: you bounce and roll around until you find your slot. I just found my slot." I was letting him off the hook, and I knew it. He *had* pushed me, complained that I needed to "get a start," a phrase that meant I should find a good-paying job and work at it for the rest of my life. He hadn't opposed my attending college, although the local university where I eventually received a B.A., Youngstown State in Youngstown, Ohio, was "good enough." And I should have majored in engineering, according to my father. After all, the only professionals he knew were doctors, lawyers, and the engineers at the factory where he worked. They were privileged; they wore better clothes and carried clipboards.

This new car was also made at a factory near my hometown, at the General Motors assembly plant in Lordstown, Ohio. It was one of the many factories that had been near closing or laying off workers when I graduated high school in 1974. It was an area known for manufacturing and iron and steel production, but the steel mills are gone now and with them thousands of jobs, livings. The Lordstown plant nearly closed as it had been responsible for making the ill-fated Chevrolet Vega, a car with a self-destructing aluminum block engine and a frame that routinely broke in half. Now the factory produces Chevrolet Cavaliers, a fairly solid car, and, as my father says, "the guys at Lordstown are scared for their jobs so they tighten those bolts a little better. Make sure the car's good." Those "guys" were the men and women with whom I grew up and graduated. I bought this car because I figured I owed them one.

I could be working there, too, had I majored in engineering at YSU. It would have been an effortless, predictable slot. The public high school I attended was geared toward creating factory workers. There were two tracks: "general studies" and "academic preparation." I clearly remember being selected for a track at the end of my eighth grade year. A teacher, a half-drunk physics instructor, had declared that I should be in general studies, whose curriculum included industrial arts, simplified mathematics, and no foreign languages. I was, after all, a weak mathematics student, so how could I succeed in an academic preparation program and then attend an engineering school? It was that simple: either I was to be a worker or an engineer. What else could be expected of these children?

I was adamant. I would be in an academic track; I was going to college. My father wasn't sure it really mattered, but I was. I was going to be a writer and had guessed by then that a college education and a life as a writer were complementary. But wanting to be educated and to be a writer were exotic notions. We were not supposed to lead lives of thought or imagination. In northeastern Ohio, industry was king, and steel mills constituted the palace guard. Generations of workers were born, had children who replaced them, and died in these mills. It was without question the only way of life. When a boy (or girl, though job equality for women in industry was not achieved until the factories had ceased to exist) finished high school or quit, family members worked to get him an application at one of the mills, to get him a "start." He was then expected to work midnight or swing shifts, buy a new car, drink hard, and eventually "settle down," get married, have children. If this youth had a talent that was not useful at the mill, it became a hobby— the artistic air-brushed designs on vans and motorcycles, for example. But when the mills closed, the rules changed.

Years later, at my first teaching position at a regional campus of a large state university, I saw myself in the rows of students in my basic composition courses. The conditions had not changed; the mills and factories were gone, victims of the shift to the "service economy," and students who had never considered going to college were there, general equivalency diplomas or general studies backgrounds their only preparation. I stood in an unenviable position as their writing teacher. I was the enemy, another version of some teacher in the eighth grade who had declared them unfit for academic pursuits. I stood in the way of their associate degrees, the new goal that society has hurried to erect to give these disenfranchised students a modicum of hope. So I had to be endured. I hope that over the course of the semester they found that I knew them better than they believed I could, that I sympathized with them and desperately wanted them to learn. Some wedged classes between a day job at a restaurant and a night job guarding a warehouse or a closed factory. Others locked their children in rusted station wagons in the parking lot for the hour or two they attended class. Some, though it may seem uncharitable to say so, were belligerently ignorant and were infuriated that the rules no longer permitted them to remain that way. On the bad days, it was like teaching people to drive cars who would rather walk or ride bicycles.

Their attitude toward education is summed up in a working-class aphorism: I'd rather have common sense than an education. I remember being confronted with this adage by steelworkers I met at a diner in Trenton, Ohio. I ate breakfast at a Big Boy restaurant before class at Miami University-Hamilton, sitting anonymously at the counter, shift workers from the Middletown steel mill at each elbow. Then the workers discovered what I did for a living, and one announced, "I always say that an education is nothing compared to good, common horse sense. What do you say to that, Prof?" I had long ago developed an answer for this question, having been asked it by family and friends for too many years: "I believe those who say they prefer one to the other are usually lacking in both." At a tavern, this statement would get you the broken butt end of a cue stick for a souvenir, but in the bright of day in a diner it simply shuts down the discussion. Pithy statements could carry the weight of law.

This strain of American anti-intellectualism, I am convinced, was instilled in the working class to keep them uneducated. Industrial America did not need an educated workforce, and if that workforce valued education, an unnecessary distraction, it would have thinned the pool of workers. I remember the long lines of people outside of factory gates on the days it was announced or rumored that "they would be handing out applications" for jobs. Some would camp out the night before, in those days when the working class became unnecessary, in the dark days of the 1970s when the rules changed. If you could just "get in" at a mill or factory that had survived the closings, then life could proceed normally. They were waiting in line for a chance for their lives to begin. To this day when my father suggests that I move closer to home, he names a college or university nearby and asks if I've heard when they're "giving out applications." I've learned simply to answer no rather than try to explain.

The engineers fared no better in this. The engineering graduates from YSU were simply skilled workers, not educated ones. I had tried a year of that, choosing civil engineering because it might give me the credentials to become a surveyor (which was "outside work") and allow me to make enough money to go to school to study writing and literature. I dropped out, the second time in as many years, to work full time in an endless string of truckstops, parking lots, and janitorial crews and to write. The marble kept spinning, dervish driven, on the wheel.

Eventually I found a job enabling me to support myself and still go to school. Working mornings and weekends at an automobile dealership, I attended university in the afternoons. Sometimes I showed up for class still dressed in oily coveralls, not having had time to change. In the mornings I'd help a mechanic pull a transmission; in the afternoons I'd study Chaucer. My co-workers tolerated the "college boy" because they saw I could work and would work, while my boss was genuinely supportive but for reasons less clear. I was given finals week off and could work extra hours whenever I wished, a perfectly flexible schedule. What I was studying in school was still off limits, unmentionable, however. Today, thirteen years later, if I went back to the corner restaurant where the mechanics ate lunch, I'd sit down with them and talk. "Still teaching?" they'd ask. Then the conversation would switch to which cars were moving (selling) and which ones were coming in (breaking down). I don't believe they even know what I teach.

I used to wonder how I escaped the anti-intellectualism of the working class; certainly I did not grow up in a house full of books and intellectual aspirations. I've finally credited my introduction to the world of books to a lack of child care. My mother worked as a bank teller a couple of evenings a week, and my father usually took those evenings as opportunities to go to the local Moose lodge or a steel mill juke joint to drink away the factory. With no one to tend her children, my mother would take us to the William McKinley Memorial Library in Niles, Ohio, across the street from the Dollar Savings Bank where she worked. She had a deal with the librarians to watch me, I suppose, but she also took me there because she had noticed I like to read. I could be dropped amid the stacks in the children's reading room at five o'clock, and I would not surface until she had balanced her window and returned at nine or ten in the evening.

With a dozen or more hours of time in the library each week, I quickly exhausted the books of interest in the children's section and was allowed by a very suspicious librarian entry into the adult stacks. There I found the full versions of the watered-down children's classics I had already read and reread, Defoe's *Robinson Crusoe,* for instance, or Swift's *Gulliver's Travels,* and I worked my way through them. They were somehow richer, fuller, though the words took me often to the big dictionary on the dark maple pedestal. I clearly remember reading methodically through the entire section devoted to Mark Twain, then Charles Dickens, and finally reading with great interest but half an understanding the complete tales of Poe. There, too, I developed an interest in mythology and classical history. I read about Greek architecture and, going out to the portico of the library, which housed a huge, seated William McKinley carved in soot-stained marble, I would be delighted to find its columns Ionic. I remember once carrying a large, sophisticated book on Meso-American civilizations to the check-out desk. The librarian asked me, a nine-year-old fixture, if I really read these books. I somberly answered yes, though she still thought that I was lying and made me wait for my mother to return before she would sign it out. For some reason my reading interests always met with my librarian/guardian's disapproval. Maybe she knew that once I had seen Machu Picchu or the glory of Quetzalcoatl, I would never be satisfied with a life spent inside Republic Steel. She read discontent in my future.

Even my teachers at school warned my parents that I would rather stay indoors and read than go out for recess. At home I healthily scaled trees, played, and ran. But at school there were books on history, on paleontology (a word I knew by age six because it would direct me in the library stacks to books on fossils). How could I prefer kickball? But it would not do for a working-class child to be so interested in books. I found this out in the sixth grade when I was sent to visit the principal's office to discuss my reading of Marx and Engels's *Communist Manifesto,* a book not found in our little school library, of course. I had bought it myself at a newsstand in Niles that carried worker's party papers and Gus Hall's books. (Hall, a leader of the American Communist Party, was a local resident.)

I can't say that my parents disapproved of my reading, though I am sure my father would have preferred that I had taken an interest in boxing, not books. But when he learned that I was reading Marx, he joked that he didn't care if it was Karl or Groucho, I could read what I wanted. I had heard tales of his union activism and knew about his work on strike lines. Nevertheless, I'm not sure my father has ever understood what I do. When I applied for graduate school, the entire concept was foreign to him. We had argued over whether he would co-sign a student loan and over what use "more college" would be if I couldn't find a job with an undergraduate degree. (The word *college* was always a substitute for education, a derogatory label for an unknown substance.)

I had been laid off from the car dealership shortly after graduation. It was the depths of the late seventies' recession, and people had discovered they did not wish to buy American cars that resembled sea mammals; indeed, double-digit inflation had outstripped single-digit gas mileage estimates. I had been laid off, though I had seniority over some who kept their jobs, because I had an education and, the boss rightly or wrongly assumed, other opportunities. Since then I had been looking for those opportunities while doing odd jobs and collecting unemployment checks.

Then I heard about graduate school. I had never understood graduate school or ever really known what it was. People who graduated from Youngstown State didn't go to graduate school; they went out and found work. But, with unemployment close to 30 percent in the former "Steel Valley," graduate school looked like the closest thing to a job that might come my way. First I learned that I could study, even major in, creative writing. I had never heard of this program of study. Indeed, YSU offered creative writing courses and I had taken them, but they were taught by faculty members who dabbled in writing or who took an interest, for a while, in teaching it. I was delighted to learn that there were universities where professional, established writers taught courses in writing. Then I discovered that some graduate schools offered stipends. I had earned a stipend as an undergraduate by editing the student newspaper and literary magazine, but this one was different. I would teach, something I had never considered doing, and be paid five hundred dollars each month. That was more than I was making at that time, a veritable living wage! Though it would be untrue to say I went to graduate school for the money, the availability of a stipend determined my choice of schools. Being from the working class, I simply had to make a living. Furthering my education was certainly not part of what was expected from me at this point in my life. I should be working and even settled down by now. Never mind that some rules had changed: the deeper rules remained intact.

Then I told my father what I wanted to study.

"What good is more college going to do you?" he asked, and I remembered having explained studying literature as leading to a job in journalism. It hadn't, and now I had to explain why I wanted to study creative writing as well. I told him I wanted to write poetry and fiction.

"I know what poetry is, and that's no damn good," he said, "but what's fiction?"

"It's like storytelling. Like when you make something up."

"That's a lot like *lying,* isn't it? You know, you were raised better than that," he said with what I'm sure he thought was unassailable logic.

I didn't need his permission to go. I'd been independent for quite a while and had a full tuition waiver and teaching assistantship at Ohio University in Athens. But I was broke and needed for the first time to get a student loan, which he very reluctantly co-signed. Athens was 220 miles away. I didn't have the money to rent a truck or even to pay for the gas for one.

I had been working for a man who owned a surplus materials business. I worked at his house, learning how to lay sidewalks, ceramic tile floors, sod. I did a little of everything, though what I enjoyed most was working with the carpenter, a local cabinetmaker whose work was exact and fine. I had learned a few things about carpentry, enough to make Christmas gifts for my family and to help with an addition to my boss's house. The most important thing I learned, though, was a carpenter's maxim. The cabinetmaker once told me that a good carpenter works just beyond the capacity of his tools. He said that a particular cut or joint was easy to make if you had *exactly* the required tools: the tools simply functioned as required, and the job was accomplished. A good carpenter, however, has to do things for which the perfect tools are not available, adding skill, a steady hand, a good eye, a fine touch with a rasp. Setting dowels without a drill press, cutting rabbet joints without a table saw—that's what marked a fine carpenter.

And that's exactly what I did at Ohio University. My tools had been sharpened at Youngstown State, but they were few. My fellow graduate students had already attended writing workshops with established writers, had attended schools that prepared people for graduate school. So I struggled to read works of literature I had formerly only heard about, to write stories and poems that contained polish and imagination. Now, as I teach poetry and fiction writing to undergraduates at Siena College, a small liberal arts school, I try give students what I would have liked to have known at that time, try to get them to realize that "creative" does not mean simply "anything goes," that writing is hard work.

And I continued to work as a carpenter. In graduate school I had to work weekends and summers to make ends meet despite the monthly stipend. A friend and I started doing carpentry work on weekends, and I once again kept a dual life, wearing old work clothes my father had cast off because of frayed collars and worn cuffs. (He was always an impeccably dressed factory worker, and I admired the pride he showed in his appearance.) On my first day on the job, Mark and I started stripping and refinishing a house from the 1920s recently purchased by a professor in the English Department. The professor remarked that I looked like I had come from "central casting," underscoring what I found to be the opinion of the working class prevalent in academe—a stereotype of sorts. We were Steinbeck's romantic farmworkers or Marx's radical proletariat. Under any rubric we were the loyal, noble, work-drones—steady, trustworthy, even admirable. But we were also ignorant, low-minded, and a little rough around the edges.

Even today among my colleagues and friends at Siena College, many of them Ivy League graduates, I have trouble finding the same cultural anchors. I have learned about the social assumptions of private schools and preparatory schools, the social conventions of the daughters and sons of the well-off who in becoming academics are self-consciously downwardly mobile. I've somehow met them in the middle. Nor is my family any more familiar with the lives my colleagues lead. My family is quite impressed with my degrees, though their understanding is flavored by the medical strain with which they have been familiar. My eighty-six-year-old grandmother addresses her letters to me using "Dr." while a friend in Youngstown introduced me at his wedding to his new in-laws as "Dr. Leslie," with the formal tone befitting a foreign dignitary.

My father once actually met someone else with a Ph.D. In the small mountain town of Clarion, Pennsylvania, where my father was raised, the local high school once hired as a substitute history teacher a man teaching part time while holding a post at the local teachers' college (now Clarion State University of Pennsylvania). He greatly impressed my father, a fiercely anti-intellectual young roughneck, and for years my father told me, carefully reciting the words, that this wise teacher had "a doctorate of philosophy in history" as though it were a special kind of degree, a combination of philosophy and history, that made him so intelligent. Years later, when I told my father that I would be getting a "doctorate of philosophy in English," noting that all advanced academic degrees were so designated, he scoffed—this man had been remarkable, the degrees could not possibly be similar.

Nothing is the same. I am not becoming my father, although I am more like him all the time. Perhaps my grandmother recognized that when she addressed a recent letter to "Cpl. Naton Leslie," remembering the letters she wrote to her son during the Korean War and changing my academic title to a military one. Maybe that is how my academic rank is rendered in her mind—rows of students saluting the ranked teacher. How she must imagine my life I can only imagine. The world has changed beyond recognition in her lifetime. Her fifth-grade education barely gives her the ability to write and read, and her mind wanders now, sweeping decades together and apart again.

If I had to provide myself with a title it would be "Appalachian, first-generation college graduate." But how does that title empower or disempower me in what I hear called a "system"? The system didn't offer me what has become my career; in fact, the system really seems less definable to me as a series of options and choices than it does a sequence of accidents and lucky roulette spins. When I return home, I visit friends whose accidents led them to stay where they are. The mills are closed, but the workers' bars remain, like the Falcon Club near the now-closed mill district on the Ohio-Pennsylvania border. Raymond Carver or James Wright would have been comfortable here: a simple room of beer lights and a pool table, thickly painted and repainted through a series of new looks, transformed from the flat black of the 1960s and 1970s to a church-basement white.

I go to the Falcon Club and shoot pool with Mike. He's alternately out of work or looking for work, at home or on the road. He said I was lucky that they had a degree that fit what I wanted to do, and that's about all we say about my education and my profession. Mike shoots pool like a pro.

"What are you reading?" he might ask, and I remember that it was Mike with whom I shared my earliest intellectual leanings. We were both avid readers, and books were always the basis of our friendship. We traded paperbacks, plotted reading schedules. I remember he put off reading Steinbeck's *Travels with Charley* because he had read all of Steinbeck's other works and wanted to save one to look forward to. He had recently borrowed a novel by Knut Hamsun from me, but the eagerness has gone out of him. He reads like he drinks beer or shoots pool; it is simply something he does. We talk most often now about the things that change and remain the same, about politics in furious, defiant, emotional tones and about mutual friends, alive or dead. I don't see him often—once or twice a year.

I want to tell Mike that they have degrees in what interests him too, but I know I can't. Mike wants different things now: easy money, stable times, a job. The system that spun me through college and spit me out a college professor has rolled right by him. He and I tried engineering school together, but when we both dropped out he hitched to California, where he drifted for a decade. And he was a better student than I was; everyone always said he was smarter in school. Now his brother works for one of the last mills still operating, and Mike does a little construction work. When he asks me occasionally for information on colleges, it is a tired gesture, almost as though he is appeasing me somehow, humoring me. When we drink beer at the Falcon Club we still believe in the future. I don't know if we are friends these days, but we have a mutual past. I'm glad he tolerates my pool game. His silky shots find the pockets like destinies; mine bounce, careen, and some go in. But I always miss the difficult shots and opportunities and leave some on the table at the end of the game.

6

In the Shadow of My Old Kentucky Home

George T. Martin, Jr.

The passers-by stared or pointed at us. Occasionally, one smiled or gave a friendly wave. I wondered what they were thinking as they passed in their cars. How were we different from them?

"Tommy, mind your business!" Mom yelled over her shoulders as she hunched down to pull a bunch of wild greens. Did she know we were being stared at? I turned back to the job I shared with Jimmy, scouring the roadside for spent bottles and scrap metals. Mostly we found beer bottles on this road. They were worth two cents each at the roadhouse. Thinking about what I would do with my share displaced thoughts about the people driving past us. Mom, Jimmy, and I all shared the money. I began figuring how many bottles I needed to see a movie on Saturday afternoon; maybe I could get a comic book too. Mom's burlap bag was already half full of greens; it was going to be a good day. She would have enough to give some to neighbors and relatives. Then she'd cook up the rest with fatback, make some skillet cornbread, maybe fry some baloney. I was getting hungry, picturing in my mind's eye mushing my cornbread into a glass of milk. Besides the bottles and greens, we sometimes found a discarded toy or tool or book. But the biggest find was cash money: with this Jimmy and I ran shouting to Mom and showed her our find as if it was Christmas morning. She stood up, smiled, and said, "Good work, boys!" Her reaction felt as good to me as finding the money.

We never thought what we were doing was dangerous, though it could be. Once Jimmy cut his bare foot on some broken glass, but this could happen in our own yard. What was scary was when something thrown from a passing car would whiz by, but nothing ever hit us. What hurt me was something inside that I couldn't figure out. We were having fun, but it felt like we were doing something wrong. Why were the passers-by staring and pointing?

Being different was something I thought about. I knew I was different from my family. For one thing, none of them ever seemed to have these thoughts; nobody ever talked about them, anyway. We talked about how to do things like collect greens, but we didn't talk about the things inside. I learned this early on. I asked a lot of questions from the start. One that I asked over and over was why I had a harelip. I finally gave up asking. Mom and Pop would frown or start talking about something else or get mad or just lie. I knew when they lied because they changed their story. First, my harelip was caused when the doctor's knife slipped and cut me when I was born; then it was caused when I fell on my face when I was young.

I had so many questions that weren't answered that I sometimes felt I was in the wrong family. The story in the Old Testament about baby Moses being safeguarded in the reeds in Egypt fascinated me. I was like baby Moses; I was being protected until I would be delivered to my real home. With this fantasy to comfort me, I made up my own answers: My harelip was caused by a hair from my mother getting stuck on my lip when I was born; it was cut off and left a scar.

My answer was seemingly confirmed by my sexual experiences. Sexual play was one place where curiosity was rewarded. My older cousins were encouraging. Of course we had to be creative about finding private places; that's why hide and seek was our favorite game. I can still recall the shadowy curves of little asses in bushes, under beds, and in the back seats of junked cars. Once Bettyann and I played with each other under a big, overturned wooden box with some of our cousins nearby looking for us. "I'll let you touch mine," she offered. "Can I touch yours?" We felt and rubbed each other until the others finally gave up looking, and then we just stayed there. I saw a similarity between my harelip and Bettyann's vagina; they both seemed to be the results of cuts, thus my idea of being joined mouth-to-vulva with my mother at birth and then separated.

Of course, I wasn't the only one asking questions. In school my harelip became an even bigger issue for me. The first question I was asked by any new kids I met was, "How'd you get *that?*" The questions didn't stop until I reached junior high school. Then magically the harelip didn't matter any more; it was if it had disappeared, or perhaps people were just too polite to ask me about it. I didn't learn what caused it until I was a senior in high school, when, in order to qualify for a college scholarship from the Navy, I had my first medical exam.

My questions often went unanswered. One big one was why we had had to move so quickly. Much later, I found out that we were not able to keep up the payments and were evicted from the big house, forced to live in vacant tenant quarters on the back side of the farm. At the time, alarmed at coming home from school to find our furniture in the yard, I asked Mom and Pop what happened. Their only reply was, "We're movin'."

Because the yards around the tenant houses were so big, we kept our animals, and they added to my sense of being crowded and unclean. The ponies heightened the pungent smell created by our chicken coops and the dump and packing house that were nearby. There were big rats in the sheds and under the house, and they were noisy, especially at night. It was so bad compared to what I knew existed elsewhere that I was embarrassed when, on my first date, Sue said that her father would pick me up and drive us to the dance. The only reasons I agreed were that our house sat way back off the road and I would be picked up at night.

Uncle Mack's cussing the niggers increased after our eviction. His favorite subject was race war, imminent and cataclysmic. Pop criticized him in front of us: "Mack, don't talk that way—it ain't right." Uncle Mack would stop. Pop especially did not like the word *nigger,* which we heard a lot. I never asked him why; perhaps it was because he had worked in the North and was a union man. I like to believe that it had to do with one of his grandmothers being full-blooded Cherokee. I know that he was proud of this by how he talked about it. But Aunt Eloise and Uncle Mack had the same blood, and they were always cussing about niggers. Mom's views on blacks were like Pop's. She was a Republican whose grandfathers had fought for the Union. Mom voted for Nixon while supporting integration when it came to our schools. She believed the scriptures endorsed racial equality, although I never saw black faces in our Southern Baptist church.

Mom and Grandma were the religious bulwarks of the clan. With Sunday morning and evening services, Wednesday prayer meeting, revivals, vacation Bible school, the Royal Ambassadors youth group, suppers and picnics, we were in church three or four times a week. Grandma wanted me to be a Baptist preacher and for a while I was going to be. For us it was aiming high. Church was another outlet for my curiosity. I was a champion at Bible knowledge and the winner of citywide Sword Drill competitions in which we had to find a given verse quickly and recite it. I became a medal-winning orator in the Royal Ambassadors for my Gettysburg Address.

The church was a sanctuary for Mom and Grandma, and they had standing there. For Pop and Grandpa, the roadhouse served a similar purpose. I was the only one who knew both worlds, and I sensed the conflict between them. Grandma and I carried out regular searches around the house for Grandpa's liquor bottles and poured water into them. It was another hide-and-seek game. Pop and Grandpa would take me to the road-house but told me not to tell. In our house the men never went to church and the women never drank. I didn't tell either side about my allegiance to the other.

In my family, only Mom, Jimmy, and I collected on the roadside, but the entire clan was involved with the horses and ponies, all twenty-five of us: Pop, Pop's younger brother (Uncle Mack), Pop's younger sister (Aunt Eloise), their spouses, ten kids, three grandkids, two sons-in-law, Mom and her parents, Jimmy, and me. Living within hailing distance of each other, we were together a lot. The twelve of us cousins were really like brothers and sisters. My fifty-odd other first cousins were more like real cousins in that I didn't see them every day. They lived all over the place, as far away as Michigan.

On weekends and holidays we loaded the ponies into rented trucks and drove them to picnics and fairs to sell rides. This was one of the many ideas Pop had to make some extra money. Over time, we collected about a dozen animals for this purpose. It was hard, sweaty, and smelly work, but it was fun. Every kid I knew wanted a pony and I had one, even though I did not have a bed of my own, a bathroom, or a TV. His name was Blackie because he was jet black; riding him and being seen riding him were worth all the work. There was something for all of us to do with the ponies. The men took care of the trucks and loaded and unloaded the animals, the trickiest job. The women sold the tickets, brought the food, and watched over the younger kids. We older kids fed and groomed the ponies and led them around the track. Everyone pitched in to clean the trucks after the day was over. They had to be scoured spotless because it was against U-Haul rules to carry animals. It took an hour or so to scrub the trucks down, and then we had to clean ourselves before we could go to bed.

Pop would have had us clean the trucks even if there had been no animal rule. He was fond of anything with wheels and took good care of his vehicles. Teamstering was the family vocation for men; for the women, it was serving others as maids, cooks, and waitresses. Although Pop was by then a railroad man—his ultimate wheels—he had been a long-haul trucker. He got his start by carrying moonshine during Prohibition. He was off and on involved in labor troubles, and other troubles. He even knew Jimmy Hoffa when he drove out of Flint. I remember visiting my dad in hospitals where he was recovering from wounds. As bad as he looked he always pulled through. It was in a hospital that I first heard Pop use the word *scab* like Uncle Mack used the word *nigger*.

The pony work was physically exhausting. My muscles ached and fatigue reached the point where I felt separated from my body. When the family worked together it seemed that parts of our bodies were interchange-able. When I needed a third hand, it would appear, unsolicited. In these and other unspoken ways I felt very close to the people around me.

The work also put me in touch with people outside our clan and neigh-borhood, people who had money. They were cleaner and better dressed. I remember feeling shame when a mother cautioned her child as I was put-ting him in the saddle, "Now, don't get dirty." This got me so mad that I brushed up against the kid just to get dirt on him. But the worst part of working with the ponies was Pop getting drunk. Often on these occasions, if he did not fight with some patron, he fought with us. It was after one of these picnics that I saw Pop hit Mom. He slapped her a few times, and I was petrified. Was Mom hurt? Was I next? What was wrong with Pop? The next day, Mom, Jimmy, and I ran away to stay on Uncle Heber's farm. I recall looking out the Greyhound depot window watching for Pop. I wondered if I would ever be with him again and whether I wanted to be, but after a week we went back home. I was glad and sad.

I found it impossible to hate my Pop for long. Besides his taking me places, like for rides on his locomotives, and bringing me things, like real cotton from Alabama, I could see how hard he worked. One of the first times I felt unbounded admiration for his strength and caring was when he made a fire in the pitch dark on winter mornings. He was always the first one up, and he built the fire. I remember thinking I didn't want to grow up and have to do that. The cold was especially bitter as we had no heat through the night and our little house sat exposed on a rise of ground. The cold was a constant preoccupation. We were always gathering paper and kindling, fetching coal and kerosene, cutting and hauling wood, emptying ashes, covering windows, and pushing rugs up against doors. The cold made tasks out of the simplest body functions. I liked school a lot from the first because it was warm and it had indoor toilets. In winter I tried to time it so I could get by using only the school toilets during the week.

There was something bad in the way the ponies affected Mom too. After all the work was done, she would sometimes just sit and cry. I tried to com-fort her, but she pushed me away, saying she was just "plumb tuckered out." She worked as hard as Pop. She canned food for the winter, made clothes out of chicken feed sacks, killed and cleaned chickens, picked blackberries to eat and sell, and did all the cleaning inside the house. On top of this, she worked paying jobs.

It was also Mom's job to get Jimmy and me up in the cold mornings and off to school. She was good at it. Jimmy did not miss a day of school through high school, for which he got a commendation, and I did not have any absences after the third grade. I remember one rainy and cold February morning when I was in the second grade, Mom bundled me off to an empty school. On the way I didn't see my usual pals and I thought I was late, so I ran. When I got to the building and couldn't get in, I sat on the steps and cried. Later, I found out that it had been Lincoln's birthday. I really liked going to school. It was a whole new world, one where my questions were answered and where I was praised for asking them.

Other than the ponies we all had our special work. My job was caddying. On weekends I earned as much as eight dollars a day for carrying two bags for thirty-six holes. I split the money with Mom. On some days, as many as one hundred boys and twenty winos caddied—all of us "poor white trash." These were guys I never saw in school because they never went. New caddies were hazed, which consisted of being thrown high in the air off a steep hillside and then taking sharp, hard-knuckle punches on the upper arms from everyone. At first, every day I went home tired and bruised. The hill toss was a one-time affair. The farther you were thrown and the more cuts you got, the bigger your reputation. But the punching went on for weeks, until mysteriously one was accepted and it ended. Being accepted was marked by getting a nickname. Everybody had a nickname. I was known as a smart-ass kid, but my nickname became Liberace because I had lots of wavy hair and big dimples.

With caddying there is a lot of idle time waiting to go out. It was like school to me. I was always asking questions of the old-timers. I loved hearing about exotic places and women. I learned a lot, especially from Harold, a wino who had been to New York City and, best of all, Paris, France. Harold always said "ParisFrance" like it was one word. I figured it was for his rep; after all, lots of folks had been to Paris, Kentucky. I also learned how to cheat in card games and in tossing coins with a partner, usually my cousin Joey. We could beat a younger mark by dividing heads and tails between us—we caught sight of the coin in the air. But I also hustled money by knowing things. The caddie boss bought a world almanac to check on me after he lost a bet that I could not name the capital of Nepal.

I hustled some in school, too. Once in grade school I had a homework assignment for which I had to measure the lengths and widths of the rooms in our house and calculate their areas. I fretted about this, fearing that I would have to share my work in class. We only had three rooms. Rather than suffer the expected embarrassment, I counted a walk-in cupboard as a bathroom and a built-on, utility back room and a crouch-space attic as bedrooms. This gave me what I knew was the norm—five rooms and bath. I got an A on the assignment.

Pop and Mom were barely literate, but they were smart, and they encouraged my schoolwork in their own ways. My most memorable Christmas gift came when I was in the sixth grade—a set of World Book encyclope-dias. I wonder if I was the only kid who treated the volumes as a single work to be read from cover to cover. I was fascinated with all the mysterious-sounding places in the world, beginning with Aachen. Probably the most instrumental thing my folks did was to move to a better neighborhood and school district and to a house with a toilet when I entered ninth grade. Without this kind of opportunity I would probably today be working at the kinds of jobs that my male cousins have—in auto factories, driving trucks, or in the military. As it was I became the first in my family to graduate from high school. My brother was the second, and he's a banker now.

Pop had little formal education, but he respected knowledge and he had an instinctive interest in learning. He made it a habit to read the newspaper every day. And Pop was proud to have been in all the states but Alaska and Hawaii and to know a lot of different kinds of foods to eat. He was a curious person, open to new experiences, and he was a tinkerer who could fix anything. I remember watching with my cousins as he replaced the engine in his car in our yard. He had to use a hoist and a tree limb to get the job done. The word was, If it's busted, take it to George.

Mom had a different slant on learning. She had great respect for the institutions and the titled persons of education. She was always involved in my schooling, and she knew all my teachers. She was the one who came to my National Honor Society initiation in high school. Mom had a lot of admiration for education and educated people, but she did not have Pop's searching spirit. Maybe it was because he was pretty much on his own by the time he was fifteen years old, while Mom grew up in a large, stable family. Also, being respectable folks was always more important to Mom than to Dad.

Despite their coping skills, Mom and Pop were always worried about something bad happening. Every year some neighbor or relative was driven from their home by fire, flood, or eviction. Every year somebody got in-jured, very sick, killed, or died. Every year somebody lost their job or went on strike. Every winter there was a bad fire and every spring a flood. We lived in flatland not far from Beargrass Creek that emptied into the nearby Ohio River. The worst part was that we always expected bad things to happen, even when they didn't. Then Uncle Mack was killed, and things were never the same again after that.

Uncle Mack was working on his car on a hillside in the yard while we kids played. The car started to roll, heading across a road and toward a house. Just as Uncle Mack tried to jump into the car to brake it, it hit a tree, breaking his neck. We screamed and Pop ran from the back where he had been hoeing the garden. Afterwards he said, "If I had gotten to Mack sooner,

I could've straightened his neck and maybe saved him—but I told him never to work on a car without chocking the wheels." Only a few months later we were gone, and the whole area has since become a subdivision. But the tree still stands; Pop used to drive me by it.

Not being able to talk about all the threats we faced made them even worse for me. It was as though we believed that if we talked about our fears, they would conquer us. Perhaps the corollary was more important: if we didn't talk about them, they wouldn't happen. We paid a price for this. Once, out of curiosity, I asked Pop if he was ever going to die. His retort was consistent with family practice: "Shut up!" On another occasion, I was terrified at seeing a cousin slapped hard in the face at supper by Uncle Mack, just because he had asked a question. Pop wasn't there, and no one challenged Uncle Mack.

It was very different at school, where I was praised for asking and telling. One experience stands out. I had transferred to a new school and knew no one. My first assignment was an oral book report, something I had never done before. Despite being nervous, I delivered an impassioned report totally from memory. At the end the teacher and the class were applauding. It was about the same time that my imagination seemed to go wild. I conjured up an entire idyllic country and filled it with cities, farms and factories, highways and railroads, and people. I spent hours in my classes writing. I accumulated hundreds of hand-written pages of history, geography, and miscellany about Marand, an island nation in the South Pacific. Marand was an acronym for Martin and Andrews, its founders.

In high school I began to see learning as a path to a better life. I was paid for intellectual work for the first time when I became a reporter for a weekly newspaper. I liked it that in intellectual work the inequities in the rest of my life were not decisive. Doing well in school came easily to me. My first mentor was a highly educated man, the father of a high school love. He encouraged me to think about going to college. I began to feel that I wasn't so different after all. We had moved to our new house with indoor plumbing in a good neighborhood, both Mom and Pop were working steady, and things were looking up for us. In high school, I was part of different social circles but not defined by any of them. Because of my interests and background, I ran with jocks, intellectuals, greasers, and farmers. The quote chosen for me by the editors of the high school annual was, "He was a man who had many friends."

A recruiter for the Navy visited our high school, and I competed for a college scholarship. When I won one to Vanderbilt and gave the good news to Pop and Mom, they were pleased but not excited like I was. I think they were proud of me, but they also wanted me to stay in the family and not to become different from them. To them, Vanderbilt was very far away. For a while things went well at Vanderbilt, but in my junior year I crashed. It was the stress of upward mobility (for me, feeling very much out of place); more precisely, I did not have a role model for educated, working-class manhood. Anti-establishment intellectuals like James Baldwin became my heroes. I frequented a local tavern so much that I had to take a job there to pay down my tab. That was a mistake. When finally I was kicked out of college, I owed the place more than when I had started working there. Although I had stopped going to classes, it took a noisy drinking session in my dorm for the university to expel me. I really wanted out but didn't know how to go about it, especially since I was committed to the Navy for my livelihood. After a time-out I returned and managed to graduate on time, although the Navy wanted nothing more to do with me. I didn't realize how fortunate I was. It was 1963, and most of my Navy buddies ended up serving a tour in Southeast Asia.

But at the time I had no plans, not even thoughts, about what I would do in the real world, wherever that was. So I took the first job offered me, selling industrial life insurance to poor blacks and whites in my old neighborhood. At least once a week I would end up drinking the night away with one of my clients and paying their small weekly premium for them. After two months of this, two loose threads of my life came together and things changed for the better.

The first thread was a woman. I met Ariadne at Vanderbilt. She was a few years behind me, and I returned to Nashville regularly to be with her. In those years (1963–65), the civil rights movement came to Nashville with all the force of the youthful SNCC. Through Ariadne, I became involved, and it proved to be one path of deliverance. At that time, Vanderbilt was not integrated, and one of her girlfriends was expelled for dating a black organizer. Our marginal group of poets and incipient feminists threw itself into marches, protests, and black culture.

The other thread of deliverance was a job I took. There was an appeal in the local paper for workers at a settlement house. Although the pay was much less than I got selling insurance, I immediately quit and went to the settlement, whose clients were poor, inner-city blacks and whites. Two years later Ariadne and I were married and living in Chicago. She was working for the Urban League and helping to organize Chicago NOW, and I was attending social work school at the University of Chicago and agitating for welfare rights; we were both in "the movement."

I found my field placements in social work uncomfortable and constraining; agencies reminded me too much of home (where "there's one right way to do things"). However, my classes and classmates were inspiring. We mobilized a national conference on guaranteed income attended by activists, academics, and welfare recipients. We were young, change was everywhere, and the range of our ideas was matched only by our boundless energies. By applying knowledge in the interest of social justice, we could see the end of poverty and racism. A sociologist, David Street, lectured in the social work school and through his lectures I was recruited to sociology. We learned early on that we shared a bond of stigma. Mine was a harelip; his was hemophilia. I was struck by Dave's idea for relating to sociology: "Develop a tolerance for ambiguity." It struck me as prophetic, for my life as well as for social science.

At Chicago my political activism, begun with the civil rights movement, deepened and broadened. The antiwar movement became my major passion, and I was active in the New University Conference, a sort of SDS for graduate students. At the same time Ariadne, through her job with the Chicago Urban League, was working hard in support of Dr. King's campaign in Chicago. My most enduring memories of this period include marching with Dr. King in Gage Park and, later, seeing expanses of Chicago aflame from my tenth-floor apartment after his assassination. However, my most intense experience of this period was the protest at the 1968 Democratic national convention, at which I crossed a fateful line: I have never recovered my former feelings of reverence for the United States flag. My political activism helped to form lasting bonds of comradeship with my graduate school classmates. Several are among my closest friends and colleagues today, thirty years later. A community of students developed under the polarized conditions of Chicago and the University of Chicago in the mid-to-late sixties—a generational community bound not only by left politics but by common interests in social science, the counterculture, and, yes, sex, drugs, and rock and roll.

My conflict over upward mobility intensified as I worked on my dissertation; it was the final step separating me from my former world. I felt guilt over the privilege in my life. Dad used to ask me, "Son, when are you gonna start working?" I was almost too embarrassed to tell him that I did not have to work because of money from the National Institute of Mental Health and the National Defense Education Act. The US government supported me well for my whole run through college and graduate school. I had been born at the right time to benefit from the reaction to the Soviet Union's Sputnik.

Despite much that was exciting and hopeful during those times, they were also difficult for everyone at Chicago. Two of my graduate school friends killed themselves; several other friends drank or drugged themselves to death. Relationships were intense and fragile in such a personally and politically superheated environment. Ariadne and I separated and reunited on several occasions. I survived by making a number of intuitive choices. One of the most important was to get a job as a bartender. This working-class job allowed me to feel that I was being true to my roots while taking the final step away from them by completing my dissertation. The subjects of my dissertation—black female welfare recipients—were difficult ones for a white male researcher to secure data from. However, the fieldwork came easily for me. In fact, much like the bartending job, working with welfare recipients kept me in touch with my background at the same time I was making my most significant move away from it. It helped that many of the welfare recipients and I shared a rural, poor, Southern background. We were "down home" folks to each other—once, that is, they knew whose side I was on.

Pop lived long enough to see me start working and to see his grandson born. I felt that I could see clearly into Pop when he died, maybe for the first time. He wound up in the hospital one evening after work. Despite his physical discomfort, he seemed very clear and at peace—not so fearful and cut off as he had so often been in his life. I recall well his huge, gnarled hands, clasping them and thinking how out of place they looked on the immaculate sheets of the intensive care unit. He said he expected to go to work the next day, but his searching eyes, bloated body, and contorted face all said something else: I ain't gonna make it this time; glad you could get here. He died the next morning while we waited for visiting hour. His overworked and sewn-up aorta had ruptured yet again, and the end came quickly. He lived only two and a half days after the original rupture, but it was time enough for him and us. The doctor said that the two days were a miracle. The old man had finally busted his last gut working.

My mother, brother, cousins, and many other relatives still live in Kentucky, but I'll never return there to live. The remaining friends from my Kentucky youth have also moved away. My academic work goes unread by my family, even though I send them copies of it. But they are proud of my accomplishments and are always glad to see me when I visit. We talk family, food, and basketball but not politics or religion. Meanwhile, where I live and work, white Southern working-class culture is known only as a caricature. Yet I have strong and rewarding intellectual and personal relationships with my colleagues. (It helps if they are female, black, or working class.) I have been the only person equally active in the women's studies program, the African American studies program, and the union on my campus. I will probably always be most comfortable on the margins. Indeed, I feel that sociology is a calling for me, allowing me fully to explore my curious bent about life, especially how and why people are different. Also, by remaining on the margins I am in the shadows; I do not have to call attention to myself.

Thus, I avoid subjecting myself to the possibility of again encountering my childhood bogeys—ridicule, shame, and overt conflict.

I have thrived in academia because here I have been able to address, openly, questions that have haunted me since childhood, questions about social justice and inequality. My research and publications have focused on poverty, welfare, and social policy. But I have thrived in academia in larger measure, I believe, because I have been at an institution whose students are largely working class, poor, or lower middle class. They, too, are often first-generation college students. I find satisfaction in trying to help young people who may be traveling a path similar to the one that I took, and I have developed lasting friendships with several of my former students. Also, I was fortunate in finding among my colleagues a number of people who shared the sense of community that I had felt in Chicago. These colleagues were at other places in the 1960s, but we shared common experiences; several have been cherished friends now for over twenty years.

For my son, George Thomas Martin, III, who has grown up middle class in Manhattan, I am both sad and glad that he does not have my class roots. Although my greatest sadness is that my father never had a relationship with my son, I am glad that Tom has had advantages I didn't have; I'm also glad that our relationship is better than the one I had with my father. I feel that Tom and I have a fuller relationship because we share an intellectual curiosity. As a child, Tom got answers to his questions, as I did not. Still, despite his identification with New York City, Tom has Kentucky in his blood. He was there two or three times a year while growing up. Several years after my father's death, Mom, Tom, and I took one of our frequent day trips, this one to the plantation, My Old Kentucky Home, in Bardstown. Although only about forty miles from where I grew up, I had never been there. Said Tom, "Daddy, was this where you lived when you were a kid?" "No," I said to then-eight-year-old Tom, "*my* old Kentucky home was very different from this one." It is only now, with the telling of this story, that both Tom and I can take in the full meaning of our old Kentucky home, far away.

7

Todos Vuelven: From Potrero Hill to UCLA

Rosa María Pegueros

Todos vuelven. No importa lo lejos que estemos, siempre estamos con nuestro pais, con nuestra tierra en el alma, en la mente. (Rubén Blades)

(Everyone comes back. It makes no difference how far we wander, we always have our country, our land, in our souls and our minds.)

LA SELVA (THE JUNGLE)

Vince and Richard became trash collectors like their fathers; Joe became a store manager for Sears; Bobby is now a captain with the San Francisco Police Department; Ricky teaches high school. I was much too bookish for the boys I dated in high school; they married women who stayed at home. I became a lawyer and a historian.

I was born in San Francisco and grew up on Potrero Hill in the eastern part of the city, south of Market Street. Market Street was known as "the slot" because it housed the underground cables for the trolleys. Running diagonally across the city, it has historically been the dividing line in San Francisco between the middle- and lower-class neighborhoods. South of Market is to San Francisco what the lower east side is to Manhattan. During the last ten years, Potrero Hill has been gentrified; gay people and young professionals have moved in to renovate the houses and open small businesses as industry has moved out of the city. During the 1950s when I was a child, The Hill was a working-class neighborhood along the bay waterfront, surrounded by the huge Kilpatrick and Langendorff bakeries, the Safeway coffee-packing plant, the Hexol disinfectant factory, the Hamm's Brewery, the old Seal Baseball Stadium, as well as other factories, slaughterhouses, tuna canneries, and shipyards. Throughout my childhood, the stench from the slaughterhouses and canneries filled the air. It was impossible to get the fetid taste out of one's mouth. At night, we slept with the clamor of trains coupling noisily in the nearby train yards.

Whenever I rode the bus out of Potrero Hill, I would think to myself, "I'm going out of the jungle." To me, The Hill—my jungle—was safe and dark, thick with hardship, connections, and complexity. Beyond The Hill, the world was pellucid; it was as if I were looking into a limpid pool where every fish, every anemone, every occupant of the deep was in clear view. I even thought that people with blue eyes could see things more clearly.

My earliest memory is of a sunny June day, sitting between my parents in the cab of the Atlas Paper Company truck as my father drove across the San Francisco Bay Bridge to Vallejo to deliver his load. I was five years old and had not yet started school. My father worried aloud because his teamsters' local was about to go out on strike. My mother argued against his participation in the strike. She refused to understand that he, too, hated the picket line but that as shop steward, the nominal head of his union at his warehouse, there was no question that he would take part. I came to dread the month of June because it was always a time of worry, when the local's contract would be up and the union would vote to strike. My father would have to walk the hated picket line, and we would have to depend on our savings and the strike fund.

I grew up knowing that union membership meant we would have good health care and money for education. Christmas meant Santa and presents at the union hall; summer brought picnics sponsored by the local. We lived by one cardinal rule: We must never cross a picket line. I was so naive I believed that everyone respected it. Once, as an adult far removed from my father's gaze, I crossed the picket line at a movie theater. I felt so guilty that I have never done it again.

In those days, Potrero Hill was predominantly Italian. My friends were already second-generation San Franciscans; their grandparents had been immigrants. Unable to speak English, Mama felt snubbed by our Italian neighbors. Her response was to be insular, overprotective of her children, and critical of the few friends I brought to the house. I spoke little English when I started first grade at St. Teresa's School, but I had already taught myself to read from Spanish comic books. They had brightly colored cellophane covers and plots in which someone was always crying "¡Auxilio!" (Help!) My only Latina classmate, a girl whose parents, like my mother, came from Santa Ana, El Salvador, refused to speak Spanish and avoided me because I embarrassed her. Forbidden by the Irish immigrant Sisters to speak Spanish, I quickly learned English.

My father, who is Mexican American, had no relatives but his mother; I grew up surrounded by my mother's relatives and their friends in the Salvadoran immigrant community of San Francisco. While I was grounded in its rituals and mores, I knew little about my mother's family history until I was in graduate school and broke the taboo against inquiring into what had happened in El Salvador. As a child, I was discouraged by my mother and her family from asking questions; their reply to any inquiry was usually, "Why do you want to know? That is in the past." I had not even been told about the pivotal event in modern Salvadoran history, La Matanza, the massacre of thirty thousand Indians and peasants in the western provinces of El Salvador in 1932.

My great-grandfather, el abuelo (grandfather) Aurelio, was a highly educated man who fled his native Cuba at the turn of the century during the Spanish-American war. He settled in El Salvador after traveling throughout the world, earning his law degree, and becoming an architect along the way. Even though he was a Jew, he used his skills to build Santa Ana's cathedral, as well as a maternity hospital, theater, and other public buildings, and he brought the railroad to Santa Ana, the second largest city in the country. Mysteriously, his belongings, collected from travels all over the world, suddenly disappeared and the family was dispersed. As a child, I wondered what terrible calamity could have befallen this prosperous family to cause el abuelo's house to be emptied and razed. My great-grandfather's estate was lost long before I was born. During my childhood, my mother's family was poor though not starving. They had fled El Salvador for Guatemala only to be caught there in the revolution of the late 1940s; a few years later, my mother and her sisters moved to San Francisco, leaving their mother and brothers in Guatemala.

They say that all beginnings are hard. My mother's arrival in San Francisco was no exception to this rule. Coming from a Guatemalan household where she had had a measure of comfort, she found herself running a sewing machine at the Levi Strauss factory. Fortunately, her sisters, both nurses, were soon employed at St. Joseph's Hospital in San Francisco, and they got her a job in the hospital cafeteria. She was not particularly happy at the hospital. The nursing Sisters, all German immigrants, were kind, but she hated the work. Within a short time after her arrival, she met and married my father.

My mother has had a hard life. Fleeing revolutions, she came to the United States to live the immigrant's dream, only to find that the streets were not paved with gold. Closely tied to her family, she saved every cent she could spare to send to them. We were never impoverished, but neither was anything wasted. Every outgrown item of clothing was packed into duffel bags and sent to Guatemala. My mother sent enough money to her brothers in Guatemala to put one through law school and to help her other brothers with their educations.

My father's background was far more humble. My paternal grandmother, Carlota, fled Mexico during the Mexican Revolution; little is known of her family. She was a wily yet undisciplined woman who outlived five husbands in turn. I remember her as angry and abusive. My grandfather, a merchant seaman, seldom saw his only son; when he did, he beat him with whatever was at hand. He died in 1932 at the height of the Great Depression, when my father was only twelve years old. As the depression deepened, my grandmother could not earn enough to support herself and her son. After years of fishing off the San Francisco pier and raiding the trash cans behind grocery stores for wilted cabbage leaves that his mother would make into soup, Dad lied about his age to get a job as a truck driver. Until this day, my father cannot abide the smell of cabbage or fish: for him, they are the stench of poverty.

I am their oldest child. My mother was so ill during her pregnancy and after my birth that her doctor said she should have no more children, so for the first four and a half years of my life, I was an only child. Then my younger brother was born and soon after a sister and another brother. The fact that there is such an age gap between my siblings and me, eleven years between me and my youngest brother, means that I had no allies as I was pushing at the borders of acceptable behavior for a Latina. Of course, there is no way to know if I would have had any help if we had been closer in age, but as it was, they were too young for me to be interested in them. We are far closer now as adults than we were as children.

To my family, I was an oddball: bookish, self-absorbed, reaching beyond my family to make friends with people who were different from anyone in our immediate circle, falling in love with classical music when I chanced to hear it. Both of my parents were bewildered by my love for books. My mother, blind in one eye and partially blind in the other from a childhood accident, uses her eyesight for sewing, crocheting, and other utilitarian handicrafts, but she seldom reads a book and only occasionally a newspaper. She often said to me, "You can't eat books; you can't marry books. What are you going to do with all those books?" They worried that my solitary devotion to learning would injure my health. "You'll get consumption!" an uncle once warned me.

My father, working twelve to fourteen hours a day for almost fifty years, had neither the time nor the energy to read. When he saw me reading, he fretted about my future. "Pegueros," he'd say, "I worry about you. You have no ambition; all you want to do is read." Still, they were persuaded by a door-to-door salesman to purchase an *Encyclopedia Britannica Jr.,* as well as the set of children's classics that came with it, including *Black Beauty, Treasure Island, Robinson Crusoe,* and a children's version of Shakespeare. These books whetted my appetite for more literary riches. After listening to me beg for months, my father took me to the public library when I was nine years old; it changed my life. If I was lacking a wide circle of friends, I was rich in my fantasy world. Language seemed to explode in my brain. I discovered *Grimm's Fairy Tales,* the wonders of science, and the comfort of poetry. I hurried to the library every day after school, neglecting my homework while I indulged myself in the treasures the library offered. The nuns would write concerned letters to my mother, but since she did not read English, I would write a response for her without showing her the missive. This continued until I was in the sixth grade and the Sisters determined that I was a discipline problem who should be kept back. I confounded them, however, when they gave us our first Stanford-Binet tests. My score was far about that of my classmates. The Sisters didn't know what to do with me, so they made me take them again.

The Sisters could hardly be blamed. Each teacher was assigned fifty children of differing capabilities and had to manage without teacher's aides, enrichment materials, or any of the modern-day accoutrements. They had neither the time nor the training in pedagogy to ponder why one student never did her homework. I was bored; I had understood the lesson in class and had little need to reinforce it by doing the homework. The lure of the library books was too strong. Grudgingly promoted to the seventh grade, I had the luck to be assigned to a teacher who recognized my abilities, guided my reading, and enrolled me in classes for gifted children at a local public high school.

One of these, a summer class in journalism, sealed my fate. Never had I experienced anything so pleasurable as writing for publication. My identity began to come clear. I imagined myself a famous author. I even decorated a room—"my study"—in the basement with prints by Cézanne and Utrillo and slowly began to fill my bookshelves. I read anything the librarians would let me take home, from the best of children's literature to magazines like *Popular Mechanics* and *Scientific American.* By the time I graduated from St. Teresa's at age thirteen, I was a budding intellectual, loving books, ideas, and music to the exclusion of almost everything else.

Although I had always loved books, I was just beginning to realize that a university education was to be the fulfillment of my dreams, but to attain that goal, I had to do some basic planning. My choice, Presentation High School, was a college-preparatory school. It was across San Francisco, an hour's bus ride away from my home. Located on the edge of the infamous

Haight-Ashbury district, it was adjacent to Lone Mountain College and the Jesuit-run University of San Francisco. My mother preferred that I go to a local Catholic girls' high school that was a mere fifteen-minute bus ride away, but its curriculum did not prepare its students for college. It was the first real test of my willingness to defy her. I locked myself in the basement and blockaded the door. I swore not to come out until she gave in. We screamed at each other through the door; I knew that I was earning a beating for myself by my obstinacy. I negotiated my conditions: no beating and the right to apply to the school of my choice. After a day, she gave in to me.

Presentation High School, a girls' school operated by the same order that ran my grammar school, the Sisters of the Presentation of the Blessed Virgin Mary, was better than I imagined. It was a world of women, free from the hormonally induced preening and posturing that goes on in a coeducational high school. The library was larger than our local public library. We were encouraged to excel in every area of endeavor. It had a reputation for academic excellence. Eventually, I became editor of the high school newspaper and president of the speech club, winning prizes in oratory and debating tournaments throughout California. I learned photography and darkroom work. I had my first experiences doing political work when I helped one of the Sisters collect food for the nascent Farm Workers Union. Later, I worked on Bobby Kennedy's presidential campaign.

During my time there, I became acutely aware of class differences among my classmates. As a child, the phrase *working class* had puzzled me because all the adults I had ever met worked for a living. *Old money, nouveau riche, capital gains, the stock market* had no meaning for me. That there existed an upper class that lived off the interest from inherited wealth or investments was simply beyond my imagination. Nor had I realized that there was a middle class that went to work every day and lived very comfortably from their income. In fact, when I watched the 1950s TV series *Leave It to Beaver,* the Cleaver family looked very wealthy to me. I used to wonder just how many rooms their house had. I had no clear idea what a den was for, except perhaps for the father to hide out from the rest of the family.

At Presentation, as at St. Teresa's, we were required to wear uniforms, and the Sisters also restricted other displays of wealth that could have set us apart. Nevertheless, making friends often brought the reality of class differences home to me. I remember my amazement when I went home with a friend after school, only to be driven home in her father's Mercedes. My father had never had a new car, and I had never seen a car with a polished wood dashboard and leather seats nor had I imagined that such luxurious automobiles existed. I visited another friend whose house had plush wool carpets. I shall never forget the feeling of my feet sinking into the thick pile;

for a few moments, I sprung gingerly forward and back until her mother saw me and asked what was wrong. Once I suffered the embarrassment of a friend being denied permission to come to my house because her mother said it was "on the wrong side of the tracks." Nonetheless, my academic success, aided by the strict determination of the Sisters to treat us impartially, led me to believe that I could earn a college degree.

While my father worked so his children would have the life he hadn't had, it never occurred to him that a daughter would want anything more than a high school diploma. Thus, when I told my father that I was applying to college, he was stunned. Even though my parents had put us in Catholic schools because they did not trust the quality of the public schools, my decision to continue with my education was a surprise to both of them. My father cried as he told me that he didn't have the money to pay for any more schooling for me, but I had never expected him to pay for my college tuition. By the time I announced my intention to take the entrance exams, the librarian at our local public library gave me a job that would finance my college education.

The fire that destroyed Atlas Paper Company, my father's employer, on the day after I graduated from high school was a pivotal event in my life. I had not expected my father's financial support while I went to college, but the fire could have delayed or even ended my college plans until the family was again on its feet. I wept all that awful night, fearing that I would have to go to work full time, terrified that my dreams had gone up with the paper warehouse, and I worried about my family's survival. Fortunately, my father was given full-time work by a car-parking corporation. My worries were unfounded. However, since in 1968 there were student riots at San Francisco State University and at the University of California at Berkeley (Cal), he vetoed my decision to go to either of those state universities, leaving me only with the choice of the Jesuit-run University of San Francisco. While he was never able to help me with the tuition, I continued to live at home, and he did give me the money for my school books. I knew this meant a tremendous sacrifice for him, with my younger brothers and sister in Catholic schools all needing tuition, books, and school uniforms. He worked twelve hours a day, arriving home exhausted and covered with grease, but I never heard him complain or express the slightest resentment.

Mama was not happy about my choice. She worried that I would not make enough money to finance it and that going to college was an impractical decision. She urged me to take a secrretarial or nursing course. Ultimately, faced with a personality as stubborn as her own, she grudgingly accepted my choice. Despite her opposition, my mother's dignity, frugality, and rectitude coupled with her belief in us enabled me to envision the unimaginable. Her brother in Guatemala had become a judge; my great-grandfather had been a lawyer and architect. Now she found herself defending my choice to her sisters and other immigrant friends, all of whose children went directly to work in blue-collar jobs upon graduating from high school. I was oblivious to the criticism. I never thought about my cousins or family friends or considered that I had chosen an unusual path. I just loved my books, loved learning, and loved to stay awake late at night to write essays and to create something original.

The University of San Francisco was across the street from my high school, but in many ways it was a world away. Presentation had seven hundred students; USF had several thousand. For the first time, I met non-Catholics, foreign students, and people of great wealth. I felt like a child in a candy store. Rather than focusing on attaining a good grade point average, I took classes in everything that had ever interested me.

I soon found that my twenty-hour-per-week library job was not enough to pay for the tuition, which was raised every semester I was in college. Within a short time, I was working in the library, holding a cafeteria job that gave me two meals a day, and grading papers for pay. I saved an additional fifteen cents a day by walking the two miles from the university to my job at the library instead of taking the bus. At the end of the month, I would have $3.50 to spend on a book—my splurge. My rigorous work schedule made it impossible for me to study very much.

I encountered some prejudice from my classmates, usually expressed in insinuations that I had displaced other, more qualified students. Most of my professors, the majority of whom were Jesuits, were bemused by me, but a few were openly hostile. Once, my Greek professor, in his cups, took it up himself to phone my father to tell him not to waste his money on my education because I would never be more than a C student. My father was devastated. In tears, he told the priest that he would have to take it up with me since I was paying my own tuition. I was hurt beyond words. The fragile acceptance I had won from my father for my academic work had nearly been destroyed by a drunken cleric.

Most of my teachers were supportive, however. My algebra professor, who was also the dean of students, secured a three-hundred-dollar scholarship for me from the American Business Women's Association, telling them that I really needed the money. Fortunately, he didn't tell them that while diligent, I was about the worst student of algebra he'd ever had. It was my only scholarship in college; I applied for no others because I thought they ought to be reserved for the truly needy. I don't suppose it ever occurred to me that I was about as needy as they got at that school. It was also a matter of pride. Having to endure snubs and snide remarks about "affirmative action students," even though I wasn't one, I declined to give my critics any ammunition.

Mostly Jesuits or unmarried men, our professors were generally gentle, loving souls who had a great deal of time for us. (I had only two women professors during my entire undergraduate education.) My happiest memories are of the long, rainy winter days in San Francisco, arguing over Plato or Aristotle in our tiny classes. The largest philosophy class numbered fifteen people. My favorite professor, Dr. Vincent Moran, was a bachelor, and he gave us much of his leisure time. His home, located two blocks from the university, was a haven for intellectual discussion, classical music, and good art. Never did I experience a hint of prejudice from him because I was a woman or a Latina. His greatest contribution to my education was his careful attention to my papers. I wanted to follow in his footsteps, to earn my doctorate in philosophy at the Pontifical Institute of Medieval Studies at the University of Toronto, but my dreams had limits. I could not imagine how to finance such an ambition.

In an abortive attempt to fund my graduate school career, I enlisted in the United States Marine Corps. The recruiter gave me a written promise that I would be stationed in Germany for at least two years of my four-year enlistment. I reckoned that I would learn German, then stay on in Germany after my enlistment was up, using the GI Bill to earn a doctorate in philosophy at Heidelberg. I had to give up that dream when the Marines discovered that, unknown to me, I had arthritis. I had always thought that my legs hurt because of my running. Moreover, as I entered my senior year, I was warned by my department chair to forego the pursuit of an academic career because there were virtually no tenure-track positions available.

I was completely ignorant about the hierarchy among colleges. I had never heard of Harvard, Princeton, or Yale. In my naïveté, I thought that by going to USF, I had "made it." I didn't understand that even though its tuition seemed almost prohibitive to me and though it produced San Francisco's mayors and police chiefs, in the estimation of those in the ivory towers of academe it was a third-rate school. As a junior, I told Father Albert J. Smith, a Harvard alumnus and one of my mentors, that I wanted to do graduate work at Yale. He laughed. I was so wounded I could not even ask why he was laughing. His derision made me realize that in the great scheme of things, the University of San Francisco was not even a player. Father Smith had always been very kind to me, and I had always excelled in his classes. In retrospect, I realize that I cannot assess how much of his reaction was racism, classism, or sexism. Was he laughing because in 1970 there were no women professors in our philosophy department and few elsewhere? Was he laughing because USF couldn't compete with the academic superpowers? Was it because, despite my academic success, he could not imagine a Latina in the halls of an Ivy League school or because he knew I could never afford it?

He taught me a bitter lesson: Being working class means never knowing with certainty why someone is laughing at you. If you are a member of an ethnic minority, it is impossible to separate the disadvantages of class from those of race or ethnicity. If you are a woman, these considerations are further complicated by gender.

Throughout my undergraduate career, I struggled with the fact that my friends at UC-Berkeley or UC-Davis looked down their noses at USF. Since my education was so hard won, I wanted to believe that it was the best. Many of my professors had taught in the great European universities. If the most effective undergraduate education is in small classes where there is direct contact with the professors, why were the overcrowded state universities considered superior? During my five years at USF, I never had to attend a lecture with four hundred other students; my papers were graded and our classroom discussions led by professors rather than teaching assistants. It was ironic that I was at USF during the years when the state campuses were in continual turmoil due to the protests against the Vietnam war; there were threats to withdraw San Francisco State's accreditation, and Cal was on the verge of being shut down. Yet the intense, uninterrupted education I earned at USF was looked down upon when I applied to graduate school at UCLA in the early 1970s. It took years for me to understand that the reason that USF was considered inferior to Stanford, UC, and the others is because universities are judged by the research conducted therein rather than by the effectiveness and caring of their teachers.

It is in this regard that I feel the most alienation from my profession, an alienation that arises from the values with which I was raised. While I enjoy research and writing, I place a greater value on teaching than on research. Much of the research that I see seems to me a waste of time, an exercise in hair splitting. Responsibility for educating the next generation is unimportant to many professors in the large research institutions because the priority placed on research is structural, and gifted teachers are seldom rewarded as generously as gifted researchers.

I believed it when my teachers told me I could pull myself up by my bootstraps, but I was misled, in a well-intentioned way, by the American credo of individualism as well as by the efforts of the nuns at the Catholic schools I attended. The Sisters at little St. Teresa's School and at Presentation High School did their best to minimize the class differences among us. Without a political consciousness, their teaching led us to believe that we faced "a level playing field." No one warned us that Mexican Americans,

African Americans, and Native Americans had been systematically excluded from housing, employment, and higher education. When we failed, when we could not find housing or jobs, we blamed ourselves in the naive belief that we had only to work a little harder to grasp the brass ring. Despite pervasive rhetoric about a color-blind society, since my siblings and I entered the world of work, we have not been allowed to forget that we are Latinos. My sister Hilda works as a social worker in the San Francisco Department of Social Services, Children's Services Section. Her ability to speak Spanish is an essential part of her job. When my brother Manuel was in the Coast Guard, he was routinely berated by his commanding officer for being a "stupid beaner," a common anti-Mexican slur. After his enlistment was up, he joined the San Francisco Fire Department but stood to lose his job if white firefighters had succeeded in undoing the affirmative action program. My brother Kenneth scored very high in the written and physical examinations for the California Highway Patrol, but he was never called. I realize now that even though our teachers' encouragement was couched in rhetoric about excellence, their expectations for us were low. The bootstrap philosophy is entirely adequate if that is all you want. But if you aspire to something more than just making a working-class living, then pulling yourself up by the bootstraps rarely suffices by itself. I was fooled into believing that equality was the logical by-product of higher education. Now that I have become a university professor, with far more education than anyone from home, I struggle with the task of reconciling the standards expected of academics with my own values.

THE DEEP BLUE SEA

I was twenty-two. I had earned a bachelor's degree, but I didn't have the means to get the doctorate that I coveted. It was then I moved to Los Angeles.

For all its cosmopolitan trappings, in some ways San Francisco is a small town masquerading as a big city. Born and raised in the city, I found it impossible to walk around without meeting an old friend or classmate, a relative or a neighbor. When you live in the city, there is little need to go outside of it. In describing this phase of my life, I am struck by the irony of being a San Franciscan choosing to leave the city where others come to find themselves; the city that was to others a place for freedom and openness was limiting for me, both because of the constraints of my Latino upbringing and the expectations of my working-class parents. I had to leave San Francisco as certainly as others flee Big Pine, Wyoming, or Wichita, Kansas.

When I left San Francisco, my life, which had been following an orderly, linear, if somewhat rocky road, changed dramatically. In attending college, I had chosen a road different from that chosen by my peers and different from what my parents had planned for me. In leaving the city to go to Los Angeles, I left roads altogether to explore the vast depths of the ocean that is Los Angeles. The summer of my twenty-third year, when I moved to Los Angeles, was the real beginning of my adulthood. I put down roots in Los Angeles and forged a circle of friends. Hot while San Francisco is cool and foggy, vast while San Francisco is small and manageable, choking with smog, cars, and people who are seldom at peace with each other, Los Angeles is a wonderful, terrible place. Free to travel anonymously, I could be whoever I chose to be; I could walk the streets in Westwood or Hollywood, never meeting a soul who knew me. Instead of having to share a bedroom with a sister who resented my books and my clutter, I could re-create myself in a little house with book-lined walls, live with whomever I chose, without a phone or a television. For the first time, I was in charge of my own life. Even a small choice, like my decision to buy a dog, was an occasion for celebration. In Los Angeles, I could be an individual instead of the protected eldest daughter of Latino immigrants. For the first time, as we say in California, I had my own space.

How does one distill twenty years of adulthood into a few paragraphs? I married, I bore a daughter, I graduated from law school but quickly quit the legal profession because I was completely unsuited for it. I became a card-carrying feminist and civil libertarian. I worked as a social worker with the homeless, and I was partially disabled for two years after being beaten by a policeman. I spend little time on that period in this essay because I lived this nesting time in a middle-class environment far from my working-class youth. It was an odyssey where I doggedly ran away from myself and everything that tied me to my working-class roots. I had converted to Judaism in college, and some time after moving to Los Angeles I married a Jew. It was the easiest thing in the world to drop my Hispanic surname to adopt his name. For a few years, I deepened my understanding of Jewish history and tradition by attending a variety of Jewish colleges. It was during that time that I fell in love with the study of history. Indeed, for a while, I practiced an Orthodox form of Judaism. Tradition gave me a way out. Of course, my father expected me to take my husband's name. As easily as I slipped out of my name, I slipped into a middle-class life. I strove to feel at ease with my new identity, and I thought that I had succeeded until Passover in 1977.

My husband, Yehuda Lev, and I were attending a Passover seder at the home of some very close friends. As is their custom, they had invited a large number of people to the seder, including some newcomers to the community whom they scarcely knew. I was seated between Yehuda and our host's father. Next to him sat a young woman, a social worker who worked in East Los Angeles, an old Mexican American community.

The social worker was complaining about her job to anyone who would listen. It was clear that she hated it in general and that she particularly detested her Mexican clients. She said that she was sick and tired of working with those dirty, lazy, greasy Mexicans who were always beating their wives and the women who were too stupid to leave them. Yehuda glanced at me with alarm; my friend's father squeezed my wrist gently under the table. It was Passover and I didn't want to make a scene, so I struggled to control myself. Then she turned to me and said, "Oh, you have such long, beautiful hair and such pretty dark eyes; are you Sephardic?"

Without raising my voice, I glared at her and replied stonily, "No, I'm Mexican. My father works twelve hours a day and has never hit my mother; my whole family bathes every day." Then I stood up and walked out.

Outside, gasping and crying in the cool spring air, I realized that I couldn't run away from who I was nor did I want to. I had taken what seemed to me the easy way out, allowing others to mistake me for generic Mediterranean. Shortly thereafter, I took back my own name—over my father's objections!—and set out to discover how to integrate my working-class past with my middle-class present.

My Passover dinner experience was bitter, not only because I was furious at hearing my own people degraded, but also because I held Jews in high regard. I had adopted Jewish culture, taking back for myself the religion of my great-grandfather. I love Jewish culture deeply, and it was this that enabled me to isolate that bigoted woman from my Judaism. Nevertheless, I had to find a way to integrate the two halves of myself.

THE ELYSIAN FIELDS

Education is learning to use the tools the race has found indispensable.

(Josiah Royce)

[Legend engraved in the marble arch over the proscenium at Royce Hall at UCLA]

The University of California at Los Angeles is a splendid place. Standing on the terrace on the third floor of Royce Hall, I survey a campus that looks as though it could be in the Italian hills. The red-tiled roofs, the jacaranda trees with their delicate lavender blossoms, and Lombardine architecture lend power to this image. The physical beauty of the campus is a soporific that drugs you, making you forget the ugliness outside. In my program at UCLA, I found a real peer group. I was happy there.

I came to UCLA to become a historian. Modern women live to their eighties; at thirty-eight, when I started graduate school, I was squarely in middle age. If I were a nineteenth-century pioneer, I might be dead by this age. Instead, I am embarking upon a new career. Pursuing a doctorate in Latin American history long after the time, some would say, that I left the working class forces me to address questions that I thought were long settled.

As an older student, I experienced graduate school as a process of infantilization. I was told to trust my professors' judgment and came for a while to distrust my own. My economy of motion, developed by long experience, was undermined. Instead of doing only what needs to be done, graduate students are put through meaningless exercises and rituals, often for no better reason than that our professors had to do them. Yet the process is a socialization to a culture that is in a state of transition. The current "downsizing" of the university and the attrition of faculty due to aging mean that within a decade the university will have a very different appearance. Large numbers of women have acquired higher degrees. While the number of minority faculty is small, there are still many more of us than there were a decade ago.

Returning to school as adults, we find ourselves having to curb our disagreements with the administration or with powerful professors because outspokenness could bring punitive "ratings" (the system by which assistantships and fellowships are determined) or denial of access to academic jobs or funding. Some of us are veterans of struggles for civil rights and/or civil liberties, but we are denied access to our own files because of an archaic system that values secrecy over the civil rights of a student to know who is judging him or her and what is being said. I came back to school as a confident adult, secure in my ability to manage a life balanced between work and love, only to have my priorities questioned and even displaced by a profession that places little importance on being a successful *person*.

As a mother, I found it particularly frustrating that, in order to maintain my academic credibility, I almost had to keep my daughter in the closet. When it became known that I had a child, one of my professors gave me an evaluation that criticized my "inability" to devote myself wholeheartedly to the historical profession—this because I had to leave a seminar immediately at the end of class to pick up my daughter from day care. On another occasion, a professor criticized me for devoting too much time to extracurricular activities such as taking care of my daughter. I have noticed that young women without children or older women whose children are grown get more support from their professors than women with children at home. Furthermore, I have never heard the extracurricular activities of any of my male classmates criticized in their evaluations. Presumably a devotion to racquetball or chasing women is above reproach.

Nevertheless I have been fortunate. My entire graduate career has been financed by the University of California. I have had research and teaching assistantships in the History Department and in the women's studies program and fellowships of various kinds. I have also had the solid backing of my committee. Moreover, I have had my husband's love as well as his moral and financial support. I believe that my law degree helped me in the eyes of those making the decisions, in addition to helping me to develop the tenacity to endure despite many bureaucratic obstacles to success. But other Latinas have not had my good luck.

While the university administration worries aloud about "minority retention," little, it appears to me, is done about it, if the rate of attrition among Latinas in my department is any measure. The university is designed to "help those who help themselves." Unfortunately, this is a culturally biased issue. Little is done by the university to help people of color to adapt to the graduate school or to stay there when the pressures from home are overpowering. I have had many of my Latina students ask me for advice because they were being subjected to overwhelming pressure from their families to contribute to the family income. University officials forget that success is predicated not only on native ability and hard work but also on a supportive home environment and a hospitable atmosphere at school. As a Latina, I have enjoyed the official approval of the administration as evidenced by the financial support for my work, but I have seen little personal support from professors, particularly male professors, or in support services from the university. To be fair to UCLA, there is a limit to what the university can be expected to do for adults. But in light of its willingness to impose other rules—for instance, requiring the recipients of student loans to come to a meeting explaining their obligations—I do not understand why there is not a more active effort to help its minority and working-class graduate students.

One of the biggest personal obstacles I faced in pursuing my education was my deep reluctance to incur debt. The middle and upper classes are accustomed to manipulating debt to their advantage, but for a working-class person debt is a ball and chain. My father has always paid his bills in cash or has used credit cards only to pay them off monthly. He so feared debt that he refused even to take out a veteran's home loan. The house my parents own was left to them by his mother. While I am aware that many of my friends owe several thousand dollars in educational loans, I was terrified of incurring such debt.

The other obstacle I encountered in graduate school was the resentment of some of my classmates. Over the years, pointed articles against affirmative action were left anonymously in my mailbox in the history department. Many of my women colleagues (not women in my own field, however) have expressed their anger that there "just isn't anything [funding, jobs] out there unless you're a minority." Once, waiting for an elevator, I overheard a discussion carried out in stage whispers between two graduate students in medieval European history. "Oh, I had two good interviews, but I'll never get a job," said one. "There are just too many minorities and women after these positions." I bit my tongue to keep from asking him how many Mexican medievalists he knew. One classmate has told me many times in both subtle and overt ways that he doesn't expect to find a good job because he's "just a historian, not a specialist in African history before the Civil War or some such rot." Another male graduate student in our department complained recently that he had lost a second job to "an affirmative action hire." I suppose the affirmative action candidate was to blame when he failed to fulfill his contract by not finishing his dissertation. This kind of hostility and harassment has forced other Latino scholars out of academe. In truth, the university has traditionally expressed all sorts of preferences, for example, for veterans, for athletes, or for the children of alumni. I believe that increasing the number of minority and working-class faculty is a valid goal, and I will not allow myself to be harassed out of a dream that I have had all my life.

Society benefits when all social classes are represented in higher education. While we all aspire to a higher standard of living, not everyone has the opportunity to make large amounts of money in our chosen life's work, nor is higher education a guarantee of higher wages. A professor who understands only those students from comfortable circumstances will seldom do justice to those whose struggle for education is the end of a long and difficult road. The participation of working-class and minority faculty in higher education assures that the university reflects the diversity of viewpoints found in the society at large.

My circle of graduate students created its own support network. Most of the women are from working-class backgrounds. Four of us are Latinas, three are Jewish (two of the Latinas are Jews, one by choice), and one is of Central European/French/Native American origin. During our years in graduate school, we shared our joys and frustrations, joined together to face difficulties, held teaching assistantships at the same time and shared our resources, coached each other through examinations, and critiqued our dissertations as they were being written. We believe that our ad hoc support system made it easier for us to succeed. The university's insensitivity to the needs of nontraditional students, the low priority it has given to the special issues they present, and its ineptitude in dealing with diversity doomed the others. Without a good support system, they dropped out.

When I was first in graduate school and I railed against the hierarchical nature of the university, one of my professors, a woman, told me, "But you CHOSE this. This is the way it is." It's true that I chose a life of learning; I *didn't* choose the medieval autocracy that goes with it. Before I started at UCLA, I had thought that the greatest difficulty I would face in graduate school would be learning to study again. Even though I had street smarts from working as a social worker with homeless people and from studying law, nothing prepared me for the labyrinth of academic politics. The political questions that I face arise not from the work of research and writing, with which I became adept as a lawyer, but from the experience of maneuvering through the maze and from teaching a college class as an academic from the working class.

I am no longer the naive working-class girl that I was at seventeen. My education, values, and choice of leisure pursuits are far removed from those of my family and the milieu from which I came, but the values and experiences that inform my thinking are solidly working class. When I step into the voting booth, my choices reflect my lifelong bond with the labor movement, my commitment to feminism, and my concerns about poor and working people, not out of altruism but because in my heart I continue to be the teamster's daughter who won't cross a picket line and who worries about strikes every June, the parking lot manager's daughter who was too proud to apply for a college scholarship, the Catholic schoolgirl whose opportunities were created by the Sisters and an all-girls high school.

While I was a graduate student, dependent upon grants that were announced in June for the next year's livelihood, June was always an anxious time. It was in graduate school that I recognized the characteristics that distinguish the working class from the middle class. The first of these is the middle class's material security. Even when it is having cash-flow problems, the middle class always knows that there will be money for essentials, for plentiful food on the table and a home that's big enough for one's family. There may not be enough for the trip to Europe—this year—but eventually it will work out. In my family, there were never any leftovers because our food had been carefully rationed. Trips to Europe, new cars, expensive jewelry were for other people, not for us.

Applying for grants, I was acutely aware of the items that were missing from my applications. For instance, my middle-class colleagues could point to a year's study in Mexico during college when their interest in our field was sparked by a particular experience. Others could point to travels in Central and South America with their parents. A close friend of mine reported attending a national meeting of the recipients of a major grant; all of them, herself included, were the children of academics. She jokes that as an adolescent she rebelled by going to Brown University instead of Harvard. I wish I'd had that choice.

Middle-class people are not at the mercy of the system in important life decisions, but we were faced with the choice of attending a poor public school or squeezing every penny to attend a slightly less poor Catholic school. We went to the Catholic school and received an education that made it possible for us to be upwardly mobile. Manipulating the system is a given for the middle class. If there had been magnet schools when I was a child, we wouldn't have known about them.

As a college student, I didn't apply for a scholarship because I thought that financial aid was scarce and that it should be kept for the "truly needy." I didn't realize that anyone needier than I was would not have had the education to qualify for the university in the first place. At UCLA, I saw that the attitude of my mostly middle-class students was quite different from what mine was as a student. They believed they were entitled to support and complained bitterly when it was not forthcoming; I was always insecure about my right to higher education. As a graduate student, I knew that if the university ceased to fund me, it would be nearly impossible for me to finish my doctorate.

Being working-class, I always felt that I was in the university at the sufferance of others, as if I should apologize for filling the space. Later, as an instructor in a college classroom, I was sensitive to the shy working-class students who believed deep down that they didn't belong in it. When I took these students aside, shared my own struggles with them and urged them to utilize the remedial tutoring services offered by the university, I understood the pride that kept them from availing themselves of these programs. They trusted me because they knew that I know what it's like. Nevertheless, I maintained good relations with my non-Latino, non-working-class students. No one chooses the class into which she or he is born. Why should students born into comfort or even wealth and privilege be resented or disparaged? Seeing me as their teacher was a lesson in itself. Furthermore, I wanted to teach them that what they might do with their wealth and privilege is more important than living a comfortable and unexamined life.

I share the memory of having slept in the same bed with all my siblings; I know what it feels like to want desperately to get an education when all your friends are already working at adult jobs; I have written my school papers on a noisy manual typewriter late at night in a room where my sister was trying to sleep. I understand the Latina women who face pressure from families who don't understand why they are going to school when they could be out working and contributing to the family income.

Like my parents, my greatest commitment is to see that my daughter receives a first-rate education. Toward that end, we sent her to a Jewish day school that is known for its academic excellence. It is very American, I'm told, to want for one's children better lives than we had ourselves. But my working-class background makes me yearn for something more. I want all of our young people to have better lives. I believe deeply that our society should make decent education for all children one of its highest priorities. Through my teaching, I intend to do my part.

I do not want anyone to think that I would have traded one minute of my long pursuit of an education for someone else's easier life. I am nobody's victim. I would have liked guideposts and role models along the way (it would have been less scary), but I prevailed even without them. I look upon my experience as a boxer regards the miles of running, the hours of pounding a punching bag, and the years of sparring with partners in a ring. Having to work so hard and come so far has made my resolve rock-hard. I know who I am and what I believe. When I stand before my students, they learn that hard work can lead to triumph. Marriage and education have changed the material conditions of my life, but they cannot change my internal landscape. They cannot take from me the lessons I learned on the way to my doctorate. My lifestyle may be middle class, but my heart and soul are Latina and working class. I want to offer the benefit of my experience to young people who come from circumstances like my own as well as to those who have known only privilege.

Novelist Henry James once told his sister-in-law, "Tell them to follow, to be faithful, to take me seriously" (Edel 554). Artists, musicians, and academics who emerge from the working class have a particular tentativeness, a special need to be taken seriously. I have come a long way from the boys on the hill, the factories, and the slaughterhouses, but I am never quite sure that I am being taken seriously. These days, ensconced in my tenure-track job in New England, so far from home, I am living the dream I dared to dream while hoping that I will someday feel as comfortable on an academic panel as in my kitchen.

WORKS CITED

Blades, Rubén. *Rubén Blades y Son del Solar: Live!* Elektra Entertainment, 1990.
Edel, Leon. *Henry James: The Master, 1901–1906.* New York: Lippincott, 1972. Vol. 5 of *Henry James.* 5 vols. 1953–72.

8

Another Day's Journey: An African American in Higher Education

Gloria D. Warren

When I consider what a privilege it is to have come this far, from Detroit to Minnesota, and to be just months away from completing a doctoral degree, I am in awe of what God can do and thankful for my upbringing—for my family and the community that gave me spiritual resources and an understanding of those resources in the hands of a faithful God. I grew up during the turbulent sixties in a place called Motown, the Motor City. I was surrounded by spirituality, hope, and life lessons that were often echoed in gospel and rhythm and blues songs that both children and adults would sing and listen to as if they were words to live by.

My community consisted of the poor, the working poor, the working class, the middle class, and some who chose not to work. All seemed to have a tacit agreement about the sacrifice required to insure a future for the children. They understood that segregation and racial injustice were like plagues that have no respect for persons. When children passed by, the sometimes wise and dignified winos eyed them with parental authority, curtailing their language and behavior until they were out of sight. The middle-class African Americans who were our landlords, doctors, and cultural brokers always spoke to the children, both the clean and dirty, about the importance of staying in school. We had a family physician and counselor whose name was Dr. J. B. Martin. He would say to me, "Twin, you making good grades in school?" I'd say, "Yes sir." He'd glance at my mother, who nodded in agreement. Then he'd say, "All right, Twin, you better not let me hear tell you not doing good in school." And there were the nosy grandmothers, old, sometimes reclusive or senile, who watched from windows and porches as we walked to school, always mindful of our safety. There was no one person, family, or group that we modeled ourselves after because the whole community was our role model.

My father worked at Acorn Iron Works, one of many small plants that serviced the Big Three auto manufacturers (General Motors, Ford, and Chrysler). My mother worked as a waitress at a number of places, Vicki's Barbecue for one, and later started her own day-care business. My parents are representative of African Americans of the 1940s and 1950s, particularly men, who fought alongside whites as equals in World War II and upon returning to the United States migrated from the South to the North, no longer willing to tolerate segregation, in search of equality and jobs.

I knew as a child that both of my parents had to work to provide for us. We lived in a large two-bedroom apartment that my Southern Baptist-bred mother always kept tidy. We always had food and nice clothes. My parents often provided goods and services for other members of the extended family who from time to time might have been unemployed or might have needed something when there was a new baby. I knew from these exchanges and from watching my parents pay for groceries, rent, and other family necessities that you should work to provide for your family and yourself. Work was labor and its reward was to be paid a wage that allowed one to provide for the family. I never heard any conversation about work as a career or about careers with any upward mobility.

My parents organized our lives around work, church, and school. My mother would lay our clothing out before we went to bed and make us check for missing buttons and unraveled hems. My sister and I would awaken every morning to the smell of grits and sausage, pancakes, or Cream of Wheat. My mother would be dressed, ready to go to work. Daddy had already left for work at 6:00 A.M. My mother would braid our hair, direct us to check our hair and clothing before leaving the house, and then she would take another look at us as we left for school. Work must have been important because Daddy never ate breakfast with us. I suppose we were latchkey children, but it did not feel that way because it seemed as though all the mothers in the community could care for us. My special community mother was Mrs. Davis. She was the person who greeted us from school, removed any notes pinned to our dresses, and prepared us a snack. She even had a nickname for me, Sugarfoot, and I knew she loved me. I didn't feel neglected but rather a little indulged by having more than one mother.

Although my immediate family was small (I have one sister and one brother), my host of cousins were like brothers and sisters. Cousins Net and Deb, my neighborhood friends, and I waited for hours along with thousands of others to get into the Fox Theater to see the Motown Review—go little Stevie Wonder, "everythang is all right, uptight, out of sight." To keep in touch with our Southern roots, I, like many black children in the North, spent summers with my extended family in the South. I did my time in Enterprise, Alabama. My best memories were times visiting with my grandfather, Uncle Frank, and his wife, Lila Mae, and bike riding with cousins down dusty roads that stretched into forever. We ate Aunt Inez's breakfast of biscuits, chicken with gravy, and her famous homemade ice cream that never lasted more than twenty-four hours. I never recall any visible signs of segregation or tension, but in retrospect I realize the adults shielded us from such things. They would whisper or make us leave the room whenever the conversation shifted to adult themes of any kind.

During these visits to the South, I learned that Aunt Ethel, in the days of separate but equal, had attained what the family called a great accomplishment by earning a Ph.D. in education at Florida A and M University, and she was a high school principal in Pensacola, Florida. I saw her on occasion but was never really close to her. I knew what she did was important and deemed a worthy achievement because in the black community, whether in the South or North, education was believed to be a panacea for racism and to assure the upliftment of the Negro. Daddy felt proud of her but, oddly, he never spoke directly about her achievements to me. I learned years later as an adult that Daddy had attended a summer precollege program at Boston College, but he never followed up on this opportunity to get an education and he never said why.

Belief in education was evidenced in my own years at school. My community and school were black, and I was taught by black teachers in ways that prepared me to function in both white and black worlds. My teachers were an extension of the community. Teachers and parents respected one another highly. The last thing any student wanted was to have a note sent home requesting a parent to come to the school. Teachers and parents collaborated in chastising students for misbehaving or for foolishly wasting time that should be spent on "gettin' all the education you can get." This was further evidence of that commitment by everyone—communities, teachers, and parents—to my generation so that we would have opportunities that so many of them missed and would never have.

I learned Shakespeare and Langston Hughes. Once, some black college students from Wayne State University came and performed Shakespeare's *A Midsummer Night's Dream* at my elementary school. I was fascinated by the idea of a Shakespearean play performed by people who looked like me. We had a weekly ritual of presenting oral reports on important contributions to society made by members of the Negro race. My teachers taught me about the creative genius of the Harlem Renaissance, the strength of Sojourner Truth, the medical acumen of Dr. Charles Drew, and the wisdom of the peanut scientist, George Washington Carver. Overarching this knowledge was the principle that I and my race were made in the image of God. I possessed the ability to do anything my heart desired.

My mother would ask me to read my reports on Langston Hughes and the Harlem Renaissance and my favorite, Dr. Daniel Hale Williams, to her in the kitchen while she prepared dinner. Ma would talk to me about the things I learned in school. I remember telling her one day, "Mommie, I'm going to get a Ph.D. just like Aunt Ethel 'cause that's the best I can do in school." She smiled and responded, "Yes, you will, Gloria, yes you will." Every morning she would get up and pray aloud. I heard her praying for me, my family, and my community. I especially recall hearing on the phonograph the song by the Roberta Martin Singers, "God Specializes (in things so impossible)."

For my mother, rising early and having that daily devotion time became a way to understand and cope with the uncertainties and disappointments of life but also to celebrate its joys. For people who have neither access nor privilege, faith in God is a resource. Coming from a working-class family, my mother, like so many women of her own and previous generations who had neither access nor privilege, talked to God for "de Lawd will make a way, somehow." Faith in God and what He can do has been my resource along this journey in higher education.

My mother attended college for one year at Tuskegee but had to drop out because her parents became seriously ill. Shortly after, both of her parents died, and she had to move up North with her older brother. She soon married my father and began having children and never was able to finish college. She had gone farther in school than anyone in her family by finishing high school, but at that time extended family responsibilities superceded personal goals. I would be the first person in Smith family history to graduate from college.

During my years of growing up, spirituality was the cohesive force in my world. My family, church, and community were not made up of perfect people; they wrestled with the same imperfections and weaknesses that we do today, but they strove to live in a godly fashion before their children. An important aspect of spirituality was community parenting, which is consistent with the West African spiritual and community principle that "it takes a whole village to raise a child." The mothers would pray not only for their children but for other mothers and their children as well. They helped to raise all of the children on the block. One day I used some profanity, thinking that no one had heard me or that no one would tell my mother. I was immediately chastised by Crystal's mother, who called Mrs. Davis (my special community mother) to tell her what I had said and sent me home. Mrs. Davis in syncopated time spanked and preached to me on why profanity was wrong. She told me that she wanted me to grow up to use good words and not bad ones. She said that good words help people and make you look good, but bad words hurt people and make you look bad. All behavior whether good or bad touches the community. Last year when I went home, I visited Mrs. Davis. I brought her flowers and I thanked her for loving and disciplining me.

At Sunday morning worship service at Messiah Missionary Baptist Church, Reverend T. C. Simmons would preach. When I was a child I imagined that the wailings and moanings of the congregation made the building bulge out and lean to the side, a sign of a spiritual and cultural energy that no man-made building could contain. There was something wondrous about this space on the corner of Humboldt and Poplar in southwest Detroit. I can still see maids, common laborers, and janitors walking with the authority and commitment of kings and queens. In this house, common folk, who to the world outside have neither access nor privilege, are the royal priesthood, engaging the sacred and entertaining angels unaware. I remember the senior choir, especially the voices of the women, moaning and singing with conviction, "Walk in the Light, Jesus the Light of the World." They could sing with authority because they could see God opening doors of opportunity for their children and their children's children, and they committed their daily lives to that goal. In this atmosphere I learned that the fear of God is the beginning of knowledge.

I grew up with the expectation that I must go to college and be successful, do something that would benefit myself, my family, and community. That meant nothing but As and Bs on my report cards from kindergarten to high school. I remember often burning the midnight oil to get that A. The only question my family and I had was which college? On Saturday, my mother gave me permission to go to the Utley Branch Library. I was excited to have a library card and to carry books from the library home in my arms, meeting the approval of passing adults who smiled and nodded in admiration. I loved to sit in my rocking chair reading, traveling back in time or going to other parts of the world. From junior high to high school I had teachers, mostly African American, who told me I was college material. I was always in the college-prep track.

In my senior year in high school, the teaching staff and school administrators arranged a college fair. One profound impact of the civil rights movement was the establishment of funding—scholarships, loans, and other forms of financial aid for the children of the working class, the working poor, and the poor. Representatives from different colleges and universities visited us and reviewed different programs and admissions material. I took my admission packet home and examined the information. I sat both my parents down and discussed with them the three colleges I was interested in: Michigan State University, the University of Michigan, and Wayne State University. Both of my parents were in favor of my going to college but were concerned about the costs. My mother was instrumental in helping me decide which college. I had received four-year scholarships from both Wayne State and Michigan State and a two-year scholarship for the University of Michigan. I favored Wayne State University or Michigan State University because their scholarships were for four years, but my mother suggested that I would have a much more rewarding experience if I went away to school. Wayne State is located in the heart of Detroit; Michigan State is in East Lansing, very different from the world I grew up in. I chose Michigan State and declared a major in veterinary medicine.

The transition from high school to Michigan State University was a cultural shock. My father drove me up to East Lansing. On my first day I kept looking for black people and didn't see any. I knew that several of my classmates had been accepted to Michigan State, but we were assigned to different dorms. Robin, a friend from high school, and I had agreed to be roommates at school, so I knew eventually I would see her. I stayed in Hubbard Hall, the penthouse dorm on campus where at first sight I felt out of place. I saw some student housing in the area that looked like housing projects, and I thought maybe I could move there if that's where black folk lived. I was relieved when a black aide introduced himself and some upperclassmen and women. His role was to help black students get acclimated to the campus, both socially and academically. The upperclassmen and women became my extended family and community at the university.

My first encounter with racism occurred when I saw white students and their parents surreptitiously protesting the students' room assignments, insisting that they weren't going to room with "niggers." Innocently, I avoided this ordeal by choosing Robin, my high school classmate, to room with, but there were many other episodes that I could not avoid. I had an adviser who did not advise anything but ambiguity, instructors who constantly questioned my topics for papers, experiences with drunken white males who yelled "niggers" at us out of their dorm windows, and lab classes where we played the game of "who's going to be stuck with the dumb nigger?" One of the highlights of my college study was a chemistry lab class in which the experiments assigned were ones I had performed in my advanced chemistry class in high school. (Thank God for Gladys Brown, my high school chemistry teacher.) I was teamed with a young white man who was ostracized because he was "poor white trash." We often finished our experiments first and consistently received the highest scores. After a while, race did not matter for my white lab partner and me. My fellow classmate's ostracism eliminated those boundaries and created solidarity between us. We empowered each other as we discovered that our knowledge and expertise matched and at times surpassed that of our tormentors. It was a sweet victory.

In my junior year I declared a new major, nutrition. One other black woman had the same major, and we sat together in class. It was comforting to have another black student to sit next to; many times I was the only black person in my classes. I recall seeing only two black faculty members, one of whom never spoke to me; the other was Dr. Richard Jones, a professor in urban affairs. He cared about black students and often spent time talking with us. The only other professors that I felt truly encouraged me as a budding scholar were my Chinese humanities professor, Dr. Lee, and my English professor. I received As in both their classes. My lack of mentoring or encouragement may be somewhat typical of the undergraduate experience, but it was compounded for me by issues of race and class. I remember during my last year trying to figure out why all my classmates had been encouraged and instructed in applying for internships while I was not. When I persisted in asking for internship information, I was referred to a program that was viewed as undesirable and was eventually discredited.

What little guidance I had in creating a successful experience in post-secondary education came from upperclassmen and women. But even then, middle-class black students had additional resources in that they had been prepared by their middle-class families to climb the career ladder. They knew the language of academia and corporate America and could operate in both black and white worlds. I envied them. My very low tolerance for whites came from not being prepared to socialize with them; this was an experience that my all-African American upbringing of faith and community had not included. At least middle-class blacks knew how to play the game. I was from a working-class family that had never been in the game, had always been marginalized by white America. At best, I could stand on the sideline.

Upon preparing for graduation, I found myself going it alone and finding internship programs that would give me job experience. The best way I can describe my treatment compared to my white classmates is that while I was only one of two black students in my department, I was never given advice by the predominantly white departmental faculty on networking and career opportunities. Instead they would refer me to the bulletin board where career-related materials were posted. I knew I was tolerated at best.

Consistent with the more subtle, sophisticated forms of racism that lead us into the twenty-first century, they didn't have to call me a nigger, only to engage in behavior that said, "You don't quite come up to the standard." That did not stop me. My pride would not let me beg them for the same chance they gave other students, so I kept checking the board daily, making phone calls, and going on interviews. I found employment with the help of two black women, sisters whom I am eternally thankful for because they gave me a chance. They gave me opportunities to learn the application or service aspect of providing nutrition services.

At graduation I had decent grades and some job experience under my belt similar to what my white counterparts had, but I encountered problems finding employment. In college I was rarely able to establish trust or a meaningful rapport with white professors, administrators, or classmates. Not having skills in communicating with whites limited my ability to network. I had letters of recommendation but not from anyone affiliated with the university or anyone who was white. Over several months I saw white former classmates gain employment fairly easily while I ended up working as the office manager at a seedy contact lens agency. This period of my life was revelatory because I was finding out in an adult way that the world is black and white. I turned to one of the church mothers I grew up with, Mama Gandy. I had finally landed a job at a health department clinic near where Mama Gandy lived. I would go to her house for lunch, to visit and talk about life. Sometimes she would talk to me about my relationship with God and the church. She would speak about Jesus as savior and as the answer to my questions, doubts, and fears. She served up sermonettes with homemade apple pie, preserves, or candied yams. She helped me to see my work at the clinic and any other work I might do as performing services for others. Her wise comments and our time together confirmed that my education could make a difference. No one in the academy had ever suggested that or told me that my knowledge was valuable.

One day about eight years ago I met Reverend and Mother Crawford, two of the joys of my life. They live in a working-class/working-poor neighborhood, one having too many people and too few jobs. They are like precious jewels God has tucked away for his people. Reverend and Mother Crawford are well past seventy and full of wisdom. Mother had agreed to start a Bible study for my friends and me because we said that we wanted an older spirit-filled woman to teach us how to be godly women. Mother gave of her time and self. Many a day I have sat and listened and watched.

Over the years of working with families and at community-based organizations I began to see that I needed additional knowledge and training. My heart was still set on returning to school for my master's and doctoral degrees. I applied to various schools from time to time, but I kept getting rejection letters. I was disappointed and discouraged but after a while I began to enjoy not being in school and understood that I needed to develop certain skills before returning. I was also beginning to have serious problems with my vision that required surgery. Further, Reverend and Mother Crawford were teaching me things about myself that would strengthen me in ways that would be essential for my future success. For people of color, one's intellect is not the determining factor in staying the course but rather tenacity and a strong sense of who one is. That means meditating on our legacy of strength and what we have endured throughout our journey as African Americans. My African ancestors survived the Middle Passage; whom or what should I fear? The stories that Reverend and Mother Crawford would tell and sitting and listening to them expound on the scriptures reinforced my faith as a resource that, unknown to me, would sustain me in my journey in higher education.

I decided to reapply to graduate school but this time to a black institution, thinking that there I would be in a supportive environment. I settled on Howard University. My best friend had moved to Washington, D.C., and she had a friend who could help me get a scholarship. I visited Howard for an interview, and the department head spoke seriously with me about pursuing a doctoral degree. I was empowered by seeing African American faculty for the first time and by their assumption that I could be a scholar and a potential colleague. The Howard faculty's validation enhanced my belief that I was going to earn a doctoral degree. At last someone from the academy said I was doctoral material.

There was a great deal of turmoil going on within the upper echelons of the administrative circles at Howard University because shortly after my visit they lost their law school accreditation and their president resigned. I had my heart set on going to Howard University, but suddenly there was no scholarship for me. I drove over to Reverend and Mother's place with tears streaming down my face. I couldn't stop crying, but Papa with his calm and wise spirit sat on the porch with me, his hand holding mine. He spoke with the faith of one who has been on the journey for a long time. He said, "God has something better for you." We went inside the house, and Papa made coffee while Mother hugged and held me. She sat me down at the kitchen table and heated up a piece of sweet potato pie. Her words were like a balm, soothing to the spirit. She read from the Bible that "all things worked together for them that love the Lord who are called according to His purpose." Eventually, my spirit was calmed. As I drove back home I was deeply thankful to God for Reverend and Mother. Deep down I knew they were right. I learned that God was saying to wait in faith.

If God indeed had something better for me, then it was my responsibility to find out what that was. I began to conduct information interviews with people in my career circles. One black woman told me that I should check out the University of Michigan's program in public health. I could commute to school and still be close to my family and community. I met with the minority recruiter several times. She suggested that I get information about another graduate program and compare it with the package the University of Michigan offered. She had met the minority recruiter from the University of Minnesota, and obtaining graduate information seemed fairly simple. I completed both sets of admissions materials, knowing that the University of Michigan was my first choice. Besides, where the hell was Minnesota? I knew it was north, the Twin Cities are there, they have a small African American population, and most of all, it's too cold! Then something unforeseen happened. I received a personal letter and phone call from the home economics education department head asking me to consider a doctoral program at the University of Minnesota. I talked it over with the minority recruiter, my mother, and Reverend and Mother Crawford. I would be one of a small group of African Americans who had been recruited for the graduate program. Everyone agreed that I should go, for they and so many others had sacrificed for me to have such an opportunity, and because my success would help bring resources into the family and community. An African American from a working-class background in an upper administrative position can make decisions that directly impact her community.

At prayer meeting, Papa asked that precious handful of the faithful to gather in a circle and pray for me. Here stood prayer warriors, the glue that holds the church together, noble old ladies who keep their money tied up in handkerchiefs because they can't afford purses and men who in time past labored from can to can't. I felt surrounded by their hopes and their strength. I marveled at their faith. Many times while I was trying to relocate from Detroit to Minnesota and felt like giving up, I remembered that they were praying for me. That prayer would calm my spirit. It still blesses me today. The prayers of the righteous availeth much.

My nephew and I drove to Minnesota to look for an apartment. After several days of looking, we had found nothing. On the day before our day to leave, my nephew and I stood in the middle of the hotel room and prayed. The cousin of a friend of the family, Birdie Martin, lived in Minnesota. That very same day, Sister Birdie came by and took us apartment shopping. We found a nice apartment in St. Paul, where I live today. That evening I remember saying to my nephew, "Do you see, Phillip, how God answered our prayer?" I returned to Detroit fretful but thankful because getting a place confirmed for me that God was with me in my decision.

As I lay awake in bed contemplating my move to Minnesota, it seemed as if all of my years of studying, listening, and learning about faith in God culminated in my decision to attend graduate school in Minnesota. From an academic standpoint, I had never felt unprepared in terms of my knowledge or intellect. I never needed remedial courses, even in undergraduate school. It would be other things, such as networking and understanding the language and politics of higher education, that I would have to learn. I had to stand on the promises of God in faith, believing that somehow He would work it out. I had done my part—gathering information, asking questions, and saving money. Bible study with Sister Strong and with Reverend and Mother Crawford, in which I spent hours researching Sunday School lessons and various documents, sharpened my research skills and reacquainted me with the habit of concentrating on one topic for hours at a time.

Everyone who had agreed to help me move backed out at the last minute for a host of reasons, most legitimate. I contacted Mother Crawford and she spoke with John, a Bible study friend, asking him to help me move to Minnesota. John graciously agreed without any hesitation. Like Abraham, I was thankful that God had sent me a ram in the bush. But I was to learn another lesson about life and people, this time through my mother. My mother is a community mother who has the gift of agape, the ability to look at the heart, the inside of a person and not the outside. She had befriended and cared for Erwin, who to the world was just another alcoholic. To her, Erwin was a man who helped her with maintenance around the house and garden. He responded to her respect for him by being faithful to her in his work, always keeping in mind "how Mrs. Warren wants her house to look." John, Erwin, and his friend helped me to move with just twenty-four hours' notice. I once read in my Bible where God advised Samuel after several attempts at choosing the next king of Israel to look not at what appears on the outside but rather on the inside, at the heart. With this advice, Samuel was able to identify David as the next king of Israel. I learned, like Samuel, that the true measure of a person is the heart, their ability to help and care for others. I would have more lessons like these in the days ahead.

I had moved to Minnesota and was getting ready for the start of classes. The day before they were to begin, I drove around Como Lake tearfully praising and thanking God for this marvelous opportunity while listening to the gospel song "Standing on the Promises." All the lessons and examples of what people in the Bible had experienced in their walk of faith were being reinterpreted and synthesized in my own life. God had moved the hearts of strangers to help me with the major task of moving. In the process, my heart and my ways of looking at the world changed. John, Erwin, and Sister Birdie had done for me what I probably would not have done for them. I had a haughty spirit. I knew that I must change my attitude and begin to reach out and help people as freely as these strangers had helped me. God had used this experience to begin to sweeten me. I stood at a crossroads in my life as I was just beginning truly to walk by faith and not by sight.

Now that I was in graduate school, I plunged myself into my books and into getting acclimated to the campus and my department. I joined the graduate student council and developed a community among the small group of African American students that I was recruited with. I studied, completed all my assignments on time, earned better than a 3.5 average, and participated in social gatherings in the department. I also attended the orientation for graduate students, where I was one of three blacks in a room of one hundred whites. I signed up at the library for classes on using the databases. I was thirsty for knowledge. Since my undergraduate days, I had learned some ways that would help me assert myself in the academy. I was determined that this time around I would get all of the benefits of higher education.

My first inkling that something was not right was when I discovered that the scholarship package promised to me had been changed. Upon inquiry I was informed that the amount I was promised would be all the scholarship monies I would ever receive and that they preferred that I did not take on additional work, which might jeopardize my studies. I was in a catch-22. I slowly began to see that racism was very much a part of higher education in 1989, just rationalized under the guise of excellence in education and something called "Minnesota nice," which means whites discriminating against people of color in a courteous manner and deluding themselves that because they have the veneer of courtesy they have not been discriminatory. For example, I attended a meeting where someone stated that all African American families are at risk or dysfunctional. One assumption that underlies this belief is that the African American family is not capable of being a productive social unit or of contributing to the good of society. What struck me most about the incident was the silence of the faculty, professors in home economics education who at least should have offered a scholarly rebuttal. No one said anything. I responded with a rebuttal to which the person did not reply. At this same meeting, information was shared regarding a faculty exchange with a historically black college. Although no one responded openly against it, I felt tension rise in the room. Faces became flushed and people squirmed in their seats. They then went on to engage in an academic discussion of why this was not viable. I found it interesting that no one argued in favor of the proposal. Finally, the department head provided a dignified way out by saying they could discuss it at some other time. I knew from community politics that when issues are deemed important, proposals are presented in the affirmative, individuals are assigned tasks, and a time frame for completion of the tasks is outlined. Now I wonder: If these professors felt threatened by a short-term relationship with a professor of color, how do they feel about me as a doctoral candidate?

As a way of networking I served on different committees as a student representative. I needed to be in circles where there was some validation of me as a scholar. My adviser was supportive, but that was not enough to sustain me. Somehow I knew from staff meetings like the one I just described that there would be problems, and I would need to know people who could help me get an assistantship or other funding. My faith and community resources had taught me that I have a right to the best, just like everyone else, because God is no respecter of persons. The quality of work I performed on those committees was my way to show that I had what it takes to be in the academy. My participation allowed me to meet faculty and administrators who believed that students of color and the perspective we bring are assets to the academy. We worked together as colleagues. These persons were sensitive to the issues of class and race and were instrumental in helping me with funding, networking, and negotiating in the university.

My experiences were mixed for the first three years, but academic life was still stable in terms of scholarship funding. My cohort group of African American graduate student friends became my family. We went on picnics and to plays together and formed a research group to help each other review papers and learn more about the conceptual underpinnings of different methodologies. I kept my girlfriend's daughter when she went to conferences or had a big study load. We ran errands for each other, and Walter did maintenance work on everybody's car. We shared resources. From time to time we went to church, but it was Minnesotan and black middle class. African Americans from the Twin Cities are different from African Americans who have grown up in other metropolitan areas where the black populations are larger and where major changes in city hall and economic development have taken place. Detroit has some infamous aspects such as its high crime rate, but Detroit is also a city where African Americans play a role in every area of the city politics. It strengthens one's spirit and raises one's vision of the power of a people when one has been socialized in that kind of setting.

Every time I go home to Detroit, I spend time with Reverend and Mother. Before I leave on the plane, I always stop to have breakfast with them. Papa reads a chapter from the Bible, and then we get on our knees and pray. Papa can see things, rivers of disappointment afar off. Papa always prays for me to endure things that stand just on the horizon. My family of friends at Minnesota and my family and friends at home became the community of support I surrounded myself with.

When I initially applied for the graduate program in home economics education, I had talked about the historical role of the Black Church in African American family life and parenting. During my years working in the Head Start program, I found myself and others counseling parents with values and beliefs steeped in the traditions of the Black Church and the African American legacy of spirituality. Some of our parents had complex and chronic problems and desired something to help their spirits to live in ways that would be constructive for themselves and their children. African Americans have historically used the Black Church and spirituality as a support system for problem solving and coping. For my master's thesis I was interested in studying the impact of a church-based parent education program on parenting abilities. I, like many of the women in my own and previous generations, received informal instruction about parenting in the context of the Black Church. Many times the older women, usually church mothers and the wives of deacons, would take some young couple under their wing and help them with a new baby. Or a church mother might see you act in a way that was inappropriate and get your attention, saying: "Baby, may I see you for a second? Baby, be consistent with your children. Don't keep saying 'Stop, I'm gonna get you' and then not do anything 'cause that means you lying to them and that's confusing; learn to be consistent with them." The elders teach the younger or novice parents. These were patterns of socialization in which I and others learned how to parent.

Although I was encouraged to pursue this topic of study in both my master's and doctoral work, no one validated my dissertation topic with any research funding and resources. I was on my own. When I came into my fourth year, there was no funding for my doctoral study, and I was consistently told that the doctoral degree was not something that the department had agreed to provide funding for. Could I have made this major transition on hearsay? I later found out from talking to other students of color and administrators that reneging on scholarships or funding for students of color at the second year is a common practice. No, my perceptions were right; it was not me. There is still some pain and anger around this that makes it difficult to discuss. People of color know what I'm talking about; some things are best said when they cannot be used against you.

In the fourth year of my program I had no funding. I was preparing for my written and oral exams and writing my dissertation proposal. My bills were past overdue, and I feared any moment that my landlord would give me an eviction notice. I made all the rounds talking to administrators, going to all the appropriate offices, interviewing for jobs, and writing the president of the university, but to no avail. I was frightened. I had always been able to pay my bills, always had a job that covered my living expenses, but not anymore. After many days of going in circles and being faced with the reality of no scholarship funding, I felt pressed out of measure—a feeling of anguish and turmoil with no relief in sight. I felt that God had abandoned me. Where was this marvelous Jesus they spoke about when they prayed for me? Why was God allowing this to happen? One night I heard a voice crying out, "Oh, Lord, help me, please help me." I woke up to find that it was me. Somehow my spirit, my very being, was crying out to God. I never had that experience before. The next day I attended revival at a local black church, and one of the church mothers stood up and sang, "I Must Tell Jesus." When a church mother sings, it sounds like the voice of the ancestors. And then she just moans, for words cannot express the soul's anguish and expectation. These are women who, despite their circumstances, believe that God cares and will make a way out of no way.

The next eighteen months I found myself working at temporary assistantship positions. I received funding to conduct my research with the help of an African American faculty member. I had also passed my written and oral exams, and I was thankful for that. However, I found that my spirit had become bitter. I began regularly to attend the church whose revival I had attended because it had been my choice for a site to conduct my research. This church reminded me very much of my home church in Detroit. I was collecting data, but in this space I also felt a healing of my wounded spirit. I'd make my rounds saying hello and hugging Aunt Diddi and Mother Williams. It was like a balm.

During the summer of 1993, I was working on the first three chapters of my dissertation. I still had no funding for the year. I was frantic, and my sporadic morning devotions and Bible study were indicators of the distance between myself and God. All these years of being in Bible study and trying to live right and this is what I got? From time to time, I would listen to the tapes Mother Crawford had given me at Christmas to help me cope. Listening to them ministered to me in ways that I cannot explain. I do know that something kept me from almost committing suicide. That's how isolated I had begun to feel.

There is a spiritual that says, "Jesus, he will fix it—afterwhile." In August, something strange began slowly to happen. A couple of years before, I had befriended another African American graduate student, Renee. We attended classes on different campuses and only visited with each other quarterly, but Renee and I began to become close friends. I was able to share how crazy and out of control I felt. Although I had written the first three chapters of my dissertation, I had almost lost my sanity, and that was scary. I knew she was a godsend. She sat me down and helped me to reevaluate my timeline for completing the dissertation. She also told me about some temporary employment that could help pay some bills, at least for a couple of months. I ended up reassessing my values, particularly in relation to money and the graduate-school experience. One issue that stands out is that of taking on debt. In my family, it was important to owe no one, especially institutions or white people. Many African Americans, particularly those who migrated from the Jim Crow system in the South, were taught that accepting a loan from whites made one more vulnerable; generations of economic disparity in slavery and sharecropping have left an imprint of caution on the minds of African Americans. I had to adopt the middle-class view of educational loans as an investment.

My friend Renee was also experiencing her own set of difficulties. As she ministered to me, I was able to minister to her. Somehow that motivated me to begin to be attentive to my time with God in devotion and in faithful attendance at church. I could see as each day passed that I was really on the edge, more than I could previously have imagined. I became ever more thankful, knowing that the line between sanity and insanity is thin. Now I understood what those old folks meant when they opened their prayers saying, "Thank you, Lawd, I woke up this morning clothed in my right mind."

I was also thankful that I had chosen to conduct a study on socialization and parenting in the Black Church. Collecting data through observation, recording the services, and conducting interviews had played a role in ministering to me. As I sat and listened to stories, particularly those of the older people, I was reminded of the historical faith and endurance of my people. Mother Crawford reminded me that being a doctoral candidate was a privilege granted by God and a prayer answered by those who had sacrificed so that I could have such a marvelous opportunity. There was a story to be told about the role of the Black Church in family life that would benefit my generation and generations to come. As a researcher and scholar, I believed that these oral teachings and social dramas were valuable contributions to understanding the role of rituals and symbols in the construction of knowledge about parenting. I grew confident in advocating for other students and faculty about the uniqueness of the research experience as an opportunity to achieve excellence in higher education for researchers of color.

As the fall quarter was in full swing, both Renee and I felt that something good was about to happen. We began to talk about forming a coalition through which graduate students of color could support each other academically and emotionally. I met with the director of the Minnesota Women's Center, whom I had worked for on a diversity project. She was part of that small network of persons I referred to earlier who encouraged me as a scholar and potential colleague. She listened to me and was instrumental in helping me network. She encouraged me to start such a coalition and gave me some information on a small grant program that could provide some start-up monies for it. Renee and I developed a strategy for approaching faculty. We also generated a list of graduate students who might be interested in joining such a coalition. At that time I was also involved with a group (mostly composed of white women from varied economic backgrounds) who were working to improve the climate for women in higher education. Renee and I agreed that a gathering on mentoring sponsored by this group might be a good place for talking to women graduate students of color about the viability of starting a graduate student coalition for women of color. All of the vice presidents would be there, a priceless opportunity to network.

Renee and I prayed about it and then wrote the proposal. Like our ancestors, we used our faith as a resource. The Lord answered our prayers, and we received some money to develop a program. Immediately following the acceptance of the proposal, God answered another prayer: I was hired as an administrative fellow. Now I had a stable source of income, hallelujah! On sharing the news of my job with another friend, she said she knew of a position that I could have had a while earlier. My response to her was, "No, God wanted a coalition to be formed to help graduate students of color. If I had been comfortable and secure and not had the experience of being crushed, I would not have been motivated to help others." Although it would not have been my way, it was God's way; as God told Isaiah, "For my thoughts are not your thoughts, neither are your ways my ways, saith the Lord. For as the heavens are higher than the earth, so are my ways higher than your ways and my thoughts than your thoughts." God, in his infinite wisdom, had used this experience to strengthen, sweeten, and bless me so that I could minister to others. I see the faces of the elders who sing with authority, "Jesus, He will fix it—afterwhile."

It's another day's journey and I'm glad about it. I titled this essay "Another Day's Journey" because like my ancestors before me who struggled through pain and much sorrow I can look back and see that God was with me. He had taken what was meant to be for evil, the marginalization of an African American doctoral student, and turned that experience into something good. I am thankful for my upbringing of spirituality in the community, home, and church. These experiences have laid a foundation that I can build on as an individual and as a scholar. For my journey, God placed family and friends—my parents, Reverend and Mother Crawford, Renee,

Mother Strong—to succor me along the way. My time in Minnesota seemed bitterly cold, but God performed a work of grace in me. I am a little stronger and a little sweeter, I have met people from different walks of life. I have developed a rapport with administrators and faculty that I would never have dreamed of before. I am even more committed to African American families and communities. Surely it's another day's journey, and I'm glad about it!

Part Two | Border States

9

Useful Knowledge

Mary Cappello

To Whom It May Concern: I am not what I have tried to be! Will I ever be able to write a few words correctly? Will I ever learn not to misspell words? No. Never. I am a cobbler. (From the journal of my grandfather, John Petracca)

In the process of becoming official, of gaining the authority to reproduce knowledges about the history of private and public utterances in the United States, in entering the academy as an assistant professor of English, I have experienced in many ways the not-so-subtle necessity of having to move as far away as possible from who I am. When I think "working class," pictures come to me more readily than words, thus signaling this aspect as perhaps the most unspeakable feature of my identity in academe. I am, after all, much more aware of how even my lesbianism, an obvious site of censorship, shapes my interpretations of literature in and out of the classroom than I am of how my working-class upbringing does. My working-class background may be my best kept secret.

Woman/lesbian/feminist/Italian American no doubt intersect *working class,* and yet I only narrate myself as working class through the figure of once-within-a-place. Insofar as I have learned to affiliate my class position (in contradistinction to other subject positions) with its material evidence, its signs, it makes sense that *working class* in my story conjures architectures: row home; playgrounds like minefields of unsuspected debris, rusted shopping carts that scarred faces and legs; resounding edifice of Catholic church and Catholic school, hallowed heights and peculiar smells of incense or the sawdust meant to quell the tang of vomit. Yet I also suspect that my affiliation of class with the somewhere that I left when I entered this profession is the fresh retelling of its sequestering by the middle-class authority of the academy.

Why have I not, after five years in graduate school and four years as an assistant professor at both a prestigious private and a sprawling state university, been able or compelled to position myself as from the working class? Are there ways of imagining working-class experience vis-à-vis higher education that wouldn't presuppose a movement up? (Up and away?) What's at stake in the refusal to implicate one's working-class markings in the work of teaching people how to reinterpret the representations that shape their real lives?

In the pages that follow, I hope to begin to articulate a present that is at once continuous with and disseevered from the past, a past remembered in ways that my academic present would have me deny, even as academe offers the occasion to write about it. What happened in the university—undergraduate studies at Dickinson College, graduate work at SUNY-Buffalo, tenure-track positions at the University of Rochester and the University of Rhode Island—must not be imagined as antithetical to what happened in Darby, Pennsylvania, where I grew up. Even though each locale played its part in negating the other, each was and is always complicit with the other. Each was and is equally threatening to the other though not equally damaging or devastating, for the violence with which academe keeps working-class people from entering its domain is not exactly equivalent to the resistance that working-class people might have to that space.

First, my working-class credentials. My father, a sheet-metal worker at the Philadelphia Naval Base for forty years, currently suffers from asbestosis as a result of one of his jobs. My mother was a housewife/poet and closet political activist who suffered from agoraphobia for many years. Credentials aside, what I remember and affiliate my working-class identity with are (too thin) walls and broken, split-open bodies accompanied by the eventual dawning of the illusion of upward mobility. To be working class was always to be in a simultaneous state of surround and transparency. Surround: my neighborhood was cacophonous with the noise of work and rage. Someone inevitably had his visor lowered to extra welding in his garage on the weekends; or a hammering job that threatened to split the fragile foundations of the neighborhood would pound out from the small fenced-in patch that was an amateur boxer's backyard. Houses did not communicate with one another so much as they interfered in their married proximity with one another. No community to speak of, except at church where contributions were the key to success no one could purchase. Transparency: being astonished and embarrassed to discover that I could see my family's unselfconscious movements from the window of my friend's house across the street.

But the violence of seeing and being seen and of being forced to listen and being wholly heard was outdone by the violence of body opening body, of male against male or male against female. He spun him round and threw him onto the cement; he grabbed him by the shirt collar and threatened to choke him; the father beat the small boy/as the boy grew older, he ordered the father to beat him; the boxer smashed the face of a gang member in a public place/the victim's buddies sought revenge and "accidentally" shot the boxer's little girl (she was eight) through the back of her head. Such violence was not, as is stereotypically assumed in the United States, a way of life for Italian Americans per se. The neighborhood was mostly populated by Anglo, Irish, and African Americans who shared, though never exactly or equivalently, a rage-inducing class status. On Concord Road, my family were the minority "wops" among wasps. Take, for example, an incident I recall from elementary-school English class. We were learning about characterization in literature, and the teacher, Miss DiBonaventura, asked David Lemon to characterize me: "She has little feet, curly hair, and she's a wop," he said. Obviously, he had never considered that our teacher's mellifluous name might have a Mediterranean origin, and so he was forced to apologize to her and to me.

This is the narrative that brought me to school: escape, study, read, apply, and the world of the Ivy League will open up to you its contemplative flower and the noise will subside. Following a dominant mythology that persists in our national consciousness today, I had equated higher education with the Ivy League, and I had pictured the Ivy League as a world of richer textures and finer sounds than those I knew. It was a fantasy reserved for a select number of us in high school. One inspiring English teacher who was deeply connected to certain of nearby Philadelphia's pulses, film and theater in particular, occasionally chose a few of us for the golden opportunity to join her on excursions to such events. *The* university from our parochial point of view was Penn; Princeton, though, was not far off. It's flower, I thought, would open up to me. I was sensitive and it deserved to be mine.

The flower crumpled in one short interview and one clipped rejection— two out of three of my postsecondary-school options, for my family could only afford for me to apply to three schools. Nearby Swarthmore College had sent a representative to our high school (Darby-Colwyn) to interview those of us at the top of the class. We were told they had a full four-year scholarship that might be offered to one of us. At my interview's end, my interlocutor jokingly asked, "Do you play football?" then went on to offer his evaluation of me to our guidance counselor: "She's short but perky," he said.

There must have been something wrong: I'd worked hard, I was the class valedictorian and a class leader. Soon after this disappointment, I received a rejection from Princeton University, only to learn that a less scholastically able football player at my high school was accepted there. The repetition made the message clear. Not only was passage to higher education going to be rare, but the only ticket in might be the body, and at that, only a particular version of the body: the brawniest child of labor, the buxom male body burst from the working-class frame was recruited to carry the transcendent-of-class Latinate insignia.

Ever after this and in spite of the richly creative years I have known in higher education, there always has lurked a feeling of lack of fit between the contours of my knowledge and the academician's garb. I falter in announcing it, however, for a subordinate class position is already over-accompanied by that most impoverished of emotions, pity. Sympathy, understanding, will not do. Rather, I mean this essay as an intervention into institutionalized self-definition and, most importantly, as a map that might be applied to the terrain of academe and then explored for the differences that emerge: riffs, valleys, bulges, bluffs, blindnesses.

The borderline state, the sense of being neither here nor there persists: the working-class academic can never fully "move in." The people from your former life refuse to understand what you do; in your new one, what happens at the dinner table will always give you away: arranging silverware was not part of your training. You know and you don't know, and what you don't know is worth more to your professional position. You know how to play Italian folksongs on the mandolin; you know how to play beeries and basketball; you know how to plant an unpatterned garden (weeds can be beneficial too); you know what a gunshot sounds like; you know the fear of impending violence, the padding of feet down a corridor of no return; you know to expect the spillage of somebody's pain into the festivities. You don't know how to color-coordinate your wardrobe; you've never found glasses to fit your face; you don't know how to play tennis. You know how to shut out external noise, yet you don't know how to shut out demands that will exploit you as a junior woman faculty member at any university. You feel you have missed something. All the awards and honors cannot convince you "you're in." You still think analogically in a profession that welcomed you into its precincts for your clarity and logic.

This is where some new vantage is required, where the fissures created by the narrative of was and is need to be puzzled out without being figured into a middle-class penchant for neatness. The most obvious observation I can make about the preceding diagnostic profile is its emphasis on lack. Feminist writers especially have exposed the myth of lack as it has been applied for centuries to the marginalized—women, African Americans, and the working class, among other subalterns. We're told women lack aptitude for the public sphere; blacks lack the ambition to better their position; working-class people lack consciousness of their condition. These are some of the readiest instances of dominant displacement, and while they are easily enough exposed for their invalidity, easily enough indicative of the fragility of the center that insists upon them, they have wreaked forms of havoc in people's psychological dispositions that are none too easily repaired or are all too easily given over to the "cures" of the systems that oppress. Higher education in the United States has done much to reinforce lack across the bodies and minds of women, working-class people, and people of color, in part by insisting that they sever themselves from an identity designated as "prior" to their entry into academe, as though it were as simple as leaving one's baggage at the door.

But what had been deemed lack is now better understood as delegitimized knowledge, knowledge that needs to be acknowledged—a task that is difficult for student and teacher alike. As a working-class student, I should have been encouraged to interrogate aloud the homogeneous student body that I was ever aware of—redundantly thin and appallingly white. Rather than quiet the noise of the working-class neighborhood now internalized along with other cultural voices, rather than transmute the distracting din into a convincingly serene Muzak, we might learn to mine such sounds for their worth, their instructive tension. I am reminded of Henry James's governess in *The Turn of the Screw*, whose escape from lower to upper class provokes hallucinations. Shocked by the repressions exacted by her new world and by the disillusion of the so-called real world she's entered, she starts to "see things." I want to suggest that we can't afford to get sick like the governess on realizing how the middle class uses the working class as a screen for what's most aberrant about itself; we can't afford to work our psyches into a permanent grimace because of the lack of fit of working-class face to middle-class mask. Instead, we need to tell the things we see as what we know: a knowledge that is just as valid as any and possibly more instructive than most. But this would require from the outset that students be encouraged NOT to assume they already know everything about themselves, the student sitting next to them, their teacher, and the texts we put in front of them. Students become disappointed and confused to learn that their teachers—people whom they've come to enjoy and respect and who may even have changed their lives—might not share their upper-crust background or their heterosexual disposition because college has taught them to desire same, to become same, to adjust to the status quo.

There are very high stakes involved for teachers and institutions in fashioning a curriculum that would do something other than reproduce the values of the capitalist culture that we serve. It would require, for example, challenging the assumption that we educate people so that they can enter the middle class. A year or so ago I was asked to serve on a board at the University of Rochester consisting of faculty and administrators who were to evaluate a questionnaire meant to measure the university's strengths and weaknesses in the eyes of seniors exiting the university. I took issue at the contradistinction embedded in these two questions: "To what extent have you learned to appreciate literature, music and art?" and "To what extent have you learned to understand the role of science in society?" Since I had been teaching my students to deconstruct binaries like "appreciate and understand," "art and science," and especially to analyze literature in terms of its material circumstance and ideological implications, I felt that the questionnaire would misrepresent what I do. I also hoped that any student who had studied with me would not have known how to answer the questions. When I announced my position to the group, they looked confused and aghast. I tried putting it another way: "I don't teach literature so that my students will know what play to go to in their leisure time after a hard day in the lab." Rather than persuading my audience with clarity, I provoked further disdain as another faculty member retorted that surely I must know that we have an obligation to help our students to "become bourgeois." (He wasn't kidding.) Another responded that it would be a crime if we didn't help our students to "enjoy fine music." Now I would never deny that as an educator I am complicit with the middle-class establishment. Education is pretty high on Althusser's list of "ideological state apparatuses," and I do enjoy the privileges of the middle class: a space that shelters me from pain and enables me to escape oppressive forms of labor, a space for making my version of class intelligible and valid, enough room to make choices in, material comfort, and mobility. But I also still have hope that the university can be an agent for social change even if my working-class students (though it's hard to know who they are) may want this kind of knowledge least, and I feel most disabled when it comes to finding ways to use precisely the space of this privilege to meet my working-class kin where they live.

My role as a working-class person enjoying the privileges of middle-class existence is circumscribed, directed by the system I participate in to serve only those people who are inside, not those outside its walls. If, as I have been suggesting, working-class knowledge needs to get in, the insight and experience gained in higher education needs to get back out to the people who fled scared from the place, people like my brother, for example.

My oldest brother wailed on the piano in our row-home basement for much of his youth. My mother found some way to get him formal lessons; it was better to spend money on lessons, she decided, than on the tranquilizers prescribed for his hyperactivity. He was an autodidact—a word with pejorative class resonance—on several other musical instruments as well. At the end of an increasingly alienating high school experience, with only his music to go on, he applied to the Berklee School of Music in Boston and was accepted. But something snapped at some point in the entry process that I still cannot locate. He became increasingly, violently ill on the long train trip from Philadelphia to the Boston campus with my other brother. Was it the flu perhaps? They arrived. They visited the campus. They got right back on the train. My brother announced he had decided not to go to the Berklee School and that he would pay back the nonrefundable admission fee to my parents in time.

My brother only reports one reason for his decision now: "I was afraid I'd be alone," he says. Since then he has worked as a roofer, and he complains about the back-breaking, finger crippling, and mind-numbing consequences of his job. He married, had two children, and was left by his wife; he has been a single parent for the past five years. He has periodic gigs that reawaken his compositional abilities, but mostly he suffers long bouts of unemployment that result in my niece and nephew receiving substandard medical care, food, educational privileges, and child care.

Is it possible my brother's position would have been any more financially secure had he gotten the degree in music? It may have made a difference for his self-esteem, it may have afforded him insight into the socially constructed mechanisms that impinged on his choices, and this would have. . . ? I can't really fill that gaping space with a what-life-would-have-been for my brother. In fact, to do so would be to evade *my* trouble: a perceived gulf between my life and the lives of those I love and have left behind, the unresolved anger I feel as I devote myself to helping the privileged become more privileged while I feel hopelessly unable to affect the quality of my relatives' lives. I feel it as a gross discrepancy. I feel my energies caught in a medium, singular and unbending. Is my knowledge only useful to those who are able to cross the threshold? Perhaps my problem is qualified by the concept of direction. I want a geometry that can yield more crossover of knowledges and less boxing in. I need to understand what is obscured by my privileged perspective on working-class experience and identity. I need to hear what people like my brother can observe about me and my institution.

To mis-remember. To close with a story never delivered to me by popular American culture or in any classroom in my educational history. My version of *Italian American* working-class experience could only disappoint the American mythology of the Italian immigrant as a creature with a propensity for sinking his dumbfounded face into his shoulders, and, just when you least expect it, pulling a machine gun up against his pasta-stained shirt, burping a series of violent "ehs" into your unsuspecting body. I close this set of reflections on the working-class scholar with what Michele Wallace calls in another context "double jeopardy"[1]—that is, "the confusion that can result when two or more problems of oppression which have very different contingencies and specificities happen in the same place" (664).

Wallace describes the kind of methodological stammering or, worse, muteness that attends most attempts to accommodate politically more than one "mode of alterity" at a time—for example, "Black and poor, gay and Asian, Puerto Rican and female, Mexican and mentally ill"—doublings that are refused signification within the regime of the normative American cluster: "white middle class male" (665). Analyzing one's experience of double jeopardy as it relates to dominant discourse, Wallace suggests, remains a potentially alienating if not impossible enterprise, especially within academic frameworks. Cultural studies offers the rather fanciful if unintentionally organic depiction of double jeopardy in the word *imbricate*. Picture a pine cone whose tiers overlap. The image the word conjures is almost too pretty in the face of the compensations and vulnerabilities involved in the meeting of ethnicity and class.

My family is dark complexioned and curly-haired, except for my grandmother, who always expressed a feeling of good fortune at having fair skin and blue eyes. "Most people," she would proudly announce, "think that I'm Irish." Even if the formation of Italian American immigrant identities can in no way be compared with the history of the African or Chicano in the United States, shared class affiliation and broadly conceived ethnic features within white hegemony render us familiar. It may be that in the United States we *really* and not just imaginatively have lives in common. Nevertheless, I am not aware of any work in cultural studies on the real and fantasized identifications forged between people of color and Italian Americans in the United States, and film director Spike Lee's attempts to represent serious neighborhood rivalries in New York City between blacks and Italians unfortunately depend upon brutish fabulations of Italian-American sensibility, now reduced to a rude or beautiful face.[2]

In popular cultural representations of the Italian American, words fail her or make him out to be dumbly poetic. Indeed, the ideological linkage of my particular ethnic identity with my class made me a highly unlikely candidate for higher education, even if my own experience of being Italian in America was daily marked by my family's unfailing attention to the nuance, power, and range of voice, an unacknowledged literacy. I can only hope this last part of my tale can be forgiven for remaining within the frame of the family; there are, after all, other collectivities that hail my identity in ways I cannot begin to explore here.

To return to the epigraph from my grandfather John Petracca's (1900–1972) journal, a kind of letter to the world: "To Whom It May Concern: I am not what I have tried to be! Will I ever be able to write a few words correctly? Will I ever learn not to misspell words? No. Never. I am a cobbler." The "No. Never" in this passage haunts me. It's a dead weight that contradicts my grandfather's life's work—the mountains of lore, short stories, letters, aphorisms that he composed in his shoe repair shop and jotted onto the material of his trade, whole treatises squeezed onto the backs of the tabs used to mark down what part of the shoe needed fixing, with a word inevitably broken by the hole-punched O at the top or bottom of the tab. My grandfather hoped to be a writer, and he was. My grandfather hoped to express his thoughts and feelings in the language of the new culture he had entered, but this presented a variety of problems. To be a laborer and a writer in this culture was not allowed; there were no means by which his writing could become public. He wore the mantle of English uncomfortably; sometimes English simply was not adequate to his task. Two generations later, I am unable to read the passages he produced in Italian: the language, and with it, the ineffable and therefore perhaps most pressing aspects of my familial and class identity have been erased from the realm of useful knowledge.

In spite of what I have yet to know, I remain sure that speech, song, and the written word were survival tactics for my family. In the Depression years, my grandfather seems to have used irony in his journal as a strategy for getting by and as a tool for restaking his dislodged self:

> It is cloudy and warm. The water company served notice threatening to close my supply of water if I don't pay my bill! Is it not grand? And to think that here we have no public water places where I could fetch it home! 1 PM—The Gas and Electric Company has sent its two cents in. I must be a prominent person, for everyone points his finger at me!

While my grandmother suffered through multiple pregnancies, my great-grandmother told her comic tales from her peasant town to make her laugh and danced for her to ease the pain. My mother gave to my father some of the most impassioned and persuasive speeches on civil rights that I have ever heard. In the early seventies, she wrote feminist sermons for a progressive parish priest; she used her poetry to leave the church and the bad marriage to which it yoked her and to enter a new, more various, city-bound community as a small-press editor and an organizer of readings and forums. But, powerful as writing, music, or the spoken word might be, none of these media could ever really materialize as divining rod. If the water company turns the water off, so shall it be. Poetry readings won't bring the bacon home, so my mother struggles daily as a legal secretary against the delegitimizing of her experience and knowledge, her identity. A working-class person's daily thoughts, a shoemaker's poetry, may be just the resources higher education needs to divine itself, to plumb the depths of its mechanisms of exclusion, its refusals to know or to find marginal knowledge(s), in the best sense of the word, useful.

NOTES

1. I am referring to the discussion that follows Michele Wallace's essay, "Towards a Black Feminist Cultural Criticism."

2. See *Do the Right Thing* and *Jungle Fever,* both of which miss the opportunity to expose the white-authored systems that pit these people against one another.

WORK CITED

Wallace, Michele. "Towards a Black Feminist Cultural Criticism." In *Cultural Studies,* ed. Lawrence Grossberg, Cary Nelson, and Paula Treichler. New York: Routledge, 1992. 654–71.

10

A Carpenter's Daughter

Renny Christopher

BUILDING

New buildings appear on campus. I think my colleagues see them just "appearing," but I see them being built, in all the intimate detail of construction. I see each floor joist, each sheet of 4 x 8 ¾-inch tongue-and-groove subflooring, each 2 x 4 in the framing, each cut with the hole saw to put through conduit, each piece of sheetrock cut around electrical boxes and plumbing pipes, around doorframes and windows, each nail dimpled, each joint taped to accommodate the joint compound, each stringer in the roof, each bale of shingles placed along the peak ready to be laid out and tacked down with the nail gun. And I see the men doing the building. Most of the students and faculty pass them by with less attention than they give to the squirrels and the birds.

But I don't want to romanticize building too much because while its sensuality and satisfaction call to my memory the smell of pine pitch in a newly milled 2 x 4, the heft of a framing hammer, the solidity of a well-built wall, and the sounds of the words *plumb, level,* and *square*—the very tangibility of it all—I also remember the other side of it. I remember the running sore turned to scar covering the whole of my father's left knee—the result of contact with cement while he worked a slab dry, kneeling at the edge to smooth and level it, crawling on the kneepads, with the caustic cement oozing inside the rubber and eating away skin right through the cotton pants. I remember the stiffness and pain of the frozen muscles in my shoulders and back after digging pier holes by hand with a pick and shovel. I remember the grinding effort of trip after trip to move a stack of sheetrock in out of the rain, one of the guys on one end, I on the other: lift, turn vertical, walk, carry the weight in one arm pulled down hard by the 10 x 12s, lengthening out the arm tendons. Balance the sheet with the other hand, turn horizontal, slide onto the new stack. I remember the work of it all, the coming home with no resources left in body or mind—too tired to read a book, almost too tired to eat, to think, to be. And now mostly I wonder about my relationship to the guys making the new college buildings appear and to my colleagues who will work inside these buildings. I am an academic worker now, an intellectual worker, not a construction worker.

I make it a point to say hi to the guys working, to recognize that they're there, but I know that they see me as one of the college people. I want to show them my scars, my still-present callouses, but they'd just think I was flirting with them. And the truth is that I was never wholly one of them, just as I am not now wholly and unreservedly an academic. In that last year of working, when I was doing my master's degree at the same time, I never told the guys I was working with that I was taking that two hours in the middle of the day, four days a week, to go to classes. They thought I was going to the lumberyard or the other job site or to deal with subcontractors or something. Only my dad, whom I was working for, knew what I was doing. I couldn't have told them because it would have made the guys I was working with look at me as a geek—the old, about-to-retire electrician who thought I was sort of cute doing this work; the plumber who was my age but secure enough in his identity as a stud that he wasn't threatened by working with a woman and told me about his girlfriends as if I were one of the guys; the concrete cutter who told me at lunch, sitting in the bed of my pickup, about how much fun he had had in Vietnam. More important, it would have undercut my authority with the labor crew of teenage boys I supervised. They would immediately have seen me not as the competent worker that my performance day after day forced them to recognize, but as an egghead, a snob, an "intellectual," with all the pejorative force that word carries among anti-intellectual working people who would never use a word like *pejorative*.

So I never told them that I was going to San Jose State to get a master's degree in linguistics. I wanted to be one of them. I worked with them, drank beer with them, and I fought hard to win acceptance as a woman working in a job traditionally reserved for men. Like on the day when I was putting up a redwood lattice on top of a brick wall, a lattice that my dad had custom-designed to the owner's specification, and a guy walking by on the sidewalk stopped and watched me. After I'd gone through the motions of picking up a slat, placing it so the slant cuts at top and bottom lay even on the edges of the framing beam, and stapling top and bottom, the guy says, "You know you can buy that stuff premade?" in a tone of voice that indicates that he really believes I don't know that and I'm going through a lot of work for nothing.

Or the time I was mudding drywall—laying the mudlike joint compound over a sheetrock wall to smooth the joints and nail holes for painting—and a guy watched me for a while and finally said, "I guess you do know what you're doing, after all."

Or my own grandfather, who watched me lay hardwood floor—fit in a piece, drive a chisel underneath it, pull it over so the tongue-and-groove joint is tight, nail it down with the air gun—for fully a half an hour, then said, "I guess your dad taught you how to do that okay."

To be a woman doing carpentry (or any such job) is to be a target for stares. People behave as though you were performing a spectator sport instead of a job. But in spite of all that, I loved it. I wanted to do well at it, and I did.

When I left the jobsite between twelve and two Monday through Thursday, I drove to San Jose State and went to class in my work clothes—paint-splattered boots, jeans with a hammer loop on the right leg, a screwdriver pocket on the left leg, and T-shirt. I took off the rolled bandanna I wore around my forehead and put it back on to drive back to work.

It was a small program, and everybody got used to me. They had to. I was the most successful student in the department: I got the best grades and the highest scores on the comprehensive exams. But I was never wholly present in that program. I resisted. I had a crisis of identity, a crisis of epistemology. I had believed in science with an understanding formulated far away from it, a (what now seems) naive belief that there really was knowledge. In the academy, I discovered that there was only theory; theory in the academy is far removed from experience, especially the kind of experience one gains working with wood and steel and concrete. I had always been bookish, drawn to the world of school so alien from the world of my family. But my first experience in graduate school, which I had dreamed about from far away with a sort of romantic notion of what it would be like, had turned out to be a disappointment.

Now, with my Ph.D. in literature almost in hand, I work in a classroom rather than a construction site, and I no longer wear my workboots to class, but I feel as much outside as I ever did. I speak in class as if I were giving orders to my crew or shouting up to somebody shingling a roof. I try not to. I've tried for years now to change the tone and timbre of my voice to match the way I've changed the vocabulary and syntax of my speech. I've tried to disengage how much I care about what I'm talking about in order not to let my voice slide up that register. I've tried to make my gestures less florid, to look like I'm pointing a pencil instead of swinging a hammer. But the workboots and yellow bandanna are still there, ghost-presences, marking me.

There are other consequences of the past I carry into the academy with me. "Work" is a relative term. Because of my background, I have a hard time defining the activities of reading a book or writing a paper as work. Teaching is borderline: sometimes it seems like work, and sometimes it seems like a privilege. Teaching is the only thing I have no doubts about, the only thing about the academic world that I love. I do not love scholarship; I love being in a classroom, working with students. But still it doesn't feel like *work* because it isn't hard, it isn't unpleasant, it isn't boring or frustrating. It's rewarding; it's an amazing privilege to be given the opportunity to influence so many people.

Work, to me, is something one does with one's hands. My academic boyfriend says that's labor; thinking is work. But because I can't really believe it's work—I hear my mother's voice saying to me, "Get your nose out of that book and go do something!"—I take on too much, I overcommit myself. Do half again or even twice as much as my colleagues, work seven days a week, long hours. My old self doesn't respect my new self. My old self says I'm living a lazy, overprivileged life. My new self says, what more could I do? My old self says, you're not doing anything productive. My new self says, you don't know how to think.

Of course what I call my "old self" was never really myself: it was the internalized voices of the world around me, to which I never really felt I belonged. Now, living in the new world, I tend to identify with that semi-imaginary "old self," just as, at the time, I wanted to identify with some as-yet-unimagined "new self." Because I am now here, on university ground, feeling ill at ease, I take the values of my old world as a baseline. Back home, feeling equally ill at ease, I hear myself arguing for (some of) the values of the new world (mostly racial equality and feminism, two things that my grandfather and various other relatives objected to stringently, although my mom and dad approve in principle of the first and are almost silent on the second).

There are other consequences. Having been raised among women who do not speak in public, I am often left after asserting a position, arguing an idea, wanting to apologize for having spoken, for having taken up the time in class to speak. Once I did apologize to a professor for speaking up in class. Surprised, he answered, "This would only happen in California." My unspoken answer was that this would only happen in a university where there are students like me.

I watch a carpenter carrying shingles to a new roof. He stands on the plywood that has been nailed over the stringers, and a conveyor crane brings bundles of shingles up to the roof level. He lifts them off the conveyor, carries them up the roof, lays them out so they can be opened as they are needed. Two roofers will complete the job, one of them laying out the shingles, the other tacking them down witn an air gun, the compressor chugging on the ground below. My brother and I took turns laying out and tacking. But I've never done a roof as big as this one. I've only done houses, and this is a large building that will hold classrooms and offices. I want to be up there with that guy, carrying the shingle bundles across the roof, showing off my ability to walk on the roof's slant, to balance the bundle, to flop it down just right.

So when I walk by the building sites, I say hi and wave to the guys working. It's not enough, of course. Nothing will never be enough to stitch together the before and after of this life.

AT THE PHOTOCOPY MACHINE

I run into Kate, a fortyish reentry student with an annoyingly breathy voice, at the copy center. Kate says, "Do you ever wonder, when you're reading all this theroetical jazz, and you think about your mother or somebody, do you ever wonder who you're doing this for?"

I tell her that once I gave my mother a paper of mine, one I'd written with her in mind, defending women who read romance novels. My mother said that it was very nice, but she couldn't follow what I was talking about because she'd never read any of "that stuff," that is, the critics I'd mentioned.

Kate asks, "Does that hurt?"

And I say, "It makes me feel like a misfit in both worlds."

Her face takes on an animated expression of comprehension, of revelation. "Yes, yes, yes," she says, nodding so hard her whole body sways. "Yes. It's a real liminal feeling."

I think about what the academy has done for me, for Kate. It has taught us the word *liminal*. That's something, I guess.

QUALIFYING EXAMS

For four months I have read books all day long. If anybody had told me when I was a teenager that a future awaited me in which I could do nothing but read books, I would have thought I was being offered paradise. But in fact it has not been fun at all. It has not been fun because it has funneled down into one compressed point all the pressures of graduate school. All this reading has been aimed at a target date when I'll be examined to decide whether I'm fit to write a dissertation and receive a Ph.D. In other words, this is a sort of trial to see if rich and powerful people will accept me as a colleague.

I'm smart. I know I'm smart. But that's not the issue, and that's why four months of reading books has not been fun. I'm still just me, a working-class kid from a small town who knows the theme songs to *Gilligan's Island* and *Gunsmoke* and *Hogan's Heroes* but doesn't know Plato from Herodotus and doesn't care. And I feel like this exam is where I'm finally going to find out that there are a lot of secrets that they all know that they've been keeping from me so that I won't make it into their cozy inner circle. This is either paranoia or good sense; it is impossible, in my position, to know which.

On the morning of my exam it is raining. As I drive to campus, the rain falling on my windshield makes me start crying. I don't want to cry, but I can't stop. I keep thinking about my grandfather. He died a year ago. He came to California from Ohio, from his father's wagonwright shop, and signed on as a carpenter to build the new General Motors plant. He had a wife and a sick two-year-old son. When the plant was finished, he heard they were hiring millwrights, so he filled out an application and wrote "millwright" on it, even though he didn't know what a millwright was. They hired him, and over the course of thirty years he worked his way up from the assembly line to being plant manager, supervisor of the entire manufacturing process. My own life has recapitulated his in some ways. When I wrote my very first college English paper, "The Symbolism of the Rose in *Portrait of the Artist*," I didn't know what a symbol was. Since then I had worked my way up to almost having a Ph.D. I kept thinking that he would have been proud of me, even though he wouldn't have had any idea what it was that I was actually doing.

As it turns out, I pass my exams. The only person who ever seriously thought I had a chance of failing was me. But it wasn't just worry about failing that had been driving me; it was worry about who I would be in my new life. Afterwards I walk across the campus, the beautiful, fertile grounds that look like farmland but that are used to grow something else. I miss the long, straight furrows, the strawberry plants creeping over the black earth, the walnut trees with trunks painted white, the sprinklers making prisms in the summer air.

PENCIL PUSHERS

On the way across campus on the shuttle I see Richard, a former student of mine who started at Cabrillo and has transferred to UC-Santa Cruz. He was a carpenter; he had a disabling on-the-job injury and went to college on vocational rehabilitation, studying finance in order to become a stockbroker. He is succeeding very well. He tells me that he's going to graduate this year. I congratulate him and tease: "So, you'll be wearing a tie and all that."

He chuckles, shakes his head. "No, no. I'm hoping I can be different a little, break the mold. I don't want to be another pencil pusher."

A vista of memory opens up for me. I haven't heard the term *pencil pusher* for years, but I instantly remember with what scorn my parents and their friends used to talk about pencil pushers, who included everybody who worked in an office and everybody in the government, anybody in any white-collar job. I remember how we disrespected pencil pushers, considered them lesser people who nonetheless had all the power. Now I have become one, as has Richard. And yet we bring with us our old selves and all that scorn we had for people like our new selves.

Richard and I get off the shuttle and head in different directions. "Take it easy," he calls, and I reply, "Take it easy." That parting phrase comes from my old world, familiar yet distant, and rings out between us here in the land of the pencil pushers.

STILL IN SCHOOL

My mother was a contradictory role model for me in the activity of reading. She taught me to read when I was three because she didn't have the patience to read to me. She read a lot herself, but only at night after everyone else had gone to bed, on her own time, time created by her insomnia. As I got older, in grade school, she would tell me as I sat reading by the window after school to "go do something!" as if reading a book weren't doing something. She meant something active, something with my body. That made it hard for me all those years later as I studied for my Ph.D. qualifying exams: I had to ride a stationary bicycle while I read or carry a book with me while I cleaned up the kitchen so I wouldn't be sitting still and "just reading" too long.

I grew up reading "junk." My mother (being contradictory again) gave me a subscription to *Reader's Digest* when I was eleven. I read every word of it every month for six years, until I went to college and learned that it was trash. Paradoxically, I had a good vocabulary and scored well on the vocabulary test on the SAT because I did "It Pays to Increase Your Word Power" in every issue. When I was eleven I abandoned kids' books and started reading adult books borrowed from the storefront library in the shopping center or bought at the library book sale for a nickel. I started with mysteries. I read all of Erle Stanley Gardner's Perry Mason series. All of Agatha Christie. Then I moved on to historical romances—not the kind my mother liked, which went back no further than the nineteenth century, but the medieval ones about castles and royalty. At twelve I thought *Gone with the Wind* was classic literature and felt very superior for having actually read the book rather than just having seen the movie. The next year I discovered Ayn Rand and read all her books because I mistakenly thought all that talk about superior men was addressed to me.

My reading didn't make me any friends, though. The kids I went to school with thought I was a geek; my family thought I was lazy. (One summer I used a broken big toe as an excuse to do nothing but read, and nobody could yell at me for it because the doctor said if I moved the toe a loose bone chip would migrate into the joint and I'd have a stiff toe for life.) And when I got to college, I discovered I'd been reading all the wrong things.

I took a UC-Berkeley extension course by mail in my last year of high school, an English course. For the final assignment, we could pick a book from a long list, read it, and write about it. I chose Robert Louis Stevenson's *The Black Arrow*, a book I fell passionately in love with because it had a female character who got to masquerade as a boy for most of the book and therefore had all sorts of adventures unavailable to girls. In his comments on my paper the professor said, "When I was your age I enjoyed simple adventure stories like this, too." I was devastated. I thought I was reading a classic of literature, not a "simple adventure story"! I'd selected it from their list, after all, and then they patronized me for it! I knew there was a world of hidden knowledge somewhere, but how was I supposed to find it?

I did eventually find it and now rest very uneasy with it because it entails not only a list of facts, which I expected, but also a value system whose existence I never suspected, one that clashes with the value system I grew up with. I find myself caught between them, wishing for the best of both, but most of the time merely being stranded, caught on a skewer. For example, middle-class, college-educated society really believes that college-educated people are worth more as human beings than non-college-educated people —it's an absolute hierarchy. I can't believe that, of course. And the knowledge of that hierarchy makes my stomach flutter when they praise me for all I've achieved. I know they're telling me that I'm a more valuable person now, more valuable than my father or mother or brother. I want to punch them. I think they think I'm ungrateful.

In the working-class society I come from, connection comes by blood, not by achievement. There's also an absolute dictum that you don't talk about your problems in public. This includes going to any sort of counseling or therapy—or, indeed, doing what I do constantly, talk about my background and my differences from my colleagues. Or writing this essay.

The feeling of homelessness these conflicts leave me with is hard to describe. My brother is four years younger than I am. He is married. He is the manager of a racquetball club, a position he obtained by sheer perseverance. He started as a desk clerk and hung in there until the company that owns the chain of clubs decided to promote him to a temporary managerial position (they were very reluctant because of his lack of a college degree), and he did so well they kept him on. He has been upwardly mobile, as I have, although along a different and much more recognizable (to my family) route. I saw him after an absence of a couple of years at our grandfather's funeral. I explained the Ph.D. program to him, which I had entered after being out of school for a while.

"You're still in school?" he asked, incredulous. "For how long?"

A CARPENTER'S DAUGHTER

Barbara is another graduate student at the university. She and I have always gotten along well; she has an acerbic sense of humor that I appreciate. On a cold, clear December day I run into her on the footbridge over the ravine between Kresge College and the bus stop. We stand in the center of the bridge, surrounded by redwood trees. We talk about graduate student stuff—taking qualifying exams, our fellow grad students. Virginia, another graduate student, joins us. Barbara and Virginia start talking about how awful the proseminar, the first class you have to take in grad school, was for both of them because they had never known anything about literary theory before. I say that I already knew about abstract theory from my master's degree but that I still hated the proseminar because I thought theory was all such bullshit, and now I just mostly ignore it.

Barbara snorts. She says to Virginia, "Have you ever heard this woman talk theory?" Virginia hasn't because we've never been in a class together. Barbara continues. "She can do it better than anybody. She talks theory all the time."

I decide to joke with Barbara about it, so I rattle off something that I intend to be recognized as pure garbage: "Well, of course, when I say *hegemony*, I mean it not in the literary sense, as commonly used, but rather in the Gramscian sense. . . ." But Barbara doesn't get the joke. "See what I mean!" she shrieks to Virginia. "She can talk about all that stuff like nobody else. And she's always talking about her working-class background and how deprived she was. I bet none of that is true." She turns to me. "I bet one of these days we'll meet your parents, and it'll turn out that your father is a professor of philosophy at Harvard!"

Barbara and Virginia laugh. I laugh, too, because that's all I can do. I say, "Well, come to my graduation party and find out." As I walk away, my hands start to shake in my jacket pockets. For days I think about what Barbara said. If my father really is a carpenter, her reasoning goes, then I couldn't possibly be as smart as I am. So, in order to be as smart as I am, my father must be a professor of philosophy at Harvard. That means that we have not a class system but a caste system because no working-class kid can be smart and upper-middle-class kids will always be smart.

What Barbara said reminds me of something my friend Jessie Virago wrote. Jessie is an undergraduate, a late-entry, working-class student who's done a lot of thinking about these issues. Jessie wrote:

> During lunch with a professor of literature with a PhD from Yale, I mentioned my social background and the years I had spent as a secretary prior to attending school. He replied, "But you always knew you were smart, right?" Hear how the conjunction "but" juxtaposes smart with secretary or smart with working class. I consider the equating of social class position with intelligence to be one of the most common, egregious, and offensive examples of classism in America. It does insidious damage to working class people's sense of intellectual and academic entitlement, and it is particularly galling to hear it from one's professors.

Reading Jessie's words over again made me feel better. It's important for us to stick together, just as it's important for the members of any marginalized group to support one another.

But the more I think about it, the angrier I get. My dad is smart. He's not educated, but he's smart. I fantasize sometimes about my graduation party, the event that will finally bring together the two halves of my life. I imagine my father shaking hands with my friends. His hands are so calloused and scarred and weathered that his fingers no longer have their full flexibility. I imagine those hands meeting the soft hands of my professors and my friends. I imagine that his hands might teach them what all my words can't seem to get across.

My dad joined the Coast Guard at seventeen, came home after the war and drove midget race cars, went to college to study architecture but dropped out after less than a year, became the skipper of a fishing boat, then learned to build boats and then to build houses. He's got a skipper's license, a radio operator's license, a contractor's license, and a real estate license. He taught himself each new skill as he needed it, including carpentry, painting, cement work, welding. When we first moved north, he went to work in a factory that made paper containers. He told them he knew how to fix all their machinery, which he'd actually never seen before, but he sure enough figured it out. Now, at sixty-two, he's the maintenance man for a chain of health clubs. Over the last year, he's taught himself how to do upholstery in order to fix the benches in the clubs' weight rooms. He set up an upholstery shop in his garage, bought himself an upholstering sewing machine, and started taking in outside upholstery work. It's his kind of ability to learn these skills, to continue to tackle new areas, that has allowed me to succeed in graduate school. But while my colleagues appreciate my ability to learn new discourses, they do not value my father's ability to learn new trades. They wouldn't even be able to see it. Blue-collar work is simply invisible to them.

I've been thinking a lot about my dad recently. He's taking a correspondence course in boat design. He's completed the first three lessons and gotten As on each one. He showed them to me with the same pride I used to show my grammar school and high school report cards to him. He used to give me a dime and later a quarter for each A on my report card. So when he showed me his first lesson, I pulled a quarter out of my pocket and said, "I guess I owe you this." He was proud to be able to do what I do—succeed in school—just as I was proud to be able to do his work with him.

Another working-class friend of mine, Cheryl Gomez, said to me once that it is a natural human desire to learn new things, and it is a crime for the university to be so class-based that it denies the desires of working-class people to learn. I used to think it was the structure of the university that created the problems. But maybe it's not the structure. Maybe it's the individual, middle-class people. Even the well-meaning ones who call themselves my friends.

NEAR THE END

I went to the university bookstore to buy the acid-free paper that is required for dissertations. A clerk took me to the shelf and said, "Yeah, this is good stuff. My grandmother's dissertation is printed on it, and it's still in the library."

I am arrested in motion, a ream of this stuff in my hand, halfway off the shelf. "Your grandmother has a Ph.D.?" I ask.

"Yeah. You wanna know what's worse? So does my grandfather. Only his dissertation isn't in the library."

Okay, I'll bite. "Why not?"

"It's classified."

Of course. The kid looks pretty smug. Also looks like the stock has gone downhill since his grandparents.

Later in the day I had a senior oral exam to give. The student was Cathy, who had been in my working-class literature class the year before. The other examiner was Louis Owens, a senior professor of Native American lit. Cathy did a great exam, and afterward we sat around and talked for a while. Cathy didn't get into graduate school because her GRE scores weren't very good, and she's worried about finding a job to support herself and her two kids.

Now that she's got a degree, she really doesn't want to waitress any more. She's so worried about her job situation that she can't even enjoy having done well on the exam. I remember being in a similar position when I got my B.A., only I found a full-time editing job and had actually started working before my last semester was over.

We talk about what Cathy's experience as a working-class student in this elite university has been like. I tell Cathy and Louis the story about the clerk in the bookstore and add that my grandmother only graduated from sixth grade.

Louis says, "I can beat that. My mother had a fifth-grade education and my father had a third-grade education, and I have ten brothers and sisters and I'm the only one who graduated from high school."

Cathy nods. She, too, is the first person in her family to graduate from college. We're all in this together, allies. Louis says something about how he usually works with students of color and how they always feel a lack of entitlement, the same way white working-class students like Cathy and I do. I tell them about the graduation ceremony fantasy I've been having: the Dean reads off my name, then he stops, looks up, says, "No, there's been a mistake," and they don't give me my degree after all. Cathy laughs; it's clearly something she recognizes.

Louis doesn't laugh, though. He looks dead serious. "Yeah," he says, "that could happen."

A feeling of home washes over me here in Louis's office. That was exactly the right response to my fantasy; everyone else I've told it to has scoffed. But Louis knows. Cathy knows. They're right here with me. Yes. This moment is what makes the university a home to me. This is what makes it worthwhile. If I can always find people like these, students and faculty, then I can go on, then I can remember what I came here for. We speak without translation. This is rare for me now and because of its rarity, all the more perfect.

PH.D.

Then it was finally over. A day came and I went to the Office of Graduate Studies and turned in my signed dissertation and it was over. But first I had to fill out some forms. One of the forms was a "Survey of Earned Doctorates Awarded in the United States, 1991–92." The first paragraph said this: "Congratulations on earning a doctorate degree! This is an important accomplishment for you. Your accomplishment is also significant for this nation, as the new knowledge generated by research doctorates enhances the quality of life in this country and throughout the world. Because of the importance of persons earning research doctorates, several Federal agencies—listed above—sponsor this Survey." That stopped me completely.

No no no, my heart said. I am not a more important person. If the ship is sinking, I shouldn't be the first in the lifeboat.

Mostly I think the survey is directed at science people, but among the federal agencies sponsoring it are the National Endowment for the Humanities and the US Department of Education, so it isn't only directed at scientists. But certainly my research doesn't improve the quality of anyone's life, not even my own. It certainly doesn't touch the lives of people like my family or my students at Watsonville. And neither does the research of science Ph.D.s, for the most part, except in negative ways—more effective weaponry, and the like. Still, the nation puts a lot of resources into higher education. I suppose the degrees are important. But it's that—the degree, the achievement—that's important. It doesn't make the *person* more important. My human worth is equal to that of the fieldworkers picking strawberries. But they will never, never, have anything addressed to them telling them how important they are.

CULTURALLY DISADVANTAGED

I've been teaching Richard Rodriguez's autobiography, *Hunger of Memory: The Education of Richard Rodriguez,* in my community-college class, where most of my students are Latino. His story of growing up a working-class Mexican American in California, then going on to school at Stanford and eventually doing dissertation research in London, strikes deep chords of recognition in me. He speaks eloquently of cultural dislocations similar to the ones I've experienced.

But Rodriguez has always been a controversial writer because he speaks out against bilingual education and affirmative action and is perceived as deeply conservative. My students hate his book because he seems to be ashamed of his ethnicity. When we've worked our way through the issues of ethnic identity the book raises, we move on to the subject of class and culture. I pose to the class a question for discussion: Does a person ever stop being disadvantaged? Rodriguez points out that despite upward social mobility, blacks stay black and women stay women, but he goes on to say that not "all blacks are equally 'black'" (150). He believes that middle-class status ameliorates the disadvantages of color and gender.

But what about *culturally* disadvantaged people, those of us who started out working class, no matter our color or gender, and moved "up"? What does "culturally disadvantaged" mean, anyway? You're culturally disadvantaged if you don't come from the mainstream bourgeois culture. But aren't you only disadvantaged if you want to move into that culture? Nobody's at a cultural disadvantage within their own culture. In fact, my current colleagues who come from middle-class backgrounds would be at a distinct disadvantage in my culture. They'd be shouted down and never get the potatoes passed to them. So it's my very mobility that created my disadvantage.

To return to the original question: When will I stop being disadvantaged? As I get an academic job, get tenure, get increasing institutional power, publish books, succeed by every external measure, how long can I call myself disadvantaged?

Dan, my lover, who is largely responsible for encouraging me to go to graduate school and to stick with it, recently read *Strangers in Paradise: Academics from the Working Class*. He said he was almost sorry for getting me to go to graduate school since it seemed from what he read in that book that it would make me permanently miserable. I thought, at last, he's beginning to understand. I will never stop being disadvantaged as long as that familiar pain remains centered in my chest, the pain that has come from so much dislocation, separation, and loss.

WORKS CITED

Rodriguez, Richard. *Hunger of Memory: The Education of Richard Rodriguez*. New York: Bantam, 1982.

Ryan, Jake, and Charles Sackrey. *Strangers in Paradise: Academics from the Working Class*. Boston: South End Press, 1984.

11

Paper Mills

Heather J. Hicks

To talk about myself as an academic coming from a working-class background, I have to begin by recalling what I was *before*—before the American educational system processed me through its vast and creaky machinery and transformed me into something of its own. Such recollection comes hard. Frankly, now that I have reached graduate school, the institution has so unequivocally taken on the role of surrogate that my background seems reduced to segmented memories, brief visits home, and phone conversations that provide only a weak distillation of the life I led before I left my small home town in Maine for college in 1985.

I don't reflect often upon the details of my childhood and youth in a rural working-class family, but, perhaps curiously, I do think of myself as a product of the working class in general terms more or less constantly. This is more odd still because, in truth, I was less "working class" than "rural class." I believe it was our rurality more than my parents' type of employment that informed my family's class status. Only three miles and two generations separated my family from my great-grandfather's farm, where for many years he had combed and cut the dry Maine soil with a team of workhorses. My parents raised my brother and me according to values that the decrepit aspect of this old farmhouse came to symbolize in my mind. Perched on the very shoulder of a straight dirt road in the middle of a flat meadow, it seemed to bear down on us on summer days when we drove past it, its white-gray dilapidated clapboards and bent spine coolly, dryly conveying an aura of mirthless hard work. The work my father did in the paper mill was only one part of the work demanded of him by rural life, and this greater engagement with our surroundings was what defined us. We were citizens of a dusty rural empire, isolated by a perimeter of trees and stone walls from the notions of leisure that undergird middle-class ambition.

Perhaps my embrace of a generic category of the "working class"—one made at the expense of accuracy—shows that I have been more deeply interpellated than I realized by the applications I have filled out over the years for this or that program or scholarship, applications in which it was understood that the invocation of some general picture of a working-class background would lend me the edge, suggesting a struggle on my part that would translate into a pinch of added diversity in program statistics. I believe this happens—I believe that the forms one fills out in one's life, the boxes one checks, become a powerful personal narrative, an autobiography ghost-written by the heavy institutional type which supplies only a line for one to fill in: "Father's occupation" (electrician), "Mother's occupation" (nurse), thus telling the applicant precisely how little value is placed on the details or nuances of one's background. These forms tell us how to tell our stories, obscuring details, reducing our lives to myth and archetype, making us forget how to tell our stories ourselves.

So, yes, I am from a (more or less) working-class background, and yes, it matters to me, informs me everyday, but how does it? Why does it? To answer, I have to think back to a childhood spent in a town of 2,400, to days spent in a school where I passed through the first six grades in the elementary building, then six more in the high school with more or less the same forty students. I knew Kim and Mike and Karen and Shawn and Debbie and Janet and Mark and Eddie from kindergarten on. For twelve years there were virtually no changes, the trip from elementary school to junior high amounting to no more than a move next door to the high school building, which stood sixty feet away across a pot-holed expanse of asphalt. In such a place, identities were established early and indelibly, and by the age of eight or nine I had taken on the role of "brain" that I would wear to tatters by my senior year without even realizing how little comfort it provided me.

What did we all do there during all those years together in the classroom? I cannot speak for my classmates, cannot say what it meant to them to be accosted by elementary knowledge day after day. But I feel that our class status must have affected us all similarly because, on the most basic of levels, it made all of us different in the same way. We were all working class. There was not to my knowledge a single doctor, lawyer, or other professional in my entire town. The category "rich kid" simply did not exist. Most of my classmates' parents worked as electricians (as my father did) in the paper mills of Rumford and Jay or as linemen for the telephone company or as truck drivers, farmers, loggers, and the like. These parents, by and large, had themselves regarded school as a necessary evil and forced their children to go on the same terms. As one might imagine, this led to a less than inspired academic environment.

Yet to leave such matters to the imagination is to defeat the purpose of this exercise. Let me say, then, that my peers saw no connection between education and success—really had no aspirations to "succeed in life" at all, which leads me to suspect that this notion itself is the property of the middle and upper classes. School was simply a place to be rather than a place to do anything, and their submission to its tedium rendered it little more than a prologue to the working-class existences most would enter fully upon graduation. This passivity to place, this helpless submission to a controlling environment, seems to me the essence of much of working-class life. How can students improve their lot if the educational system itself becomes a complicit model of power and passivity?

As for how my own class position affected my personal relationship to school during those years, it is a question too complex ever to answer fully. I was "working class" in high school, but to say that I was "affected" by this educationally or otherwise seems inaccurate. It was my life. Terms like "affected" only make sense as part of a broader historical discourse. The history of my working-class background could not start until I moved away from it, away from home, and began a new stage of my life. It was only then, after the important transition from a working-class life to a working-class background, that I felt "affected." During my high school years, my family was considered more comfortable than many in our community. My father endured periodic terms of unemployment from his job as a union electrician, but for the most part we lived comfortably. It would be very easy to paint a picture of myself as the young working-class girl, struggling through a rural high school with her eyes set unyieldingly on the brass ring of admission to an outstanding college. It would seem reasonable to expect that mine was the story of one who saw higher education as a "way out."

Yet frankly, to the best of my recollection, my academic performance in high school was almost entirely for its own sake. I did every assignment as well as I could because I could do it. My parents were, if perhaps somewhat dazed by the fierceness with which I attacked my studies, quietly supportive of these efforts. My father himself loved reading and encouraged me most powerfully when he was not even aware of his effect, by unconsciously demonstrating the agility and grace of his own mind. In terms of class, however, I think neither I nor my parents credited education with much transformative power. For them, school was finally the work expected of me, the pattern of diligence prescribed to me. And while I could imagine my academic achievements taking me to a new physical setting, I had no special ambition for them to transform my class status. This is not to say that I had not seen rich kids in other towns, at other schools, and that I was not fascinated by them. But I never really began to make the connection between class and education until the very end of my high school years.

I applied to a number of Ivy League schools, expecting to find, if I got into any of them, students distinguished exclusively by their records of academic excellence. It had really not even begun to dawn on me that, as much as anything, schools like Dartmouth, Princeton, Yale, and Brown constitute concentrations of great wealth, an archipelago of privilege running down the East Coast. It seems difficult to believe that this fact had escaped my rural consciousness, but few students from my community went to college at all, and only one or two students had ever gone to a competitive college or university.

In fact, the infrequency of migration of students from my high school to high-profile colleges protected me from much of the stress I now understand many upper-middle-class and upper-class students—children of professionals and students at America's elite private schools—must endure. Had I had so much as an inkling that there were students out there who took a whole course just to prepare them for the SATs, my confidence doubtless would have shuddered and collapsed. As it was, the SAT seemed less stressful to me than the exams I took day to day in high school. Those tests were much more personal: the stakes were my position in an academic hierarchy (such as it was) upon which I had meticulously garrisoned myself at the top. The SATs had none of that closeness. My whole memory of the test is a huge airy room full of long tables occupied by widely spaced strangers, an arrangement mirroring the answer sheet before me with its widely spaced circles for us to blacken with our bright, generic #2 pencils.

My naïveté suffered the first encroachments of class consciousness when I did in fact gain acceptance to a number of schools I had applied to. The guided tours were enough to begin to reveal the class dynamics I was poised to enter into. At one campus the student guide lingered longest in front of the university sports facility, lovingly detailing its inventory of automatic polo ponies and fencing rooms while my parents and I gaped in horror.

I would love to say that I was undaunted by such hints of financial power and class privilege, but this is not true. Class in fact became an issue in my decision. I remember a phone call from an undergraduate recruiter at another university urging me to come to her school. I explained to her that I had decided against it. When she asked me why, I recall rather bluntly stating that hers was the Ivy most known for internal social structures that maintained rigid class distinctions (information I had unquestioningly accepted from an interviewer at another university). She, probably rightly, denied this, but I had made up my mind.

The school I chose happened to be Dartmouth College, but my experience there in relation to class could have happened at any number of American colleges or universities. I arrived there toting a deeply inculcated disdain given me by my father for "the rich." A lifetime union member and the son of a union member, my father had railed against social and economic inequities for as long as I could remember. Yet this disdain had never been activated in me because of the dire shortage of rich people in my community on which to vent it.

I quickly learned at Dartmouth that being working class was not simply a matter of hating everyone from the upper classes. The well-to-do did not prove to be the faceless drones wearing Rolexes that I had expected. Some of my closest friends at Dartmouth, now my closest friends in the world, come from families of professionals, from the upper middle class. Yet there were moments of friction born of this difference, mostly when the topic of our parents was introduced or, worse still, word came of an impending visit from one or more sets of parents.

On the other hand, there were class strata at Dartmouth that I never scaled, groups that seemed to be identified largely by compatible levels of economic privilege that I remained nearly entirely ignorant of. I knew nothing of the internal dynamics of these groups, knew of them, really, only by their prominent outlines on the social terrain of the campus. In some cases these cliques congealed around Greek letters, but just as often they formed in the unofficial space of a dormitory. Always in retrospect, I see the machinery of class operating more clearly. In retrospect it is clear to me that I led a very peripheral existence at Dartmouth. In retrospect it is clear to me that this was largely because I lacked a set of social skills fostered by the suburban middle class, and this lack marked my difference even more than my lack of material objects.

Dartmouth changed me. I gradually learned not to be afraid of those of greater privilege, not to assume that they were a superior caste. At the very least this meant putting aside a type of humility that had been conflated with good manners throughout my upbringing. At most it may have meant that I had become part of the class I had once feared and hated, a possibility I will return to below. If it did change my class position, it did so without the attendant financial boost. I tumbled out of Dartmouth with a B.A. in English and a hundred dollars in my checking account, eventually arriving in Washington, D.C. I spent the nearly obligatory year there subsisting as a managing editor while socializing with a set of Dartmouth alumni, some I had known before and some I had not, but all of whom had more money than I.

Many of them had jobs that paid more than mine, and this was the first hard class lesson of LIFE IN THE REAL WORLD. The adage "money makes money" still applies in unexpected ways in our culture. The children of professionals whom I associated with gravitated to consulting and management jobs quite naturally. It was as though their belief that they deserved to make a lot of money was so strong that they could earn no less. Moreover, they had an innate tolerance for certain kinds of office work that was incomprehensible to me (happily, it remains so). Yet even those who were not earning more than I was had more money. This was hard lesson number two of LIFE IN THE REAL WORLD: Class permeates young people; they absorb privilege into every nook and cranny until they are saturated with it. My friends seemed to generate cash and objects from some well-hidden and seemingly endless personal stock. When it came right down to it, the nuts and bolts of this constant supply of capital often was as simple as a check from the parents. But there were other more subtle sources—insurance and car payments quietly provided for, newly activated trust funds, old, deep savings accounts.

That year in Washington tells me, as I look back, that I came out of Dartmouth with a new, occasionally irksome class position. The four years in Hanover overshadowed the eighteen I had passed in Maine. I had been assimilated into a community that was decidedly not working class.

Finally I arrived at graduate school, where I am writing today. While Dartmouth blindly elevated everyone to a comfortable position, graduate school seems to tend to the opposite extreme, bulldozing virtually everyone to a gradient if not below sea level at least well below the famous poverty line. Yet class remains, and graduate school for me has demanded a new, quite unexpected routine of social acrobatics.

After four years of relative marginalization at Dartmouth because I was not middle class enough and a gradual process of assimilation that rendered me superficially indistinguishable from my fellow graduates, I arrived in graduate school to find myself too bourgeois in the eyes of some. It soon became evident that for the purposes of graduate school it would have been expedient to leave the hayseed in my hair or the grease of the industrial complex on my hands. As it is, I arrived looking like a prep, and this is a statement in graduate school—a statement one would probably be foolish to make if one actually had the money to back it up. Self-representation is rather a large part of academic life, particularly with the compelling work being done today on identity politics. I wear relatively nice clothing as a marker of an upward mobility that has nothing to do with money (I have no money) and everything to do with knowledge and power. Yet I am aware of a contempt for such markers that may eventually overtake me and once again refigure me into something new, something not working class or middle class or upper class. What then? Where has all of this education brought me? Where is it taking me?

It seems to me that what is being interrogated in any anthology of works written by working-class academics is the effect of education on class status. Is "working-class academics" an oxymoron? Conventionally, class lines have divided laborers from the intelligentsia despite comparable economic distress. Am I still essentially working class despite my proximity to a Ph.D.? Was I ever working class, just because my parents were? If I was and if I am not now, at what point did I stop being working class? When I first read Shakespeare? When I first read Foucault?

From where I stand, it is apparent to me that those filling new academic positions in America today are primarily from the middle class and the upper-middle class. There is an edginess among my peers in graduate school about how they will ever be able to afford a house or children or a car, and underlying it, I think I hear the anxiety that they will not live the life they became accustomed to in youth. For many a career in academia means downward mobility.

I wonder where I fit into the question of mobility. My trajectory has always felt upward to me, but I don't have any material evidence of this—no CD player, no color TV, no microwave, and a car that is two years older than I am: not much to show for a college education and two years of graduate education.

But finally for me, this matter of material objects has never been what the term *working class* is about. A moment stands out in my mind with complete vividness that illustrates my mobility in a strangely literal way. I recall setting out with my mother to drive to Dartmouth at the end of one of my mid-semester breaks. It was unusual for me to be going only with my mother. Usually both parents enjoyed any opportunity to make the four-hour drive to Hanover. They were proud and curious about the place, I think. But on this morning, very early—it couldn't have been later than 6 A.M.—my father could not go. Instead, he had to go to work. While the details are hazy, I suspect that the paper mill was engaged in one of the perennial shutdowns of some part of its machinery. This always meant extra-long hours for my father and his crew.

My father had left a bit earlier to make the drive to Jay or Rumford, and as my mother began the drive out of town with me in the passenger seat, I remember being struck with the feeling that my father was out there somewhere, driving too, but on a very different road. With the greatest clarity I have ever experienced about the question of mobility, I saw myself on the road to my life of bright and interesting friends, a glut of culture and ideas, comfort and privilege. My father was on the road he took every day to the paper mill. Huge and noisy and noxious, the mill was where my father spent lonely, dirty days among men who shared none of his interest in reading and ideas.

I promise myself: I will never have to work in *that* paper mill; I will never experience the intellectual isolation of a man like my father, who reads avidly but finds no one among the roaring machinery to discuss his thoughts with. In academia—the other "paper mill" where I have made a place for myself—my life is rich with thoughts and people to share them with. It is free of the pollutants and toxins that threaten the physical health of the working class, free of the unshakable hierarchies of authority that threaten their mental health. When I look at the sheets of paper that are the currency of my career, I can, if I choose, keep my focus on the elevated ideas that they bear on their work-a-day surfaces; I need not see the grain, feel the texture, inhale the bleaching acids.

But I will never believe that education is a one-way ticket out of the working class. As long as I find a place in an academic institution, I will not perceive myself as working class. I escaped the working class not when I first read Shakespeare or Foucault but when I first found others to discuss them with, when I took shelter with a class that insulates its financial vulnerability with a rich fabric of shared ideas. But if tomorrow I left the university and began working in the paper mill, down on the floor among the pipes and vats of pulp, then tomorrow I would become working class. Outside, I would grit my teeth against the deafening noise, inhale the close, sulfuric air, feel the heat, and inside, I would feel the stress of alienation one feels when disempowered, like a child among grown-up machines, and I would know that I was working class again.

12

The Social Construction of a Working-Class Academic

Dwight Lang

On September 23, 1950, I was born in Billings, Montana. My father was a coal miner and a World War II veteran with ten years of formal education. As a result of his involvement in union activities and legal proceedings surrounding a labor strike over unsafe working conditions, he decided to leave the mines in Roundup, Montana. Dad continued to be active in the union movement and work with his hands until his retirement from the plumbing trade in 1986. My mother, like many women of her generation, worked in the home and devoted her energies to the family. Mom's high school diploma made her one of the most highly educated people in my childhood social environment. An only child, I became a focus of attention, although my parents swore that I would never be spoiled. My parents hoped that I would do well in school and were always very concerned with my academic achievement. I actually surpassed their expectations, thereby creating a source of unanticipated strain. I became an anomaly in a childhood social setting that did not stress academic achievements. Little did I know that these achievements were more highly valued in communities not a fifteen-minute drive from my home.

Like many "providers" in our community, my father was a steady worker. He enjoyed his labor, felt creative, and described his work as a pseudo art form. He had maximum autonomy in his everyday work activities and, as a union plumber, was a fortunate member of the blue-collar aristocracy. Our family benefitted from that status as well as from the unprecedented post-World War II economic prosperity. While we were comfortable in our material conditions, the family was unambiguously working class in the cultural sense.

Many aspects of American working-class culture were evident in my community and upbringing. My parents preferred to live in a working-class neighborhood of Sacramento, California, even though my father's income as a plumber would have made it possible to purchase a home in a suburban setting. Dad said that he was more comfortable in Rio Linda, among "his kind of people." Working-class children constituted the majority group in the schools I attended. I remember that most parents were in the construction industry or worked in factories. We would often talk, especially in the winter months, about whether our fathers were working. If unemployment hit a family in November or December, children knew that presents around the Christmas tree might be scarce.

Extended vacations were rare, especially in the dry summers when construction moved at a rapid pace. While middle-class families vacated the suburbs in the summer to take advantage of the weather, working-class families stayed put. Men might be able to get in some overtime on those long, hot summer days. Women could can fruits and vegetables from the garden for the coming winter months, and children would roam late into the evening in the vacant fields surrounding the Rio Linda neighborhoods. Leisure was taken around my house in the form of yard work or home improvement projects. Late afternoon and early evening fishing trips to local rivers, complete with my mother's well-stocked lunches, were enjoyable and memorable and constituted a major form of family leisure in my childhood years. Mosquitoes from the rice farms north of Sacramento always made catching the Big One a skin-slapping event. I remember arriving at the sloughs that drained the rice fields and the American River and seeing hundreds of other working-class families around campfires, spending the entire weekend. That image still reminds me of a scene from the *Grapes of Wrath,* with the smoke slowly rising from the fires and older cars and trucks parked near the campsites. Travel within California or to other states always involved visiting family or friends. Traveling simply to explore new regions or points of interest was rare, and few stops were made along the way to enjoy the surrounding areas. I tried to imagine what it must be like to be these other people living in the communities we passed through and wanted to stop and explore, but we did not have time. Trips were made as quickly as possible, largely as a result of pressures to return to work. Employers did not like workers taking time off in favorable weather when good progress could be made on construction projects.

Of course, the busiest time in the construction industry coincided with school vacation, so I and other kids spent much of our summers just hanging out in the neighborhoods. Symbolic summer journeys involved riding my bike to the local library and checking out science fiction stories. Our library was a small, older house that the county of Sacramento rented in downtown Rio Linda. It was always cool and always deserted. I relished my visits and for some unexplainable reason enjoyed the presence of those books as well as the slightly cranky librarian. These and many other aspects of working-class culture constituted an everyday world for me. I absorbed a specific class culture during my childhood years, a social structure that left its mark on all of us. Throughout this essay I explore other norms, values, behaviors, and cultural characteristics that set working-class people apart as a distinct social category.

Others—for example, Lillian Rubin in *Worlds of Pain: Life in the Working-Class Family*—have described with great clarity and precision the social environment and everyday experiences of the working class in America. It is not my intention here to debate the existence of social class in this country. I assume that we create and sustain these social categories. Those who deny social class in America ignore the obvious and live an illusionary existence. We can let the extensive sociological literature shape our understanding of the dynamics of social class statuses and cultures in American society.

As I write this essay in the spring of 1993, I am forty-two years old, having just completed my first year as associate professor of sociology at Madonna University in Livonia, Michigan. During the fall term of the 1992–93 academic year, I was visiting associate professor in the Department of Sociology at the University of Michigan, Ann Arbor. I have moved across socially constructed boundaries. At times, I feel that I am propelled by forces beyond my direct control. My self-image is, in part, that of a traveler. I have left one social structure and am now making my way within another. My children are part of a social world that my parents, grandparents, and great-grandparents never experienced and one that does not represent my social origins. I am a link in social time and space. I am both insider and outsider in my new and old worlds. Many years ago I began an expedition and am still making my way. Having traveled across class lines, I am conscious of the realities and meanings of social class in America, perhaps more than others who remain in their class of origin. In many ways, I am carrying on a strong family tradition of geographical and social mobility that dates to the waves of European immigration to North America and to earlier decades when family members in Europe and Russia were mobile by choice and lifestyle as well as because of dramatic political and economic changes.

As a result of my own family history and socialization, I do not take social-class position in the United States for granted or assume that all in this society share or should share my status, values, and beliefs. Social class in the Western sense is a relatively recent historical development within the economic system we call capitalism. What we think of as social class may evolve as economic and political conditions unfold in the twenty-first century. I see the illusion of our social creations, but I also recognize how these constructions are reified by those who view them as inevitable. Social constructions are real, however, in their effects and are potentially destructive or constructive in their consequences. This essay explores these outcomes.

Viewing society in this manner, I lack the connectedness of those who are born to one class and remain there. My movement through social boundaries creates perspective, objectivity, and at times a sense of terror. Periodically, I feel an acute elation as I realize that one cannot take social creations seriously and that I am not determined by my history. When one first travels across these class boundaries, a central emotion is the fear associated with realizing that sacred social beliefs are essentially myths. This reconstruction of social beliefs is a natural by-product of social mobility, but one is often left searching for a new worldview. The search for and acquisition of new organizing principles can be terrifying for someone in their early twenties but also intensely liberating. The absolute freedom and dismay of this realization have never totally subsided. This contradiction is always present. I eventually became comfortable with the uncertainty inherent in our social constructions. This is a difficult task for any person learning a society's terrain, and it is compounded when one is negotiating social hierarchies that are often represented as being set in stone.

I continue to ask how society can come to grips with the notion that our social beliefs are myths. I have come to base my deepest understanding not on a blind faith in social myth but on the existence of others and the relationships we forge with them in a changing social context. We help to structure one another's consciousness and thus provide meaning. Cooperation, the pursuit of collective ends, and linkage become the basis of existence. The short-term and myopic navel-gazing of the ultra-individualist leads to meaninglessness and chaos. For me, in part, significant others in the family environment provide this sense of meaning. I devote time, energy, and love to family because it seems natural and right. This is not to say that family represents the only avenue to fulfillment, but I find intense personal satisfaction in the home, perhaps at great risk. For an equally compelling reason, home has become an authentic refuge, a type of coping mechanism as I continue to ply the social byways. I continue to derive gratification and energy from my journey, the expansion of perspective, and the breaking of boundaries. My personal and public lives are linked in a mutually reinforcing dynamic. In this I take refuge and find peace. In this way I find meaning.

While my own journeys across class boundaries are highly personal in nature, they also reflect social forces that shape and drive all of us to act. My story and the stories of others often remain hidden in the broad strokes of social class that push, pull, massage, and compel us. This essay is an attempt, in part, to tease out some of the complexities of social mobility. I explore how we encounter and endure that venture. My own experiences are certainly shared by thousands of others and therefore represent patterns of social relationships found in our society. I do not claim that my experiences are unique, although some may be. But to the extent that I am a creature of this society, the experiences and ideas that reflect my own journey may be representative of others who also have moved through class boundaries and perhaps had an opportunity to reflect on their meaning. If I successfully communicate my own ideas and suggestions as an academic with a working-class heritage, those academics who interact with working-class students struggling with class issues, as well as the complexity of human motivation in a society characterized by a definitive social-class structure, might also better understand the context of everyday interactions in our colleges and universities.

The exact nature of the social forces that have propelled me across class boundaries is clear and simultaneously in a constant state of flux within a society characterized by rapid social change. Social forces, therefore, are not separate entities, easily discussed in concrete terms. For purposes of this essay, allow me to list and discuss important and distinct, yet overlapping, considerations.

The first and perhaps most pervasive factor influencing my class movement is the massive and unprecedented growth in higher education after World War II. An academic hierarchy was created with older colleges and universities at the top and the newer schools occupying mid- and lower-level positions. These newer institutions were and continue to be attended primarily by first-generation college students. I was one of the thousands of working-class students who were told and believed that upward mobility was possible as a result of acquiring a college credential. I was never informed nor did I ask whether the prestige of the credential mattered. A college was a college, whether in your hometown or in Berkeley, Ann Arbor, Eugene, Kalamazoo, Albion, Cambridge, or Livonia. Despite the subtlety and significance of the academic hierarchy, the fact remains that thousands of working-class students attended and graduated from college. Clearly, this greater access was primarily intended to fuel economic expansion, but in the process the life options of millions were impacted. Without this expansion, I and thousands of others would never have set foot in a college classroom, but a well-defined and purposefully structured academic hierarchy helped to insure that our feet primarily walked the halls of the less prestigious schools and preserved the largely homogeneous class composition of the elite colleges and universities.

A second series of events or forces also shaped my movement across the social landscape. Unprecedented economic growth after World War II expanded opportunities for families who did not feel the impact of racial discrimination. While my grandparents experienced ethnic and religious discrimination, my father and mother were sufficiently integrated into American culture by the 1940s and 1950s to avoid the worst aspects of the country's poor treatment of foreigners. Part of my early socialization was hearing in vivid detail about the perceived injustices in America during the early part of the twentieth century. By my childhood years, however, most white ethnic groups were sharing more or less equally in the general economic prosperity of this period. I was a direct beneficiary of these economic and social developments.

A third factor that influenced me, more on an individual basis, was my own particular family environment. My parents stressed academic accomplishments to a greater extent than other families in my working-class environment and expressed genuine concern for my studies. The primary emphasis was on getting the assigned work finished. After the seventh or eighth grade they were less directly involved with my schooling. My education, however, extended beyond the classroom.

My father's interest in politics was persistent and robust. No topic seemed to be off limits. This was reflected in his running commentaries on Chet Huntley and David Brinkley's *NBC Nightly News*, which we watched on a regular basis after dinner. No topic seemed to be off limits. It seemed that he never agreed with anything anyone said during the program, and we received analyses not only from Huntley and Brinkley but also from my father, well positioned on his recliner in the corner of the front room. My mother sat quietly on the couch reading the *Sacramento Bee,* periodically suggesting that his choice of language was inappropriate, often to no avail. In this way and others, my parents provided links to worlds outside the family and community. This home environment was critical in laying the foundation for my interests in education and my long-standing interests in social settings beyond my own immediate community.

The everyday experiences of work in my family were not unlike those of other households in Rio Linda. Few mothers worked outside the home, or so it appeared to me. No one seemed to question the division of responsibilities between the women and men. The rhythms of daily and monthly life were driven by the fathers and their employment. My father was gone by 7 A.M. for a lengthy drive to another area of town, always to arrive fifteen minutes early to chat with the boss and fellow plumbers. He generally seemed to have cordial relationships at work. The weeknights revolved around his arrival slightly before 5 P.M. I would often meet him at the corner and ride to the house down a pot-holed street on the truck's back bumper, always aware of my mother's admonitions to be careful. I might have been able to convince my tired father to throw around a baseball or football for a few minutes, but he usually went inside to rest and talk with my mother after a long day. He always seemed fatigued, and this fact shaped and influenced family events and activities. On some very hot, hundred-degree summer days, for example, he might rest and cool off for a half hour or so on the front-room floor before we ate dinner. We always enjoyed the swamp cooler that provided cool air and moisture in the dry, hot Sacramento Valley summers. In the 1960s when lighter-weight plastic pipe and materials replaced the older cast-iron and galvanized materials, my father acknowledged that many plumbers would lose their jobs but anticipated that his own days might become considerably easier as a result. After that shift in the industry my father seemed more energetic and willing to pursue leisure activities with the family.

My father's ritual "washing of the hands" took place at the washroom sink just off the kitchen as my mother put the finishing touches on dinner. It involved vigorous cleaning for several minutes with a harsh detergent like Tide. I remember marveling at his hands as they changed color after much scrubbing with a brush. The dirt in and around his fingernails was always present, however, as were the thick and rough calluses. In my parents' household, to have a job in an office, not to get one's hands dirty, to think rather than build, was the work of another group of people who lived in another area of Sacramento and whom I knew little about. My eventual location in this other group still seems somewhat contradictory and illusory. My past is relived whenever I see or talk to working-class people.

While my parents exhibited a very real encouragement for education in my early years, this support was counteracted by their later and equally genuine fear of loss. Tension emerged between my parents and me regarding the personal and social implications of pursuing levels of formal education beyond the bachelor's degree. They were only ambiguously in favor of my graduate-level studies. For many in the working class, family ties involve regular and close association with nuclear and extended members in the same geographical area. One may lose touch with family members who move to other regions of the country. Many would never jeopardize family relationships by leaving the region, even for work-related reasons. In middle-class culture, geographical mobility for career reasons is readily accepted as a fact of life. Siblings and cousins, aunts and uncles, parents, grandparents, and children may be scattered to the four winds. Modern communication and transportation systems, as well as the ability to pay easily for their use, make regular interaction possible. There is minimal fear that family ties may be disrupted by children pursuing educational and career opportunities in distant areas of the nation.

For my parents, however, promoting educational aspirations, part of a national value system, had unanticipated consequences. As I progressed to the point of graduate education, it became increasingly clear that I, as well as their daughter-in-law and future grandchildren, might be separated from them by thousands of miles as social boundaries were forged, careers pursued, and new lives built. As we communicated on a great variety of issues during my graduate years, it became apparent to them that I was traveling to a new and distant place in the social structure: a middle-class milieu. The journey and place entailed new values, beliefs, and language patterns, and I believe my parents asked themselves, directly and indirectly: Will we know them when they arrive at their destination? Will they want to continue an association with us? Will we be able to communicate with and understand our grandchildren? Will they all feel that they are one notch above us? These issues persist in one form or another to this day.

A fourth factor shaping a personal and social environment conducive to movement up the social-class hierarchy was my marriage to a woman with similar goals and dreams. The daughter of a carpenter, she and I shared a common culture. At young ages we discovered mutual interests in challenging the social constructions of our class of origin and testing other societal assumptions. In 1971, when I was about to begin my senior year of college and she her sophomore year, we married and went on, side by side, to complete B.A.s, M.A.s, and Ph.D.s. Ours was a complementary support system. As sociologists, we recognize the social forces that brought us together. Our families emerged from a similar social class and religious and ethnic heritage. Both sets of parents migrated to California after World War II in search of economic opportunities, completing a generational migration across two continents, the Atlantic Ocean, and several national boundaries. Ironically, that journey, starting in the same region of Europe and Russia, involving many families, and extending over several decades, culminated with my wife and me growing up within three miles of one another in Rio Linda. At times, it becomes strangely evident that the events of our meeting and marrying were constructed by people long since dead and by historical events both purposeful and serendipitous. Today we are acutely aware of the mutual support that we provided one another in our academic pursuits and in our rocky journey over the social class paths and boundaries. Our common experiences and history continually generate purpose, perspective, and a sense of wonder. What each of us has accomplished as individuals we have also accomplished together.

Finally, one cannot ignore individual drive, an obscure combination of innate qualities and environmental forces. During my sophomore and junior years of college I began to realize that another world existed that I knew little about, one that was not part of my social heritage. It was during my junior and senior years that I truly became obsessed with the life of the mind. It was almost as if I had discovered an alien culture from a distant galaxy. I did not converse easily with others, was rough around the edges, had something of an attitude problem, and did not have the academic polish of others in my age group. For these reasons, few of my undergraduate instructors took notice of me. During my senior year, I began to take great pleasure in spending hours in the library reading and preparing for class. My wife and I spent weekends just hanging out at the campus. While our families and friends pursued the work and leisure associated with working-class culture, we headed for the calm of our newfound world. Academia became a home away from home, a refuge, our new focal point, and higher education became our primary reference point. College campuses became depots in our journey through the social terrain. To this day we enjoy stopping by college campuses when we visit other communities. For us they symbolize personal transformation in all of its complexity and intensity.

When we entered to our new home in those early years, we encountered lifelong residents: students and faculty who seemed to have been born and bred to the values, beliefs, and behaviors of a middle-class academic environment. We knew there were other working-class people in our classes and on campus, but we did not talk openly about social class differences in those days. Ours was an unspoken communication about our travels. My wife and I were willingly adopted into this new setting but knew we were outsiders, at least initially. Many in this new home were friendly and went out of their way to make us feel wanted, but there always seemed to be barriers to total immersion in this new habitat, many that we created and others constructed by the current residents. As time wore on and through a process of resocialization, many of the barriers subsided and our adopted home became an authentic home. This came to pass primarily as a result of change in those adopted and not as a result of any fundamental change in the new residence. We literally became new people.

Our original home, our working-class home, also did not change as a result of our departure. Its structure remained intact, but when we returned our status changed from residents to visitors. Initially we felt abandoned and injured. Perhaps these feelings were in part self-constructed; perhaps they originated outside of us. Nevertheless, an invisible barrier began to emerge, and to this day we feel that the primary builders resided in our former working-class home. A class curtain descended, but one could still talk and see through it. The circumstances of this construction saddened us, and we continue to feel a degree of loss. The barrier, however, almost seems inevitable given the very real conditions of class relations in a stratified social structure. Our goal is not to forget that old home but to remember and to pass on an understanding to our children. As a result, it may be easier at some future date for them to return to our working-class home and communicate with the residents as friendly visitors. Our children will not be carrying the invisible baggage that one acquires in traveling through that social terrain.

If I try to explain my intensity at that earlier phase of my life, two tendencies come to mind. First, I simply had an unexplainable interest in the diversity and complexity of human behavior. Second, I have always had a sense of wonder about what motivates that behavior. It is almost as if I look at the world as a child does and continually ask, "Why?" I think this curiosity periodically irritated my parents and still does today. In my early years I had no one with whom to share this amazement on a consistent basis. By the time I was twenty, however, I was genuinely shocked to discover a social environment and institution that rewarded these tendencies. A new part of me was born. Was it possible to have a job where one was paid to explore one's inherent interests and where others wanted to do the same thing? I came to realize that work need not start at 8 A.M. and end at 4:30 P.M. with a half hour off for lunch. This conception of a compartmentalized segment of time where work is often unwillingly performed, often under close supervision, gave way to work linked to inner goals and aspirations that became increasingly secure, complex, and rewarded over time. This was the type of work that I knew existed for other class groups, and it was the type of work I wanted for myself. These were not jobs; these were careers. I often think about friends, family, and other members of my working-class community who might have had similar aspirations but never had the opportunity to develop their potential within the structure of the social class hierarchy.

Various societal forces certainly help to explain my travels across socially constructed boundaries. Other specific facts surrounding these experiences are equally straightforward in the context of my own history. I graduated from California State University-Sacramento (CSUS) in 1972 with a B.A. in social welfare. CSUS, a college with a high proportion of first-generation college students, was close to important family and community ties. I grew up hearing about "Sac State," formerly Sacramento State College, down near the state capital's American River. Even though I often went with my father to the plumber's union hall across the street from the campus, I never visited the college as a child. To this day I say "Sac State," remembering the buildings, the classrooms, the library, the footbridge, the parking lots, Shakey's Pizza, and the winter fog shrouding the campus.

At the time, I was not aware of the prestige ranking system of colleges and universities and how that particular social construction shapes life options. I had taken several sociology courses as an undergraduate and had done well. With limited employment opportunities in the field of social welfare and a developing political consciousness that questioned the wisdom of trying to solve the problems of social stratification at the micro, psychological level, I applied for and was accepted conditionally in the M.A. program in sociology at CSUS. After one year of course work in theory, methods, and statistics, I was formally admitted to the program. I was hooked; I was particularly fascinated with how we collectively understand social class stratification and how we attempt to justify that social construction.

During 1973 I decided to pursue the Ph.D. but was not sure exactly how to go about accomplishing what appeared to be a somewhat mysterious task. I first needed to complete the M.A. at CSUS while my wife finished her undergraduate and master's degrees. One member of the sociology faculty, someone with undeniable upper-middle-class origins, became my informal mentor. I had enjoyed his class in the sociology of work, and the subject matter of the class led to conversations about my jobs in the construction industry. He indicated an interest in my past, how I was negotiating the present, and my aspirations for the future. He was the first college instructor to take a serious interest in me, and my association with him represented a major turning point. He eventually chaired my M.A. thesis in the sociology of education, and I will always remember the concern he expressed in my early research interests. My experiences and ideas were validated when I could freely talk with him about a wide range of intellectual and personal concerns. As I explored sociology, he reinforced my enthusiasm by listening to me and reflecting with me on the substance of the discipline. Without the topic being directly addressed, he seemed intuitively to understand my journey through the social class structure. As I look back on that time, it almost seems that I was seeking permission from something or someone to enter this new world. Strangers always step lightly in new communities.

Completing the M.A. program and writing the thesis was no easy task as a part-time student, but I never felt more alive. The classes were stimulating, and my thesis research became an ongoing creative act. My wife was enrolled in the same program and experienced a similar sense of adventure. We actively maintained common goals, but the really difficult task was economic survival. There was little financial support from the university. Our parents viewed us as independent, married adults and really did not understand why graduate school was necessary. For them, a B.A. seemed quite sufficient to secure a comfortable life.

Many of the students at CSUS worked full or part-time, and my wife and I joined the ranks. Not having any social connections into the middle-class world, I pursued work that I was most familiar with and knew best: construction. After graduating from CSUS in 1972, I worked for the county of Sacramento repairing sewer and water lines. During the summer and fall of 1973, I was an apprentice plumber for a private company in Sacramento. As I worked in the construction of new homes for the middle class, I was still contemplating long-term work in a blue-collar trade. At the same time, I was enrolled in graduate courses in sociology at CSUS. My faculty mentor was intrigued, but I was pushed and pulled. People I worked and attended school with thought I was curious. My boss questioned my commitment to the plumbing trade. Here I was with an undergraduate degree, enrolled in a master's program, but still employed in a working-class capacity. I was continually aware of the contradiction.

In the summer of 1973 a significant event changed my course of action. I was helping to repair a sewer main; it was well over a hundred degrees at the bottom of the six-foot ditch where I was standing ankle deep in flowing sewage water. A new section of pipe was about to be lowered down, and, as the young guy on the crew, I had the privilege of "getting my hands wet." That event represents a moment of clarity for me in two ways. First, I realized that I had to take definitive steps toward a new life, steps that would leave behind once and for all a working-class world. I had been struggling with this transformation for a number of years, but for the first time I seemed capable of taking direct action. I felt the fading of a part of me; something new was emerging. Second, I recall, as the hot afternoon wore on, thinking of my father working deep in the earth in a Montana coal mine at the time that I was born. I thought of the cave-in that he endured and his experience seeing a friend, standing not four feet from him, crushed under tons of rock. I recalled his description of the disrespect mine owners displayed toward the workers. He had traveled from that place underground, helping to supply coal to generate electricity for the nation's industrial base, to other places and opportunities in California. I, too, needed and wanted a new social arena. I began a quest for a new home that I did not truly understand at the time. I was terrified and elated. I did not despise my past; in fact, I left it with a sense of regret, little knowing then that one cannot totally forget one's heritage nor is it very satisfying to try.

I sensed that I could not continue to straddle two social worlds. My working-class past had provided a basis for an identity that I felt compelled to change. A more complicated identity, reflecting a new place in the social structure, required direct action. I could no longer delay at this way station. In my studies I had only read about a middle-class world; now I needed to cross over the boundaries and begin my journey, begin to walk however hesitantly. Today, in my early forties, in my new location in social time and space, I feel a relatively young twenty years old. As we have no choice over our physical maturation, I too could not prevent my social journey.

After the summer of 1973, I made a serious effort to find employment more in line with my graduate training. In the spring of 1974, after another year of graduate school, I submitted résumés to the research units of various state offices in Sacramento. In June I was offered a summer position as a graduate research assistant in the Department of Education. My wife had just graduated with her degree in sociology and our bank accounts were empty. This was my introduction to middle-class work, middle-class people, and middle-class culture. I quietly and intensely explored and enjoyed this new world. During the summer of 1974, for example, I drank my first margarita with co-workers. Beer and whiskey and Seven-Up had been the drinks of choice in my working-class environment. I started buying and listening to Joni Mitchell and jazz records. I had never heard of a bagel and cream cheese. The middle-class inhabitants of the state bureaucracy introduced me to these new habits, but I just ate, listened, and kept quiet. Exposing my ignorance of middle-class ways would have made the early phases of my journey more difficult. So I observed and learned as an isolate. And while there were probably other working-class transplants around who had had similar experiences, I never really connected with any of them. The pain and uncertainty may have been reduced somewhat if I had known someone who had already been through the gauntlet. Fortunately, my wife and I had one another to rely on as we negotiated the journey.

In the last year of completing our theses (1976–77), my wife and I applied to various Ph.D. programs on the West Coast. The sociology department at the University of Oregon was the only program to accept both of us, and so, in the summer of 1977, we embarked on another journey into uncharted territory. We felt invigorated and adventuresome as we moved to the great Northwest. In the years we traveled Interstate 5 between Eugene, Oregon, and Sacramento, Mount Shasta, a dormant volcano in the Cascade Range, became a symbol of social and personal change.

In seeking entrance to what appeared to be a complex academic culture, it seemed appropriate to continue to jettison working-class traits in favor of a new set. At the time, I remember struggling with this decision, feeling I had no choice. If I continued to look, eat, and dress in line with my class origins, I knew that I would set up unnecessary barriers between myself and the inhabitants of this new place. While I could never be totally like them, I sought their acceptance and ultimately a credential, and there were many aspects of this new culture I liked and admired, especially the inquisitiveness. I often envied middle-class peers who seemed to be so comfortable and confident in class, at department parties, and other social events. I had to force myself to attend the various functions at first, but by the end of my stay at Oregon, I no longer felt disconnected.

I took what I liked about this new world, especially the intellectual aspects, and was variously amused or uncomfortable with the rest. One element that continues to amaze me is the obsessive attention grabbing. The desire to be unique, to be on the cutting edge, is central to academic culture. It is, in part, linked to the strong sense of individualism that is first and foremost middle class in origin. Competition, rather than cooperation, is the predominant mode of interaction. This runs counter to the stronger sense of community that organized my working-class worldview. My father had always stressed union and working-class solidarity. I asked myself, How can everyone be the best? How can we truly be unique in a society where we are *all* asked to be individuals? As travelers through the terrain of social class, my wife and I attempt to blend the importance of the individual and community in the way we live and work as well as in how we socialize our children.

Since graduate school I have explored and attempted to reconcile these and other contradictions. One person who assisted in negotiating these early experiences was my dissertation adviser, who not only supported and guided my academic pursuits but reflected on aspects of the personal side of my journey with me. I think her own origins in a rural community of eastern Oregon, as well as her status as a woman in the male-dominated academic culture of the 1970s, gave her a similar position as an outsider. She too traveled, but through a social gauntlet constructed differently.

One comforting aspect of graduate school was my eventual discovery that the majority of graduate students in sociology at Oregon in the late 1970s also had working-class roots. In our first few months of graduate school we did not reveal our common heritage. Newcomers to any social setting are always reticent, assessing the situation, deciding what they will reveal about themselves and what they will not disclose. In discussing books or articles in the classrooms or at coffee shops, with faculty or fellow graduate students, I watched for direct and indirect evidence of social class elitism. Offhand comments about "those people" who "work with their hands" threw up all sorts of red flags for me. In my early graduate school years, disclosure was an important organizing principle of my social interaction.

A consideration of our graduate school experiences would not be complete without recognizing two other individuals who participated in our re-creation from 1977 to 1983. A member of my M.A. thesis committee at Sac State, who continued to contribute to my development by serving on my dissertation committee, and his wife provided critical support during our years in Eugene. The trips down Interstate 5 to Sacramento always included a visit to their home, where we could count on a friendly ear and support. They gave of themselves, laughed with us, and listened closely to the details of our resocialization as they recounted similar experiences at Berkeley during the 1960s. When family members did not always understand, they did, and for that we will be eternally indebted. The facts that they shared a similar social class heritage and had crossed national boundaries from Canada to live in the United States made them empathetic with our own experiences. We will never forget these fellow travelers in our lives.

We completed our dissertations in early 1983 and formally graduated in March of that year, five and a half years after starting the program at Oregon. At the graduation ceremony, many of the Oregon faculty we invited seemed surprised at the size of our nuclear and extended families. Some appeared to be caught off guard by the fact that approximately thirty men, women, and children, including friends from Sacramento, had traveled from various locations on the West Coast to see us graduate. For many of the faculty, the acquisition of their educational credentials had been routine and expected. The small and more serene middle-class family events presented a stark contrast to the hustle and commotion of our celebration. This occasion was the symbolic representation of our journey and the intermingling of two class cultures that now resided within my wife and me.

That weekend marked another moment of transition. While our families never fully understood why we persisted in school so long, the rituals and ceremonies legitimated to some extent our long-term efforts and our new status. While the ideal of bettering oneself through education is part of the American ideology, once a member of the working class accomplishes it, he or she becomes "one of them," with different ideals, values, and behaviors. As many from the working class do not trust and sometimes even despise those from the upper-middle class, my wife and I also noticed a real tension between ourselves and many family members. This tension can be illustrated in two comments made to me in the months after I finished graduate school. During a visit to my parents' home, while discussing career goals and aspirations, my father referred to me in a somewhat sour tone as "my son, the intellectual!" He waited for me to respond, but I didn't push it. Then a brother-in-law, months after my graduation, suggested that he could never trust an intellectual. His rationale centered on the perception that intellectuals never seem committed and will talk in contradictory and circular ways. My explanation of competing theories and how new data can transform our understanding of the empirical world fell on deaf ears. In working-class culture, where intellectuals are generally not trusted and are often viewed as promoting the interests of the affluent and powerful, my wife and I had become one of "them," at least in the eyes of certain family members. While I have resolved many of the tensions with family members, strain continues in varying degrees.

For two years after completing our Ph.D.s, in a very tight academic job market, my wife and I remained in Eugene. I worked in the Sociology Department as a research associate and managed to have five articles accepted for publication: four drawn from my dissertation and one coauthored with my dissertation adviser. In the summer of 1985, we moved to the San Francisco Bay area, where I worked as a research associate at the Center for Studies in Higher Education, University of California-Berkeley. The center, located near the Campanile, as well as supportive individuals, facilitated my further explorations of class stratification in American higher education. The images of the noon carillon concerts, the Telegraph Avenue coffee shops, Sather Gate with thousands of students rushing to class, the open mike on the steps of Sproul Hall, and the August fog drifting over the campus and the Berkeley Hills are vivid in my recollection of this western outpost in higher education. At Berkeley, I had four more articles accepted for publication and completed additional research while working in a number of capacities: lecturer and research associate in the Sociology Department, postgraduate researcher in the Graduate School, and student affairs officer. I also received a small award from the National Science Foundation to do research in my area of specialty, the sociology of higher education. These and other experiences continued to expand my understanding of academic culture, and I became immersed in many of the diverse aspects of Berkeley life. The students, faculty, staff, and visiting scholars I became acquainted with contributed to my expedition across social boundaries. I met and came to admire several minority faculty in the Sociology Department, all of whom had working-class backgrounds. Berkeley in all its complexity and diversity provided me with new and additional insights into what is possible in academic life. It represents what large, racially diverse universities will become in the next ten to twenty years. I hold the greatest respect for people on the Berkeley campus who struggle with the complexity of race stratification in higher education, a struggle I was involved in at the classroom level. The open recognition of class inequality in America will be Berkeley's next and perhaps greatest institutional challenge.

During my four years at Berkeley (1985–89), the academic market remained incredibly tight, and at times I felt extraordinarily discouraged. For a period of time in 1988, I found it very difficult to devote any energy to my work. After years of hard work and effort in graduate school and beyond, I still was not able to locate an academic position. I knew the problem was essentially structural: too many Ph.D.s and not enough academic jobs. However, it was hard to persist in looking. The fact that other newly minted Ph.Ds, even at Berkeley, experienced similar frustrations did not help: All of us were discouraged. I think, however, that in many ways it was slightly easier for me, having already come through the class gauntlet. I never viewed education as a right, always as a privilege. Those who understood education to be a right, something they were entitled to, felt much more betrayed, but they found it difficult to identify a clear target at which to direct their anger. In the end, many blamed themselves and suffered immensely as a result.

Finally, in 1989 I was offered a position in the Sociology Department at Madonna University in Livonia, Michigan. I could continue my academic career, and my wife could pursue opportunities in the large, social science community at the University of Michigan in Ann Arbor. Our families again questioned our move to a distant region of the country, but we had taken chances throughout our marriage and careers—why not again? So our next adventure began, and my wife, children, and I looked forward to experiencing the four seasons. I played Vivaldi as I traveled Highway 80 alone, driving the largest U-Haul truck and towing our 1973 Plymouth Valiant. The music from jazz, classical, and country and western radio stations represented a historical and symbolic mix for this next leg of the trip. After an introspective and soul-cleansing seven days and six nights on the road, feeling dramatically isolated but still part of the working-class trucking culture, I arrived in Ann Arbor on a very hot and humid day in early July. My wife and children arrived by plane several hours later, and the next phase of our journey began.

Ann Arbor has become our home. We are immersing our children in much of what this city and university community have to offer. They are growing up in a world we never knew as children and that their cousins, aunts, uncles, and grandparents have limited knowledge of, distrust, or do not care about. Our children have no choice, as all children do not, about the ideas and experiences bombarding them. We often talk to them about the social forces that have brought all of us to this social time and place.

After three years of teaching at Madonna University, I was promoted to associate professor in the fall of 1992. It was somewhat anticlimactic. At times I wondered, Is this all there is to it? After twenty years and intense effort and striving associated with my journey across social boundaries, there were no fireworks. We woke up the next morning, got dressed, ate breakfast, got the kids off to school, attended movies, went shopping, and planned vacations. These everyday pursuits are now of critical importance to me, and I intensely, almost fanatically, enjoy my activities as father and husband. Unlike the adult-centered household of my own childhood, our family plans and activities take the children's desires into consideration.

The intensity of my journey has lessened as I continue in the cycle of life. I will, however, never allow myself to forget the journey as it happened and as it continues. I would like others somehow to find something of value in one person's exploration of the social terrain we construct. While much has changed regarding my own perceptions, what has remained constant is my eager exploration of the human condition and that creation we call "society." I try to pass on this devotion to my students, my children, and to those around me. If we are willing to study and to question social structure, anything is possible, and we will not be enslaved by what we construct.

As I continue my work in mid-1993, I have come to a greater sense of balance and perspective. When I pick up my daughter Vanessa from pre-school today, I must bend down and gaze at the ants, bugs, and flowers with her. This is where wonder exists and where it can be encouraged. I must attend my son's school activities and continue to practice for and run ten-kilometer races with him, after my routines of teaching, research, and writing. Charles is discovering the complexity and mystery of the world he is inheriting. I must plan at least one weekend date each month with my wife, Sylvia, a fellow traveler through social time and space. Our love, marriage, and partnership of twenty-two years will continue to nourish a sense of adventure. After I teach my last formal class and write my last paper, sometime in the twenty-first century, it will be my wife, my children, and perhaps my grandchildren whom I will return home to and with whom I will experience the final phase of my life and social odyssey.

13

Working-Class Women as Academics: Seeing in Two Directions, Awkwardly

Nancy LaPaglia

It's hard to be politically conscious and upwardly mobile at the same time. (Lily Tomlin's character Edie, a 1970s radical feminist)

Much as in Edie's dilemma, it is hard to come from the working class (and remain politically conscious of it) and be an academic (with its implication of upward mobility). For some of us, it means not really belonging to either culture. To choose one over the other might also mean opting for the selective sight that ambition confers on the upwardly mobile or to be narrowed by the constraints imposed on working-class women.

I like academics as a group: They are smart, funny ("witty"), reasonable, and they usually talk rather than hit people. But I still think of them as "them," although I have graduate degrees and have been on a college faculty for decades. I am not comfortable with middle-class gentility, for one thing. My upbringing did not equip me with polite (which I often read negatively as "passionless" or "distanced") manners. This decorum is what I mean by gentility, I think, and the great majority of academics come equipped with middle-class manners.

When I was a college student, I often felt out of water among the genteel and thus made many mistakes doing foolish things with great energy. My behavior seemed to receive a kind of silent disapproval from people who never said what they actually meant or felt, to my mind. Are academics maybe too clever or adroit, in addition? Their very reasonableness can strike me as hair-

A portion of this essay appears as the preface to *Storytellers: The Image of the Two-Year College in American Fiction and in Women's Journals* (DeKalb, Ill.: LEPS Press, 1994).

splitting; their articulateness can become wordy or precious. I was raised working class, and I think what I am describing is suspicion generated by class difference.

I grew up in an ethnic factory neighborhood, and my father was an ironworker when he wasn't a sort of itinerant gambler. (I don't mean that my father bet on anything; he thought people who gambled were stupid, throwing their money away. He ran card games as a dealer, usually for other, better-connected men, but occasionally on his own.) My mother was a housewife and the designated caretaker of the sick and elderly in an extended family. Her life served as a cautionary tale for me rather than as a positive model; it was a clear example of what I did not want to be. While one or two relatives on my mother's side gave lip service to the value of an education, I was the first person in my family to graduate from high school.

When I think of the impact of this background on my life and work, I picture someone with one foot in the working class and one foot on a ladder going up, unwilling to commit to a single, more stable stance. To do so would mean betrayal and treachery in some nebulous way. My awkward posture is made easier, if not more graceful, by the fact that although I have a proper academic rank (professor), degree (doctorate), and discipline (the humanities), I am on the faculty of a community college, which is not seen as "really" academic by most who are affiliated with four-year schools. I usually don't feel like an outsider with my community college colleagues, though interacting with a few of particularly WASPish bent can still make me uncomfortable. I identify strongly with my working-class students, so when I finally got around to writing a doctoral dissertation, I chose to write about them, and thus about myself.

I will describe my dissertation topic later, but let me back up before I discuss my academic life. I grew up feeling an outsider in my own immigrant neighborhood, located in an old industrial suburb of Chicago that was and is famous for gangsters and racism. (My grandmother never criticized Al Capone because "he always took good care of his mother," who lived in a nearby bungalow. Martin Luther King later threatened to march in this town, which served as a symbol of American racism in the North.) Except for the few Greeks who maintained their language and customs with ferocity, there was a great emphasis among all the various eastern and southern European nationalities on becoming "American," a determination usually not spoken aloud to their children but clear nonetheless.

Becoming an American meant speaking only English and getting a good steady factory job if male or a temporary clerical job until marriage if female. An occasional very bright boy whose father had moved up to a white-collar job could think about college and a better-paid profession. Boys from mob-connected families had another path they could take. Bright girls who wanted to fit in "knew their place": They were expected to dampen any impulse to excel intellectually and to follow the pattern of their mothers.

In my working-class milieu I was partly an insider. I had friends, did well in school, I was even a leader at times in sports and student organizations. However, I had inappropriate interests in things like books (I tried to read my way through the public library) and sociopolitical reform (I was called things like "n— lover," and I still can't write or say the word). And I was an outsider also because my mother was Jewish. The eastern Europeans in the area were strongly anti-Semitic, and simple childhood quarrels could end with someone screaming, "You killed Jesus!" I never felt that I actually did kill Jesus, but I learned that my own neighborhood held no happy future for me and that I needed a way out.

By my sophomore year of high school I already knew that college was a possible escape from my mother's life and the narrow biases of the neighborhood. I enrolled in the college prep program, and, at my father's insistence, I also took a full load of office practice courses. I am not sure why I chose to go to college. I knew no one who was an academic, and even my K-12 teachers did not live nearby. I knew about college only from reading. I had read a book by Bertrand Russell called *The Conquest of Happiness,* a brief guide he wrote in 1930 for ordinary readers, and I retained a strong memory of a chapter that declared, in essence, if you are unhappy, maybe you're in the wrong place. I needed another place. I was looking for happiness, whatever that meant, rather than status or money, for a place where smart girls were accepted. (Skimming through this book recently, I was unable to find a paragraph, much less a chapter, on the topic of being in the wrong place, but I must have gotten the message somehow, perhaps out of my own psyche as I read it.)

I went to the local junior college my first year until I found the audacity, the tuition scholarship, and the room-and-board money to leave for the University of Illinois at Urbana-Champaign. That freshman year at a two-year college prepared me well academically for downstate but did not constitute stepping off the flat earth. It enabled me to make the break in culture gradually, in stages.

I understood that I would have to learn a new set of rules, one that I believed to be more sophisticated than that of my factory-dominated neighborhood. For example, I had never eaten in a restaurant that was much more than a beanery. In high school, I sometimes dated University of Chicago students who liked me because they thought I was smart enough to appreciate just how smart *they* were but too naive to be threatening. One nice boy from the university took me to a "real" restaurant—as I look back on it, just an ordinary Italian place, but with tablecloths. I pretended I was not hungry and drank black coffee while he ate a meal. What if I did something wrong with the silverware!

Before I left for Urbana, I earned the money I would need as a carhop. I liked the uniform (white cowboy boots, abbreviated red shorts, prim Peter Pan-collared blouse), the generous tips, and the hard work that made the time pass faster than the secretarial work I had done earlier at Western Electric. The other employees at the drive-in were not saving for college, however, and I had to work equally hard at not appearing stuck-up. Admitting to ability or intelligence was a great sin and indicated that you were "stuck on yourself."

One hot Sunday morning, waiting for opening time, we sat around outside with the cooks, reading the newspaper. I asked for the funnies; they were taken. "Well, give me the book section, then." "The *book* section, she wants the BOOOOOK section. La-di-dah." And most nights after our midnight closing, the car hops went to a local bar where we were supposed to treat each other and friends to drinks. I was never able to make a clear decision about what to do in this situation. I did not want to be an outcast, but I was saving my tips for college. So I would go along sometimes, but not frequently; I would drink a little and maybe buy a round, but not always. I was unable to conform well, but I was not strong enough or insightful enough to reject that part of working-class life completely. Academics plan for the future—they have "career paths"; working-class women live in the present. I was trying to do both.

There were good times. *Guys and Dolls* was playing in Chicago, and a U. of C. friend took me. I loved it, thought the other carhops would as well, and organized an excursion downtown. This was an early example of the missionary impulse I would later have as a teacher, trying to connect cultures and social classes. I think I was not being patronizing to my co-workers at that point; I genuinely wanted to share the great pleasure I felt when I saw the musical. I was not yet a true missionary, perhaps.

I think the other carhops liked it, but what I remember best are the outfits they wore. They matched those worn by Nathan Detroit's ladyfriend, Miss Adelaide, on stage: tight, lots of draped fabric, heavy makeup, and fishnet stockings. Maybe I looked much the same to others in the audience, but I did not think so at the time. I don't remember what I wore, but I was not embarrassed by the group I was with or by my own attire. I already knew I was not a real member of their circle, nor yet of any other.

All missionaries think they are correct, that they possess the only truth. I had no such surety. I am, however, embarrassed to admit that at a later point, after I began my teaching career, I tried edging closer to academic life and sought to reject my background. I considered my mostly white working-class students "culturally deprived." They were not as sophisticated as I thought I was, and I treated them accordingly. Whatever sense of political consciousness I had at the time did not allow a complete break with the past, and eventually I think I outgrew my condescending attitude. What is left of my missionary impulse now is partly directed toward educating middle-class colleagues and friends who are distanced from working-class life and thus from my students and from myself. I am not sure this can be called patronizing since that implies the act of one in a superior position.

Just before I left for Urbana, I was taught a lesson by the carhops, so I wouldn't go away thinking I was better than they were. The drive-in was a hangout for guys who did expensive things to their cars—souped them up, chromed the engines, etc. They would drive in, pop the hood for admirers, and only later order hamburgers. I stayed clear of them pretty much, but when the handsomest to my mind asked me to go out with him on my off-night, I agreed. I spent a long time getting ready for the date and had trouble hours later accepting the fact that I had been stood up. Still later, I had even more difficulty realizing that the incident was deliberately planned. Perhaps in their view, it was retribution because they were somehow being stood up by me. I was deserting my class; they knew their place. I supposed that they were angry because I could just quit and walk away, and some of them felt they could not even take time off for a high school prom. Actually, although I did not realize it at the time, they had the same financial options as I did, but for other reasons, chance or choice, they made the drive-in and its romantic/sexual entanglements a center of their lives.

So I went off to the university and never came back home to stay. And never stopped going to college, off and on, despite four children and a full-time job. I am happily married to a carpenter with a degree in English literature, a man who also refuses to commit himself to a single group allegiance. (Do I need to mention his degree because I still bend to the prevailing value system that elevates academics over artisans?) For many years now, I have felt like a middle-aged Alice in Wonderland, wandering around academe, discovering and trying out new things. Virtually everything has been interesting. I had the great fortune to find something that I liked to do for a living, and it took me a long time to get over my astonishment that someone was willing to pay me for doing it. This was not work as I knew it from my background.

A few years ago, I became a little more focused on research and meant to achieve my final academic degree. I wrote my doctoral dissertation on the image of the community college and its inhabitants, a topic that allowed me to straddle, like my stance. Why did it take me so long? I think I am a passionate teacher, for which my early working-class schools offered models, but research is the only true currency for most academics. I choose to do it from time to time. For instance, in the late 1970s and early 1980s, I wrote articles on women painters before the nineteenth century. However, once more and better-trained feminist art historians started publishing, I was happy to leave the field to them and use their discoveries and their slides in my classes. Finally in the 1990s, there was some knowledge I wanted to produce or discover or share about another group of women, those affiliated with community colleges as students and faculty. They are considered marginal to academe and by the larger culture and have not often been the subjects of study. Now I had another mission—to examine the disparity between the fictional image of these women in our society and their own perception of their lives as taken from journals they wrote for my study.

A brief history of the difficulty I had convincing anyone that these working-class women (or two-year colleges in general) are worth studying at all will illustrate the selective vision of academe. I tried three universities before I succeeded, each time approaching a less elite campus. My first choice, the University of Chicago, listened to me politely. I had been a student there in the past and had come with an introduction from a high-ranking professor on their own faculty. Nevertheless, it did not seem believable to them that anyone would go through their program out of intellectual curiosity or mission, but only if one wanted to become an administrator in education. I didn't.

My second choice, the University of Illinois at Chicago, accepted me readily, but my adviser kept recommending books about the dismal failure of the two-year college system and asking if I didn't want to write about something else. I got pretty cranky and left. Then Northern Illinois University offered a new doctoral program that actually *focused* on the two-year college, and it was there that I finished my dissertation and received my degree. The program was begun by some faculty members who are considered politically radical in education circles, people who deem university establishments to be elitist gatekeepers hindering "inappropriate" groups from entering and thus moving upward. NIU liked my topic from the start.

All art reflects the values of its time and place, or at least the values of those who pay for its production. Thus the image of the working-class two-year college that is portrayed in American fiction, including the popular fiction that appears in film and television, is generally mocking and pejorative. Although almost half of all undergraduates in this country, as well as nearly half of all faculty in higher education, are at two-year colleges, they rarely surface in our art forms. When they do, the view is mostly negative and condescending. Curiously, the fictional stereotype of a community-college student is a white working-class woman of "nontraditional" age who has reentered the educational system some years after high school. She is presented as a loser, passive and unenlightened, too unaware to realize that she is marginalized by her culture. I call this stereotype "curious" because reentry women in actual life are usually warmly welcomed by experienced faculty because of their high motivation and exceptional insight.

I am convinced that the demeaning generalizations about community college people come as much from class bias, sexism, and racism as from any actual presence or absence of academic standards. The reentry women students I studied frequently undergo a transformation that rewards any on the faculty who care to see it. Not the transformation into physical beauty that our fairy tales and advertising extol for women, but one marked by the joy of learning and accomplished in the face of adversity. The prize won is not a handsome prince but one's own life. I also collected journals from women faculty, colleagues I admire who are dedicated people maintaining college standards despite overwork and a society that considers them beneath notice.

Feminism has helped me reconcile the two different worlds of the working class and academe. There is an attempt by many feminists to bridge the gap, and I can see that women face some common problems everywhere. I am allowed to ally myself with women at four-year schools and not feel like a deserter. On their part, there is sometimes, unfortunately, that condescending apology made on my behalf: "Don't feel bad that you're only at a community college—some good work can come out of those places." This can still take me by surprise, as I was not feeling bad before I heard them say it. Slurs of this sort can be found almost everywhere in academe, certainly not just among feminists. The underlying, but sometimes openly spoken, assumption is that anyone who works in such a lower-status institution is not interested in even *reading* research, much less producing it. American society is not supposed to be class-based, but I have encountered this particular bias even among professors of adult education who are at four-year schools. It must be strange to spend your professional career studying and presumably advocating for those you consider total dopes.

The informal, conversational style you are reading here is what I usually insist on using. "Breezy," a dissertation committee member called it; "flippant" or "too casual," I think she meant. My writing style is part of my unresolved stance. I continue to identify academic writing with jargon and obscurity, although the academic authors I admire, like Wayne Booth and Jill Ker Conway, write with grace and clarity. A lot of evidence contradicts my negative generalization about traditional academic expression, and I am working on getting past my own bias when my prejudice is unwarranted.

Despite the inconsistencies of my balancing act, I have a rewarding professional and personal life. When I was young it seemed to me that this came about almost by accident, "accident" in the way that working-class heroines operate in Bobbie Ann Mason's or Joyce Carol Oates's stories, though their characters usually have less fortunate experiences than mine. Much of my life just sort of happened, I used to feel, and I saw things mostly in the present tense even when I was trying to think ahead. This lack of a sense of agency, of taking credit or being in control, is, I think, partly due to being raised working class and partly to a prevailing pattern of female development. It does not fit well with the values of academic life, which purports to reward standing out and excelling rather than blending in and conforming. Long-range planning is an academic virtue; living for the present is common in the working class, perhaps due to necessity.

What I have been discussing in this essay cannot be explained totally as the difference between working-class and middle-class ways of behavior. There is a specific antagonism between working-class people and academe, even beyond the general anti-intellectualism that runs through much of American history. Let me give one example. At one point I was the president of our faculty council and naively decided I would try to solve a long-standing problem, a small running sore that erupted at every campus meeting: the perceived lack of convenient parking spaces.

At first I met separately with the various groups that would be involved in bringing about any improvement—security (all men), maintenance and engineering (all men), administration, clerks, and faculty. It soon became clear to me that there would be no resolution because these groups hated each other. Every meeting with security began with the same litany, a recitation of incidents where the faculty had shown disrespect to them, had behaved snobbishly. And, they added, this treatment came from people who never did any "real work"! Maintenance took the same tack. The only people that they despised more than the faculty were the administrators and that was because they were too spineless to stomp on the teachers. Unfortunately, some of the faculty actually did regard these men as a kind of necessary riffraff, so I had some sympathy with the immigrant Irishmen who run our physical plant. I had even more sympathy with the clerks (all women) who received much of the same treatment. I wound up feeling for and against all sides. The normal occupations of the working class run counter to the life that academics are supposed to lead, but that need not mean that each side must treat the other with disdain. The clerks, at least, seemed able to distinguish between those faculty who treated them contemptuously and those who did not, maybe because respect is not as great an issue with working-class women as it is with men. In any case, I have seen this mutual antagonism and disrespect often on my own campus and elsewhere. A relative of my husband who was a maintenance worker at a large university regarded their faculty, at best, as something like a herd of giraffes—interesting curiosities to talk about, but not "real people" who worked for a living. For their part, university faculty that I know rarely mention maintenance workers or other hourly staff except to complain; they are usually just ignored as unimportant.

A possible advantage to my straddling position between the working class and academe is that it can afford a kind of double vision, insider/outsider, if I am careful to look in both directions. Recently I listened to a bright University of Chicago student, one who presented herself as a radical feminist, dismiss a largely working-class and minority university in her own city because she had "never even *heard* of it," although it supports feminist practices she admires and has established an effective women's center when her own university has none at all. I should not be too hard on her: she is young, and her vision is typically elitist. And yet, here she is, among the most prominent of students advocating for radical change, and her assumption is, "Only if I've heard of a place, through its reputation acquired in ways that colleges and universities become notable (through traditionally approved research), are those places worth my care, or worth anything." While the carhops see from one direction, she sees from the other.

Those who teach her usually share her viewpoint. In my experience, academics, for all the radical talking that some of them do, are basically conservative. Anyone who has tried to bring about innovation on a university campus can testify to that. Every privilege and prerogative, however minuscule or archaic, is defended as a natural right, no matter what its effect on student progress. And here a voice in the back of my head says, "But some working-class groups you have known act in the same way." My double vision, as usual, interferes with my easy generalizations.

The view from each side has its problems, and sometimes they are the same problems. I try not to make the mistake of seeing singly, although constantly attending to two sides can lead me to be hypersensitive and quarrelsome. What I want to do is to remain open to the fact that good things and bad can come from many directions.

Although I recognize that dissimilar domains exist, I want to be everyplace. I am not actually alienated from either sphere—the working class or academe. Maybe I can justify my attempt to be in two places at once, or at least make myself feel better about my awkward posture, by quoting Balzac: "I belong to the party of the opposition which is called life" (quoted in Guerard xii). I am not simply rebelling against one position or another. I am opposing fixity and trying to have the best of both worlds.

WORKS CITED

Guerard, Albert J. Introduction to *The Adventures of Augie March*, by Saul Bellow. Greenwich, Conn.: Fawcett, 1967. v–xviii.

Wagner, Jane. *The Search for Signs of Intelligent Life in the Universe*. New York: Harper and Row, 1986.

14

Ambivalent Maybe

Wilson J. Moses

Two souls dwell, alas, in my breast.
The one wants to separate itself from the other.

Two souls, two thoughts, two unreconciled strivings; two
warring ideals in one dark body, whose dogged strength
alone keeps it from being torn asunder.
　　　　　(W.E.B. Du Bois, The Souls of Black Folk)

I am increasingly uncomfortable with clichés about double consciousness, even when they issue from the pens of such literary giants as J. W. Goethe or W.E.B. Du Bois. The two-souls paradigm is essentially reductive, for even a man as unremarkable as myself must have more than two souls. To reduce oneself to two souls is almost like reducing oneself to two dimensions. The personality of every human being is complex and contradictory. It is true enough that my feelings as a black man have sometimes been in conflict with my sense of American nationality. But over the years I have become resigned to the fact that my interests, so far in this life, have always been inseparable from those of the United States.

I am restless and vulnerable, here at home. But in Europe or in Africa I have never felt any less vulnerable or alienated. Much of this certainly has to do with being black, but a portion of it simply derives from the human predicament. We must all feel lost and lonely and threatened by inevitable doom. Every age in the history of mankind had been an age of anxiety.

In order to explain myself it is necessary to explain not one but several sets of contradictions

This essay appeared originally in *Lure and Loathing*, ed. Gerald Early (New York: Penguin, 1993), 274–90.

that I believe to be perpetually irreconcilable. I have to be specific about the several contexts in which I have experienced my raciality and other dimensions of my personality. I find it necessary to say something about my parents, about my ambiguous class background, about the regions where I grew up and where I presently live, about my religious background, about the university I attended, and—within the bounds of taste—about my marriage.

I grew up in Detroit, a city where geographical common sense is contradicted by the fact that Canada is due south, separated from Detroit by a river that is not a river. The Detroit River is actually a mile-wide strait connecting Lake Saint Clair to Lake Erie. Lake Saint Clair is small enough to be forgotten on some maps, and yet it stretches to the horizon, and standing on its shore can be like standing on the shore of the ocean, so that Detroit has sometimes the feel of a coastal city.

My father was employed by the Detroit Water Works, so he spent a lot of time on the river. One day while he was out on the river taking samples, a man jumped to his death from the Ambassador Bridge, narrowly missing my father's boat. My father was interviewed by the police and his name was given on the radio. But he never mentioned the incident until my sisters and I heard about it from the corner grocer and came bursting into the house with questions.

During the summers, he liked to fish on the river and sometimes he took me along. Once or twice we were joined by his friend Sterling Wilhite, one of the smoothest, darkest men I have ever known. His speech was sometimes clipped and ironic, at other times soft as the bittersweet poignancy of Scott Joplin's "Elite Syncopations." Like many black men of his time, he was that sharp juxtaposition of high culture and jazziness that one saw and heard in Count Basie and Duke Ellington. He lived on the west side with his graceful, pretty, almost-white wife and his two daughters, who were friendly but very gentle and refined. I would listen to the quiet conversation of the two men until I dozed off with the rocking of the boat. They had cool Atlanta University accents, and their language, while always free of profanity and solecism, could be hard and serious. I think they had the quality that is called *negritude*.

Downtown Detroit is laid out like the spokes of a half-wheel, with Jefferson Avenue, its base, running along the river and Woodward Avenue, its main street, running north by northwest; the other two spokes of the half-wheel, Grand River and Gratiot Avenues, fan out to northwest and northeast. The old black ghetto, Paradise Valley, is on the near East Side. That was the side of town where Malcolm X preached and where Joe Louis and later Diana Ross grew up. During the 1950s, the fashionable black bourgeoisie began to move onto the west side, but it was the east side that could boast of the most interesting history and the most local color. I grew up on the east side, although quite a distance from Paradise Valley. Our family lived in a "changing neighborhood," where white ethnics were being displaced by black working-class people. But Paradise Valley was still the center of black life in Detroit, usually referred to as Black Bottom or simply "the bottom."

The bottom was where my father went to the dentist and to the barbershop; it was the center of the black business community. In the bottom were colorful storefront churches, as well as the mighty dome of Ebenezer Baptist Church. There were exotic rib joints where you could see the sportin' crowd, with their "processed" heads and Cadillacs parked out front. There were bars where hardened factory workers with scarred faces drank whiskey and listened to "gut bucket" blues. There were also the offices of tough-minded lawyers, dignified old black men, who used big words and tolerated no nonsense. There were colorful costumes, barefoot prophetesses, and men wearing fezes. There were fish markets and vegetable stands with giant black round watermelons and little grocery stores where people gossiped, joked, and told the greatest lies on earth. The Great Lakes Life Insurance Company was in the bottom, and so was the *Michigan Chronicle*—always printed on green paper. The fraternity houses of Alpha Phi Alpha and Kappa Alpha Psi were in the bottom, and so was the lodge of the Prince Hall Masons.

During the 1950s, a new black district was developing. Prophet Jones had his palatial mansion on Arden Park, a fact that provided much clucking and head shaking among the respectable working class and roused the indignation of middle-class people who were forced to be his neighbors. During the years of my young adulthood, much of the black business and church activity expanded out of the bottom and onto the west side. The Nation of Islam, which had flourished in the bottom during the 1930s, was relocated on the west side. The Shrine of the Black Madonna was established on the west side by the late sixties. With middle-class blacks settling along Linwood and Twelfth Streets and into the Jewish neighborhoods out Dexter Avenue, synagogues were converted into churches. Elsewhere, the sacred tradition in music flourished, with Aretha Franklin singing in her father's choir. Some of the black churches were big on Handel's *Messiah*, and at St. Paul's AME Zion, the future Metropolitan Opera tenor George Shirley sang at Christmastime, "Comfort ye. Comfort ye, my people."

The east-side/west-side division strongly affected the social lives of black teenagers because there was a false, overly simplistic distinction between west-side "elites" (pronounced E-lights) and east-side "hoods." The topic of "E-lights and hoods" was discussed at Reverend Albert B. Cleage's Sunday afternoon Youth Fellowship, which met in his elegant west-side home. Most of the people of the east side were not hoods, however. I, for example, was not a hood, but a lot of the E-lights never could get that straight. There were a few E-lights on the east side, but I was not an E-light because I was socialized outside the values of the "black bourgeoisie" and did not attend fellowship. And not only was I a Catholic, I went to the wrong kind of Catholic school.

The Catholic schools of Detroit were divided into two classes, those outside the parish system, styling themselves prep schools, like University of Detroit High School or De La Salle Collegiate, and those that were parish-based, like Nativity of Our Lord and St. Catherine's. The prep schools were usually single-sex and had pretensions to classiness that were not always founded in fact. Their graduates were supposed to go on to Catholic colleges like the University of Detroit or Marygrove. The parochial schools often, but not always, had a more working-class character than did the Catholic preps. Nativity of Our Lord, which I attended, was lower middle class. The kind of people who went to Nativity lived in single-family houses on quiet streets. The mothers were usually housewives; the fathers were mostly semiskilled workers or small businessmen and white-collar workers. The boys stayed out of trouble, played sports, and avoided use of the "F" word. I always assumed all the girls were virgins. They wore crisp navy uniforms with white blouses.

I shall never forget the day my father brought me to the dark old building with the words over the door, "The truth shall make you free," and deposited me in the classroom of Sister Lydia. My stomach was constantly tied up in knots from the time I started to Nativity in 1952 until I graduated in 1960. Attendance at mass was compulsory, and we marched back and forth between church and school in straight lines. Nativity, like most of the older Catholic churches in Detroit, was a gigantic red brick structure. Its style was eclectic—mighty pillars, Roman arches, and lofty coffered ceiling. It was an inspiring vision to witness all those virgins with their blue beanies, navy uniforms, and white blouses, beneath the stained-glass windows, in procession to the communion rail, while Cesar Franck's "Meditation" played in the background.

The Catholic schools were very good at what they did. They stressed neatness, cleanliness, chastity, discipline, and obedience to authority. In those days, Catholic schools did not encourage the matriculation of non-Catholics. Pupils were expected to make their first communion in the first grade and to be confirmed in the fifth grade. Since there were few black Catholics in the city of Detroit, there were not many black youngsters in the

Catholic schools. I was alone in my class of seventy from the fifth to the eleventh grade. But starting in the eleventh grade there were two of us—me and Ronald Mosely. Ron was a little fellow who played football a lot better than I did and performed well academically, graduating in the upper third of the class. He was a good friend who stood by me and gave me heartening pep talks, but about a week after graduation he disappeared. His family suddenly moved out of the neighborhood, and to my continuing sadness, I never learned what happened to him.

The rest of my classmates were mostly Italian and German, with a sprinkling of Irish and Poles. I must admit that, in light of the social conventions of the times, the other pupils dealt with me rather kindly and rarely took advantage of my racial vulnerability. I thus view the entire experience with nostalgia. On the other hand, there were occasions when I had to stifle tears, and I daily experienced queasiness and pain in the pit of my stomach when I walked to school.

Thomas Murrell was my friend, and it was he who introduced me to science fiction. He was also interested in music and art. I talked him into taking art appreciation classes at the Detroit Institute of Arts, and we both made use of the collection of classical recordings at the Mark Twain Library.

I suppose I should have worked a lot harder during the years at Nativity, but I have neither excuses nor apologies to offer. Religion, history, and English were the only subjects I cared for, and even in these I did not prepare my daily homework assignments, nor did I seriously prepare for examinations. I regret that I squandered the opportunity to develop a solid grounding in Latin grammar, but I found it impossible to study. It was those knots in my stomach. On one point I wish to be definite, however: I was never made to feel that my abilities were in any way inferior to those of the white children. In fact, the nuns constantly admonished me for not working up to my abilities and warned that someday I would regret wasting my talents. They were right.

On the other hand, I read constantly. I read frivolously. Mostly, I read fairy tales, mythology, and science fiction. I loved Shakespeare, but I foolishly neglected to complete my assignments for English classes. I listened to Tchaikovsky, Mendelssohn, and Mozart on old 78-rpm recordings (Vivaldi had not yet become fashionable) and wasted a lot of time strolling around in the Detroit Institute of Arts. Nativity Church was itself a kind of museum, and I have idyllic memories centered in my fascination with the medieval character of the Catholic ritual. I never knew Catholicism as a social experience, but I appreciated the Church greatly for its music, architecture, dogma, statuary, and incense. I still appreciate the cultural heritage of Catholicism and feel, in a cultural sense, more Catholic than African.

Of course, I accepted the agenda of Catholic education, for the most part. I hadn't started drinking, but I occasionally smoked a cigar. Sexually, I was a good boy. I discovered a collection of *Playboy* magazines, owned by a friend's older brother, when I was around sixteen, but *Playboy* was comparatively chaste in those days, and I never saw a page of hard-core pornography until I was in college. I did not think much of sex as sex because I believed it a sin to keep impure thoughts in my mind. Following the injunction of the Baltimore Catechism, I committed no sins of impurity, either alone or with others, and I had never seen a condom. My youthful fantasies were of romantic love, derived from the few sonnets of Shakespeare, Petrarch, and Michelangelo that I had memorized. My view of women was largely controlled by women, and it was completely ethereal and idealized. I was, in short, a chaste and often solitary nerd.

For four years, I played football, astonishing my teammates with a clumsiness and ineptitude that evoked something bordering on awe. I had a high tolerance for pain and was pretty strong, but I was not agile, I was not deft, I could not sense the drift of a play. I believe I fumbled every single pass that was thrown to me in the entire four years. I had my nose smashed, got my shins bruised, and missed every tackle that came my way. Finally, in my senior year, I overcame my lack of talent and *earned* a letter in football. I was allowed to start in several games and once won the praise of our handsome backfield coach, Gino D'Ambrosio, whom we all passionately adored. Athletically gifted people may find it difficult to understand what I am saying, but I am prouder of that letter than of almost any other accomplishment in my life.

During my high school years, I did not, of course, know the term "cultural relativism," but I certainly received a basic introduction to the principle, if not the concept. I developed respect for two pantheons of heroes. At school, I idolized the English martyrs, Saint Alban, Thomas à Becket, and Thomas More. Isaac Jogues and Thomas Aquinas, the angelic doctor, were also among my favorites. I also learned black folklore. My Aunt Mary believed that God had sent the iceberg to sink the wealthy bigots on the Titanic. My friend Marvis Lee Butts told me that the Bible predicted the black man would rule the world someday. I realized that certain people in the neighborhood corresponded to stock figures in the African American Carnival of Animals: Brer Weasel, Brer Bear, Brer Snake, and the Signifying Monkey. I also got to know Pepper and Mustard, the Jack Leg Preacher, and Shine.

One day, my mother asked me if I knew that there was a Negro national anthem, and when I said I did not, she sang it for me on the spot. Someone was always singing around our house. If I began humming the barcarole from *Tales of Hoffmann,* Mom would pitch in and harmonize. We especially liked snappy spirituals like "I Want to Be Ready to Walk in Jerusalem, Just like John." Another favorite was "Ezekiel Saw de Wheel, Way in de Middle of the Air." From early childhood, I was fascinated as much by the language and the lyrics as I was by the rhythms and the melodies. We almost always spoke standard English at home, but we enjoyed speaking dialect, as well. We always knew that whenever Mom spoke in dialect she was ready to go on the warpath. Dad wasn't so much into dialect, but he could talk like a preacher when he wanted to—humorously and with an artful quaver in his voice.

It had always been taken for granted that I would go on to college after high school, but little discussion was given to the question of where. The sisters at Nativity had warned us about Wayne State University, a citadel of atheism and communism, and encouraged the brightest ones among us to think in terms of the University of Detroit, which was operated by the Jesuits. But the University of Detroit was on the other side of town and much more expensive than Wayne State. I sometimes wonder if I might have been happier at the University of Detroit, but at the time I was in rebellion against the church, and furthermore, I had romantic notions that I would be happier at a school with a large black enrollment. Just to be safe, I applied to Highland Park Junior College, where I was pretty certain I would be admitted.

This was before affirmative action. Still my grades were okay and I was a Michigan resident. I suppose my chances for admission to East Lansing or Ann Arbor would have been perfectly good, but I never thought to apply. In 1959, lower-middle-class kids who wanted to attend college had to learn the ropes on their own. My family thought scholarships were only for gifted athletes and impoverished geniuses. Since I couldn't play football or improvise on the piano and my father had a job, I didn't think of myself as deserving a scholarship, so I didn't apply for any. In retrospect, I can see the need for the various supportive structures that later developed in American universities. Black students have not been the only beneficiaries of such structures. There have been many indirect benefits for all working-class students. The trickle-down effect of equal opportunity and affirmative action programs on public attitudes in such areas as counseling, student aid, and campus employment have benefitted all young people. White students have often been better positioned to exploit the indirect benefits of affirmative action than have the mass of black students, who must still overcome poverty, violence, naïveté, and racial prejudice in order to leave their home communities for the university. In any case, affirmative action had not yet been invented, and my high school did not have a guidance counselor to show me the ropes.

Wayne State University was in a period of rapid physical expansion, and its enrollment grew from thirty to forty thousand students during the 1960s. Tuition was cheap, and there was no distinction between day and night school, although a large number of courses were offered in the evenings to accommodate working students. The student body included wealthy matrons returning to college after their children were grown and chic young women who worked as secretaries in the College of Liberal Arts. There were businessmen studying the humanities as a hobby, schoolteachers meeting the requirements for advanced certification, children of Grosse Pointers who for various reasons had not gone off to Dartmouth or Bryn Mawr. I encountered Jewish students of all varieties for the first time, including both the devoutly orthodox and the suavely atheistic. And there were black students, most of us from unsophisticated but aspiring families, children of factory workers and civil servants, working part-time and taking the bus to school every morning.

One of my professors, George Naknikian, told us he had been brought up in the Armenian Orthodox Church, but he called himself an atheist. I remember one student walking out of class when he criticized the Catholic Church. Milton Covensky and Jason Tickton always insisted on referring to their Jewish religion and culture in lectures, and their lectures were all the richer because of this. I am glad that I was not instructed by generic de-ethnicized white folks. Within a year of matriculating at Wayne State, I first ate meat on Friday and stopped attending Sunday mass. The opera buffa that was my young adult life opened with my denunciatory sisters calling me "Jeremiah the Apostate," and leaving for church singing, "Oh, sinner man, where yah gonna run to? On de jedgement day."

My intellectual life at Wayne State was focused almost exclusively on European culture. That was how I wanted it. During my undergraduate years, I took only two courses in American literature and none in American history. I loved opera and must have seen at least fifty between 1960 and 1968, most of them during the Metropolitan Opera's annual visit to Detroit. I made an annual pilgrimage to Stratford, Ontario, where I saw perhaps twenty Shakespeare plays and where I met my future wife, Maureen Connor, a stunning Irish redhead from Minneapolis.

My intellectual and cultural life had absolutely no relation to my formal academic work. I continued to read frivolously, and I listened to Schumann and Brahms, but my performance in terms of grades and courses went from bad to worse. In the summer of 1963, I was working at the Chevrolet Gear and Axle Plant in Hamtramck, Michigan, and doing very poorly in college. I found it impossible to study and had little idea of what I wanted to do with my life.

The turning point in my academic career came when I was married in the fall of 1963. On June 3, 1964, my first son was born, and my grades began to improve. I read British literature, heard German and Italian music, and studied classical mythology.

Gradually, I gained some exposure to the writings of black Americans. The Miles Modern Poetry Room at the university library was next door to the music listening room, where I spent inordinate amounts of time. There I discovered Langston Hughes's *The Ways of White Folks* and *I Wonder as I Wander*. By the time I graduated from college in 1965, I had read Lerone Bennett's *Before the Mayflower* and Rosie Poole's anthology of Afro-American verse, *Beyond the Blues*. I could never bring myself to finish James Baldwin's *Another Country*—absolutely boring. I found Richard Wright's *Native Son* powerful, but I thought the final courtroom scene embarrassingly naive. I found Wright's *The Outsider* a far more satisfying and truthful depiction of the mind of the black man. I was impressed by Booker T. Washington's *Up from Slavery*, and I discovered Du Bois's *The Souls of Black Folk*, which I consider the greatest piece of writing by a black American. Du Bois's *The World and Africa* was my first experience with Du Bois that led to my career in African American studies.

In 1968, I read Harold Cruse's *The Crisis of the Negro Intellectual*, which I consider the most important theoretical work in the field of black studies. For an American, it must be even more important than Fanon's *The Wretched of the Earth*. I am perplexed by the present dependency of young African American intellectuals on French theorists. Perhaps this is because I preferred German to French in college, or perhaps it is only because I am growing old. But I do not believe that any French theorist—even Fanon— can teach us as much as Cruse can. Fanon's *Black Skins, White Masks*, although a fascinating book, will never be as significant to me as Cruse's *Rebellion or Revolution?*

Not long after reading Du Bois and Cruse, I abandoned British literature for African American studies. I left the English Department at Wayne State for the doctoral program in American civilization at Brown. My original intention was to write a dissertation on Du Bois, but around that time I became aware of William Wells Brown's little book, *The Black Man, His Antecedents, His Genius, and His Achievements*. This book contained an excerpt from one of Alexander Crummell's speeches that I found poetic and forceful:

> Amid the decay of nations, a rekindled light starts up in us. Burdens under which others expire seem to have lost their influence upon us; and while *they* are "driven to the wall," destruction keeps far from *us* its blasting hand.

We live in the region of death, yet seem hardly mortal. We cling to life in the midst of all reverses; and our nerveful grasp thereon cannot easily be relaxed. History reverses its mandates in our behalf: our dotage is in the past. "Time writes not its wrinkles on our brow"; our juvenescence is in the future. (167–68)

This was the same prophecy, although more formally expressed, that was boisterously proclaimed by some of the boys in the neighborhood. This was the prophecy that Ethiopia would soon stretch forth her hands, the prophecy that the black man would rule the world someday! It was the confident message of black messianism and black nationalism, on which I had secretly fantasized since childhood!

"Who was this Alexander Crummell?" I soon learned that he was the great black nationalist conservative of the nineteenth century who had devoted his life to the cause of Pan-African nationalism. He had been educated in classical and biblical languages at the University of Cambridge and had served the cause of Liberian nationalism for almost twenty years, between 1853 and 1872. He had founded the American Negro Academy after his disillusionment with Liberia and return to the United States in 1872. Du Bois had met him and described their first encounter in chapter 12 of *The Souls of Black Folk:* "I spoke to him politely, then curiously, then eagerly, as I began to feel the fineness of his character,—his calm courtesy, the sweetness of his strength, and his fair blending of the hope and truth of life. Instinctively I bowed before this man, as one bows before the prophets of the world. Some seer he seemed, that came not from the crimson Past or the gray To-come, but from the pulsing Now" (170–71).

In Howard Brotz's anthology, *Negro Social and Political Thought, 1850–1925,* I found additional excerpts from the writings of Crummell and other black nationalists of the "Golden Age," including Henry Highland Garnet and Martin R. Delany. Hollis Lynch's biography, *Edward Wilmot Blyden: Pan-Negro Patriot,* convinced me that there was more to black nationalism than the black-power advocates of the sixties realized. Dorothy Porter's anthology of early black American writing contained the nineteenth-century writings of Maria Stewart, which anticipated the most impassioned jeremiads of Malcolm X. I was fascinated by the genius and power of Marcus Garvey's program, but hostile to the racial chauvinism contained within it. Years passed before I came to appreciate the importance of Harold Cruse's insights on Garvey, especially Garvey's emphasis on economic power as the basis of intellectual independence.

Inspired by Cruse's injunction that black intellectuals ought to concentrate on the internal dialectic of the black American experience, I focused on the irony that black nationalism had historically functioned as a vehicle of assimilation. This contradiction became the subject of my doctoral dissertation, which was published as *The Golden Age of Black Nationalism, 1850–1925*. I came to believe that any work in African American studies must be solidly grounded in a thorough study of primary documents by the major black authors of the nineteenth century. I devoted a chapter to Crummell in *The Golden Age of Black Nationalism,* and I eventually made Crummell the subject of a lengthier work.[1]

The furies that pursued Crummell during his life continue to plague black intellectuals in these times, and yet black intellectualism seems to be completely out of touch with any sense of its own history. In an American culture that is obsessed with newness for its own sake, we seem unable to create any sense of a black intellectual tradition. The American penchant for planned obsolescence favors innovations rather than continuity, and black studies is inescapably American in its adherence to the cult of newness. Innovation has its negative as well as its positive consequences. It often destroys an environment in the name of progress and growth. But growth may be either healthy or cancerous, and the growth that is taking place in the black studies movement may not be all to the good.

College professors are not supposed to compete with professional athletes, movie stars, and talk-show hosts. Our agenda should be defined by what is good for our students. We should be in the business of convincing young people of the value of spiritual and intellectual struggle and the inevitability of tragedy. Most of our students, baptized in the inanities of Ronald Reagan and the profanities of Eddie Murphy, have been taught a profound contempt for the spiritual. We, their parents and teachers, must share blame for their apostasy if we have, in the words of Du Bois, "worshipped the whores of Hollywood."

But Hollywood is seductive, and I admit I sometimes dream of a motion picture called *The Adventures and Travels of Alexander Crummell*. It begins with the clatter and splash of a horse-drawn buckboard over the filthy gutters of New York in 1834. The times are rough and so are the people. This is the summer of a great race riot, and the bespectacled fifteen-year-old black boy driving the wagon is suddenly pelted with rotten vegetables by a gang of young toughs. We cut to the chase, as the gang pursues the cart through the narrow, jolting streets. But in later scenes, we witness Crummell's travels through the idyllic English countryside and his sojourn among the stately towers of Cambridge University. We follow him to Africa, where he sees elephants and hippos, howling monkeys, exotic birds, gorgeous foliage, beautiful, bare-breasted native women, and puritanical missionaries suffering from heatstroke. The movie would portray the horror of Africa's first military coup and the public lynching of E. J. Roye, Liberia's president and Crummell's friend. It would conclude with the struggles of Crummell's later years, his fire-and-brimstone sermons, his friendship with the young W.E.B. Du Bois, and a deathbed denunciation of Booker T. Washington.

Two souls? All thinking people have more than two souls. Alexander Crummell was an Afro-American and an Americo-Liberian, a black chauvinist and an anglophile, a black messiah and an Uncle Tom. Many struggles took place in his soul, and certainly there was more than one dialectic. The same was true of Du Bois, who was both a revolutionary and a traditionalist, an aristocrat and an egalitarian, a democrat and a totalitarian. Goethe, too, had more than one war waging in his breast; his classicism struggled against his romanticism, his cosmopolitanism against his nationalism, his traditionalism again his inventiveness. The "fashion of our life," in Crummell's words, "fills us with perplexities and breeds constant anxieties, but these are the heritage of all God's spiritual creatures . . . created for the unending, the everlasting ventures and anxieties of the spirits in the deep things of God."

It is the job of the black intellectual to teach our young people the importance of this inner struggle. Our youth are at some times disturbingly credulous, at others skeptical to the point of cynicism. Our task is to hearten them in their internal warfare against both credulity and cynicism. And our obligations are not limited to black students. Black scholars today often find ourselves teaching predominantly, or even completely, white classes. It is not uncommon for us to feel that we are ambassadors for the race and that we must achieve by our examples the mighty task of racial vindication. We feel that if we reveal small human flaws we will provide excuses for discrimination against all black people. We fear that any mistakes we make, any deficiencies we reveal, will reflect poorly on our black colleagues or make the path worse for black students. We have an irrational dread that if we are mediocrities in our profession, we will hold back the progress of the entire race.

Many black spokesmen speak mainly to white audiences. We do not have to apologize for doing this, any more than Malcolm X had to apologize when he lectured at Harvard and the London School of Economics. We should, however, be honest enough to admit that our perspectives arise out of the rather milky conditions in which we live. E. Franklin Frazier recognized fifty years ago that the black liberal intellectual, immersed in the bohemian-proletarian culture of his white peers, is often incapable of intellectual independence. So thoroughly have some of us caught the thought and speech of postmodern intellectualism that the spectacle of a desperate and abandoned young black man in the squalor of a Chicago tenement, naively attempting to find God's truth in *The Protocols of the Elders of Zion,* evokes more of indignation than of pity. Even those of us with the sincerest intentions have not learned how to reach that black youth, and it seems unlikely that we will reach him so long as we teach in predominantly white classrooms.

Twenty-five years ago, Martin Kilson sniffed at black studies and thought he "smelled a rat."[2] More recently, John Hope Franklin said that "most African American scholars went into so-called black studies, not by choice but by the force of racism that dictated the nature of scholarship, as it did in virtually all other aspects of American life" (74). There is no question that I, too, have sometimes smelled a rat and wondered if I should have "re-treated," as Franklin puts it, "to the study of Negroes."

In one of his visionary poems, "Children of the Moon," Du Bois invented the story of a self-sacrificing demigoddess, who, "in Time's weird contradiction," brings to the "Children of the Moon/Freedom and vast salvation" (187). The salvation of a race is a lofty goal, and an educator who aspires to it should beware the pitfall of hubris. The "weird contradiction" is something that we have all known. Internal contradiction and ambivalence are part of the human condition, and African Americans, no less than other human beings, are destined to confront them as long as we are human.

NOTES

1. *Alexander Crummell: A Study of Civilization and Discontent* (New York: Oxford University Press, 1989).
2. "Anatomy of the Black Studies Movement," *Massachusetts Review* 10 (Autumn 1969): 718–25.

WORKS CITED

Brown, William Wells. *The Black Man, His Antecedents, His Genius, and His Achievements.* New York: Thomas Hamilton, 1863.

Du Bois, W.E.B. *The Souls of Black Folk.* Chicago: McClurg, 1903.

———. "Children of the Moon." *Darkwater: Voices from within the Veil.* New York: Harcourt, Brace and Howe, 1920. 187–92.

Franklin, John Hope. "Illiberal Education: An Exchange." *New York Review of Books* September 26, 1991, 74–76.

15

Class Matters: Symbolic Boundaries and Cultural Exclusion

Sharon O'Dair

"I believe this community is a hard-hat community and very few hard hats take in Shakespeare. They're more *Oklahoma* types. I'd like to see [the company do] more things that the citizens of Garden Grove would come out to." So reasoned City Councilman Raymond T. Littrell as he and other members of the council in my hometown of Garden Grove, California, decided in June 1988 to withdraw an $83,000 subsidy from the Grove Shakespeare Festival (Herman). City councils sometimes debate the value of subsidizing arts organizations, and often the debate is conducted over cultural taste, the relative merits of *Oklahoma* and *Othello,* but seldom, I think, do naysayers suggest, as did Councilman Littrell, that the subsidy might be justified if the Grove Shakespeare Festival produced dinner as well as theater.

Five years later, in 1993, the Grove Shakespeare Festival still limps along, each year securing funding from various sources to make up the shortfall and to contribute to Orange County's cultural life. Shakespeare *is* hard to shake, even in a city almost adjacent to Disneyland, whose principal claim to fame is, locally, its part in a burgeoning Little Saigon and, nationally, its status as the corporate headquarters for a successful television preacher. In 1993, as I read and think and write about Shakespeare or the canon or literary theory, the fuss over the Grove Shakespeare Festival often comes to mind. When it does, I know that what bothers me about the councilman's remarks is not that they almost deny the very possibility of me, the daughter of a hard hat who grew up in Garden Grove and became a Shakespearean, nor even that they homogenize and stereotype the working-class constituents the councilman is elected to represent. The problem is that basically the councilman is correct, and that as an academic I am implicated—seriously, strongly, probably permanently—in reasons why "very few hard hats take in Shakespeare."

I wish to discuss several of these reasons, reasons that, because I left the working class to claim a career in the academy, strike me as undeniable realities, obvious truths. These, shall we say, deeply experiential truths, however, are ones that colleagues in English departments, who usually lack the weight of my experience, tend to resist or to qualify when they consider them at all. Yet I am convinced that, until progressive academics in English confront rather than dismiss these kinds of experiences and arguments, we will be unable to extend to the working class the kinds of opportunities successfully extended in recent years to women and racial minorities. John Guillory, I believe, is correct: the category of class is incommensurable with that of race or gender, and the marginality of the working class "cannot be redressed by the *same* strategy of representation" that has worked, more or less, for women and racial minorities (11). Unless, therefore, we rethink our critique of the canon and of the university, "the category of class in the invocation of race/class/gender is likely to remain merely empty" (14).

To make that invocation less empty requires an understanding of why few hard hats take in Shakespeare, which in turn requires one to confront what are perhaps some hard truths about academic work and its functions in society. My first point, therefore, is that academics must acknowledge what one might call the liminal importance for the working class of reading books or, later on perhaps, wishing to write them. In a working-class milieu, a child's desire to read books or to succeed in school signifies difference— not just emotional or intellectual difference but material difference as well. Consider this, for instance: the child must leave the home and even the neighborhood to find novels or stories to read, cajoling her skeptical, even fearful, parents to drive her to and from the public library, because in her own house, if she is lucky, the library consists of *Reader's Digest, Guideposts,* and her neighbor's fingered *National Enquirer.* The desires of this working-class child, if acted upon successfully, eventually separate her from her peers and family and from her culture, as Annie Ernaux points out in her autobiographical novel *Cleaned Out:* "Books . . . books . . . [My mother] believed in them, she would have given me books to eat if she could have, she carried them as if they were the Holy Sacrament, with two hands. . . . She told me to look after them, not to get them dirty. What she didn't realize was that these same books were shutting me off from her, taking me away from them and their cafe, showing me how awful it was" (77). What the books offer is, partly, a window onto the attractions of a life of the mind. They also offer a glimpse of a life in which the culture of the school—taste, manners, a standard language, in short, the culture of the middle and upper classes—is not jarringly discordant with the culture of one's own everyday life. That culture, that life, is where you look for space, look for privacy, look for books—and find none. Instead, you do your homework under bad light at the kitchen table, ignoring as best you can the noise and noise and noise that surrounds you.

For good reasons, a desire to read books or to succeed in school is often seen as a betrayal of the values and the integrity of the community. Working-class kids play sports or work on cars or take care of younger siblings; they don't read and study. Thus, "'smart' boys are often labelled 'fags' [or] 'ass-kissers' . . . when they do well in class . . . [and] working-class girls suffer similar ostracism," report Stanley Aronowitz and Henry A. Giroux (12). Novelist Paul Monette describes a more physical response to such desires: "Dad . . . used to hit me for *reading*," seethes an adult and dying Tom in *Halfway Home* (19). In a memory that might be a refrain in this novel of violence and reconciliation, he sees himself "as a little kid, black crewcut and shoulders slumped, reading in secret so my father wouldn't beat me" (97; see also 167).

Ernaux's *Cleaned Out* records a French working-class university student's burden of shame and alienation, especially with respect to her parents, whose way of life she learns to disdain, whose way of life she must disdain if she is to learn. Indeed, this is the usual destiny of a child who accepts that goal: to abandon, seemingly with few regrets, the language and culture of her birth. As Lillian B. Rubin observes, upward mobility implies a value judgment. She writes, "Those who climb up have a different sense of themselves and of their relationship to the world around them. . . . And whether they bear the lash of resentment of those they left behind, or the smile of approval of their newfound peers, the messages they get reinforce their self-image as not just different but better" (9). Nevertheless, a working-class student's shame and alienation can be aimed in the opposite direction, too, with respect to the knowledge and culture one is trying to acquire, the knowledge and culture that allows one a better life.

My parents knew early on that I was especially bright. On a trip home from college, I once found a letter my mother had written my father, who in 1960 had taken a long-term construction job in northern California because there was none at home. In the letter, amid details of siblings, the house, and the neighborhood, she briefly notes her joy and wonder at the doings of their four-year-old. By the time I was seven or eight, tests confirmed what they already knew, and I became unlike the working-class kids in my immediate neighborhood, separated from them during school hours and placed instead in a classroom of other bright children drawn from several elementary schools. They were, by and large, children who did not live the way I lived, whose families did not live the way my family lived. (The reasoning seemed to be that if I weren't tracked out, I might get on the wrong track.) To be sure, I took readily to the challenges of the advanced schoolwork—regular elementary school classes had bored me—and eventually I found it advantageous that the children of professionals liked me. I could watch their color television sets, listen to their Beatles records on big console stereos, and feel the freedom their large houses afforded. But even as a child I knew all this was not simply advantageous, and for many years I bore a double burden of guilt. Among my middle-class friends I was embarrassed by my parents and my home, and among my working-class friends I was embarrassed by my intellectual privilege. Such separation, such opportunity, is a blessing and a curse.

I remember being chastised in fourth grade by the daughter of an aerospace engineer for saying *ain't* all the time; "*ain't* ain't in the dictionary," she sneered in a voice the entire class could hear. In 1964, *ain't* wasn't, but it was in the vocabulary of my neighborhood in Garden Grove, and stung though I was, I vowed at that moment never finally to cross to the other side, the side I was already tracked onto. And I like to think I haven't. Years and years of professional training—graduate school at Berkeley under the tutelage of Greenblatt, Fineman, Barish et al., and six years teaching Shakespeare as an assistant professor at the University of Alabama—have not smoothed my rough edges. My colleagues have not liked my position or the politics implicit in an essay like this one, and some of them fought bitterly and unsuccessfully to deny me tenure. Even my parents, who understand little of what I do for a living ("You teach *how* many hours a week?"), tease me about the occasional ungrammaticalness of my spoken English, me their English professor. I have refused to memorize and then recite lines of literature in conversation with colleagues, finding it too smooth, too genteel, a part of the role to resist. Often, in fact, I keep my professor's role firmly at arm's length; parts of the role, some of the behavior associated with the role, I avoid or reinterpret to suit myself. Clothes, haircut, the car I drive, the jokes I make in class, I am making this *Hamlet* my own out of respect for my alienation and shame, alienation from and shame at what I've become, not only what I left.

No doubt all professors sprung from the working class know of what I speak, shame and alienation of various sorts, moving in one direction and then another, humiliations that should not count but do. Never knowing where to place a fork or spoon. Being told there's a proper way to skin a carrot. Laughing off awkwardness until it hurts. As Pierre Bourdieu explains:

> The manner which designates the infallible taste of the "taste-maker" and exposes the uncertain tastes of the possessors of an "ill-gotten" culture is so important, in all markets and especially in the market which decides the value of literary and artistic works, only because choices always owe part of their value to the value of the chooser, and because, to a large extent, this value makes itself known and recognized through the manner of choosing. What is learnt through immersion in a world in which legitimate culture is as natural as the air one breathes is a sense of the legitimate innate choice so sure of itself that it convinces by the sheer manner of the performance, like a successful bluff. (91–92)

In Bourdieu's view, professors from the working class by definition possess "ill-gotten" culture; our performances always reveal us. But some of us, it seems, take some pleasure in revealing ourselves, in refusing a performance that we know will only betray us.

One might thus wish to claim that a working-class professor's refusal or appropriation of her role is revolutionary practice, and perhaps not in such a small way as it might seem. For when her performance differs from that of an upper-class white male, she challenges the norms of her society, since how a person performs a role influences the role itself, either by reinforcing others' (and one's own) expectations for the role or by opening up a possibility for change in them. Surely, for example, movements to democratize the canon result partly from decisions by individual scholars to interpret part of the professor's role differently from expectation, to take as objects of study texts that had not previously seemed to be appropriate for serious scholarship.

Undoubtedly, such an argument carries much truth: *in the long run* performance counts, our choices affect the structure of everyday life, the personal is political. Yet such truth does not, I think, obviate Bourdieu's functionalist model of reproduction through education. Like much sociology, Bourdieu's model does not suggest the impossibility of change but rather the difficulty of change within institutions since, as Guillory notes (55–63), once established, institutions tend to persist. Institutions, Peter L. Berger and Thomas Luckmann observe, "confront the individual as undeniable facts" (60), facts that, despite one's potential for radical agency, will outlast the individual even as they antedate him or her.

This, then, is my second point: I am, and doubtless the reader is, part of an institution whose principal function in society is to distinguish, to separate, to launch the meritorious, however defined. The privileging of intellectual work, the judging of merit, is itself a principal way in which society reproduces itself. As Evan Watkins observes, in the United States "the boundary lines of class are drawn through a series of contact points staffed by intellectual workers. . . . [who] 'earn their right' to be intellectual workers by having demonstrated their merit for the work in school" ("Intellectual" 204–5). All of this suggests, as Richard Terdiman explains: "There is *always* class in our classes [because] the act of classing itself presupposes power in the form of a superior instance authorized to decide the membership of the categories specified. A system of classes (of whatever kind) always implies evaluation, and hence its inevitable if guilty accompanist, subordination" (228).

I am writing this essay—rather than waitressing or driving a bus or cleaning up at Disneyland like the kids I grew up with—in large part because the institution did that job on me. In class, the institution found me willing and appropriate, that is, meritorious material on which to work. It then classed me accordingly. Thus, though I know that engaging the institution through my sometimes bizarre performance in the professor's role is progressive or at least disruptive, I also know that the institution still works to distinguish and separate and that I work to distinguish and separate. I know what every ex-working-class academic or professional knows: "School knowledge is loaded in class terms" (Aronowitz and Giroux 12). The upwardly mobile working-class student is wrenched from the culture of her birth and reconstituted according to the norms of middle- and upper-class culture—standard English, taste, manners, and today, perhaps, political correctness. No more ethnic slurs, no more homophobia, no more hating everyone not of the clan. In class, we learn to class, as Terdiman points out (227). And we learn that we belong no longer to the working class.

A continuing source of frustration for me as a writer and professor of English, and this is the third point I wish to address here, is the apparent controversy of this assertion: "Professors of English are not working class." Again and again, in print, at conferences, in casual conversation, I encounter colleagues who gain a comfortable and secure living in institutions that sit atop a hierarchy of institutions geared toward the sorting and sifting of human lives and who *at the same time* claim solidarity with or deny their difference from those who have failed in or been failed by those very institutions. Among colleagues and friends, that is, resistance to recognizing the class positions of intellectuals is strong and to me almost perverse, a series of refusals and excuses such that almost any discussion of this issue becomes heated and, worse, convoluted and imprecise. Distinctions dissolve in a chorus of "but . . . but . . . but's": a professor's salary is but thirty or forty thousand dollars a year, hardly more than a plumber's or mechanic's; the angst of a family like that in *Ordinary People* proves that life is miserable, too, for those in the upper-middle class; the fact that ethnic working-class America has abandoned liberal politics, finding some comfort if not real help among the Republicans, shows that they are not worth our trouble or concern anyway.

I know and can understand, and indeed have explored in print, some of the reasons why some academics in English refuse to acknowledge their positions among the elites and why others identify with the working class or claim working-class status: guilt, ideology, politics, ignorance, sheer human kindness all play their part (see O'Dair "Vestments"). What concerns me, however, from the vantage of both theory and practice, is the possibility that attempts to dissolve class in sets of common experience actually constitute an abandonment of working-class people. Recently, for example, in light of its weakened position in the West, the Left has determined that the working class "failed in its historical mission of emancipation" and thus no longer "represents the privileged agent in which the fundamental impulse of social change resides," as Ernesto Laclau and Chantal Mouffe observe (169, 177). But such a theoretical determination, with its attendant emphasis on new agents of change such as women, homosexuals, or people of color, does not and cannot eliminate the disadvantage of the working class. (Perhaps it can only make it worse as, once again, the working class is judged wanting, this time failing not just a course in history, but history itself.) Nor, I think, can such theoretical twisting and turning dodge the fact that class distinctions exist in the United States—it is, says Rubin, "a structured reality that there's no room at the top and little room in the middle" (211)—and that educational institutions, including the academy, are vitally, perhaps essentially, involved in maintaining them—"schools appear *the* motor force where a system of class boundaries reproduces itself," as Watkins insists in *Work Time* (245).

A few years ago, I presented a paper at a conference dedicated to exploring class bias in higher education. Tension developed from familiar debates about definitions of social class and the role of education in constructing class distinctions. Discussion became highly charged as the conferees gradually confronted the proposition that class bias is different from and thus cannot be equated with racial bias or sexual bias in the academy. But as bickering and fighting and posturing continued, slowly there emerged a sense that a lot of us indeed shared a certain kind of background, upbringing, and experience of education and the academy. Slowly people came to demand of speakers and of each other that they reveal themselves, to demand that someone who claimed to speak for us in fact be one of us.

Suddenly, you had to have credentials of a different sort—not where you took your Ph.D. or where you taught now or whether you were something other than a white male but what your father or your mother did for a living. Colleagues who answered "professor" or "physician" rather than "truck driver" or "bank teller" found themselves relegated to the margins, silent and awkward.

What I experienced there was, I imagine, something quite like what blacks or women felt a generation ago when they were organizing themselves and laying claim to a particular experience of America and the academy—a great and all-encompassing relief that others understand me and I understand them. Who cares what instrument to use on *crème brûlée* or even how to spell it? What I experienced there was the matter, the weight and significance, of class: class matters in ways that are painfully obvious to us and almost invisible to our colleagues who are not from the working class.

Let me sum up what Councilman Littrell from my hometown seems to intuit. For the working class, books take you away and distinguish you from your peers, and they give you the power to judge others, or perhaps more accurately, books give others the power to judge you. The professor, situated in the academy and perhaps the supreme warder of books, institutionalizes subordination and thus class through her ability to evaluate, to pass on or to fail. The power of her authority, as Watkins points out, "visibly and immediately seems to control the outcome of the situation and visits its humiliations on you" ("Intellectual" 209).

Shakespeare, who succeeded in letters despite his small Latin and less Greek, expresses these points well in Caliban's instructions to Stephano and Trinculo about how to overthrow Prospero.

>   'tis a custom with him
> I' th' afternoon to sleep: there thou mayst brain him,
> Having first seiz'd his books; or with a log
> Batter his skull, or paunch him with a stake,
> Or cut his wezand with thy knife. Remember
> First to possess his books; for without them
> He's but a sot, as I am, nor hath not
> One spirit to command: they all do hate him
> As rootedly as I. Burn but his books.
> (*Tempest* 3.2.85–93)

"Burn but his books," for surely it is Prospero's books that enable him to "control the situation and [visit] its humiliations" on Caliban, to inflict physical punishment on the recalcitrant slave: "tonight thou shalt . . . be pinch'd / As thick as honeycomb, each pinch more stinging / Than bees that made 'em" (1.2.327–32). And, of course, Prospero's books prove impossible to burn or to possess, and relations of power and privilege in *The Tempest* remain structurally unchanged. Still, it pleases me to think that Shakespeare reveled in the irony of including in this play celebrating the power of books an "abhorred slave" who succinctly anatomizes the uses of education for most workers: "You taught me language; and my profit on't / Is, I know how to curse" (1.2.365–66).

With respect to power and privilege in late twentieth-century America, class matters, and books, like Shakespeare's, map class. So it is that "the school functions as a system of credentialization by which it produces a specific *relation* to culture. That relation is different for different people, which is to say that it reproduces social relations" (Guillory 56). That relation *is* different for different people, which is why the councilman is correct: "Very few hard hats take in Shakespeare." The hard hats who do, find themselves in a position as conflicted and uneasy as that of the professor who grew up working class.

WORKS CITED

Aronowitz, Stanley, and Henry A. Giroux. *Postmodern Education: Politics, Culture, and Social Criticism.* Minneapolis: University of Minnesota Press, 1991.

Berger, Peter L., and Thomas Luckmann. *The Social Construction of Reality: A Treatise in the Sociology of Knowledge.* Garden City: Doubleday, 1967.

Bourdieu, Pierre. *Distinction: A Social Critique of the Judgment of Taste.* Trans. Richard Nice. Cambridge, Mass.: Harvard University Press, 1984.

Ernaux, Annie. *Cleaned Out.* Trans. Carol Sanders. Elmwood Park, Ill.: Dalkey Archive Press, 1990.

Guillory, John. *Cultural Capital: The Problem of Literary Canon Formation.* Chicago: University of Chicago Press, 1993.

Herman, Jan. "Grove Theatre's Supporting Cast: Enter the Philistines." *Los Angeles Times* May 31, 1988 (Orange County ed.), VI 9.

Laclau, Ernesto, and Chantal Mouffe. *Hegemony and Socialist Strategy: Towards a Radical Democratic Politics.* Trans. Winston Moore and Paul Cammack. London: Verso, 1985.

Monette, Paul. *Halfway Home.* New York: Crown, 1991.

O'Dair, Sharon. "Vestments and Vested Interests: Academia's Suspicion of the Working Class." In *Working-Class Women in the Academy: Laborers in the Knowledge Factory,* ed. Michelle M. Tokarczyk and Elizabeth A. Fay. Amherst: University of Massachusetts Press, 1993. 239–50.

Rubin, Lillian B. *Worlds of Pain: Life in the Working-Class Family.* New York: Basic Books, 1992.

Shakespeare, William. *The Tempest.* Ed. Frank Kermode. New York: Methuen, 1986.

Terdiman, Richard. "Is There Class in This Class?" In *The New Historicism,* ed. H. Aram Veeser. New York: Routledge, 1989. 225–42.

Watkins, Evan. "Intellectual Work and Pedagogical Circulation in English." In *Theory/Pedagogy/Politics,* ed. Donald Morton and Masud Zavarzadeh. Urbana: University of Illinois Press, 1991. 201–21.

——. *Work Time: English Departments and the Circulation of Cultural Value.* Stanford: Stanford University Press, 1989.

16

Nowhere at Home: Toward a Phenomenology of Working-Class Consciousness

Christine Overall

What does it mean to ascend [from the working class] to the academy? *Because the interests of the two classes are inimical and the cultural styles antagonistic, the mobile person is often torn between competing loyalties and adrift with respect to his or her sense of membership in class culture. It is the sense of being nowhere at home. (Ryan and Sackrey,* Strangers in Paradise)

PROLOGUE

In 1989 I was invited to a birthday party in the neighborhood where I grew up in the fifties and sixties. The party was for a friend from my high school years, a friend who never went to university and never left the working-class suburb of Toronto where I once lived. At that party, surrounded by people still living where their parents had lived, still doing the sorts of jobs their parents did, I felt like a frivolous tropical goldfish in a small pond full of sensible, hard-working minnows. To the other partygoers I was both ostentatiously visible and almost incomprehensible. When I mentioned to my friend that I would soon be flying to Edmonton to read a paper, she replied pertly, "Can't they read it themselves?"

But for me the most revealing event in the evening occurred very late, after midnight, when all of us had danced a lot, eaten a lot, and drunk a lot, just as we used to twenty years earlier. A large, florid-faced, sweating man, who in high school had been a dedicated football player, drew me out into a hallway because, he said, he wanted to ask me an important question. I waited for what I anticipated would be a sexually aggressive or mocking comment. Instead he surprised me by saying in a tone scarcely above a whisper, "How did you get out?"

In an article entitled "The Structure of Proletarian Unfreedom, philosopher G. A. Cohen undertakes to show that, in an important sense, workers are forced to sell their labor power.[1] He argues that while a small minority of proletarians are individually free to escape their class position by rising into the petty bourgeois, "each is free only on condition that the others do not exercise their similarly conditional freedom"; that is, proletarians may be individually free but they are collectively unfree (Cohen 244). He uses a disturbing scenario to bring his thesis to life:

> Ten people are placed in a room the only exit from which is a huge and heavy locked door. At various distances from each lies a single heavy key. Whoever picks up this key—and each is physically able, with varying degrees of effort, to do so—and takes it to the door will find, after considerable self-application, a way to open the door and leave the room. But if he does so he alone will be able to leave it. Photoelectric devices installed by a jailer ensure that it will open only just enough to permit one exit. Then it will close, and no one inside the room will be able to open it again. (242)

The poignancy of the situation that Cohen describes lies partly in the fact that each person's exercise of freedom by exiting the working class is a threat to the others' freedom to leave. But what strikes me most forcibly about Cohen's image is his assumption that the people in the room will know that they are locked in, will believe in a world outside the room, will recognize the key as the means of escape, and will even attempt to seize it. For although workers in this culture may recognize that some persons do not sell their labor power to survive, more than this recognition is required to identify their own position and see the possibility of escape—especially the kind of collective escape that would constitute the end of class society.

The power of the class system in North America persists, in part, because of its simultaneous invisibility and apparent naturalness. Hence, to me, the pathos of the ex-football player's question was that, unlike most of the other partygoers, he believed that there is something to escape from, that there is something to escape to, that escape is possible, and that escape is worthwhile. Unlike the ex-football player, many working-class people don't know that they are locked in a room or that there is anywhere else to go. The key is imperceptible or appears valueless or is too heavy. And the few who escape from the room soon forget where they have come from.

I, however, am among those who, in the words of Carie Winslow, "spend their lives trying to get out of neighborhoods they grew up in or occupations they were slotted for by grade 4" (50).[2] At the age of twelve I decided that education would be my way of avoiding a future as a waitress, factory worker, or clerk-typist. If education was the ticket out, I was determined to get as far as I possibly could. Three degrees later, I still have not left academia, convinced as I am that education remains my only protection from what would otherwise be a working-class destiny.

Of course, I haven't entirely escaped the working class. I have not escaped in Cohen's sense, for I still sell my labor power. I am compelled to do so, for, despite Cohen's theoretical freedom to advance into the petty bourgeois, I have no sources of independent wealth and neither the talent nor the resources for becoming an entrepreneur. Indeed, the recent loss of my partner's job has only served to emphasize the total dependency of our family of two adults and two children on my wage. So I remain working-class insofar as I am, as the working-class writer Dan Nickerson defines it, "dependent on a wage drawn from the fruits of [my] own labor" (Nickerson 53). Moreover, I am still working-class in another sense defined by Nickerson: I "identify with working-class culture—the values and lifestyles of the generally non-college-educated, wage-earning people" (Nickerson 57). While working-class culture is not by any means uniform and monolithic, it socializes its participants, as my later discussion will show, to see the world with different beliefs, hopes, and expectations from those held by middle-class people. Despite my lengthening sojourn in academia, the experiences and assumptions of the working-class kid from Toronto still animate my life.

Nevertheless, my life represents my parents' vision of escape, for I have moved from the class of "people who are engaged in the direct production of goods or services and not generally paid for their thinking but for their production" (Nickerson 57) into the middle class, which Nickerson defines as "that group of workers who do not work in the direct delivery of goods and services but who work in support of the direct production of goods and services in their roles as organizers, teachers, managers and consultants" (Nickerson 54). And, insofar as I live as an academic more comfortably, more freely, and less precariously than my parents did, I have in this way at least escaped from my working-class background.

THE PHENOMENOLOGY OF A WORKING-CLASS ACADEMIC

In what follows I hope to demonstrate both the necessity and the fruitfulness for academics, particularly academics with working-class origins, of a form of feminist consciousness-raising with respect to class. It can teach us both about the ambiguities of escaping from the working class and about the ways in which academia contributes to the difficulty of escape.

I want to explore what I call the phenomenology of a working-class academic's consciousness. My inspiration is, in part, philosopher Sandra Lee Bartky's investigation in her landmark paper, "Toward a Phenomenology of Feminist Consciousness," of the phenomenology of gender and the "profound personal transformation" of becoming a feminist. But whereas her work delineates her growing awareness of the social category of "woman," I wish to delineate some aspects of my growing awareness of the social category of "academic from a working-class background."

Working-class academics are ironically described by Jake Ryan and Charles Sackrey as "strangers in paradise"[3] in their eponymous book. The autobiographical stories they present are fascinating but somewhat foreign to my experience, primarily because almost all of their storytellers are male, most entered university employment during the fifties and sixties, and many came to academia after serving in the US military. I, however, write as a Canadian woman who was an undergraduate in the late sixties and has been employed in academia—first in a junior college, then in a university—since the mid-seventies.

This essay is also inspired by my fairly recent recognition that the phenomena associated with sexism are not adequate to account fully for my discomfort within the academic community. I occupy a minority status not only by virtue of my sex but by virtue of my class origins, and the analysis by feminist scholars of the situation of women in academia—an analysis that usually emphasizes gender, race, and, less frequently, sexual orientation—seems surprisingly inadequate to account for both the reality and my perception of my situation as an outsider.

In the women's studies literature, what might be called "middle-class solipsism" prevails, that is, the assumption that membership in the middle class is the norm and goes without saying, whereas working-class membership is deviant enough to have to be signaled by an explicit allusion. General references to class are curiously empty of the experiential core that animates discussions of gender and race; "and class" becomes the tail end of a litany that includes all the usual dimensions of oppression and marginalization, yet the inclusion of class remains theoretical. As Elliott, a working-class lesbian writer, points out, "Class isn't about theory. Class is about survival, about which of us will and won't make it" (39). Discussions of class should therefore take root in the theorized experience of our class origins; we need a phenomenology of class.

Possibly the experiences of working-class attachment and membership have received less attention than experiences related to gender, race, and sexual orientation because while (apparently) one's sex, race, and sexual orientation remain more or less intact upon entry into academia, working-class people seem to leave their class behind in order to succeed in the university. In late twentieth-century North America, class is, unlike sex and race, fairly readily admitted to be a constructed identity rather than an essential one. So it appears to be a superficial characteristic, perhaps a matter of the clothes we choose to wear or the foods we happen to like, rather than what it is: a status that can be constitutive of one's sense of oneself, one's place in the world, and one's hopes and prospects.

I have noticed that my attempts to discuss my working-class origins and their current significance within the university are often received with a certain discomfort best represented by the response, "Why do you have to keep talking about it?" This is a response activists have seen before with respect to women's issues, gay/lesbian/bisexual issues, and race issues. It is a sign that something important is being discussed, something that makes people self-conscious, perhaps, about their current privileges. In a written dialogue with bell hooks on race and class, Mary Childers suggests: "Many privileged women are made uncomfortable by stories of the abuse rather than the help doled out [to working-class children] by middle-class teachers, preachers, social workers, store owners, classmates, etc. They don't want to realize that their class has been a sphere of trauma for others or to remember the ways in which they participated in mocking poor kids in the second grade" (Childers and hooks 72).

In my university department, the persons with whom I seem to have most in common and who have consistently acted as my allies over the past decade are the secretaries with whom I share a similar class background. At the same time, I experience a recurrent and shameful envy of my middle-class students, especially the well-groomed, knowledgeable, confident young middle-class women, who are able to take for granted their right to be at the university and their ability to function well there. I also sense a certain distance from my middle-class female colleagues. For example, I felt resentment (though I did not express it) toward a feminist academic who remarked at a social gathering that she and her husband were going to be "poor" for a year while they went to Oxford on sabbatical, living on one salary and renting out their gorgeous house back home. I was reminded of writer Caryatis Cardea's comment to middle-class women: "Poverty is not-having-money due to conditions beyond one's control. To choose to be relatively moneyless within an essentially self-controlled life is simply not poverty. You'll just have to come up with another term (or, preferably, knock it off!) and disabuse yourselves of the notion that your lives in any way resemble the lives of poor people" (Cardea 108).

In what remains of this paper my intent is to explore some aspects of my consciousness, as a working-class academic, of self and of social reality. This is no generalized class consciousness, although generalizations from it may be possible. It consists of a series of fairly specific internalized conflicts. As Ryan and Sackrey remark, "[T]o grow up working class, then to take on the full trappings of the life of the college professor, *internalizes the conflicts in the hierarchy of the class system within the individual, upwardly mobile person*" (5, their emphasis).

To paraphrase Bartky, working-class consciousness is the consciousness of a being radically alienated from one's world and often divided against oneself (21). Yet these conflicts can also be a source of insight and strength. As bell hooks remarks: "Contradictions are perceived as chaos and not orderly, not rational, everything doesn't follow. Coming out of academe, many of us want to present ourselves as just that: orderly, rational. We also then must struggle for a language that allows us to say: we have contradictions and those contradictions do not necessarily make us quote 'bad people' or politically unsound people" (Childers and hooks 70). Indeed, they may teach us something important about both the place we've come from and the place we're in now.

CONFLICTS

1. The contrast between class identity and gender identity is informative. Unlike class identity, one's gender identity is usually quite visible; in fact, it is socially expected and required that each of us announce our gender identity, both continuously and ostentatiously (Frye "Sexism"). Consequently, in the academy there is a growing awareness of both the dimensions of gender construction and its oppressive consequences. By contrast, one's class identity is and is expected to be much less obvious, especially at the university where wealthy students dress in ragged jeans and poorer students inconspicuously work twenty or thirty hours a week, "part-time," in order to be able to afford the same academic life funded, in the rich kids' cases, by Daddy. It is hard for working-class people, whether students or faculty, to recognize the difference that class makes; after all, we're all here at university, aren't we? In fact, I had been teaching for thirteen years before I explicitly identified my origins as working class. Whereas university women—faculty, staff, and students—are more and more feeling and expressing solidarity around issues of sexism, there is little or no discernible sense of cooperation or communality among those from working-class backgrounds. There is little or no awareness of the dimensions of class construction and its oppressive consequences.

At the same time, and apparently paradoxically, despite the relative difficulty of detecting and appreciating people's class identities, I have succeeded in internalizing considerable contempt for my own class origins. Regrettably, like many others, I have naively and unwittingly bought into the oppressive connotations of escape: that partially escaping my working-class origins somehow makes them not important or that anyone can leave, if they just work hard enough, or even that my working-class roots weren't real, never existed. Like self-described "working class intellectual" Martha Courtot, "In order to succeed in the world I [have had] to deny my deep root system and to become something different, a social construct of an upwardly-mobile working person who would succeed or fail depending on how much of myself I could remove, forget, leave behind" (Courtot 89).

The difficulty of recognizing one's working-class origins and their significance is a result of the operation of internalized oppression. While G. A. Cohen does not explicitly acknowledge the importance of internalized oppression, he provides the possibility for it when he distinguishes in his paper between the freedom to do something and the capacity to do it, arguing, "If one lacks the capacity to do A as a result of the action of others, then one is not only incapable of doing A but also unfree to do it" (254–55). The lack of capacity to recognize one's working-class origins is, in part, the result of internalized limitations on freedom—limitations created by a political system that encourages acquiescence and hopelessness, a mass culture that values fulfillment through material acquisition, and a primary and secondary education system that discourages children both from dreaming and from criticizing.

My first conflict, then, is between, on the one hand, the invisibility of class and the consequent mystification of my class identity and, on the other hand, the internalization of disdain for my working-class origins and the desire to transcend them.

2. What has recently been dubbed the "imposter syndrome" is not just a phenomenon of gender; class refugees are also subject to it. Like Carie Winslow, "I still have a high investment in not being found out. My mom taught me that it was important to hide being poor" (49). I have to cope with feeling both intelligent and stupid at once: intelligent enough to have succeeded, in the ex-football player's words, in "getting out," but not bright enough to become just "one of the boys" in the university environment. The legacy of a working-class upbringing is the shame of being a misfit, the feeling of not being good enough or smart enough to succeed in middle-class academia. At any moment, someone may find out that I am not really the scholar and intellectual I have tried so hard to be. It is not surprising that, after being a nonstop talker all through primary and secondary school on my working-class home turf, I became completely silent at university and only slowly, painfully, regained my voice when I saw that speaking out was part of the price of success. And so my second conflict is between the sense of false superiority and uniqueness at having been "smart" enough to escape from the working class into academia and the feeling of being a scholastic fraud, a working-class bull in the university china shop.

Growing up in working-class Toronto, I had, unlike my middle-class colleagues, little or no access to foreign travel, classical and contemporary art, dance and theatre, fine cuisine, elegant clothes, middle-class manners, and influential people. Before I went to university, no one in my family had ever written a term paper or sat in a lecture hall, and no one could explain to me how to communicate with professors (none of us had ever met a professor), how to dig out obscure information in the library, which extracurricular activities would be useful, what magazines and journals to read, how to handle myself at social events, or where to find a summer job that would complement my studies rather than just exhaust me (we didn't have the right "connections"). Like the philosopher Robert Nozick, I am an "immigrant to the realm of thought" (viii). As a result, I never felt that I knew the academic rules, especially the unwritten ones, well enough to participate as an equal with my supposed peers. I had to learn, slowly and painfully, to "pass" as middle class.

3. Because we were not exposed to and governed by the same rules as children of the middle class, working-class kids may not be "nice." As writer Tammis Coffin notes, people from working-class origins often are potential "trouble-makers" (48) insofar as we have less commitment to the middle-class rules, practices, and niceties that we never entirely learned or understood. Less burdened by notions of what is "proper" in social situations, we may be more "direct and able to get to the point" (47) and more expressive of our feelings (not all of which are positive). As Childers and hooks observe, this openness can be threatening to middle-class people (70–71). Often, we have seen more of the gritty, hard-working, dangerous side of life than have our colleagues who have spent their lives in the middle class.

In discussing her experience as a woman of color in a predominantly white world, the philosopher María Lugones suggests that "the outsider has necessarily acquired flexibility in shifting from the mainstream construction of life where she is constructed as an outsider to other constructions of life where she is more or less 'at home'" (275). Similarly, for the ambitious working-class person, the capacity for what Lugones calls "world-traveling," that is, the ability to shift from the "dominant culture's description and construction of life" to a "nondominant" or "idiosyncratic" construction (281, 282) becomes a necessary skill. And, as Lugones suggests, world-traveling can be a source both of insight and of ambivalence; it can result in being "nowhere at home."

When I was sixteen, a high school teacher chastised me for using what he called "bad grammar." That same year, a friend was amazed when I used the word *inebriated* to describe a drunk. But at that age I already understood that I had to speak two languages: the vernacular of working-class adolescents and adults, complete with slang, neologisms, and linguistic constructions that do not follow the grammar textbook, and the jargon of (semi-) educated middle-class adults with both its more sophisticated vocabulary and its greater constraints on acceptable speech. We have different characteristics within different worlds, says Lugones (281). As an adolescent, I was bilingual, but I had to avoid displaying my bilingualism inappropriately within each of the worlds I inhabited. This difficulty persists. Within academia, I must remember to tone down my expressiveness and exuberance, be sure I know how to pronounce words that I have learned only through reading, and curb my tendency to use a relaxed, colloquial speaking style. On the other hand, I have been greeted with incomprehension, laughter, and even contempt among those from my own background when I accidentally used a word such as *demographics* in ordinary conversation.

Even while acknowledging the strengths of my working-class background, it is important for me not to romanticize its impoverishments—of understanding, education, opportunity, and thought. There is a certain moral error in speaking of one's working-class upbringing "as a kind of accomplishment" (Jeremy Seabrook, quoted in Steedman 15). It is the error of inappropriately applying what philosopher Marilyn Frye calls "the arrogant eye" to one's own background. The arrogant eye "organize[s] everything seen with reference to [itself] and [its] own interests" (Frye, "In and Out" 67). For me, the working class was something to survive, overcome, and escape, but for my parents it represented the best they could provide while raising their children, and for my childhood friends it remains the only life they know.

And so the third conflict is between feeling that speaking out about the reality of my working-class roots is a disloyal, even pretentious, appropriation of my family's struggles and also believing that my origins have conferred special strengths, including the determination to persist in work for which my background never prepared me.

4. Despite my sensation of being an outsider, a displaced person in academia, I am also dogged, especially in these recessionary times, by the feeling that I should be grateful to have a job at all, especially one that *looks* so much easier than anything my parents and grandparents had to do in terms of pay, self-determination, and comfort. As Ryan and Sackrey express it, "Career consciousness and its careful nurturance . . . is [sic] a skill much more easily learned in a middle or upper class family. . . . Alternatively, *having* a job and *keeping* it, is [sic] more a working class perspective on the world of work" (90, their emphasis). One of their contributors writes, "Middle class folk expect to have rewarding careers. . . . Other folks have jobs. And if they're lucky, the jobs aren't too bad. Compared with the rest of my

family, I'm lucky" (293). And writer Marilyn Murphy suggests, "Most upwardly mobile working and poverty class women feel like frauds in our middle-class jobs. The jobs are not *really* work to us. We feel guilty about the money we make, so much more than our parents made for standing on their feet all day and taking abuse" (39). As a result, as Murphy points out, upwardly mobile working-class women may overwork and take abuse on the job because it is harder for us to recognize when a job is exploitative. After all, the work is clean, reasonably quiet, not obviously physically dangerous. How can subtle harassment, a workload of one hundred fifty students and nine committees, and the expectation of constant availability to students and faculty alike be considered bad working conditions? In general, while I am highly critical of academia in general and my own institution in particular, I also feel inordinately thankful for the things it gives me: a library full of books, an office all to myself, interesting students, and legitimation for thinking and writing.

And so my fourth conflict is between, on the one hand, bemusement at the fact that I can get paid for activities that seem not to be "real work" but "mere" reading, writing, and speaking and, on the other hand, pride in and gratitude for my job. It is no mere dilettantism, it is my very life.

EPILOGUE

This newly developing consciousness of myself as an academic from the working class has effects on my teaching, my research, and my perception of the university. There is room here for just one example.

At my institution, in an attempt to compensate for declining government funding of postsecondary education, there are plans to institute hefty increases in tuition. Our students, the vast majority of whom come from comfortable middle-class families, enthusiastically support proposals for increased fees, which they believe will improve learning conditions. They also think that less wealthy kids will not be unduly burdened because of the planned provision of increased scholarships and bursaries.

I know, however, that no matter how much financial aid is improved, high tuition and fees discriminate against working-class students and contribute to the preservation of class distinctions in academia; they make escape more difficult. I chose my undergraduate institution entirely on the basis of financial considerations: it was nearby enough to enable me to continue to live at home and thus not incur the expenses of independent living, and it offered me full funding for tuition and books, unlike the other, newer university in town whose programs I preferred but which could offer me only a partial scholarship.

Back where I come from the proposed higher tuition fees will be perceived by prospective students as a real obstacle. The public perception of an increasingly expensive education will prevail over any added information about financial assistance. In my old neighborhood, people are reluctant to take big financial risks. They won't bet on a mysterious system that might or might not give them money to compensate for its high costs. Students from working-class families will not assume that they will be the ones to receive the extra funds; after all, their families don't have a history of luck with money. If they decide they need more education, they are more likely to choose the less expensive community college. And so, as a result of reasoning such as this, I find myself more radical than my students. While they happily contemplate and even vote for increased tuition fees, I hold a view they regard as archaic: I support a policy of zero tuition.

For working-class kids, higher education is a curiously ambiguous phenomenon. Ironically, it is a way out of some working-class limitations while it also contributes to making that escape difficult. In other words, to use Cohen's terms, the university is a route to individual freedom even while it helps to preserve collective unfreedom. As Ryan and Sackrey emphasize: "Academics contribute, consciously or not, to the reproduction of the system itself which keeps cultural and class relationships more or less in order. . . . [The academy] does much to support the meritocratic ideology which claims entitlement to privilege and reward for those capable of high levels of achievement and the hindmost for the most ordinary plodder" (108–9). The presence in the university of faculty from the working class appears to confirm the myth of upward mobility. We must buy into academia in order to get out of the working class, but in doing so we also buy into the denigration of our origins and the preservation of class inequities. In the end, it seems the price of successful escape is to be intellectually and socially "nowhere at home."

NOTES

1. I am grateful to my working-class colleague Henry Laycock for drawing this article to my attention.

2. I am grateful to Dawn Tunnicliffe for drawing my attention to the Winter 1991–92 issue of *Sinister Wisdom,* in which several articles on class issues quoted in this essay appear.

3. I am grateful to Chuck Barone, who in 1988 led a support group for academics from working-class backgrounds that I had the fortune to join and who half-ironically encouraged us to consider seeing ourselves as strangers in paradise.

WORKS CITED

Bartky, Sandra. "Toward a Phenomenology of Feminist Consciousness." In *Femininity and Domination: Studies in the Phenomenology of Oppression.* New York: Routledge, 1990. 11–21.

Cardea, Caryatis. "All the Pieces I Never Wrote about Class." *Sinister Wisdom* 45 (Winter 1991–92): 105–17.

Childers, Mary, and bell hooks. "A Conversation about Race and Class." In *Conflicts in Feminism,* ed. Marianne Hirsch and Evelyn Fox Keller. New York: Routledge, 1990. 60–81.

Coffin, Tammis. "The Situation for 'People Raised Working-Class Now Working at Middle-Class Jobs.'" *Present Time* 24, no. 2 (1992): 45–48.

Cohen, G. A. "The Structure of Proletarian Unfreedom." In *Analytical Marxism,* ed. John Roemer. Cambridge: Cambridge University Press, 1986. 237–59.

Courtot, Martha. "Confessions of a Working-Class Intellectual." *Sinister Wisdom* 45 (Winter 1991–92): 88–92.

Elliott. "Funeral Food." *Sinister Wisdom* 45 (Winter 1991–92): 34–39.

Frye, Marilyn. "In and Out of Harm's Way: Arrogance and Love." In *The Politics of Reality: Essays in Feminist Theory.* Freedom, Calif.: Crossing Press, 1983. 52–83.

——. Sexism." In *The Politics of Reality: Essays in Feminist Theory.* Freedom, Calif.: Crossing Press, 1983. 17–40.

Lugones, María. "Playfulness, 'World'-Traveling, and Loving Perception." In *Women, Knowledge and Reality,* ed. Ann Garry and Marilyn Pearsall. Boston: Unwin Hyman, 1989. 275–90.

Murphy, Marilyn. "Did Your Mother Do Volunteer Work? An Introduction to the Class Issue." *Lesbian Ethics* 4, no. 2 (1991): 28–40.

Nickerson, Dan. "Being Sensible About Class Divisions." *Present Time* 22 (January 1991): 53–58.

Nozick, Robert. *Philosophical Explanations.* Cambridge, Mass.: Belknap Press, 1981.

Ryan, Jake, and Charles Sackrey, eds. *Strangers in Paradise: Academics from the Working Class.* Boston: South End Press, 1984.

Steedman, Carolyn Kay. *Landscape for a Good Woman: A Story of Two Lives.* New Brunswick, N.J.: Rutgers University Press, 1987.

Winslow, Carie. "A Poor Girl Comes Clean." *Sinister Wisdom* 45 (Winter 1991–92): 49–52.

17

Past Voices, Present Speakers

Donna Burns Phillips

I am the child of an earthbound New Englander with opinions and an erstwhile Bostonian with aspirations. Thus I began as a hybrid, an offspring of opposites, neither this nor that nor anything in between. Torn by the resulting dissonance, I chose an exit route that would by definition eliminate the paradox. I have lately discovered, however, that the path merely circles; in the end is the beginning.

On the paternal side, I was born into a family descended from independent Scots, a family that believed in the Protestant work ethic, capitalism, and strong women. My paternal grandmother, the matriarch, was adamant that a man should be educated for work, a woman for marriage. Within this mindset, the male is the primary breadwinner, the female the primary breadmaker. A definitive example of this attitude can be found in the family's pronouncement that obviously my marriage wrecked on the shoals of my culinary ineptitude.

Grandmother Burns's two oldest sons were stable providers and childless; this combination of circumstances allowed their wives to choose to work in or out of the home. These women could afford their nine-to-five secretarial or sales positions, and both found their jobs most satisfying. Grandmother's daughters, on the other hand, did not marry well; they not only had to work, but they were obliged to take better-paying shiftwork in the factories or, in one case, to do housework. I never heard any of them complain about the quality of their lives, but they did want something better for the children.

This attitude is certainly not unique to the working class; almost all parents want something "better" for their children. My mother grew up in the context where "the Cabots speak only to the Lodges, and the Lodges speak only to God." Within this milieu, "better" is directly tied to class consciousness. But in a New England working-class household, "better" is not connected to social status, for New England workers—even those no longer earning their livelihoods off the land or the water—seldom recognize anyone as their better. Instead, "better" is usually an economic issue. Schooling is important insofar as it is tied to earning capacity. Perhaps part of what prevented my cousins from achieving anything that could be considered much better on any level was their parents' lack of imagination, their inability to conceptualize possibilities beyond the very next step. Although my paternal uncles had both finished high school, none of my paternal aunts graduated. So, depending on the gender of the child, a high school diploma and maybe some technical or secretarial school signified their version of success.

My father, however, a maker of iron castings in his work life, refused such rigid moldings in his personal life. The baby and rebel of the family, he had managed two years of technical school for himself, where his vision had expanded. He was determined that all of his children would be able to write the letters B.A. after their names, regardless of what letters identifying gender and marital status came before it. Possibly, having seen his sisters widowed or married to men who were "no good" use up first their youth and then their lives on the assembly line, he had promised himself that the only man his daughters would ever need to depend on was their father.

The result was an incoherent version of women's liberation. It was characteristic that to most of our pleas for help he would reply, "Stand on your own two feet" while at the same time charging to our rescue behind the scenes because he feared our own feet weren't sturdy enough. Defying his mother's dictum, he insisted formal education was the one certain means for his daughters to be financially independent if and when that were necessary. On the other hand, he taught my brothers—but never my sisters or me—to change the oil in a car, to run an electrical connection, to hang drywall. After his retirement, he made the rounds from one of our houses to another, building things, fixing things, and generally making certain we understood that things would soon have fallen down around our heads had we not had the good sense to summon him in the nick of time.

There is a perception that children in working-class homes are brought up with language attitudes and experience that will work against their needs in school. Research studies like that of Shirley Brice Heath support that assumption.[1] But at best it is a generalization, certainly one that held true only peripherally in my case. I don't recall ever seeing either of my parents open a book, yet reading was an integral part of our lives. Someone read to me until I could do it myself. Whenever we complained of being bored, my father would say, "Go read a book." Of me, he often bragged to his family in tones of mock disapproval, "She's always got her nose in a book." I remember holiday dinners when aunts and uncles took turns testing my spelling ability, showering me with applause for my performance. And they loved my using "big words," oohing and aahing over me with affection. Aunt Lillian, with only an eighth-grade education, taught me to play Scrabble, Anagrams, and Crossword Lexicon while I was still in grade school, and she never minded my taking interminable lengths of time deciding on my words. Aunt Amber gave me her collection of books about writing, then a typewriter, then a complete set of the Harvard Classics, and finally a copy of *The Writer's Market.* In retrospect, I recognize that they not only saw me as different from the rest of the family but also saw that at least in part it was my language that made me different. They encouraged that difference even though it would lead me to places where they could not follow; I sometimes think they secretly believed that, having skipped a few dozen generations, the muse of Robert Burns, their only famous ancestor, had now inexplicably chosen to reappear in his namesake's daughter.

My mother's siblings, meanwhile, were busy overcoming having been birthed by a one-time vaudeville performer of uncertain origin who had gone through more husbands than anyone cared to count and who occasionally still arrived on the doorstep resplendent in feather boa and dyed-to-match hair. Theirs was a formidable task; Grandmama was a shock to everyone, a kind of poor man's Auntie Mame—eccentric, flamboyant, and utterly unreliable. The family insult went something on the order of, "You're just like your grandmother!" My mother spent her whole life being not-her-mother, and she never missed an opportunity to admonish her daughters that "a lady never . . ."

One thing, of course, that a lady never does is use nonstandard grammar. Taken out of the proper Bostonian environment provided by one of Grandmama's husbands (none of us has ever figured out exactly which one) and misplaced into a New England mill town, my mother was unashamedly patronizing toward the many French-Canadian workers because, she explained, they spoke broken English. Naturally, her constant corrections and prescriptions were supported by my teachers. Although mine was predominantly a blue-collar community, my friends, the other "smart" kids, came from white-collar families. I walked carefully in their worlds, always aware that my clothes didn't measure up, certain that I was there on a temporary pass that would be withdrawn if my brain or my manners failed. Only in retrospect do I recognize that Bobby Burns and his daughter were welcomed everywhere; while my mother often made everyone just slightly uncomfortable, people smiled when my dad came into a room. It seems I had learned very early to equate education and propriety in general and language in particular not just with internal family approval but with external social approval. When my father said, "He don't know no better," I wanted to die.

My mother's brothers, by contrast, were glamorous creatures, seldom seen and consequently idealized and idolized. The eldest managed one of Boston's most famous drinking establishments, the second was a foreign correspondent, and the youngest was a career army officer stationed abroad. All dressed beautifully, behaved beautifully, spoke beautifully. It is hardly surprising that as an adolescent I wanted the approval of these men. I was certain they knew the proper thing to do in any situation—how much to tip the cabdriver, which wine to order, what to wear to a Sunday brunch. Fitting into their arena meant knowing both which fork and which pronoun to use.

By the time I began high school, the company had recognized that my father had the rare gift of being almost universally loved and trusted; as a result, workers listened to and preferred to deal with him, and customers valued his expertise and his word. My father exchanged his denims for a tie and moved us into the "right" neighborhood. We still didn't have any money, but we were poor at a higher level. When it came time to apply to colleges, I ignored my English teacher's suggestion that I try Vassar. I refused to go to a school where I would be the token charity case—or worse still, have to wait on tables to earn room and board. For all the wrong reasons but with all the best results, I went to the state university. Everything was paid for by scholarship; I didn't have much spending money but neither did most of the students. It was a place where I thought I would stand on what I could do, not on what I didn't have.

This expectation proved to be both true and not true. What I didn't have was of no particular importance; what I didn't know, however, seriously compromised what I could do. I discovered I hadn't read any of the right books. I was stunned when I realized that none of the hundreds of books I had read—my whole allowance usually went to fines for overdue library books—had any worth. One Shakespeare play in school. That's all. Who was this Dostoyevski everyone kept talking about? Why hadn't my teachers or the librarians thought to provide some guidance? To make matters worse, I had never listened to classical music, never seen an opera or ballet, never been to the legitimate theater, never walked through an art museum. We lived fifty miles outside of Boston, one of the country's finest cultural centers, but it occurred not even to my mother that literacy in the fine arts was a vital component in an education. In my experience, this cultural black hole is the origin of one of the most significant differences between students who come from a working- rather than a middle-class background.

In our adult lives, my sisters and I have reacted to this genetic and environmental hodgepodge in different ways.[2] Susan, who now admits to having been part of a motorcycle gang in her early teens, has become the matriarchal heir apparent, steeped in propriety, duty, endurance, and nobility but blessed with a sense of humor. Melissa the Irreverent bubbles through life on an HBO comedy routine; absolutely nothing fazes her. I have proceeded in waves: I smoked on the street after winning an "I Speak for Democracy" contest; I majored in theater but never wore white before Memorial Day; I taught my daughter to shiver at the sound of a double negative but took her out of private school when she announced that anyone who didn't regularly vacation in Aruba was poor. I rejected my father by dropping out of college to get married and I snubbed my mother by joining a bowling league. What my parents had wrought was a snob unlucky enough to recognize and regret her own elitism.

Our society assumes that education is the great leveler. In a democracy, equality means equal opportunity, which means, in turn, that society does what it can to neutralize the physical, psychological, economic, and cultural disadvantages that its young citizens inherit and bring with them into the classroom. Crime, chemical abuse, racism, moral lapses, technological lags, and a host of other social and economic ills are blamed largely on poverty, inequality, and ignorance—all of which we assume can be erased by sufficient and appropriate education. Within this framework, a Ph.D. presumably certifies that one has no relevant prior self. Academics are acceptable in most social strata. What the old-monied have rightfully inherited, the professorate has presumably acquired: cultural sophistication, a patina of good breeding. Academic poverty is genteel, respectable, connected to the romantic notion of the genius whose mind is focused on higher matters, whose sensibilities render him or her too delicate to attend to petty monetary concerns. Knowing takes the place of having.

When I rather belatedly became an academic, I thought I had outwitted the conflicts inherent in being a halfbreed by discovering a framework wherein oppositions can achieve coherence. In this arena, one may be both smart (say about ancient Armenian pharmacopoeia) and stupid (say about the need for water in car batteries). One may criticize color, texture, line, and proportion in a piece of art but appear to have dressed in the dark. Most inviting, perhaps, is that one can for practical reasons perpetuate social and linguistic niceties while philosophically espousing Marxism or one of the other egalitarian isms. With an easy conscience I can insist upon behavioral and lexical decorum in my classroom even as I am lamenting student passivity. I have my own definition of civil disobedience. As a bonus, I thought I had achieved gender unmarkedness. In these times of fashionable political correctness, no one talks about female professors and never have there been inflected abominations like *professoress* or *professorette*.

It seems I have been wrong on both counts. Two years ago, for example, I invited a senior colleague to sit in on my class in composing theory. One of the few things he and I agree on is that our students seldom have the opportunity to watch us model the kind of dialectic we want them to engage in. During one class, while he and I had a heated (but, of course, civil) debate over the merits of a commentary on New Criticism, my students sat mesmerized. Later congratulating myself on having created so perfect an example of intellectual inquiry, I turned around just in time to hear a student say, "Wow. I've never seen a woman stand up to a male professor like that before." The student had learned that women do have a voice; I learned that I can't consider my gender irrelevant to my teaching. So I should not have been so surprised, perhaps, to discover that I am qualified to wear yet another qualifier. The socioeconomic sins of the father have been visited on his daughter: I am a working-class academic, a blue-collar intellectual.

My first instinct was to ignore this oxymoron: academics by definition are not working class. The gold call-for-papers flyer tacked to the bulletin board, an attempt at undermining homogeneity, the moving of a group to the margins on the basis of a circumstance no longer pertinent, seemed insidious. Perhaps even invidious. My second instinct was to deny membership. (Could I plead that my father eventually donned a tie and became management rather than labor?) Yet upon reflection, I see that it matters, it makes a difference. A trivial example: in conversation with colleagues, I notice their sentences often begin with "When I was at Princeton/Yale/Harvard . . ." Mine begin with "When I was in graduate school . . ." Then, too, I had elected to accept a position as a composition specialist at an open-admissions university, confident that I could use my own experience to effect a positive change in my students' attitudes toward both written language and education. Before long, I discovered that this field of study relegates me to the outer—and lower—reaches of intellectual prestige. Once you discover that difference moves you from not-same to less-valuable status, its effect on more significant matters becomes evident. The choice left to me is not acceptance/rejection but embarrassment/embracement. The tension of being caught between irreconcilable worlds reemerges. Like Orpheus, I have looked back and thus forfeited my prize.

Epistemological assumptions and their resulting pedagogical practices are indelibly marked by a working-class origin. For example, in an urban open-admissions university, the role of postbaccalaureate education is especially problematic. Those who believe a university education should be reserved for students who will go on to become scholars themselves, or for students who believe that education is valuable and ought to be had because it enriches life, see little or no place for the nontraditional student who is not only often underprepared but also values the wrong thing—the diploma rather than the education. On the other hand, those who insist that a university education should be available to all who want it, regardless of motive, aim, or aptitude, are often torn between their belief in and love for the traditional curriculum and a fear that it is largely irrelevant for nontraditional students, no two of whom can be expected to have the same background, knowledge, motivation, intelligence, or needs. What becomes of the teacher who has learned the wrong thing?

In either case, when trying to decide upon what epistemological assumptions to proceed—to decide how knowledge is constructed—we realize we must first decide what counts as knowledge. Is that which is experientially known equivalent in worth to that which is cerebrally known? The academic who believes his or her responsibility to be self-replication (a notion antithetical to the working class, which wants to produce better, not same) cannot accept the ramifications of theories of the social construction of knowledge because a true social constructionist, for example, privileges no knowledge over another. Students, not teachers, set the learning agenda. Even in a watered-down version where interpretive communities (themselves a social construct) decide what counts, the knowledge constructed by students has equal validity to that possessed by the instructor. What becomes of the professor who cannot profess?

Furthermore, while social constructionism, particularly as it manifests itself in Paulo Freire's work, is an elegant theory, it is problematic in practice.[3] My students are almost always the first generation in their families to go to college. A few are traditional in the sense that they are here immediately out of high school. But most are older, most are underprepared, and most are working to pay for their own education. Many have families of their own for whom they are responsible: children whose needs have to come first, husbands or wives whose financial and moral support is uncertain. It is hardly surprising, then, that they carry with them a trade-school mentality, which means they are here to qualify for a higher-paying job, not to get an education. Most important, perhaps, they are terrified that they can't measure up, won't understand what they're reading or we're saying. They see no likenesses between themselves and us; we are alien and too often alienating. In their eyes, those who live in the ivory tower are unaware of and unfit for the realities of life.

Consequently, the abdicating of authority that a social-constructionist approach requires is especially difficult. My students are uncomfortable with taking charge; they are suspicious that what I label as empowerment for them is really laziness in me. They prefer me in my role-model mode: I did it, so can you. Work hard, follow the rules, stay out of trouble. Learn this, that, and Shakespeare. Earn your credential before you try subverting the system; Kenneth Burke is unique.

Then, too, I find myself struggling when I want to teach a course whose concerns are purely theoretical but my students constantly demand that I talk instead about practice. All sorts of dilemmas arise from this tug-of-war between competing agendas. When I teach composing theory, for example, I really want to examine, speculate on, the way literary criticism, reading theory, and writing theory interact. My students don't. They want information about how to teach someone to fix a comma splice. Should I discuss linguistic referentiality when they want to talk lesson design? The working-class side of me, the one that has been boiled in New England pragmatism, demands that I give them what they need to succeed in the world, give them ways to create good assignments and to correct grammar, and let the abstract come as it will. Moreover, on the combined principles growing out of the Protestant work ethic that no one can ask you to do more than your best and that success is directly proportionate to effort, my working-class side demands that I give them credit for their efforts.

All of this wars with the scholarly side of me. I want my students to have voracious intellectual appetites, to be unable to rest until they have solved whatever riddle we articulate, to look for answers because they simply must find them, not because they find some use for them. Who cares what grade you get if you learned? Who cares if you can't use Roland Barthes in the classroom? I care if you dangle your participle, a fault you should have corrected long ago (though I care in the politically correct way of providing you with the means to come in from the margins). I care about standards, and the truth is, effort doesn't count. Talent counts. Analytical ability counts. Creativity counts. To strive for competence is meaningless; the only worthy goal is excellence. I don't want to hear that you didn't finish your paper because your car broke down, you were up all night with a sick child, you had two other exams scheduled for today. You have to make up your mind that your education (especially as it is tied to my class) comes first.

And yet, these thoughts are consistently suppressed. I believe I have been shaped by my father's notion of taking responsibility for those to whom we are tied by virtue of position. My mother was active in charities; she worked hard for causes she believed in. But for her, it was charity; for my father, it was responsibility. My mother was distanced from those she helped; they were abstract beings. But a genuine concrete being used his one phone call to let my father know he would be absent from work the next day because he was in jail for shooting his wife. In a very real sense, my father saw the men who worked for him as kin. Their trust in him was absolute and unswerving—only he could safely cross their picket line during the strike, only he could persuade them to work overtime, only he could see to it that they sought medical or legal help, only he could bring Christmas baskets that wouldn't be refused as charity; in return, he belonged to them, he owed them, he was responsible to and for them.

I do the volunteer work required by my middle-class self, but it is my father who comes with me into the classroom. I hear him whispering that if my students trust me, then I belong to them, I owe them, I am responsible to and for them: I am responsible for their learning. If they don't get it, the fault must be mine for not explaining it clearly, so I will lie awake nights until I come up with a new way to present the material. If they are in the middle of an emotional crisis, I will give them what advice and support I can—I'll probably also give them an Incomplete. If they try hard, I'll try harder to find a way of rewarding the effort. Intellectually, I believe this to be wrongheaded. Intellectually, I believe students to be responsible for their own learning. But emotionally, when my students fail, I fail. They are kin to me.

That stance can have adverse effects on one's professional life and attitudes. I want all the people who believe teaching freshman composition is charity work to teach something else, preferably somewhere else. I want time for my own scholarship, but as I haven't discovered any practical application for it, I keep putting it off in favor of immediate pedagogical or service needs, which may or may not be a particularly pernicious version of hubris and is certainly detrimental to a career. My students see (and often take advantage of the fact) that I belong to them; they are sometimes unpleasantly surprised to discover that my brand of moving them toward self-sufficiency is far more difficult than they had anticipated. Some will see my effort as betrayal; some will see it as respect. And some may even see in my attempts to be the combined and regendered Alberts, Schweitzer and Einstein, the shadow of their own futures.

Referring to a passage in Lévi-Strauss's autobiography, *Tristes Tropiques*, Jerry Herron writes, "But the rum, like the forgetfulness, is only a trick—a trick that people play on themselves when they imagine the story they have told is ever more, or less, than that: as if writing a thing out could really get you off the hook; as if it could absolve you of being who, or where, you are (936). But if Mikhail Bakhtin is right that our language results from the weaving of all we have heard spoken before, and if getting our language in front of us is a way of discovering what we think, then autobiographies can narrate the construction of our heteroglossia, placing our stories before us for analysis and interpretation.[4] They provide a kind of Burkeian grammar of motives, allowing us to inscribe who we are, what we do, to whom we do it, by what means, in what context, and for what purpose.[5] I believe that academics have to be just as clear and deliberate about their attitudes toward the students they teach as they are about the theories they teach.

No doubt most academics hear, although in differing voices, many of the same words. My language is not unspeakable or inaudible for anyone concerned with education. No matter what qualifiers go with my professional designation, I am probably more like than unlike my colleagues. What does seem distinctive to the working-class academic is the persistence of past voices opposing present speakers, the antitheses refusing resolution, refusing synthesis, refusing even compromise. If finding a coherent identity is so difficult for me, one who has had an entire life as well as a career in which to reconcile the influences of hostile value systems, what must it be like for the students who come into our classrooms wholly unsuspecting, wholly unprepared for the changes we intend for them? Do they think these ends can be accomplished only by the death of the original self? Do they fear these ends will require the rejection of the original self?

My story suggests that education is not, in fact, a transformation. It is not a subtraction. Education is addition. As such, education sets up a dialogue among past, present, and possible selves. I have learned to value my internal conflict for the very same reason that I value debate in general: it pushes me to think and rethink what I believe, to inscribe and reinscribe who I am until I get it right. What I hope my students will learn from me is to live with and to revel in the unresolved tensions, to believe they will find a voice, a way to write their stories in the spaces left between the lines and in the margins of the traditional text.

NOTES

1. In *Ways with Words: Language, Life, and Work in Communities and Classrooms* (Cambridge: Cambridge University Press, 1983).

2. My brothers have always seemed blissfully unaware of the contradictions.

3. See, for example, Freire's *Pedagogy of the Oppressed* (New York: Continuum, 1970).

4. The terminology comes from Bakhtin's *The Dialogic Imagination,* ed. Michael Holquist, and trans. Caryl Emerson and Michael Holquist (Austin: University of Texas Press, 1981).

5. See the introduction to Kenneth Burke's *A Grammar of Motives* (Berkeley: University of California Press, 1945).

WORK CITED

Herron, Jerry. "Writing for My Father." *College English* 54 (1992): 928–37.

Part Three The Intellectual Worker/ The Academic Workplace

18

Workin' at the U.

Milan Kovacovic

My mother was a seamstress, my father a laborer. Thanks to the meritocratic tracks of the Republic, when the French school system still worked, I found myself catapulted into the high University. There, I made my way through the cracks of a schizophrenic system which nurtures both the same and its contrary. I now find myself among those in the faculty who are very critical of the University; in itself, the institution is a highly respectable spiritual principle, but its temporal incarnation is rather regrettable. (Marcel Gauchet, editor of the French intellectual journal Le Débat)

As a tenured associate professor of French language and literature, I am extraordinarily privileged, though not in income, for I earn only a modest living. My two college-age children fall in that vast American lumpenmiddleclass that does not qualify for financial aid yet cannot afford education, except on loans, scholarships, or disruptive concurrent employment. No, my privilege derives from another source, incomparably more important than money: my matchless working conditions. Furthermore, I am able to appreciate them fully and not take them for granted. Prior to ending up in my present enviable position, I also experienced the opposite, on what I expected would be a permanent basis. A proletarian background gives one a perspective on things.

Hubris aside, and knock on wood, I now enjoy solid employment security and, according to Teachers Insurance and Annuity Association actuarial tables, decent odds for longevity, although these two historical characteristics of the college teaching profession are eroding, the first under the assault of budgetary retrenchments and right-wing ideologies (tenure is already abolished in the UK), the second following the intrusion during the late 1970s and early 1980s of pathological levels of stress in this previously genteel occupation. During that period, ambitious, aggressive, insecure public universities in the broad IIA ("Comprehensive") AAUP category, such as the one in which I teach, as well as many private liberal arts colleges, succumbed to delusions of grandeur and began to emulate the ever more demanding and capricious "publish and/or perish" dictums of the established IA research centers, whose number of approximately thirty was, ironically, beginning to be considered excessive at the same time. On the heels of unfettered capitalism, the successful professor came to be defined as an individual entrepreneur with allegiance only to his or her career. The most effective way to prove one's worth or gain leverage was to obtain an employment offer from a competing institution. Loyalty became an archaic value. In that context of reduced emphasis and rewards for the nonportable, difficult-to-evaluate commodity of teaching, undergraduate education was viewed as a nuisance and its quality plummeted while its cost to students climbed tremendously, with greater increases yet projected for the future unless the excesses of the past twenty years are corrected in the academic perestroika looming on the horizon. However, as with the perverse effects that followed the collapse of bureaucratic communism, the forthcoming upheavals in academe may also result in the destruction of whatever pretense of access and excellence remains in public higher education.

A tacit compact of low demands and low expectations has set in, between faculty trying to juggle their various responsibilities within the infamous "reward system" (thus only nominally paying attention to teaching) and students employed long hours to defray the cost of their degrees (and perforce only nominally involved in their studies): "Just give me my diploma and let me out of here!" The disparaged cafeteria curriculum of yesterday may soon look like an educational cornucopia; it is giving way to spartan fast-food fare consumed in small portions at a snail's pace. Whereas in most countries a college degree requires three years to complete, the traditional four-year American baccalaureate now listlessly drags on to five, six, seven years at most public urban universities. Meanwhile, shades of class polarization: some of the elite US private institutions are beginning to offer turbocharged three-year programs.

While I deplore certain aberrations in the recent professional trends, particularly the new "productivity" expectations for tenure-track faculty and the grossly unfair three-tier stratification (tenured, tenure-track, temporary) that prefigured the disturbing evolution in the general economy toward marginal employment (it's not always honorable for universities to play a vanguard role), I have nonetheless benefitted greatly from the climate favoring writing and research, which I enjoy fully as much as teaching. The problem is how to make those activities compatible because, facile rhetoric to the contrary notwithstanding, they aren't. Perhaps the solution lies in providing alternating periods of full engagement in each rather than simultaneous halfhearted attempts at both.

Still, personal complaints seem unbecoming at this point. Tenure, which I was fortunate to obtain in 1980 before the full onslaught of the current insanity, gives me the option of determining my activities freely and thus maintaining my self-esteem and integrity at some tolerable cost to my career. And my working conditions are truly incomparable! To wit: no boss, no dress code, no shift work, no weekend or holiday duties; summers off, plus quarter breaks; a private office in a clean, quiet, well-heated building (no air conditioning needed in my region) with a direct telephone line, voice mail, and the Internet for instant communication with colleagues from France to Oregon; in my office, a wide window that opens on a vista of sky, lake, lawn, and foliage; reserved parking less than sixty yards away; swimming pool and recreational sports facilities, if I care to use them (I haven't for the past thirteen years, but it's nice to know they're available); university letterhead and mailbox; some secretarial support and use of a sophisticated photocopy machine; a captive audience of bright young people presumably eager to hear me think aloud; social if not financial status, allowing entry, if desired, to all levels of society; and not least, a readily available community of colleagues, some of whom have "nevertheless" become friends, as we facetiously say in the profession.

Or perhaps not so facetiously, as intimated by the quintessential, hence revealing, academic joke about the professor who receives a get-well card in the hospital following a heart attack: "The Department wishes you a speedy recovery. Signed: Five for, three against, one abstention." In the strange mix of cantankerous individualism and groveling submissiveness that characterizes the culture of academe and the temperament of its denizens, one finds little evidence of working-class solidarity. (In fairness, it must be recognized that the instinct to organize has also diminished, if it has not disappeared, in society at large.)

This lack of solidarity bothers me deeply. At my institution, which is better than most on this point, a collective bargaining agreement has been in place for more than a decade. But the egalitarian spirit of syndicalism remains conspicuously absent. Department heads, who are fellow union members and therefore simply *primi inter pares,* continue to evaluate their peers yearly for merit pay, which is added to base salary and grievable only at the dean's level; by ranking their colleagues, the department heads, without bearing any managerial accountability, thus collaborate in the predictable (and intended?) generation of horrific divisiveness, disgruntlement, and conflict. It is well known that academic politics are particularly vicious because the stakes are so small. Thank God professors are not physically brutal; most campuses would erupt spontaneously into mini-Yugoslavias. In the case of salary distribution, the monetary amounts are often too insignificant (I have seen differences as small as $29 per year) to qualify as merit, yet symbolic enough to create paralyzing demoralization, particularly when compounded over time. It is pathetic to see presumably intelligent Ph.D.s wasting so much time, effort, good will, and energy on endless administration, discussion, evaluation, and grievance over such a patently dysfunctional nonsystem. It leads one to agree with Ralph Nader in his critique of standardized testing that SAT/GRE-type intelligence can have severe gaps or shortcomings. The bewildering salary wars at my institution also reveal a certain level of immaturity; after all, most academics are people who have never left school.

In my long and indecent enumeration of advantageous working conditions at the university, I have overlooked two additional important ones: the possibility of obtaining sabbaticals or travel grants and the unparalleled freedom of scheduling and movement. I am restricted to a specific place, the classroom, only eight hours per week, MWF, and even there I can sit, stand, or walk as I please. My office hours are likewise self-defined and hardly burdensome. Utopia!

Indeed, I am given the means to lead a dignified life, free from the relentless dehumanization that so many people endure simply to earn a living. And as regards my relatively enfeebled purchasing power (considering the enormous length and cost of training required for this profession), I am sheltered from embarrassment or ridicule by a tradition of tolerance for eccentricity in the absent-minded professor. Thus, if my bicycle (yes, a bicycle, at age 50, weather permitting), shoes, or sweater are not of the latest fashion or if they are somewhat ragged at the edges, it is not because I am a pauper to be pitied but because I have no time or care for such trivial concerns. My mind is occupied with much more important intellectual matters, for instance the examination of La Rochefoucauld's seventeenth-century maxim: "Contempt for riches was among the philosophers a hidden desire to avenge themselves from the injustice of fate, through scorn for the very things of which they were deprived; it was a secret way to protect themselves from the humiliation of poverty; it was a devious means of obtaining the consideration they could not get through riches" (#44).

Truly, I have no right to complain when I think that so many people earn their living as I once did, from unhealthful if not dangerous occupations, on graveyard, swing, or rotating shifts, in freezing or scorching surroundings, under artificial light and deafening noise, doing repetitive, monotonous tasks, watching the clock tick away the seconds until the first fifteen-minute coffee break, until the thirty-minute unpaid respite of lunch, until the second fifteen-minute coffee break, until quitting time or mandatory overtime, until retirement decades away, and death shortly thereafter. That's for the lucky ones who have full-time jobs with fringe benefits such as health insurance and a two-week paid vacation yearly.

The only industrial injury I face as an academic is the risk of contracting "tennis elbow" from excessive or improper keyboarding. (How embarrassing to hear this diagnosis from an orthopedist specializing in sports medicine!) OSHA seldom finds the need to intervene in the university, although lack of complaint is not necessarily a good indicator of satisfaction. Americans, notoriously litigious in most other realms, feel they have no rights in the economic arena and are therefore surprisingly tolerant of substandard working conditions. For instance, this is the only country in which supermarket cashiers find it normal to stand rather than sit. "Take it or leave it" is the most widely accepted principle of US labor relations. In that context, grumblings about windowless offices or foul-smelling labs tend to be viewed as frivolous.

While tendinitis or torticollis are extremely painful, debilitating, even disabling ergonomic ailments afflicting countless sedentary employees lashed to computer screens, myself included, they are not qualitatively comparable as occupational hazards to the threat of silicosis that I endured for an entire year in my first full-time job immediately out of high school at Ace Metal Refinishers in Chicago. This exhausting and filthy work required wading, to the din of compressors, into swirling clouds of pumice powder and lacquer spray in order to clean and refinish the metal surfaces on the façades of various downtown buildings. We worked from scaffolding enswathed in dingy tarps, often at night so as not to inconvenience the nattily dressed office workers. I can still feel the abrasive dust filtering into my sleeves, down my collar, and through the face mask, irritating my nostrils, and leaving grit between my teeth, my eyelashes itchy from sticky sweat, red hair turned white before midshift in the powdery mist. And, supreme humiliation, this was not even a heroic, essential blue-collar undertaking like coal mining or steel-beam riveting but mere cosmetic work to make the metal surfaces shine brightly, at the expense of my and my co-workers' lungs.

Nor is any academic ever required to ask permission to go to the restroom or then have to endure the boss's snide remarks adding insult to indisposition, "Come on, shammer, what's the matter wit' you, you already went twony minutes ago," as I did in my next job, an immeasurable improvement over the first, this time loading freight, baggage, and mail into airplanes at the San Francisco International Airport.

Not a single day goes by that I don't count my blessings, that I don't cherish the wonderful working conditions prevailing in my beloved second home, the cinder-block Humanities Building, whose architectural blankness I no longer even notice much less bemoan. Not a month passes that I don't retrieve my doctoral degree from its hiding place on a shelf between the pages of a large atlas, like a veteran digging out his bronze star periodically from a shoebox for reminiscence and inspection. I gaze with disbelieving and grateful eyes at this parchment of genuine sheepskin, which I own only because it came free with my generous fellowships at the Claremont Graduate School, an oasis of Mediterranean tile roofs, coconut trees, orange groves, and flaming bougainvillea framed against blue skies and snow-capped mountains on glorious smog-free January days in the L.A. basin. I contemplate the beautifully calligraphied document, similar in importance for me to that of a union card for a journeyman bricklayer, and I give thanks for this miraculously acquired passport into the paradise of academe where I belong like a fish in water, although my integration to the professional class has been far from seamless.

I continue to see myself simply as an intellectual worker. Some obscure atavism still compels me to inscribe a (w) instead of an (o) before my university telephone number. Similarly, I am uncomfortable with the title of "professor," which I use only on my IRS Form 1040 in the hope of avoiding audit in the years when I have professional expenses to deduct. My more accurate in-house title of "associate professor" is beginning to feel tarnished after thirteen years in rank, the equivalent of lieutenant colonel in the army, "Lite Bird" patiently awaiting to be deemed "Full Bird." I prefer to be called "teacher" or perhaps "college teacher" or better yet "educator," although I am aware I could not withstand the crushing workload and confinement of high school teaching in this country. Or, if it didn't sound so snobby in English, "*professeur*," which in French democratically encompasses all the above designations.

I know academe is my place; I belong here, I claim ownership, I am not a usurper, even if, admittedly, I got in through the side door at the right time, as a former student, now locked out from similar opportunities, likes to remind me. I feel at home in the university, at all hours, unlike most of the regular front-door entrants who are either more "normal" than me or less attached to the campus, from which they flee at the first chance. I can't really blame them; the place does look like a factory. My uneducated but highly intelligent mother, bless her soul, could not comprehend why I might stay inside those uninviting buildings during off hours, nor, conversely, how I could leave my place of duty with such impunity any time I felt like it during the 8 A.M. to 5 P.M. period Monday through Friday.

My indulgent wallowing in two seemingly antithetical values, freedom and security, should not be misconstrued. As a privileged academic, I work hard, very hard, damn hard, incredibly hard, much harder than imaginable. I work all the time, as do many of my colleagues, who lament that they feel caught on an ever-accelerating treadmill.

Just as self-censorship is the most insidious kind of control, self-imposed work is the most demanding. Fortunate are the tenured academics who lack intellectual initiative; possessing limited financial means but much leisure time, they become adept do-it-yourselfers or notorious hobby-ists with exquisite skills in woodworking or other crafts. At the campus club dining room, they describe their latest home improvement projects and elicit exclamations of awe, sighs of boredom, or glares of envy from their less handy colleagues. I have no time, resources, or inclination for such distrac-tions; I stand resolutely at the other extreme: the rain gutters on my house will forever remain unsightly, and I have no garage in which to tinker nor any plans to build one. My only hobby is reading, active, semi-recreational reading that then becomes part of my work, itself devoid of boundaries. I make no attempt or pretense at balance. If anything, I want to focus my life even further and eliminate all remaining distractions. And instead of im-ploring the clock to make the interminably tedious minutes tick by, my eyes are transfixed on the calendar, on the avalanche of faraway deadlines that suddenly loom close as I anguish over the scarcity of time and the realization that I will leave a number of projects unfinished, or even unstarted, in this lifetime.

My personal and professional lives have melded; I have survived for years on a regimen of five hours' sleep per night. I interpret this as evidence of absorption in a very satisfying occupation, not workaholism, although my family and friends might disagree. One thing is certain: I cannot possibly work more than I do.

I live in a frenzy. Or maybe I don't live at all. Still, I would not trade my present existence for my former one, when work stopped the instant I punched the time clock. I fantasize that when my current writing projects are completed, I will teach and do nothing else. Enough of this demented pace; "Teach well and be kind" will be my humble goal, the one I had when I entered this venerable profession. Or perhaps I will only write and not teach at all. That prospect sounds appealing, too, although I would miss the social contact and the ready forums for my musings. Trying to juggle both writing and teaching and doing neither fully is what drains me. The most fatiguing work is the work not done, the work postponed. At any rate, I will do considerably less, and soon. My current pace is not sustainable much longer.

But even a reduced level of activity would necessitate plenty of work. Serious teaching is consuming; it requires endless effort and energy. It is by definition always incomplete, imperfect, yet, paradoxically, this lack of finality, this need for constant reevaluation, is also what makes teaching such a fascinating and rewarding endeavor, like artistry or parenting. Only the teacher is aware of the shortcuts taken, what could have been done, should have been done, might have been done, even when the evaluations look good.

In the meantime, caught in the treadmill, I try to accomplish too much and experience mainly exhaustion and frustration. A friend once admonished me: "You cannot be a good husband, father, friend near and far, teacher, writer, scholar, engaged citizen, and homeowner. You have to choose. You have to accept being mediocre in some areas, you have to neglect or drop some roles." At the time, unbeknownst to him, I was also trying to be a dutiful son to my invalid mother. The same friend, then beginning his fifth and penultimate year of probation and trying to publish his seventh article out of the ten expected for tenure, had concluded his exhortation to me with a wistful confession: "You know, this horrendous workload is destroying my marriage, but it's also sure as hell keeping me from even the slightest temptation to engage in any new relationship. This profession is becoming suitable only for single people without family responsibilities." Still, as a tenured academic, I could not imagine a more desirable occupation. I felt that although my friend's assessment was right, mine was not wrong.

Through luck and some wild quirks of fate I have thus become a member of what John Updike, uninformed about the pettiness of campus politics and transcending even ethnic identity in his Ghanaian son-in-law (an educator like Updike's own father), calls the "international race of teachers and artists, . . . people who are at home with pencils and paper, with the tools of education and art . . . peaceable, reasonable people, who value civilization and trust it to offer them a niche" (172). Updike's description of the benign universal race of teachers and artists does ring true, however, when compared with the ferocious ways of the business world, although yet another perceptive joke has it that in the corporate world, it's dog eat dog; in the academic world, it's the opposite.

That I would seek, much less find, such a niche is utterly astonishing to me. The academic profession is exceedingly difficult to enter, the sacrosanct terminal degree a daunting prospect for a self-supporting, isolated working-class person with dependents. Earlier, I could not have imagined undertaking such a journey, nor did I even aspire to. I had set out into the world of work with only one expectation: Perdre ma vie à la gagner (To lose my life while earning it).

It hadn't begun that way. In fact, from childhood I was destined for an intellectual career despite my proletarian origins, a social trajectory not infrequent in France at the time.[1] My parents were Slovak guest workers in Normandy, and my father died shortly after my birth. Since my mother could not care for me in her employment as a live-in maid, I was boarded with an elderly peasant couple, Pépère and Mémère, in a village without even a steeple. We had no folklore, no religion. Our traditions were extraordinarily simple. This raw, unencumbered living created an organic spirituality: earth, meadows, clear river, morning dew, the temperate ever-changing Ile-de-France sky. We were poor, bought little, owned nothing, yet felt no lack. I attended a one-room primary school directed by an extraordinary teacher in the civic tradition of the Third Republic, Madame Mercier.

Madame Mercier had an incalculable influence on my destiny. She arranged for me to get a French government national merit (all-expense) scholarship, and at age ten I found myself catapulted (a word often used by those who have shared this experience) to the prestigious residential lycée for boys at Saint-Germain-en-Laye, an upper-class suburb of Paris. The distance of only forty miles from my archaic peasant third-world, which had not changed in centuries and where I still had not encountered a toothbrush, to the sophisticated, exclusive world of the lycée turned out to be the longest voyage I have experienced in my entire life. At that time, only 10 percent of any generation in France received a secondary school academic diploma, the baccalauréat, and private institutions were for students who had failed out of the more elite public sector, such as my school represented. Besides the French bourgeoisie, a number of my classmates came from prominent native families in France's then waning colonial empire—Indochina, Arabic North Africa, black Africa. By age thirteen, I had completed three years of Latin, three of English, one of Spanish, and I was studying trigonometry and discovering Baudelaire-Verlaine-Rimbaud. I had racked up all the first prizes in the humanities and was enjoying life at boarding school thoroughly. It allowed for greater camaraderie, better study conditions, more fun, faster maturation, and wider autonomy than our day-school classmates could experience at home.

Meanwhile, my mother had gained new self-taught skills and had become employed as a live-in cook for a wealthy Jewish family, the Kapferers, in whose Parisian mansion at 64 Avenue Henri-Martin, one of the most exclusive addresses in all Paris, I resided on weekends and during school vacations. I was tracked for the royal road, under the dual patronage of the French welfare state and the Kapferer family, whose household of thirteen included a live-in domestic staff of six, plus me. My proletarian background did not limit my horizons. After the brutal transition from the "primitive" living conditions in the village, I had quickly assimilated to the ways of the high bourgeoisie. I partook of its prerogatives, its refined manners and tastes, even its styles of clothing. (Every year, when my age-mate Alec Wildenstein, grandson of the Kapferers, returned to Paris from his family's principal residence at the Hotel Pierre on Fifth Avenue at Central Park, I inherited his New York wardrobe. Later, in 1970, when he was twenty-nine, his purchase of a Velázquez painting for $5.5 million would pulverize all price records in the art world.) I straddled the upstairs/downstairs divide. I had become a *petit Monsieur.*

But just before my fourteenth birthday, in 1956, my mother decided to emigrate to America on a whim based on abysmal ignorance that I did not counter, being, like her, of an adventurous if not reckless nature. That fateful move proved to be disastrous for both of us. I lost my two powerful French protectors and my mother an irreplaceable employer.

My adaptation to American schooling entailed a dizzying regression. Accustomed, without being aware of it, to rarefied levels of culture, I suddenly had to adjust to pervasive mediocrity and ambient anti-intellectualism. I discarded my reddish-brown leather schoolbag and my beloved Parker fountain pen, which had been my appendages since I first entered the lycée. They now looked ridiculous and were no longer needed. Unable to find anyone to share my enthusiasm for poetry, jazz, or the lyricism of great cities, I repressed my sensibilities, lost interest in school, and gravitated toward delinquency.

Four years later, the American dream was in a shambles. At age eighteen, I faced adult life with no skills, no project, no perspective for the future. In my group of teenage friends in Chicago, I was the only one to graduate from high school. Allergic to the classroom, my New World buddies had all dropped out the day they turned sixteen. They then worked episodically as construction laborers or forklift operators or at similar unskilled occupations. They drank beer, hung around, played baseball, made girls pregnant (avoiding those who had brothers, uncles, or shotgun-wielding fathers), and otherwise carried on the rest of the time. They had tattoos all over their arms and potbellies by their early twenties. A number of them died in alcohol-related accidents or languished in prison. The rest survived in a permanent cycle of hires, layoffs, and rehires. No great future, but you could actually make a halfway decent living in America in the 1960s, even marginally aspire to support a family, on one and a half or two jobs. Ironically, the oppressive task of polishing metal in Chicago was considered one notch higher in the working-class hierarchy than those "bottom-of-the-ladder" occupations; it was a semiskilled activity requiring a high school diploma. I was a victim of my better qualifications; I envied the easier life of my drop-out friends. All of us so totally lacked ambition that we did not even think of joining the military to improve our lot . . . until we got drafted, in my case at age twenty-three, in 1965, in the first wave of conscripts for the Vietnam War. The rate of rejection for physical and mental deficiencies among draftees, and even more among volunteers, was so high that it gave Congress and the Johnson administration the impetus to pass the Great Society education and nutrition programs for "national security" reasons.

Sometimes I wish I were Jewish or Armenian or Palestinian or a member of any of the diasporas that, because of the vicissitudes of history, consider knowledge the only worthwhile possession. All my overwork would be appreciated, even revered, in a milieu where education and culture are valued for their own sakes. But I am marked by my roots and my environment; my European peasant origins and the anti-intellectual atmosphere of American society inhibit me from accepting intellectual recognition easily.

I remember my otherwise beloved peasant mentor Pépère vituperating in a populist mode about politicians: "Those people don't know what work is. All they do is talk talk talk and go to banquets. They need to learn what it feels like to handle a pick and a shovel. That would straighten them out." Leaving for the lycée was for me a wrenching but necessary separation from Pépère, who wanted me to continue to attend Madame Mercier's school until the mandatory age of fourteen and then to take up some worthwhile manual occupation in the village. In his deeply organic view of the world, "living" and "working" were indistinguishable concepts. The literary critic Roland Barthes was not far off the mark when he wrote in a celebrated essay that authoritarian regimes, reflecting a sizable segment of public opinion, would reserve for the "idle, lazy, harmful" intellectuals (the regimes' blanket definition) the ultimate concrete, quantifiable work: digging holes or piling up rocks (185).

Given my background, I am often assailed with doubt about the validity and usefulness of my endeavors. I do nothing concrete or tangible, the results of my work are not evident, even to my "superiors" (I repeat, they're not my bosses—the difference is enormous), as reflected in their salary and promotion decisions regarding me. At Ace Metal Refinishers, I would have simply exorcised my anger about unfair treatment with a cathartic "Fuck 'em," but I have forgotten how to speak so clearly since learning the polite, prudent, articulate, obfuscating language of the university.

And I am troubled by guilt about how I acceded to this edenic world of academe. Given the disappearance of ecclesiastical orders, the military has until now been the only option for male upward mobility through credentials; not much has changed since Stendhal's nineteenth-century novel *The Red and the Black*. In my case, sadly, I have to thank the Vietnam War, for which I was drafted like so many young men of my generation simply because I was of the working class, hence not a student eligible for deferments or counseling. But instead of getting shipped out to lose my life, limbs, or mind in the swamps of Indochina in 1965–67, as were nearly all of my comrades from basic training company B-1-4 at Fort Ord on California's Central Coast, I was assigned by a benevolent Pentagon computer to the beautiful town of Würzburg in West Germany, in the heady days when one twenty-five-cent quarter was interchangeable with *ein Mark,* which got you *ein Bier,* a real one, served from tap in a half-liter stein with a thick head of foam on it, not the sloshy stateside stuff. In my new hilltop quarters at Leighton Barracks across the valley from twelfth-century Schloss Marienberg, I also took advantage of the freedom from responsibility and the break with the rat race of the civilian world to put my life in order and to begin gathering college credits through University of Maryland extension courses and by correspondence through USAFI in Madison. By the time I finished my two years of military service, I had accumulated ninety-nine quarter credits. Not much of an "undergraduate experience," but under such decadent circumstances and so favored by luck, how can I not harbor massive survivor guilt?

After release from the military, I was eligible, like all veterans, for the GI Bill. I returned to work part-time (with top pay scale and full benefits acquired through six years' seniority. How times have changed!) at the San Francisco Airport and registered as a student at California State University-Hayward, which I chose over San Francisco State because it was slightly closer to home and there would be no ocean fog and less traffic for the seventeen-mile commute. Even if for the wrong reasons, it was a fortunate choice. At Hayward, I met a professor, Elie Vidal, who encouraged me, restored my confidence, raised my expectations. To alter a destiny, a few words, so rare, were sufficient. His were clear, committed, decisive: "You must do a doctorate." Details had no importance; the essential, complementary conditions of *personal* (Elie Vidal) and *institutional* (GI Bill and fellowship) support were in place. *Each is nothing without the other.* Earlier in France, I had likewise progressed only because of help from both a personal advocate, Madame Mercier, and an institutional patron, the French government.

Married and with two children, I completed my studies by pooling fellowships, GI Bill benefits, and income from airline employment. I received a doctorate of arts in French studies from the Claremont Graduate School and became a *professeur,* which I think had been my calling ever since I first sat in Madame Mercier's schoolroom back in the village in Normandy. Teaching experiences at various public and private institutions, including the "selective" Pomona and Scripps Colleges in California and Carleton in Minnesota, and two years of living in a racially integrated housing project for low-income families in Los Angeles served to complete my contrastive social education, as did repeated travels on free passes between the United States, France, and Czechoslovakia and thirteen years (1961–74) of observing contemporary civilization from one of its best vantage points during the period of the sixties, the San Francisco International Airport.

But during my moments of vulnerability, instead of considering myself a teacher/writer/scholar who has attained statistically singular achievement against forbidding odds (i.e., a terminal degree and a tenured position), I feel more like a social parasite. The attitude of society at large also contributes to this occasional malaise of mine. Americans basically disdain education: "Those who can, do; those who can't, teach." Or: "If you're so smart, why aren't you rich?" And woe unto the high-achieving student: She or he faces ostracism at school. How can the United States be surprised about its education crisis and low academic standards when such attitudes prevail?

Once, a few years after I had become a professor, I returned to Chicago and was visiting a blue-collar tavern with a former friend who introduced me as his "now successful" buddy from old metal-refinishing times. He asked people standing around us at the bar if they could guess my new line of work. Someone suggested I put my hands up so they could be examined. No sooner had I done so than a derisive voice piped up, "Hey guys, lookit, with smooth hands like that, this dude can't be doin' diddly shit, he don't work at all." For a fleeting moment my sense of shame was greater than my recoil from the stupidity of the statement. Once poor, always poor; it's in your genes.

Another time, I had driven my daughter Laurie and her friend Ann to their Suzuki group violin lesson. Seated in the parents' row in the classroom, I was doting on the blissful sounds coming out of all those miniature violins and reflecting on the casual comment I had overheard from Annie in a giggly conversation with Laurie on the way to the lesson. She had said, in a matter-of-fact tone that left me stunned, "I wonder what musical instrument my sister is going to learn when she turns six like me." While pondering the social implications of Annie's statement and the distance from my own childhood experience, I noticed among the group of parents a former student of mine who had brought her niece there.

"Well, how are you doing?" I asked the now suddenly thirtysomething student in a tentative voice.

"Great!" she exclaimed. "I have a FAN-TAS-TIC job. I'm a buyer for the Emporium department store!"

"Congratulations!" I replied enthusiastically, relieved that she had not joined the ranks of the underemployed college graduates of generation X, as so often happens these days, to the point that I feel uncomfortable going to the shopping malls and franchise restaurants where I am forced to confront my privilege and to envision impending generational warfare, when anyone over fifty holding a full-time job with benefits will be slated for execution by the rampaging underemployed youth, Khmer Rouge style.

I was mulling over this delirious scenario when, after a long silence, the former student turned to me and asked, like an afterthought: "And what about you? You still workin' up there at the U.?"

Finally, I remember a third consciousness-raising episode, a visit to a student teacher in a fifth-grade classroom. She had introduced me proudly as her university professor and asked the children if they had any questions they would like to ask me about French culture or any other topic.

A wall of hands shot up. I pointed to the pupil who had lurched forward the fastest, both arms in the air, pleading, "Me, me, me, please."

"Okay, you're first," I said.

"Can you tell me how many hours you teach each day?" asked the boy about eleven.

I gulped, unable to believe what I was hearing. Could this possibly have been his family's topic of choice at the dinner table? "Those damn professors up there, all pinkos, teaching so little, eating up our tax dollars."

"Three hours," I lied, after some hesitation, omitting also to rectify the daily frequency implied in his question; furthermore, I felt compelled to add an apology, this time the truth: "But I also take a lot of work home."

Why am I so defensive, why this bad conscience? I will match any highly paid business executive with the mental energy I expend, what with the study abroad programs I have developed (and which were deemed useless if not detrimental to my career by a former dean), the international exchanges, the new courses, the countless requests for letters of recommendation, the "none-of-your-business" controversies (such as, during the early Reagan years, pointing out to the university the fact that some full-time faculty were eligible for free surplus-cheese distribution, having personally missed the qualifying mark by a few hundred dollars), my 542-page bilingual social autobiography manuscript, etc., etc. My work has by no means been only contemplative; much of it has entailed leadership, initiative, organizational skills, negotiations at ministerial and foundation levels. Still, I cannot satisfactorily explain what I do, nor can I expect anyone to understand how hard and how much I work, short of spending an entire day and night at my side, and that would amount to outright punishment, for it is not in the least interesting to watch an academic at work (unlike a welder or a cook or a beautician): "Wanna come over and see me think and write?"

In the midst of my frantic busy-ness, the lingering doubt sometimes pops up: "Wait a minute. Stop. Is what you do of any use?" For a long time I thought that this might be only groundless working-class paranoia, equating usefulness with ditchdigging. But no, I was right all along, I do have genuine cause for concern. One of the biggest shocks in my life came when my own campus administration, not some fascist regime as predicted by Roland Barthes, proposed to eliminate the entire Department of Foreign Languages and Literatures in one fell swoop! Goodbye French, German, and Spanish at a time when a huge Airbus (largely Franco-German) maintenance base was being slated for construction in this community and when world as well as US cultural diversity initiatives were being touted by the university. I would have become "redundant," as the British say, but thanks to tenure would probably have continued to teach in another field for which I was deemed qualified, perhaps remedial English composition. In ten weeks' time, I'd have to teach "writing" to university students who had attended at least twelve years of schooling in their own native language but had not yet mastered its syntax and often professed an unabashed, coddled dislike for reading. Good luck!

Fortunately, the local campus decision was overturned at the more enlightened system-wide level. So much for decentralization. A cut of one-third was ultimately imposed the following year, through attrition and the reduction of tenure-track commitments, after resistance had been worn down. It is too late to defend academe from the "barbarians" outside the gates; they are inside, in positions of leadership. Access to quality public higher education, such as I enjoyed at Cal State-Hayward in 1968–71, may soon become a memory of the postwar decades ("the thirty glorious years," as they are called in France), a unique, short-lived period that featured two other anomalies in human history: danger-free sex and middle-class aspirations for all. As we witness the dismantling of the welfare state and approach the twenty-first century at breakneck speed on the electronic information super-highway, it's full steam back to the nineteenth, with foreign languages deemed suitable only for the upper classes and the underemployed young staying at home to care for their aging parents.

NOTE

1. See Baillargeon's interview with Marcel Gauchet.

WORKS CITED

Baillargeon, Stéphane. Interview with Marcel Gauchet. *Le Devoir* (Montreal, Quebec), Aug. 17, 1992, 9.

Barthes, Roland. "Poujade et les intellectuels." *Mythologies.* Paris: Seuil, 1957.

La Rochefoucauld, Francois, duc de. *Maxims.* Trans. L. W. Tancock. Harmondsworth: Penguin, 1967.

Updike, John. *Self-Consciousness.* New York: Knopf, 1989.

19

Class, Composition, and Reform in Departments of English: A Personal Account

Raymond A. Mazurek

It is 6:00 A.M. Alone with a cup of coffee and my electronic typewriter, I am sitting in an office of a research institute at one of the small elite colleges of New England. As of two years ago, the average yearly expenses for students here, according to the catalogue, amounted to over sixteen thousand dollars. I make roughly thirty-two thousand dollars teaching at a state university very unlike this older one that serves my present employer as a kind of model.

This New England college sits on a hill at the edge of a small mill town, just as in earlier times the wealthiest farmers chose the highest ground for their homes. Walking in the grocery ten minutes by foot down the hill, I see other sorts of people: men of color in blue T-shirts, unshapely couples from the white working class. At the college, young people dress as casually but with a different style, imitating an earlier archetype. It might be twenty years earlier, when the culture's unconscious erupted into the American Dream.

Twenty years ago, I left another New England mill town and headed for a different college on a hill in Maine, escaping the suffocating love of a family just above the poverty line. Except for the family move from Chicago to New England when I was three years old, the 165-mile ride from home to college had been the longest trip of my life. The young woman I had ineptly tried to pick up at the first orientation party had spent her summer in Africa.

Now twenty years later, 1990, I am sitting at a desk in a prestigious New England college. In front of me is a picture of my mother, who seventy years ago quit school in the eighth grade to work in a textile mill. Her story is not mine. I belong here, and I do not. I will always hear the whispering voice that Mike Rose mentions in *Lives on the Boundary* telling me that I don't really belong, whatever the outward signs. The stories of class have failed us, children of the working class, both the Horatio Alger and the Marxist stories. The stories of work and class must be reimagined and retold.

It is 1981. A year out of graduate school, I have accepted my second "visiting" job: I am one of the fifteen visiting (i.e., nontenurable) assistant professors in a department of fifty. We teach four courses a semester; everyone else, three. We have no merit raises. Our jobs are referred to by the dean as part of the "floating bottom." After we organize to complain about our plight—in tones that are hardly militant, in an organization that is informal and ad hoc—attitudes of other faculty toward us become more ambivalent, and this comes to a head later in the year during the search for a new department chairperson. The younger, controversial candidate had many strikes against her, the most serious being the belief among senior faculty that she "promised" us visitors something, would ally herself too much with us. A series of "safe" choices as department chair follow, and our positions are replaced gradually by attrition: tenure-line or full-time faculty with master's degrees who will not complain replace us. It is a kind of victory. But only one of the fifteen eventually makes it to the tenure track at this university; years later, all of those I remain in touch with have had troubled careers. Few achieve tenure. Those of us who have "made it" spent energy on our own writing, energy stolen from heavy teaching loads in jobs that officially had no research requirement. Commitment to teaching was negatively rewarded.

Sitting in the library on a Saturday afternoon that first semester, surrounded by critical books, wondering at how much life it would cost to devote oneself to writing them.

It is the late eighties. I'm teaching at a two-year campus of a major university with publishing pressure plus teaching loads as high as four courses a semester. There is an out, however; one can get grants to hire a "substitute," a part-time teacher to cover part of the composition load. Some part-time faculty teach as much as full-time faculty in a given year or more. Part-timers and our attitudes toward them fill many moments of conversation. Colleagues comment: "They *choose* to do it, so for us to say they're exploited would be patronizing." (Or if the market is functioning, there can be no exploitation except in the mind.) "Most of them are doing as well or better than we are." (Or they have husbands who subsidize our department.) "I don't care who teaches it [composition], so long as I don't have to." (Or I'm burned out, and that's all that matters, sorry.) These are the comments of colleagues who have come through similar years of underemployment, some as full-time "part-timers" themselves.[1] To varying degrees we experience our present jobs at a two-year campus as underemployment, and, like many professors at lower-status institutions, most of us are from working-class or lower-middle-class origins. All of us, though to varying degrees, feel ambivalent and uncomfortable about the part-time situation, which we are officially encouraged to ignore. We grasp hesitantly at the tainted means of professional respectability and survival.

Graduate school—the least prestigious department in the Big Ten, perhaps the most camaraderie among faculty and students and almost certainly the most easily available TA positions. There were many grad students from famlies that never did that well financially, probably more than at most graduate schools, and a sharp division between our "work" (writing and research) and our workload (teaching two or more sections of composition a semester).

Back in the research institute, another fellow, politically radical, comments: "I prefer to lecture; I like the performance. Teaching small classes to undergraduates is a waste of time. Twenty-year-olds don't know anything." The teaching load at research universities like the one where she works is approximately one-half my own.

When I was growing up, my father worked in a nonunionized shoe factory in Lawrence, Massachusetts. I entered a liberal arts college in 1970, during the height of scholarship availability, and received a Ph.D. in American studies and English in 1980. Most of my teaching has been in rhetoric and composition.

That I received a Ph.D. at all is statistically unlikely, but that I would wind up tenaciously clinging to tenure at the bottom of the pack, in terms of prestige, in a hierarchical profession like English studies is not. As Jake Ryan and Charles Sackrey point out in *Strangers in Paradise: Academics from the Working Class,* the thousands of working-class academics who were assimilated into US higher education in the years after 1945 tended to be concentrated in lower-status colleges and universities. "Late arrivers on the professional scene, for the most part, end up somewhere toward the bottom of the prestige scale of the profession, if for no other reason, they are affiliated with second rank institutions" (77). Their book has been a great help to me in making sense of my own experience, which, if not representative, is far from unique.

Combining sociological analysis with the anonymous personal narratives by twenty-four academics from working-class origins, Ryan and Sackrey's work reveals the deep-seated ambivalence of those who have migrated from the working class to the professorate. Although some of their informants assimilate quite happily and a lucky few retain strong roots in both their communities of origin and academia, anger and alienation are more characteristic responses of those who have internalized class conflict. Academia is a culture very conscious of status where, unlike most professions in contemporary capitalist culture, "prestige replaces wealth as the mediating value" (Ryan and Sackrey 76).

> For academics, criteria such as publication record, prestige of the institution of association, how little or how much one teaches, one's pattern of collegial association (cosmopolitan or local), are the conventional symbols of status. Consider the opportunities for self-loathing to discover that it matters little that one has climbed out of the depths of the social order to make "something" of oneself, only to find that again one can end up at the bottom of a much approved heap, but nonetheless a heap and there is a bottom. . . . To put the matter more broadly, capitalist social relations *always* have a few at the top and the many at the bottom. Access to the top is masked as simply a matter of meritocratic selection rather than as inherited advantage. Those who hold sway in the academy are invited to be self-congratulatory, even pompous, and the persons at the bottom are encouraged, if not by persons by circumstances, to be envious, self-abnegating, or invisible. (Ryan and Sackrey 78)

As Ryan and Sackrey point out, the contradictions of the academic hierarchy are internalized; this is felt more sharply for many working-class academics than for children of the middle class, who grow up with more understanding of the internal workings of the professions and who start the competitive process with more advantages.

At lower-level institutions such as the one where I presently work, identifying with research and struggling to find the time to do it may be ways to continue to have an intellectual life or ways to continue to be taken (a little more) seriously within the profession (conferences, journals, colleagues at other institutions, that still-possible-next-job-if-the-market-improves). At none of the three institutions where I have taught did commitment to teaching provide a source of intellectual community, despite occasional efforts by some faculty to try to build some such sense, despite the fact that I teach mostly rhetoric and composition, which is probably unique among academic disciplines in producing a rich scholarship on pedagogy. Yet pursuit of this scholarship, ironically, takes me away from the local campus (with the exception of my own classroom) and toward intellectual communities dominated by those who teach rhetoric at research institutions, who have light teaching loads. I say this less to manifest sour grapes (though that sourness, within and beyond my personal biography, is in a sense my subject) than to point to the way class hierarchies structure even the most lowly and despised areas within the contemporary university.

Rhetoric and composition provides a rich example of the prevalence of academic hierarchy, for it is a field that has always been an important part of the college English department, yet it, like the working-class academics (and others) who staff composition courses, has usually been "envious, self-abnegating, and invisible." As Richard Ohmann noted in 1976 in *English in America: A Radical View of the Profession,* a work that has contributed even more to my self-understanding than *Strangers in Paradise,* the English department is large at most colleges and universities because of the perceived need for courses in rhetoric and composition, but this field is barely acknowledged as a respectable one by its members, who link their professional status to literary scholarship. As universities developed into research institutions, literary scholarship provided the "scholarly rationale of the field." Thus: "It was natural for faculty to want to teach literary scholarship as well as study it and indeed, that this kind of teaching came to be seen as the most important, the most central, teaching we do. Hence, the familiar paradox that the part of our job that justifies us to others within and outside the profession is the part we hold in lowest regard and delegate to the least prestigious members of the profession" (243). The existence of a large "underclass" of composition teachers—graduate assistants and part-time teachers and some permanent instructors, mostly women—throughout the twentieth century has been well documented in recent years in the work of James Berlin, Robert Connors, and others. As courses in rhetoric came in the late nineteenth century to emphasize writing rather than speaking, many professors of rhetoric left the profession for literature, which lacked the heavy grading requirements of the new composition courses.

But something else was also at work: composition was less attractive than literature not only because of the heavier paper load but also because of its perceived intellectual thinness. As Berlin points out, the perception of rhetoric as a nonfield resulted from a positivist epistemology that reduced the teaching of writing to teaching a few basic patterns of organization and grammatical correctness: composition was concerned with referential discourse; rhetoric was not formative of worldview but secondary to positivist science, which generated accurate pictures of reality to be reflected in rhetoric. Literature, meanwhile, studied the complex, the symbolic, the rhetorical sign exiled to the imagination.[2] These views of rhetoric—and the very existence of composition as an always-denied presence within college education—were socially functional in a new historical period. As Ohmann notes in *English in America* (and later in *Politics of Letters*), at the end of the nineteenth century and the beginning of the twentieth, the formation of corporate and government bureaucracies on a larger scale than had existed before demanded a new white-collar workforce. The new white-collar workforce needed to process written information and thus to learn to write. The German model of the research university was grafted onto the American small college to produce research workers and corporate bureaucrats. But the university itself was staffed by workers driven by the same need for professional status as the other members of the new white-collar class. Within English departments, the drive for professionalism resulted in a literature faculty that marginalized the composition courses that made it the largest faculty group in many universities.

While the composition that was taught in such universities was—and still is—often intellectually thin, "its thinness is socially useful" (Ohmann, *English* 160). Reducing rhetoric to basic patterns of organization and correctness, driving critical thinking in its fullest sense (with reflection on the rhetorical situation of the writer within her culture and history in all its rich complexity) outside the composition course (and into literature, history, and other liberal arts courses) is useful to the bureaucracies that need white-collar workers. For they need workers who will think critically and ask questions—but only to a certain extent.

English in America, very much a product of the 1960s whose historical insights it summarizes, attempts to link the thinness of freshman composition to the administered thought, manifest in documents like *The Pentagon Papers,* which refuses to question the assumptions of the organization. While a failure to be sufficiently self-critical is as much a problem on the Left as the Right, among marginalized groups as well as large organizations, much in our recent history suggests the accuracy of the connection Ohmann made between an intellectually limited approach to composition and the needs of the military-industrial complex. The sixties were a flowering of critical thought and of the liberal arts. During the recession of the 1970s, those who pursued liberal arts education were penalized economically in favor of those who possessed more specialized career training. But now it appears that this denigration of the liberal arts has gone too far; the corporations themselves bemoan the "cultural illiteracy" of recent graduates.

The decline of the liberal arts has everything to do with class, for it did not occur equally at all US colleges. At elite institutions the liberal arts continued to thrive in the 1980s:

For Wesleyan students (and for those at Yale, Stanford, Wellesley, etc.) there is *still* no penalty for pursuing the humane and pleasant activity of reading good books and trying to understand the world. These students have a reserved place waiting for them in either the professional-managerial class or the ruling class, some by virtue of having made it into an elite college, most by birth and nurture. They will land on their feet, even if they think they are risking downward mobility by studying Shakespeare instead of biochemistry. The class system, I suggest, is becoming more firmly etched as the crisis works its way out. (Ohmann, *Politics* 12)

The late 1980s and 1990s have admittedly experienced a limited rebirth of the liberal arts that has filtered down to lower-status institutions, and this has included many forms of intellectually sophisticated composition courses based in critical thinking, classical rhetoric, and cultural studies, tendencies that began as early as the 1960s but that have recently accelerated. This new liberal arts is politically sophisticated, willing to situate itself historically by looking at its embeddedness in power relations structured by race, class, and gender. Thus it is also subject to attack: the radical university professor has become one of the new villains in popular discourse on the right.

A small part of this criticism may be justified (the Left has always had its share of foolishness), but for the most part this reaction appears to result from a fear of the strength of a revitalized Left in touch with the growing multiculturalism of US culture and on US campuses. The Left may be in the process of reforming itself using the tools of Marxist class and ideological analysis in combination with other (feminist, minority, ecological) discourses and without the historical blinders and blunders of Marxism—a hope for the cataclysmic rebirth of utopia, a denigration of the discourse of human rights and democratic participation which appears to me the necessary core of any humane politics.[3] Such reform must, it seems to me, strive for moral consistency at the local level, reviving one of the most positive features of the social movements of the 1960s, hopefully without the self-righteousness and humorlessness that sometimes characterized those movements. A major part of such a revival, however, would be renewed attention to problems of class, including the hierarchical relations among college teachers and the degraded status of teaching within the university.

Academics on the left would do well to examine their own workplaces critically and even to take some of the criticism raised by the Right seriously. It is too easy to dismiss shrill but popular works such as Charles Sykes's *Profscam*, which attributes the problems of higher education to professors' selfish avoidance of teaching and their support of meaningless, trivial (and often left-wing) research. In his attack on the professorate, Sykes shows little understanding of the workloads many professors face (we do not work only the nine or twelve or six hours a week during which we teach, obviously) and makes less attempt to understand the specialized discourses of the academy. (Would Kant or Plato be less open to reductive attacks in the popular press if Sykes quoted them rather than Derrida?) However, he does touch on an important issue, as suggested by chapter titles such as "The Flight from Teaching" and "The Crucifixion of Teaching." The content of those chapters may be exaggerated and distorted, but the underlying issue is real. The Right is exploiting some of the academy's real weaknesses: its tendency to despise and denigrate teaching, to glorify publication and research, to build national and international research communities while professors labor in isolation, unable to communicate to colleagues across (or even within their own) disciplines.

For all their apparent populism, right-wing critics like Sykes (and like that more famous right-wing populist, Ronald Reagan) forebode a greater control of the academic workplace by outside bureaucrats and the triumph of managerialism. Previously, managerial control over the university was extended through the adoption of the research model; now, research and tenure are increasingly envisioned as the privileges of a few faculty. The remainder will be without the limited autonomy of tenure and subject to work speed-ups and quantitative evaluations by managers with little understanding of college teaching. The triumph of the research model in higher education was partly the result of, as Ryan and Sackrey argue:

> the rise of managerialism in U.S. Higher Education. . . . Since the bureaucratic institutions thrive on a clearly defined hierarchical order, the maintenance of such an ordering of status depends fundamentally on the same simple set of evaluative criteria that are readily quantifiable. What better device could one hope for than the published article, a discrete unit of evidence which can be offered as proof of productivity and quality? Other preferred measures of faculty worth are similar in their "concrete" quality, such as numbers of grants obtained, the dollars attracted to the campus, consultantships, and also quantified student evaluations of teaching effectiveness. (81)

The triumph of the Right would bring a further consolidation of managerialism—increasing the quantity of teaching hours and reducing the amount of research in fields other than science, technology, and business while also increasing control over the professional lives of academic workers. In some fields, such as rhetoric and composition, the proletarianization of the academy is already a reality.

The logical response of faculty to these tendencies would appear to be some sort of workplace organizing—a difficult undertaking in view of academics' view of themselves as professionals (not "workers") and a hollow one if it means organizing privileged workers (tenure-line faculty, researchers) regardless of the interests of others (unprotected full-time and part-time teachers).

These difficulties in reforming the academic workplace are readily seen in rhetoric and composition. As composition has grown in both respectability and power, composition and other English studies journals such as *College English* and *College Composition and Communication* have published many accounts of the hierarchical power relations of the profession. A movement toward reform was evident by the end of the 1980s in such key documents as the 1987 "Wyoming Conference Resolution Opposing Unfair Salaries and Working Conditions for Post-Secondary Teachers of Writing" and the 1989 "Statement of Principles and Standards for the Postsecondary Teaching of Writing." These documents grew out of the spontaneous demands to be taken seriously by underemployed teachers who attended the 1987 Wyoming Summer Conference on Composition, demands supported by prestigious scholars and other more secure members of the profession. As described by Linda Robertson, Sharon Crowley, and Frank Lentricchia, the 1987 Wyoming Conference was apparently a rare moment of solidarity and frank discussion of working conditions among people who occupy very different positions in the English studies hierarchy. The 1989 Conference on College Composition and Communication (CCCC) Resolution that eventually resulted calls for reasonable teaching loads and renumeration, as well as professional status, for teachers of composition, connecting their workplace demands to the intellectual demands of teaching an intellectually serious course in rhetoric.

It would be an exaggeration to say that the 1989 Statement of Principles and Standards has had no positive results. It has furthered the process of reflection and debate in English departments on the situation of composition and has provided a means for educating administrators. However, the tangible results have been less than encouraging. Although discussion of class, caste, and composition has continued, the situation of composition teachers in 1994 is essentially the same as it was in 1987. It is a revealing point that the 1989 resolution was conceived as a statement of *professional* standards. It is perhaps inevitable that a professional organization like the CCCC will resort to the ideology of professionalism in an attempt to further its goals, but the resolution is hollow without some means of censuring those who do not comply with "standards" (and will *all* U.S. colleges need to be censured? Ninety percent of them?) or some other means of enforcing those standards. Are "professionalism" and the petitioning of administrators to enforce professional standards sufficient ralllying points for organizing the academic workplace? Or will real progress be made only with more militant manifestations of solidarity, such as unionization?

Without solidarity within departments of English, the 1989 statement will be a failed attempt at reform. My experience, however limited, indicates that such solidarity rarely exists: at all of the universities where I have taught, tenure-line faculty have been slow to accept nontenurable faculty as colleagues. Literature faculty have tended to denigrate composition and those who teach it, and those who do research have tended to dismiss teaching as of secondary importance. Some of these divisions emerge even in well-meaning reactions to the 1989 statement. Department chairs such as Robert Merrill voice the fear that enforcement of the statement would mean that literature professors at research institutions would have to teach more (154–58). Merrill's fears are well grounded, for some such shift in work-load, including an increase in teaching and a decrease in scholarly "produc-tivity" by the same faculty, would be a good thing *if* it meant a lighter teaching load (and full-time status) at the opposite end of the hierarchy. But the possibility to enact such changes exists only if there is sufficient solidarity—if, for example, a critical mass of tenured research professors felt enough identification with those farther down in the hierarchy and enough real rewards in a renewed intellectual community at the local level to be willing to teach a bit more.

However, English departments have achieved *some* solidarity, and at-tacks on tenure in hard times may produce more of it in a profession increasingly self-conscious about the centrality of politics to its subject (which is not merely literature but also language and its uses throughout history, or, as Stephen Mailloux has argued, an expanded notion of rhet-oric). As the 1991 "Progress Report from the CCCC Committee on Profes-sional Standards" noted:

> Between 1972 and 1986, the percentage of English PhDs finding tenure-line work dropped from 93% to 40%. During this period there was a concomitant drop in the number of faculty lines. This erosion was justified by the assertion that enrollments in the late 1970s and 1980s would de-crease so drastically that postsecondary institutions simply could not afford to continue their tenure-track commitments because there would soon be no students to teach. But between 1972 and 1986 enrollments in colleges and universities *increased* significantly. (CCCC Committee 334)

The erosion of professional privileges such as tenure has already begun: it is implied in both the rise of managerialism and the right-wing attack on the professorate. In this situation, the reassertion of traditional rights will not be sufficient. Academics need to develop more recognition of their own class divisions and more identification across class lines, more attention to teaching and to the value of all their work—not merely their so-called real work in research and publication.

Part of the impetus for reform can come from the values of solidarity and community that represent the best in working-class experience. Difficult to achieve, they can best be worked toward by engaging in local struggles and by also remembering the intellectual values and retelling the personal stories that brought us (from whatever class background) to the academic profession.

English in America, that classic work on academic hierarchy, is structured around a paradox, the paradox of reform, which can apparently only be secured at the local level through broad-based social transformation. Recounting his own mixed success after going into academic administration in the 1960s, Ohmann writes:

> Hundreds of hours of committee work, and less than exhilarating results. Working from the "other side," I expected to have a more persuasive leverage (maybe even more power) and to further the interests I knew my faculty colleagues to share. But instead of finding them allies in the attempt to humanize scholarship, make the word "community" less empty, and strengthen liberal education, I met chairmen and others asking for increases in departmental size, trying to pull out of interdepartmental courses, proposing specialized Ph.D. programs, and asking for increased research budgets and reduced departmental teaching loads. Department competed with department, humanists with scientists, and everyone with the administration. And yet these were the same friends or colleagues who, over a drink and a cup of coffee, shared by and large my own views on the college and our work. There must have been influences upon their acts, other than the general ideas they expressed and presumably believed. And, of course, I began to see the same contradictions in myself. As I invoked the general welfare, I was often just evoking professional, academic interests. (21)

Attempting to act on the desire for academic community, Ohmann encounters an institutional structure designed to meet the needs of professional advancement, institutional aggrandizement, and, most powerfully, the needs of institutions outside the university. What he encounters is the invisible wall around our thoughts and practices constructed by ideology. *English in America* concludes by calling (as did another major book on the left published in 1976, Bowles and Gintis's *Schooling in Capitalist America*) for a democratic socialist revolution in the United States. Institutional reform will not come, Ohmann tells us, without broader societal reform. Today calls for democratic socialism seem to raise as many questions as they answer; post-Marxist Leftists such as Bowles and Gintis recognize the need to balance the demand for a society that funds human needs with one that recognizes local autonomy and even the benefits of a market (Bowles and Gintis *Democracy and Capitalism*). Attempts at local change encounter resistance rooted in attitudes and ideologies (such as professionalism, the importance of individual advancement) shaped by previous experience and the multiple social pressures experienced within the broader social context, yet the social order will never be challenged except through movements for local change. At a time when the Left is reimagining and questioning what a desirable social order would look like, local struggles are particularly important.

So, too, is memory—the remobilization of history in a culture based on programmed forgetfulness in a continuous present. American culture has always tended to deny the realities of class. Academics might begin the process of reeducating others about class and other insidious hierarchies in their culture by reexamining their own workplaces and their own memories.

It is 1963. Along with other children from Holy Trinity School, I am marching in formation, holding a toy American flag in a parade "For God and Country." All the schools in Lawrence, public and parochial, are marching today. Bands play, politicians and clergy make speeches, but I remember nothing of those. I do not even remember what the nuns told us about why we were marching, though they must have told us something.

When I was a senior in high school I remember Mr. Maloney saying something about the days when Communists were common in Lawrence and people were shot in riots near the mills. (He sounded ambivalent toward those "Communists," and later that year, spring 1970, he seemed gleeful in reciting to us the names of colleges and universities on strike.) But it was only when I attended college a few years later that I learned about the Lawrence textile workers' strike of 1912, how thousands of workers, Italians and Poles and Russian Jews and workers of a dozen other nationalities, had left the mills in protest against a wage cut. With the help of IWW organizers, these conservative immigrants—or were they conservative then? It is hard to imagine Lawrence workers otherwise—produced the "Bread and Roses" strike, the IWW's most famous triumph, along with Paterson, in the eastern United States. Following a march celebrating the victory, a conservative Irish priest organized a countermarch, "For God and Country," against the strikers and their anarchist leaders.

Polish Catholic kids, we marched on the fiftieth anniversary of our grandparents' and great-grandparents' triumph, marched against our ancestors' victory. My own grandfather, who died before I was born, had moved to Lawrence just before the strike and had worked in the mill. What would his memories have been? Did triumph fade in fears of not assimilating?

Years later, in the late 1970s, Lawrence is rediscovered, and my friend David sends me a *New York Times* clipping. A reporter had traveled to Lawrence to try to find descendants of the strikers. Among them he is looking for the children of Carmela Teoli. Not a strike leader, Carmela Teoli was partially scalped in the mill as a young girl, spent months in hospitals, and testified during congressional hearings on working conditions in Lawrence. First Lady Helen Taft was in the audience on the day Carmela's testimony was recorded, and it appeared prominently in newspapers across the country. But when the reporter found Carmela Teoli's daughter, a woman in her fifties, she had no knowledge that any such thing had ever happened to her mother. The reporter had restored part of her history.

Why had Carmela Teoli never told? Was her story something to be ashamed of, her story of the working class? The pain of work written on her body, the story taken to her grave.

NOTES

1. My somewhat sarcastic parenthetical comments notwithstanding, there is some validity to all of these remarks, especially the first, which points to the difficulty of "speaking for" another.

2. See Berlin, *Rhetoric and Reality;* Berlin, "Rhetoric, Poetic."

3. See Bowles and Gintis, *Democracy and Capitalism,* for an elaboration of this view.

WORKS CITED

Berlin, James. *Rhetoric and Reality: Writing Instruction in American Colleges, 1900–1985.* Carbondale: Southern Illinois University Press, 1987.

——. "Rhetoric, Poetic, and Culture: Contested Boundaries in English Studies." In *The Politics of Writing Instruction: Postsecondary,* ed. Richard Bullock and John Trimbur. Portsmouth, N.H.: Boynton/Cook, 1991. 23–38.

Bowles, Samuel, and Herbert Gintis. *Democracy and Capitalism: Property, Community, and Contradictions of Modern Social Thought.* New York: Basic Books, 1986.

——. *Schooling in Capitalist America: Education and the Contradictions of American Economic Life.* New York: Basic Books, 1976.

Conference on College Composition and Communication. "Statement of Principles and Standards for the Postsecondary Teaching of Writing." *College Composition and Communication* 40 (1989): 329–36.

——. "A Progress Report from the CCCC Committee on Professional Standards." *College Composition and Communication* 42 (1991): 330–44.

Connors, Robert. "Rhetoric in the Modern University: The Creation of an Underclass." In *The Politics of Writing Instruction: Postsecondary,* ed. Richard Bullock and John Trimbur. Portsmouth, N.H.: Boynton/Cook, 1991. 58–84.

Mailloux, Steven. *Rhetorical Power.* Ithaca: Cornell University Press, 1989.

Merrill, Robert. "Against the 'Statement.'" *College Composition and Communication* 43 (1992): 154–58.

Ohmann, Richard. *English in America: A Radical View of the Profession.* New York: Oxford University Press, 1976.

———. *Politics of Letters.* Middletown, Conn.: Wesleyan University Press, 1987.

Robertson, Linda, Sharon Crowley, and Frank Lentricchia. "The Wyoming Conference Resolution Opposing Unfair Salaries and Working Conditions for Post-Secondary Teachers of Writing." *College English* 49 (1987): 274–80.

Rose, Mike. *Lives on the Boundary: The Struggles and Achievements of America's Underpaid.* New York: The Free Press, 1989.

Ryan, Jake, and Charles Sackrey. *Strangers in Paradise: Academics from the Working Class.* Boston: South End Press, 1984.

Sykes, Charles J. *Profscam: Professors and the Demise of Higher Education.* New York: St. Martin's, 1988.

20

Complicity in Class Codes: The Exclusionary Function of Education

Irvin Peckham

Writing specialists have necessarily been concerned with the purpose of writing instruction because by identifying our professional purposes, we are identifying ourselves. We are drawn toward altruistic claims. We say we want to empower students through writing (Elbow), that we want to teach them how to discover the world through language (Britton), that we want to uncover the means by which language shapes their illusions of self and world (Berlin). It has also been popular to turn the question of purpose toward the needs of the society in which instruction is embedded. We frequently hear discussions, for instance, about how we must prepare students for rational participation in a democracy. Code words like *rational discourse, citizenship,* and *democracy* ring like the Liberty Bell down through the years in public statements of the purposes of writing instruction, generating both sympathy and economic support.

Certainly, these kinds of laudable motivations keep many of us in the classroom, but underneath these publicly acceptable objectives lies an unacknowledged purpose that contradicts our surface reasons for teaching writing. In this essay, I want to explore this unacknowledged purpose, which I interpret as the exclusionary function of writing instruction. This exclusionary function is not, of course, unique to writing instruction; it reflects the exclusionary function of educational institutions that reproduce the existing social structure by screening out students from the working-class and consequently reserving for the children of the professional and managerial classes the privileges that attend academic success.[1] I am concerned as a writing teacher with this exclusionary function because composition classes serve as primary screening devices. Marked by linguistic and cognitive habits revealing their socioeconomic origins, students have to squeeze through the first-year writing classes in particular before they can even begin to run the gauntlet constituting higher education.

By working-class students, I mean students whose parents have not received college educations. Their parents are either skilled or semiskilled laborers. By professional/managerial class students, I mean those whose parents have received college degrees and are either professionals or employed in managerial-level positions. These categories are obviously not inclusive. Many groups of students fall, shall we say, below the working class, many are in between the working and professional/managerial classes, and many are above the latter. In making these distinctions, I am marking class by reference to people's education and working situations only. Class categories are, of course, more complicated than such an assignment suggests. They can be assigned according to a multiplicity of variables and according to the relationships between these variables.[2] I have chosen these variables and categories, however, to emphasize the differences in environments that either complement or conflict with the values and language of the academic community. I do not imagine writing teachers are implementing either a conscious agenda or one that is directed only at working-class students. Surely, most students feel they are being excluded as they struggle to learn academic discourse conventions. There are, however, significant differences when the student has to break through a class as well as a developmental barrier. The central distinction is that students from the professional/managerial class are learning to think, speak, and write in ways that are reinforced by their homes and communities, while working-class students have to make significant breaks with their families' and communities' patterns of thought and language. Some working-class students will of course make the break and academically succeed, just as some professional/managerial class students will miserably fail. I am not pretending to identify determining factors of academic success or failure. I am writing only about significant trends. It is hardly any revelation that working-class students generally do not do well in school. In this essay, I want to shift the blame, if you will, from the students to the educational system that excludes them through its complicity in class codes.

Before discussing the exclusionary function of writing instruction, I need to open up my problematic situation of being a working-class academic addressing this issue. By identifying myself as a working-class academic who has more or less made it "in," I am congratulating myself for having overcome the impediments that generally keep members of my class out of academia. I am also perhaps excusing myself for not having made it "in" with more grace. In spite of the possibility that what I say might be self-interest disguised as altruism, I hope you will equally grant the possibility that I might be describing a very real exclusionary practice.

Before discussing in general terms how working-class linguistic and cognitive habits conflict with the values of educational institutions, I want to describe my working-class background. Although inserting my history into this text may be inexcusably self-indulgent (and characteristic of working-class rhetoric), I want to establish my authority, if you will, as a border crosser. I have some firsthand memories of what the old country was like, and these memories have unquestionably shaped my current vision and the mask I wear as I try to slip past the border guards into the new country of privilege.

When I was young, I thought the rest of the world (which, in my mind, extended about to Richland Center, Wisconsin, seventeen miles away) pretty much lived as I did. My parents, my brother, my sister, and I lived in a two-bedroom farmhouse with my grandparents. My parents and we three children slept in one large upstairs bedroom. My grandparents and their December child slept in the other bedroom. We did not have a telephone, running water, or, obviously, indoor bathrooms. Although I realized that some of the families on nearby farms were a little better off, I knew some were poorer, too.

My father worked in town as a mechanic during the day and helped my grandfather with the farm in the evenings and on weekends. My mother worked in town as a secretary. Despite her extra income, our family was unable to support the farm. In 1952, we had to sell it for—as my grand-mother was fond of reminding my grandfather—less than he had paid for it (with *her* money) in the late twenties.

After we moved from the farm and bought a house about a mile outside Richland Center, my father became an auto parts salesman. He was never happy in that job, and he seemed to move frequently from employer to employer. Although it has been a long time since I was a laborer, I can sympathize with my father, and I know why he usually came home tired and angry from his job. I have only to compare what it is like to spend one's day behind a counter with the boss more or less hanging over one to being an English professor. The comparison hurts my mind.

Paulo Freire would say my father internalized the image of his oppressor by becoming the authority at home.[3] His wife and children became there what he was at work. Although I would not say he was physically abusive (or at least not abusive in any sense that working-class families would understand), I was very much afraid of my father and his hand. I can remember wishing the afternoon would never turn dark, for then my father would come home. On those frequent evenings when he came home late, I would sit in the kitchen and watch the highway and hope that none of the oncoming car lights were his. If I may be honest, I can say that I spent many of these evenings hoping that he had had a car accident and that we would be free of his anger and oppression. I understand his anger and frustration now as displaced horizontal violence (Freire 48), but when I was young, I was simply afraid.

Language use in my home was characteristically unidirectional—our father telling us what to do. There was never room for discussion or negotiation; at best, we would ask questions, make requests, or defend ourselves. My father was basically an inarticulate man. He spoke in short sentences and used the "substandard" language of rural Wisconsin. His inarticulateness probably contributed to the violence that was always close to the surface. At home, he was incapable of coping with dissent. Rather than engage in dialogue, he would shout or strike out. He was striking out, it seems to me, at life that had failed to respond to him. That is what being inarticulate means.

My mother's language was more curious. She read widely to escape a life that had unexpectedly closed her in. Her reading gave her an eclectic knowledge and vocabulary of a special sort. She learned the meanings of many words from their contexts, but she rarely had a chance to use these words in her working vocabulary; consequently, she was uneasy with their use and pronunciation. I learned from my mother how to mispronounce many words and to use them in odd ways.

My mother also characteristically tangled her syntax, or, as grammar books are fond of putting it, she switched syntactic horses in mid-gallop. Her mangled syntax stemmed from her reading habits and her social environment. She read long, complicated sentences, but she did not get a chance to practice them. In *Teaching the Universe of Discourse,* James Moffett speculates that speakers gain skill in subordinating and embedding as a consequence of frequently engaging in dialogue, exchanging points of view with other speakers. But secretaries do not engage in this kind of conversation with their bosses. There may be some give and take in general workplace conversations about family life or the weather, but this is not the sort of intensely dialogic discourse of, shall we say, two compositionists arguing whether first-year writing programs should be overhauled or deconstructed. Employer/secretary conversations are directives, queries, and dictation —not much different, in fact, from the conversations that I heard my father and mother engage in at home.

My mother had one other language habit that drove me crazy: she was persistently aposiopetic—not as a rhetorical strategy, but as if she could not trust herself to complete her thoughts. She left them, as it were, for her interlocutors to complete. Later, after I had grown older and more critical of my mother's language, I might flinch at her mispronunciations and mixed constructions, but I could not stand those gaps, and I would leap in to complete them as if I were completing something in myself.

The linguistic and social milieus of my childhood represent a reasonably typical working-class environment. I was not deprived, but I had internalized a set of class codes that made it difficult for me to do well at the University of Wisconsin because the university professors, most of whom had come from a different class, had internalized a different set of codes that marked one's educability. Within a class, ethnic group, or discourse community, codes strive toward transparency in order to transmit messages, but between classes, codes may turn opaque. Double negatives, for example, signal an emphasized negativity in working-class discourse; for members of the professional classes, they signal ignorance, and the message is obscured by the overtones of cross-class dissonance. Similarly, when meeting people in mixed company, a working-class man shakes hands with the men and nods his head to the women; this is how he says hello and signals respect to the women. But if a man shakes hands with only the men in the professional class, he doesn't signal respect for the women. He may signal instead either his innocence, his working-class origin, or a latent sexism. In any case, the message he wants to send simply doesn't get through. It gets bounced back accompanied by some unfriendly messages from the intended receiver. That's how my messages were received in college: I tried to say shibboleth but missed the *h*. Sometimes I was told in unfriendly terms that I, a fugitive, should perhaps return to E'phraim.

I survived college, but I was never an academic star. I earned the kind of grades that traditionally propel liberal arts students toward the school of education rather than graduate school. At the time, I thought my few As, my many Bs, and my sprinkling of Cs were proof of my laziness or stupidity or both. Some twenty years later, I realize now that I was neither; my grades represented my membership in the class that is systematically weeded out by the unwitting functionaries of an institution that pretends to invite them in.

I am not ignoring the possibility that several factors cause mediocre academic performance. I am not claiming to cite even the most important factor. But I am claiming that class origins, as well as racial and sexual distinctions, are a significant factor in determining whether students are weeded out or invited into the privileged conversation. Working-class students are identified by their habits of language, thought, and social behavior, and these working-class habits are precisely the habits that professional/managerial-class teachers have learned to interpret as evidence of intellectual inadequacy.

The British sociologist Basil Bernstein, in "Class and Pedagogies: Visible and Invisible," has offered a detailed description of these habits and an explanation of how they are misinterpreted by teachers who belong to a different class. Bernstein was concerned about the liberal agenda of British schools associated with the open classroom, student-centered pedagogy, and what is now known as the whole-language movement. Bernstein argued that this kind of "invisible pedagogy" supported the sociocognitive habits of children who came from the professional/managerial class but conflicted with the habits of working-class children.

In *Politics of Letters,* Richard Ohmann has sharply criticized Bernstein's research. Ohmann was concerned about the deterministic implication that because of their immersion in rule-bound environments and restrictive language, working-class people would not have the cognitive tools necessary to initiate social change (280–93). Although I respect Ohmann's concern, his critique does not alter the reality of different codes of behavior at different levels of the socioeconomic hierarchy. These are the codes that Bernstein—quite accurately, from my experience—tries to describe.

My move is not only to transport his thesis across two decades and an ocean but also to push it to different levels of education. My argument is that the "liberal" sociocognitive habits characteristic of the professional/managerial class are increasingly valued at increasingly higher levels of education, a consequence of the teachers' class origins. Although few research projects have addressed the relationship between class origin and level of academic employment, the existing research shows, not unsurprisingly, that the higher the level of academic employment, the higher the socioeconomic origin. Working-class teachers will generally be found at the elementary and secondary levels (with women notably overpopulating the former). Academics with professional/managerial-class origins disproportionately constitute the professorate. Further, the more elite the institution, the higher the percentage of professors who come from the professional and managerial classes; working-class teachers who have managed to slip into the professorate will be more frequently found in community and state colleges than they will at Berkeley or Harvard.[4] I am suggesting that elementary, secondary, and college teachers value the sociocognitive habits that characterize their own classes. Thus, working-class students may do well at the elementary and secondary level but bomb out at UCLA.[5]

AUTHORITY

The fundamental assumption guiding Bernstein's analysis is derived from the work of George Herbert Mead, Edward Sapir, and L. S. Vygotsky. That assumption is that thought, language, and social structures are dialectically related. In the thought/society dialectic, for example, individuals are born into preexisting social structures that shape the structures of the emerging individuals' thoughts. Having unique twists to their thoughts, individuals to varying degrees reshape the social structures. This dialectical shaping and reshaping is sometimes characterized as an ongoing conversation between individuals and the multiplicity of social structures or discourse communities they inhabit.

Bernstein describes the working-class social structure as *position*-oriented and the professional/managerial class as *person*-oriented. The structure of the working-class family reflects the parents' work situations. Both at work and at home, working-class individuals have clearly defined roles determined by their positions. Lines of authority are firmly established and are rarely subject to rearrangement by negotiation. Children in position families have to assume fairly rigid roles that do not change in response to the individual's identity ("Socio-linguistic Approach" 153–55). The home, as it were, is rule-bound. It seems as if authority figures in this kind of home have learned to understand the world as composed of decontextualized laws that individuals must obey, so the parents teach their children to conform to a "law and order" social rubric. This was certainly the world of my father. In my naïveté, I would have called him a dictator. Now I understand that, having been told in his work to do what others told him to do, he was trying to prepare me for the "real" world as he understood it. He did not know there is another world in which people who understand the functions and origins of rules question them and reshape them to make them fit ever-changing situations—and, further, that in this other world, rule-bound thinkers get poor grades.

Whereas parents in position-oriented families have closely supervised jobs with a narrow range of responsibilities (the extreme would be a job in an assembly plant), professional/managerial parents have open-ended jobs with wide-ranging responsibilities. The latter are not closely supervised; indeed, many people in these kinds of positions might feel as if they are essentially self-supervised. Only in the broadest of contexts are they held answerable for their daily decisions (e.g., tenured professors whose rewards depend on their publications and consequent status with their peers). According to Bernstein, parents in the professional/managerial class bring their jobs home with them by creating *person*-oriented family structures in which roles are determined not by position but by who the individuals are, that is, by their *person*. Children in position-oriented families are required to *assume* roles, whereas children in person-oriented families *make* their roles. In position-oriented families, children are socialized; in person-oriented families, children and parents socialize each other ("Socio-linguistic Approach" 154). In position-oriented families, children have to respond; in person-oriented families, children learn how to create.

Bernstein points out that children from position families may do well—indeed, they may excel—in conservative schools with rigid structures and that emphasize memorization and drills, but in liberal schools dominated by an invisible pedagogy (invisible, on the one hand, because the teacher is not the eternal commanding presence at the head of the class and, on the other, because an invisible acculturation process is being taught), these students will not do as well as students who have come from person-oriented families ("Class and Pedagogies"). It seems as if the person-oriented family is itself structured around an invisible pedagogy in which parents are training their children to face the kinds of ambiguous, problem-solving situations the parents face in their daily lives. These are, in turn, the kinds of situations students encounter at the college level—or at least at the kind of colleges that grant doctorates.[6] So one might expect that students from position-oriented families would do well in schools that ask students to memorize, if you will, the meanings of others, but they will have trouble in first-rate universities that ask students to make their own meaning. The A students in universities do not memorize; they question. They know how to face ambiguity, how to accept responsibility, and how to make decisions. They create new meaning because they had to create their roles in their families. These are the students who are invited to go on to earn their doctorates, and then they, in turn, reward students who think like them—and who, not surprisingly, generally come from the same social class they do.

LANGUAGE

Working-class language also conflicts with the language students are expected to use in the school environment. Working-class students quickly learn that their and their parents' language is "incorrect." This labeling means that they and their parents are "incorrect." Although some working-class students may, for good reasons, resist "correction" of their language, themselves, and their parents, most learn to change the superficial linguistic markers of "substandard" usage: *ain't* becomes *am not, he don't* becomes *he doesn't,* and (significantly) *me* no longer occupies the subject position. But deeper linguistic habits, reflecting their position-oriented social structure, remain embedded in the working-class students' utterances. These habits hinder their abilities to speak and write in ways that are rewarded in school, particularly at the university level.

Bernstein traces these deeper linguistic habits to the communal nature of working-class families. They often live in extended families with grand-parents in the same house or apartment. Uncles, aunts, and cousins live nearby. Although Bernstein is describing British working-class families, his description fits my home exactly. Not only did I grow up living in the same house with my grandparents and aunt, there were more Peckhams than Joneses in the Richland Center area. Shirley Brice Heath documented the same communal nature of working-class whites in the Piedmont Carolinas. These working-class people know their family members and their neighbors well; consequently, they understand paralinguistic meanings conveyed by such things as tone and gestures that an outsider would miss. Indeed, at times utterances might be thought of as place holders with the real meaning of an exchange being signaled through other channels.

Bernstein calls this *public* language because the utterances themselves are *public* property—that is, everyone tends to use the same basic utterances ("Socio-linguistic" 129). Public language tends to be composed of short, grammatically simple sentences. Often the sentences are unfinished because the listener understands, due to the public nature of the utterance, what the rest of the sentence would be. The relationships between the parts of the sentence do not have to be connected by subordinate structures because the listener knows the relationships. Consequently, extended utterances are connected by strings of coordinating conjunctions. Public language relies on idioms and concrete language—the language of description and narra-tion. One will hear in public language few abstractions or generalizations that are hierarchically related ("Public Language" 42). This language corre-sponds with James Britton's description of *expressive* discourse, the kind of language in which the speaker (or writer) assumes a familiar audience who shares the speaker's language, experiences, and associations (82). It is the language that teachers try to "correct" by making writers aware of the neces-sity of communicating to an audience who does not understand the mean-ing in the gaps between sentences. It was the language of my home with my father's commands and my mother's broken sentences. And it is the lan-guage that working-class students have to overcome if they intend to suc-ceed in college.

The language of the professional/managerial-class students, by contrast, is the kind the professorate expects. Not only are the surface conventions "correct," but the structures reflect valorized cognitive habits generated by the social structure of the professorial/managerial class. Professional/

managerial families are individually oriented both at home and in their workplaces. Professional and managerial-class parents do not have the same kind of extended family or community relationships that working-class people do. The parents may live hundreds or thousands of miles away from their parents and extended family. They may move several times in their professional lives, and they may frequently travel outside the state and country. In the course of their moves and travels, they come into contact with people from radically different discourse communities with different paralinguistic conventions. Consequently, the parents cannot assume their audiences' familiarity with paralinguistic signals, much less with the parents' contexts.

Because of the variety and frequency of unfamiliar audiences at home and work, Bernstein claims that professional and managerial-class parents learn to rely on particularistic language to make their individuated meaning explicit. They need precise nouns and verbs; they need modifiers; they need to be able to engage in extended utterances in which the relationships of the parts are signaled by syntactic structures and appropriate subordinating conjunctions ("Public Language" 55). They need to be able to hierarchize and contextualize. Above all, they need to be able to recognize the differences in audience and adapt their discourses to different rhetorical situations. Bernstein calls this kind of language *formal* because meaning is contained in the structure (the form), in contrast to public language in which meaning is contained in the gaps. Professional/managerial-class parents, of course, teach their children to speak formal language, which is the kind of particularistic language expected and rewarded in school.

A POTPOURRI OF DIFFERENCES

Bernstein points to several other habits of thought and language that encumber working-class and favor professional/managerial-class students in student-centered classrooms. The same habits clearly work toward the advantage of professional/managerial-class students at increasingly higher levels of education. The authoritarian environment of the working-class students discourages them from questioning. The open, relativistic environment of the professional/managerial-class students encourages them to question. Because of the infrequent dialectical discourse in the home, working-class students do not learn how to qualify and substantiate assertions. Because of the focus on language, on establishing one's position through language, on linguistically explaining oneself to varied audiences, professional/managerial-class students learn how to clarify, qualify, and substantiate their assertions. Working-class students learn how to use only *public* language. Professional/managerial-class students learn how to use both *public* and *formal* language and all the varieties in between. Working-class students learn that there are right and wrong answers, and they need to know what the "correct" answer is. Professional/managerial-class students have learned that answers depend on the contexts of the questions. They are used to ambiguity, to open-ended situations in which one discovers not the "right" answer but the "best" answer for the moment. Working-class students learn to focus on content—the immediate meaning of a thing or situation. Professional/managerial-class students learn to focus on structure, to relate a thing to other things, to notice similarity and difference. One might say that working-class students learn only the values of their community; professional/managerial-class students learn to situate the values of their community within the values of other communities they have visited. They learn how to compare and contrast and through these essential cognitive strategies discover the kind of meaning that counts in academia.

I could elaborate on these and other differences, but I think (from behind my mask) that I have made my case. A constellation of linguistic and cognitive codes mark students according to their class origins. Although the educational institution professes to promote egalitarianism, to offer equal chances to all, it is implicated in a social structure that marginalizes difference. Because the professorate are generally from the professional/managerial class, they reward the linguistic and cognitive codes of professional/managerial-class students but interpret the linguistic and cognitive codes of the working class as signs of stupidity.

In writing classes, we are particularly implicated in this class-based screening agenda for we are experts at evaluating students via their texts. We have been trained to valorize texts flashing with the class codes of the professional/managerial classes and to marginalize the texts betraying our students' working-class origins. We have been trained to marginalize the kinds of narrative and descriptive writing tasks that resonate with the working-class experience and to valorize the abstract, analytical writing tasks at which the professional/managerial-class students excel. We see the working class's over-coordinated sentences, their tangled syntax, their trite statements (characteristic of public language), their focus on immediate events and concrete experience, their inability to contextualize, generalize, and hierarchize through language, and we marginalize them with Cs or worse. We assume they can't think because they don't write and think like us. We weed them out by virtue of their texts.

CULTURAL LITERACY

I would like to add to these essential linguistic and cognitive differences the difference of "cultural literacy." The cultural literacy difference is manifested, to be sure, in working-class students' texts, but it seems to spread, in significant ways, further than writing classrooms. Cultural literacy differences reveal themselves in the entire ambiance of university life.

Working-class students, for example, will not be acquainted with Bartok or Van Gogh. If knowledge is predicated on experience, working-class midwesterners won't know what the ocean or mountains really are, for few of them will have traveled far from home, and New Jerseyans won't know the Mississippi from the Platte. Working-class students will not really know about airplanes, about the differences between the East and West Coasts, much less the difference between Yuba, Wisconsin, and Greece. Many professional/managerial-class students will know about these things from personal experience. They will have been to plays. Many will have been to concerts, operas, and ballets. I compare my daughter, a high school senior, to children who have grown up in South Omaha, the ghetto of white working-class children. My daughter is familiar with Puccini, the Weavers, and the Moody Blues. She knows more about literature and painting than I knew when I was a senior in college. She has frequently been in Mexico, twice to England, and once to Switzerland, France, Italy, and Greece. She has lived in a rural community in northern California, in San Diego, and now lives in Omaha. She is used to flying across the country by herself. She is conscientious, contentious, and fiercely self-disciplined. Coming up against the likes of my daughter, those kids in South Omaha don't have a chance—particularly since the educational system is *not* predicated upon equal education for all but upon competition with professional/managerial-class students starting from the fifty- and working-class students starting from the zero-yard line in the one-hundred-yard dash. And then working-class students are told the reason they don't win is because they are slow.

Granted, a few of us manage to break with our origins, denying our class histories as minorities have had to deny their ethnicity.[7] We are denying our "incorrectness" or the "incorrect" class into which we were born. I do not know how others manage the break, but I erased my incorrectness by infrequently going home. In time, I more or less forgot who my parents and siblings were. Although I hesitate to admit it, I must tell you that the only time my parents and I and my brother and sister have been together since I left home was for my parents' silver wedding anniversary. I suspect the next occasion will be a funeral. That's called erasure.

By sloughing off our working-class skins, we make it through college and become teachers. And some of us struggle through graduate school to become professors in third-rate universities. Beyond that, there may be the token geniuses who are hired in elite colleges or universities, but these are not many, for these positions are reserved by the elite for their children.

After all, there are only so many of these positions to pass around. And someone has to teach in the elementary and secondary schools, doesn't she? And someone has to sell auto parts for $5.95 an hour and get bossed around.

This is how I, as a working-class academic, see the picture of class discrimination in educational institutions. If I were inclined (which I am not) to attribute acts of will and cognition to social structures, I might claim that what we have here is a part of the organism retaining privilege for itself and its kind. It seems to me that although the educational institution claims to be promoting universal literacy and egalitarianism, it has embraced a system that institutionalizes difference, and through difference, failure, with the failed ones coming primarily from the working classes (the ones who have different habits of language and cognition). One could not of course expect otherwise when it is the dominant classes who construct the norms by which one marks success and failure. We pretend the race is even, but I see it as fixed.

NOTES

1. See Ira Shor, *Critical Teaching and Everyday Life,* p. 2, for a summary of the "revisionist" interpretation of academic purpose.

2. See Pierre Bourdieu, *Distinction,* pp. 101–9.

3. See Paulo Freire, *Pedagogy of the Oppressed,* pp. 48–51.

4. See Howard R. Bowen and Jack Schuster, *American Professors: A National Resource Imperiled,* pp. 32–33, for a summary of the research.

5. See Mike Rose, *Lives on the Boundary,* pp. 174–75.

6. See ibid., pp. 187–91; and Shor, *Critical Teaching,* p. 24 and p. 77.

7. See Richard Rodriguez's autobiography, *Hunger of Memory: The Education of Richard Rodriguez.*

WORKS CITED

Berlin, James. *Rhetoric and Reality: Writing Instruction in American Colleges, 1900–1985.* Carbondale: Southern Illinois University Press, 1987.

Bernstein, Basil. "Class and Pedagogies: Visible and Invisible." In *Class, Codes, and Control.* London: Routledge & Kegan Paul, 1971. 116–45.

———. "A Public Language: Some Sociological Implications of a Linguistic Form." In *Class, Codes, and Control.* London: Routledge & Kegan Paul, 1971. 42–60.

———. "A Socio-linguistic Approach to Socialization: With Some Reference to Educability." In *Class, Codes, and Control.* London: Routledge & Kegan Paul, 1971. 143–69.

Bourdieu, Pierre. *Distinction: A Social Critique of the Judgement of Taste.* Trans. Richard Nice. Cambridge, Mass.: Harvard University Press, 1984.

Bowen, Howard R., and Jack Schuster. *American Professors: A National Resource Imperiled.* New York: Oxford University Press, 1986.

Britton, James, et al. *The Development of Writing Abilities.* Urbana, Ill.: NCTE, 1977.

Elbow, Peter. *Writing with Power.* New York: Oxford University Press, 1981.

Freire, Paulo. *Pedagogy of the Oppressed.* Trans. Myra Bergman Ramos. New York: Herder and Herder, 1970.

Heath, Shirley Brice. *Ways with Words*. Cambridge, Mass.: Cambridge University Press, 1983.

Moffett, James. *Teaching the Universe of Discourse*. New York: Houghton Mifflin, 1968.

Ohmann, Richard. *Politics of Letters*. Middletown, Conn.: Wesleyan University Press, 1987.

Rodriguez, Richard. *Hunger of Memory: The Education of Richard Rodriguez: An Autobiography.* New York: Bantam Books, 1982.

Rose, Mike. *Lives on the Boundary.* New York: Penguin, 1990.

Shor, Ira. *Critical Teaching and Everyday Life.* Boston: South End Press, 1980.

21

Is There a Working-Class History?

William A. Pelz

The working class has always been a problem for Western society and even more so for intellectuals and their institutions. Liberal capitalist society with its contradictory belief in political freedom and the free market has always been frustrated, if not infuriated, that the former has been utilized by workers to challenge the prerogatives of the latter. Traditionally, the two general defenses employed against labor, and particularly working-class intellectuals, have been repression or co-optation (*embourgeoisment,* as Europeans might say). More recently, a new tack has been taken and the problem is being resolved theoretically by mere denial: the working class is said no longer to exist.[1]

Any class society protects itself through control of the intellectual means of production. That is, those who own the material means of production control the production of ideas[2] and thereby limit the breadth of discussion while stunting the development of class consciousness. Rather than contribute to that discussion, the focus of this piece will be my observations as a member of the working class attempting to teach history within the confines of that quintessential class institution, the university.

Raised in a working-class district on the south side of Chicago, I went to the local public school, John P. Altgeld grade school, interestingly named after the most radical governor the state of Illinois has ever had. Altgeld was to go down in history as the man who exonerated the surviving Haymarket martyrs,[3] an act that alone was sufficient to earn him the undying hatred of the local business elite. Because I was part of the postwar baby boom, attending public school meant alternatively half days or having two different grades meet in the same room. This gave me an abundance of time to sit and read during school since the harassed teaching staff's main concern was that the classrooms of sixty-plus students should be reasonably quiet.

Ironically, not receiving much attention from teachers caused me to develop into a fanatical reader. By fourth grade, I was reading at the level of a high school senior. Spelling was another matter, however. Our family received the *Chicago Tribune,* whose quirky owner, Colonel McCormick, along with an affection for fascism,[4] had his paper spell words *his* way. Thus, I thought *through* was spelled "thru," and it took years before I spelled *sophomore* without an *f.* Therefore, I was lucky even to pass Language Arts many grading periods. After a certain point, my family was unable to be of great educational assistance as well. My father, a machinist and locksmith by trade, never finished high school. At least my mother, who worked as a teller in a local bank, had a high school diploma. Yet they, especially my father, instilled a love of learning in me. My father was particularly keen on taking me to the various museums in Chicago, which opened up to me a whole world far different from the streets of the South Side.

Although I was most certainly working class, I somehow thought I was middle class. Teachers kept saying that in America there were a few rich people and a slightly larger poor group and all the rest of us were middle class. Only when my parents made the (to me disastrous) move to the suburbs did I begin dimly to realize my class. It happened when I was attempting to register for high school. The "guidance" counselors, who appeared to me to be a rather dull-minded lot, kept insisting that I take vocational shop courses. I kept saying I wanted to take college prep courses, to which their reply was, "Be practical, you have to prepare for a job." When I pointed to my test scores, they only made strange faces and oblique comments about my "background." With my parents' backing, I won this struggle but not before I began to wonder about this "classless" America I lived in.

My suspicions were heightened in high school. I found many stupid, vapid, but ever so well-dressed kids in my college prep classes while even the most intelligent of my peers who had been confined to vocational hell wasted their days making bookends in metal shop or helping the auto shop teacher fix up his wife's car. By the end of my freshman year, I understood how the school's track system worked: It worked basically on class. No amount of stupidity or low test scores could prevent a business owner's kid from wasting space in college prep classes. Meanwhile, a friend of mine whose father was a truck driver had to fight to get out of the vocational track although he was later to get the highest ACT scores in a graduating class of around four hundred.

All the same, I did avoid the shop track, as did some of my friends. Thus, we left high school with many of our illusions about "classless" America relatively intact. After all, college was going to be different. Well, we were right. It was different, better certainly in terms of intellectual stimulation but worse in terms of the number of upper-class types we had to endure. Once more the class system was not completely spelled out, but it was apparent all the same. Seated in the library one day worrying about how I would find money to pay tuition next term, I overheard two students discussing their summer plans: "Well, Daddy wants us to go to India but I'm not into it. After all, there are so many *poor* people there."

During my freshman year, I also discovered fraternities or the "Greek system." I rather quickly concluded there was little essential difference between most "frat rats" and street-gang members . . . except fraternity members were "respectable" and richer than their poorer ghetto cousins. Moreover, I soon discovered that membership in certain frats was a ticket into an American version of the English "old boys" network. Graduate school proved to be more of the same. Not to belabor matters, I made it through the higher education system and finished as a Ph.D. in comparative labor history thanks to various government scholarship and loan programs—and no thanks whatsoever, I should mention, to the much-vaunted private sector.

Once I began teaching, I naively believed that I would be able to teach eager students history from the point of view of common people. Moreover, I thought that higher education in general and the history profession specifically were in the process of being transformed. I was inspired by the civil rights movement with its demand for African American history and likewise excited as women demanded their rightful (and historically truthful) place in history. I felt sure that this signaled the emancipation of workers' history as well. I was wrong.

A number of factors contribute to the ignorance of, if not destruction of, working-class history in our colleges and universities. Among significant factors are: (1) antilabor bias within American culture; (2) elitist attitudes, particularly among middle- and upper-class students; (3) class bias within most history textbooks; (4) antilabor attitudes among most faculty members bolstered by a shortage of working-class professors; (5) the inherent disadvantages for working-class students in college; and (6) the structure of the university as a probusiness (antilabor) institution.

There is a tremendous weight of the antilabor bias in our media. To cite only one medium, glance at television programs. As a study by the International Association of Machinists (IAM) found, there are hardly any workers shown on TV.[5] When they do appear, they are often buffoons or foils for middle-class professionals. In fact, this is becoming more rather than less of a problem in terms of misrepresentation. The words *union* and *racketeer* are almost always said in the same breath while positive images of organized labor are almost completely absent. Meanwhile, labor issues like lockouts, pay cuts, or unsafe working conditions are largely absent from television, bumped off the air by more pressing stories about O. J. Simpson or a man who wants to keep a Vietnamese pig as a pet in his million-dollar condo. Few notice the irony of a TV anchor making a seven-figure salary attacking public school teachers for greed because they average $38,000. As Larry Duncan of the Committee for Labor Access noted, "T.V. is full of sensational stories of human tragedy like murders or even homelessness but rarely will they find time to even mention hopeful examples of collective human struggle like one so often detects in a strike."[6]

When I was a child at least I had *The Honeymooners,* in which I recognized people like my family. It was a comedy but not at the price of demeaning working people. Later, there was the first *Bill Cosby Show* in which he played a high school teacher who lived a lifestyle not unlike that of my working-class peers. Now, the screen world appears to be populated almost exclusively with lawyers, doctors (Cosby's most successful incarnation), cops, and the like. True, there is *Roseanne,* but a quick read through *TV Guide* will prove her the exception rather than the rule. Why aren't there more shows featuring average workers? The networks have said that they aren't interesting, the same argument used for decades to keep African Americans and women off prime-time viewing.

An engrossing complement to the rare fictional representations of working-class people on TV is the news media's coverage of union battles where people are seen united in a common struggle. These collective ventures by workers have the possibility of demonstrating how individuals of widely diverse backgrounds can join together in the face of a collective enemy. Yet if the media does mention labor, it is almost always in a negative light. The sound bite usually stresses how some strike will hurt "the public."[7] Workers are thus either nonexistent or troublesome. This issue may seem tangential to the teaching of history, but whenever I discuss current workers' struggles with my classes, I find that the words of the media are often parroted back to me, sometimes word for word. ("It's the unions asking for more money all the time that has ruined the economy.")

More insidious is that the media shape the way students think about common people. For example, in a Western civilization class, I had a student argue that the Roman slaves should have been loyal to their masters rather than rebel and follow Spartacus in 73 B.C. His line of reasoning was based on a premise of flawless elitism. After all, he argued, it was the patrician slave owners who truly created the wealth that allowed the slaves to survive. Further, if they were really good slaves, their owners might free them in gratitude. This boy will do well in corporate America.

To combat such attitudes, I begin many classes with a discussion of the poem "A Worker Reads History" by Bertolt Brecht, in which is raised the question, "Was it kings who hauled the craggy blocks of stone?" to build the seven gates of Thebes.[8] My use of this poem is an attempt to reach those middle-class students who can think past their class prejudices while reassuring working-class students that their people are part of history too. Unfortunately, while there exists a great wealth of valuable material on working-class history, the general textbooks available for most history classes tend to range from poor to terrible. Workers do have their place in these tomes, but after the chapter on the Industrial Revolution, workers vanish. What remains is, in the words of one perceptive student, "kings and queens, wars and guns. The vast 98 percent of the population may as well not exist." Whenever I review a new textbook for possible adoption, I shudder and think of the Brecht poem. Once when I proposed to a publishing company's history editor a topics book for undergraduate use focused on the common people, his response was, "Why study the losers?"

Nor is the scarcity of interest in (or sympathy for) the working class limited to textbooks and students. Most college teachers are proudly and boastfully anti-working class. If the civil rights movement, the black empowerment movement, and the women's movement have created more self-consciousness about open expressions of racism or sexism, the typical professor still thinks nothing is wrong with being anti-working class. The same person who would never use the word *girl* to refer to an adult female openly rails against "blue-collar slobs." Since most academics buy into the notion that America (for all its problems, they quickly add) is basically a meritocracy without a dominant or ruling class, it follows that the common people are where they deserve to be. Particularly since World War II, the bulk of literature that discusses power in contemporary society is, as British scholar Ralph Miliband notes, "precisely concerned to demonstrate—or simply [takes] it for granted—that no dominant class or power elite could possibly exist in the democratic, pluralist, open societies of advanced capitalism" (26). That is to say, Western democracy purports, by its very nature, to have led to a society of homogeneous class structure. No rulers, and ergo, no ruled. Thus, even liberal professors see no reason to view workers as exploited or oppressed, as they admit women and minorities are. While racism and sexism are far from defeated in academia, at least there is some awareness of there being a problem. For the working class, no sympathy is expressed since, as one of my colleagues told me, "If you're a janitor, you only have yourself to blame." I often wonder what color the sky is in the world they inhabit, where the entire population can be professionals or entrepreneurs. Over the years, I have discovered that when you peel away the superficial layers of elitism and antilabor attitudes that cover many academicians, you unearth a genuinely elitist and anti-working-class essence.

The elitist perspective is reflected in many university hiring practices. A number of colleagues have privately told me of search committees where members sort through vitae and place all applications from state universities in the reject pile without even reading them. The fact that class background may have been a determining factor in who goes to an Ivy League school never even enters their consciousness.

This attitude is more than merely an irritation for thin-skinned labor academics. For working-class students, the effect is pernicious and often devastating. These individuals often feel shame at their origins and internalize the belief that they and their families are lazy or stupid. The result is that even exceptionally intelligent working-class students often fail to finish college. Another obstacle is that, much like many working women, they commonly have two jobs: one as student and one to support themselves. That is, they typically work at least part-time to help pay tuition, borrow potentially crushing amounts in loans, and still lack the material advantages (personal computers, cars) of the well heeled. For instance, I noticed one term that one of my best students was suddenly missing a number of classes. When this student did attend class, she was tired and distracted in a way I had never noticed in her previous demeanor. After this went on for three weeks, I finally asked her to talk with me after class. Much to my amazement, I learned she had lost her job. Without that income, she had been forced to give up her apartment and was reduced to sleeping in the back seat of her car. By the time she found another job and could afford housing again, she had been forced to drop two of her courses and her graduation was delayed six months. It's difficult to believe there is a level academic playing field.

In the same course, I had one student whose family sends in a maid to clean his dorm room and another who sleeps on a friend's sofa. The working-class student doesn't have a room of his own so that he can put most of the pay he earns working on a loading dock (11 P.M. to 7 A.M.) toward school. Of course, it is also true that most working-class students are less prepared academically. Thus, the bourgeois kid may have not only a maid but years of private school education while the working-class student may have gone to underfunded, overcrowded, and generally substandard public schools.

Finally, virtually all universities have entire programs dedicated to anti-labor bias. These programs are called business schools. In these schools, students are certainly taught a wide range of useful skills, but at the same time they are given tremendous doses of anti-working-class ideology disguised as reality. "Unions have no effect on improving wages," one economics professor assures me. Another notes that "blue-collar workers enjoy repetitive work because it doesn't require them to think and, after all, thinking causes stress for most people." The problem is not just that business schools promote these opinions but that they don't realize they are *opinions*.

Therefore it is not surprising that many students walk into my history classes with an almost religious reverence for "the market." When asked even the simplest questions about their belief, they, like members of a cult, are unable to make a sensible response. They are taught that everything from prisons to education should be privatized so that "the market" can work. Naturally, some clever individuals realize, as one young man told me, "It's all crap, but even though I don't learn anything, with an accounting degree I won't have to work in a factory like my old man." Since few institutions have labor studies programs, this probusiness slant is not balanced by a "College of Working-Class Studies."

At the other academic extreme, we have the various philosophy and many other liberal arts programs that propagate the notion that there are no social classes or if there are, they aren't important subjects of study. There is something perverse about students being taught various elitist philosophers ranging from Plato to Paul de Man while scant attention is given to thinkers who believed in democracy or equality. (If there is any difference between the government Plato outlined in *The Republic* and fascism, it escapes me, and I was forced to read Plato *three times* as an undergraduate.) At best, many a philosophy course only confuses the working-class students unfamiliar with such abstruse discussion and thereby serves to reinforce their preexisting fears of inadequacy.

The point is that, at least for the working class and the mass of common people throughout history, much of the liberal arts are not liberal at all. What they are, even if cloaked in politically correct rhetoric, is profoundly conservative—conservative because while they may question the "meaning of life" or even the "problem" of poverty, they flinch like a vampire in sunlight from a concrete examination of the sources of class oppression. Rather, college education would seem most effective in allowing students to maintain their belief in the prevailing worldview, a worldview that looks only to "Great Men" or (for those with a liberal spin) "Great Women, Men, and People of Color." This reveals itself every term when I assign history research papers. Students by and large resist writing on social history topics, especially the history of common people. They prefer Napoleon or Hitler as the subject of their research unless they fancy themselves liberals, in which case they want to do Joan of Arc or Martin Luther King, Jr. When questioned about their choice of topics, they explain that their individual "had changed history." Asked about the importance of the common people, the students normally return a blank stare as if they had met their first Martian.

Being a working-class academic is like being a member of an invisible minority group. If I remember to speak only "high English" to my colleagues I can pass as one of them. (The road to the academy is paved with working-class accents.) Students assume my position as a teacher means I'm from the upper middle class. This gives me certain advantages over my more visible African American and female colleagues: I can pass. Still, the distress at not being allowed to teach labor history is as great for me as if I were a feminist historian unable to teach women's history. In the five years at my current place of employment, I have been allowed to teach labor history once. There are no labor history courses in our catalog and certainly none is required. That workers have been an important piece in the historical puzzle is a mystery that most historians choose not to try to solve. (History from the bottom up is passé; postmodernism is what's hot.) When not ignored outright, working-class history is rendered marginal (you taught that class last year), ghettoized (one lecture on workers in the Industrial Revolution), stolen (there is no longer a working class), or lost (those people didn't write so how can we really know what they thought?). Thus for most students, working class or not, history remains "the story of kings and queens, guns and wars." This is the tragedy of working-class history.

NOTES

1. Some would have us "banish class from our understanding of the making" of history, Brian Palmer argues in "Is There Now, or Has There Ever Been a Working Class?" *History Today* 42 (March 1992): 51–54. See also his "The Poverty of Theory Revisited," *Left History* no. 1, (Spring 1993): 67–101.

2. David Sallach, "Class Domination and Ideological Hegemony."

3. For further information on this event see: Paul Avrich, *The Haymarket Tragedy*, available from the Illinois Labor History Society, 28 E. Jackson, Room 1012, Chicago, Illinois, 60604.

4. Note the Colonel's long-term support for *Chicago Tribune* correspondent Donald Day, who finished the Second World War as a Nazi radio broadcaster. John Carver Edwards, *Berlin Calling: American Broadcasters in Service to the Third Reich* (New York: Praeger Publishers, 1991), pp. 149–85.

5. "Television Entertainment Report Part II: Conclusions and National Summary of Occupational Frequency in Network Primetime Entertainment for February 1980," International Assoc. of Machinists and Aerospace Workers, June 12, 1980.

6. Larry Duncan, speech, "Labor and the Electronic Media," Committee for Labor Access, Chicago, Illinois, 30 April 1993.

7. See Michael Parenti, *Inventing Reality* (New York: St. Martin's Press, 1988). Also numerous works by Noam Chomsky.

8. Bertolt Brecht, "A Worker Reads History."

WORKS CITED

Brecht, Bertolt. "A Worker Reads History." In *Selected Poems,* trans. H. R. Hays. New York: Reynal & Hitchcock, 1947. 109.

Duncan, Larry. Speech. "Labor and the Electronic Media." Committee for Labor Access. Chicago, Illinois, 30 April 1993.

Miliband, Ralph. *Divided Societies: Class Struggle in Contemporary Capitalism.* Oxford: Oxford University Press, 1991.

Sallach, David. "Class Domination and Ideological Hegemony." *The Sociological Quarterly* 15 (Winter 1974): 38–50.

22

Psychology's Class Blindness: Investment in the Status Quo

Deborah Piper

For, in fact, in the working class, the process of building a family, of making a living for it, of nurturing and maintaining the individuals in it costs worlds of pain. (Lillian Rubin, Worlds of Pain)

This essay adds to the lens of psychology a sociopolitical view claiming that thus far the work of psychologists has on balance helped to support the status quo of a socially unjust system that represses, dominates, and violates the rights of many groups of people. The discussion here focuses particularly on social class.

After five years of graduate education, five clinical-training positions in different settings, five years of inpatient work, and two years in community-based settings, I have become painfully aware that virtually *none* of these settings ever turned to the life situations, the poverty and oppression of economically marginalized clients, as the possible source of their mental health problems. It was only in my last two years of doctoral training at Antioch/New England that I saw issues of oppression seriously addressed by psychologists.

Academic and practical training in psychological theory and concepts typically maintains an intrapsychic or "self" focus, which may call on early relationships in the family but completely excludes the context in which that person lives or lived. Systems theory and family therapy have explored a broader context but still completely exclude the social, political, and economic forces that impinge on the client's life. Self psychology has questioned the hierarchy in the therapeutic relationship and made use of the transference in a less pathologizing way. Interpersonal and Self-in-

Relation theory have chipped at the hierarchical structure of the therapeutic relationship and allowed the therapist more rein to share of him- or herself and hold a more respectful, empathic stance. Some headway has been made toward demystifying the therapeutic process and increasing the respect shown to clients, yet there is no movement toward addressing the larger forces in the macrostructures of their lives that impinge upon their emotional well-being. Feminist theorists and psychologists have opened the door to examining existing mores and ways of being that have been framed by men. They have illuminated the destructive aspects of power and control. In essence, these feminists have challenged the moral and ethical codes developed by the dominant group. As Alison Assiter points out, "A particular sort of slavery, what we might call moral slavery, occurs if a person is forced to act according to someone else's moral values" (59). Inherent in the therapeutic relationship is the potential for pressuring the client to act according to the therapist's values. Social constructionism has begun to bring a broader social focus to the lens of psychology, but there is much resistance to this frame in clinical settings.

I am deeply aware of how social, political, and cultural forces affected my own growth and development and how much one's life context weaves its way tenaciously into one's behavior and perspective. Because this paper will focus on the idea of respecting and utilizing context, it seems important to note at the outset that I am a white woman. I was born in the northeastern United States in 1947, graduated from high school in 1965 (when many traditions and systems were being challenged and feminist thought was gaining strength), obtained my bachelor's and master's degrees in the 1980s (the "me" decade), and am now completing my doctorate in psychology in the 1990s. In addition to the historical times that shaped my thinking, I should add that I was born into a family that was frequently part of the welfare system. I am the first in that family to graduate from high school, let alone go on to graduate education and a professional career. My father drove a taxi, drove trucks, did construction and odd jobs; my mother waitressed or tended bar. At the age of twenty I married into a large working-class family.

I have moved through more than one social transition: from poverty to working class and then to middle class through my education. These experiences have created moments of extreme dissonance in my own life. There were stages in my journey where I wore my education like a coat, putting it on to protect myself at school or in professional meetings, then taking it off upon returning home lest I offend or distance the people I loved so dearly. In educational or professional settings, I was very much aware of how this dissonance could quickly turn to shame, how easily I could feel inferior. It was easy to be disempowered when another person, particularly a mentor, a teacher, or even more so a therapist, did not understand or respect my world and attempted to impose their values and assumptions on me. It was easy to feel inadequate and ashamed in my childhood when social service professionals failed to address the broader economic and political structures that contributed to my family's difficulties.

I am equally aware of those teachers and therapists who have eased that dissonance and helped me to integrate the changes in my life, who have empowered me to continue growing and to challenge the systems that oppress people. These teachers and therapists seemed more like guides, collaborators helping me plan my journey and assisting me over the rougher terrain. These people did not hide behind the hierarchical and distant stance that therapists and teachers usually take. They eased the feelings of inferiority and the shame and silence that often accompany histories of poverty. They invited me into the dialogue of the academic settings they taught in. Their connected stance brought me into the role of collaborator, and my voice and ideas seemed to count in this privileged discourse that was part of the academic world.

Much of my own role as a therapist and as a teacher has been informed by these experiences and also by interactions I had working as a peer tutor while attending an alternative baccalaureate program at the University of Massachusetts-Boston in its College of Public and Community Service (CPCS). This particular college was intent on educating people who wanted to work in roles of advocacy in their communities, and it drew a largely minority adult population. While there, I was asked to peer tutor other students who had difficulty with their reading or writing skills. These students were mainly minority women from inner-city communities in the Boston area.

I brought to this work my own experiential understanding of the life exigencies that result from poverty and also knowledge gained in my studies and in tutor-training sessions. These training sessions focused not only on adult development and learning styles but also on the larger macrostructures that contribute to one's learning or lack of opportunity to learn. The theorists who became frames of reference for my own work were John Dewey, who encouraged education through experience, and Malcolm Knowles, who suggested that all learning is based on the familiar. Lev Vygotsky indicated that learning is essentially a social process, that human psychology is formed by history and culture, and that learning about those structures is inherently a dialectical process, continually moving and changing. All of these theorists and the faculty with whom I was working contributed to how I viewed the learning process. In addition, Paulo Freire described in *Pedagogy of the Oppressed* the "limiting situations" that block learning. I became familiar with Bowles and Gintis, who examined the sociopolitical forces that feed oppression and the way those forces are perpetuated through the educational system. They spoke of the impact of the educational system on the lower classes, arguing that the "roots of inequality in the United States are to be found in the class structure and the system of sexual and racial power relationships" (85). These ideas deepened my understanding of the terrible bind that occurs when people are dominated and oppressed and then blamed for their dependent repertoires of behavior. I became aware of how women in marginalized populations suffer under institutionalized oppression. On a personal level, I became less ashamed of my own background and more empowered to work through these systems. I became aware of the strength and competence of the other students and grew to respect them and myself for our courage.

Continually students at CPCS made statements reflecting the "limiting situations" they had been in and their sense of inadequacy in an academic setting. They said how stupid they were, how they were doomed to fail, how powerless they felt, that others had told them they could never make it in college. The words resonated with my own experience. One woman, in tears about her difficulty with reading and writing skills, said, "My friend said I was outta' my mind comin' here—maybe I was, maybe I'm just not smart enough. I don't even know what half the stuff I read is about." She had become quite depressed and anxious and thought of quitting. Yet, this same woman had managed to raise two children who planned to go to college, had organized forces in her community and advocated for services in her housing project, such as better maintenance and security, and she was successful. She had organized a group of people who helped get a grant for her children's school. She had managed to find her way through the complex systems governing her life and to work to improve her situation. She had survived in the face of poverty and oppression. Still, she felt shamed and "not smart enough" in school. She said she had always felt like this, and she recounted many instances when her feelings of inadequacy and inferiority had been reinforced in her earlier schooling. It seemed that her sense of failure and shame had nothing to do with her cognitive ability, her intellect. Rather, her shame and depression were results of the way she, a poor minority woman, had been treated all her life in the systems and institutions that play such important parts in shaping people's lives. Beyond that, the things she was reading and trying to learn about were not familiar to her. The materials, in effect, required a conceptual leap, and many students fell into the chasm.

It became clear to me (and it was already clear to some of the remarkable faculty whom I was able to work with) that the place to begin helping these students with reading and writing skills was by building on their own narratives, their own life experiences. By choosing readings that resonated with their own life experiences, they could build on familiar narratives and experiences. We wrote poems and stories and read them aloud to each other, sharing through them vignettes of oppression, sharing with each other the pain of that experience. We read writers like Alice Walker, Toni Morrison, Jean Baker Miller, and others. This writing and reading began to illuminate the incredible talents and strengths of these women as they wrote of finding ways to advocate for themselves and their communities, as they realized they had strong, determined voices and that they were smart in their own ways. Eventually many learned to conform to the canons of academic writing and learned how to create well-formed arguments, but all became empowered by their own stories.

These CPCS students had previously felt incompetent, unintelligent, responsible for their inadequacies, and shamed. These women were struggling with their shame, they were depressed, and their families were involved with social services that made them feel even worse about themselves. They blamed themselves. Through their readings and the collaborative, respectful teaching styles of the faculty, they began to see it was not they that were shameful; the shame lay with a society that would oppress them so pervasively. They no longer internalized the problem. They became empowered and committed to their education.

This educational setting and these experiences have dramatically impacted my thinking and my work. As I have continued on my educational and professional path, I have retained an awareness of the effects of oppression while becoming increasingly conscious of the lack of attention paid to issues of social class both in educational settings and in the field of psychology. Rick Simonson and Scott Walker, editors of the Graywolf Annual *Multi-Cultural Literacy,* call for a more diverse approach to education: "The language of the academic world, of government, of business, of mass media so easily becomes abstract, distancing, manipulative. Such language cannot, with its nervous speed, its strip-mind, appropriating qualities, touch the deep, turned-over ground of our culture. Such language can, and often does, seek to bury it" (xiii–xiv).

Social class has remained a focus for sociologists, but it has not made its way with any force into the study of psychology. Any examination of social stratification or social class structures is complicated by other factors such as race and ethnicity. Income, education, and work role have been used as common indicators of social class rank. The middle and upper classes have enjoyed the dominant status and power that accompany their position while the working class and those who rely on public assistance consistently experience life from a subordinate position, oppressed by the power of the upper classes. Miller, in *Towards a New Psychology of Women,* eloquently describes the dissonance that becomes so pervasive when stratification between dominant and subservient groups becomes established and the groups evolve to a position where there is no communication between them, no understanding of each other's worlds. Such a dichotomy leads to a perspective in which one group's values are felt to be wrong and the other's right, with the dominant group deciding what will be accepted as the status quo. The problem is that we function according to a myth of classlessness; many do not want to acknowledge our class system. Benjamin DeMott calls class "America's dirty little secret" and asserts further that "its effects, though hidden, are immense and devastating" (A26). DeMott quotes former President Bush, who said in a campaign speech, "Class isn't for the United States. We are not going to be divided by class" (A26).

Psychologists also function in their research and their work as though social class does not exist. They create theories, treatment modalities, methods of assessment, and diagnostic categories, and they perform psychotherapy, without any reference to social class structures. Mary Catherine Bateson speaks of how the "caretaking professions themselves can be distorted into forms of exploitation rather than caring" and notes further that "healing and helping can become forms of domination" (156–57). I think that this is exactly what often happens when psychologists diagnose and treat clients who are economically disfranchised. Rather than helping these clients understand and deal with the life context that contributes to their hopelessness, their anger, and the manifestations of those feelings, most psychologists focus on the individual and how their own cognition, emotions, or behaviors are dysfunctional. In this way, psychology tacitly supports the status quo of an unjust system.

Though psychologists typically express a class-free perspective, they covertly pathologize clients of lower social strata for the repertoire of behaviors they develop in response to their oppressive life contexts. People from lower socioeconomic backgrounds are often considered unmotivated, unintelligent, weak of character, impulsive, and possessed of little temporal perspective. Barbara Ehrenreich quotes Oscar Lewis's 1959 study of Mexican American families to reveal clinical terminology that is clearly pathologizing. As Lewis describes these families, "[They have] a high incidence of weak ego structure, orality and confusion of sexual identification, all reflecting maternal deprivation; a strong present-time orientation with relatively little disposition to defer gratification and plan for the future, with a high tolerance for psychopathology of all kinds" (49). This description bears a strong resemblance to characterizations of economically disenfranchised patients that I have heard in many clinical case conferences. Historically, such clients have been blamed for not being motivated to change, not aspiring to attain the status of the mentally healthy middle class. The question is whether psychologists have as their goal enhancing in some way the lives of the people they work with, or if their true goal is to make their clients more like themselves.

Seymour B. Sarason points out that "earlier in the century psychologists were a far more homogeneous group, often coming from privileged families" (150). In discussing the difficulty psychologists often have in transcending their own backgrounds, Sarason wonders, "How can you confront and transcend that which you do not consider in any way problematic?" (48). If one is a member of a privileged group, if one's way of speaking and behaving is part of the dominant discourse, one's repertoire of behaviors is not questioned. Social norms are defined by the dominant group in society. Yet, it is critical that a therapist examine his or her own cultural background; it is important that this examination include a sensitivity to the influence of social class origins.

In *The Therapeutic Relationship and Its Impact,* even the popular psychologist Carl Rogers, who is hailed for his respectful client-centered approach, has this to say about clients who are economically disenfranchised: "The unmotivated, defensive and reluctant patient from a different (lower) socioeconomic background may not provide the therapist sufficient opportunity to deepen the relationship, and may thus severely limit the therapist's ability to communicate and function effectively" (quoted in Jones 314). Unless we become aware of how institutionalized class oppression is, even the most well-intentioned liberal can develop empathic blind spots.

On the broader societal level, the upper classes in general, be they doctors, lawyers, psychologists, educators, or writers, are inherently invested in maintaining things as they are; their position of power and control is not one they want to give up. In fact, as Ehrenreich has pointed out, they have a "fear of falling" from this position. She observes that the poor came "to represent what the middle class feared most in itself: softening of character, a lack of firm internal values" (51). Enrico Jones, in a review of psychological research, examined the patterns of equating higher levels of social class with mental health and concludes that attainment of middle-class standing has become "itself an index of health" (310). Jones illuminates the injustices toward economically marginalized clients in his research, pointing out that there is a direct relationship between social class and severity of diagnosis as well as in expectations for successful treatment and level of training of the therapist assigned to the client. Clients from lower socioeconomic strata usually carry more severely pathologic diagnoses, are given poor prognoses for follow through and outcome in treatment, and are usually assigned to less-well-trained counselors and psychologists. That there is class bias in the field of psychology is thus not in question: the question is what can be done about it.

The trend in psychology to pay more attention to social constructions has prompted an examination of the broader social contexts in which one makes meaning. The self, rather than existing in a vacuum, exists in relation to others. This perspective moves the interpersonal context of the therapeutic relationship out into the world. It is a macro view rather than a micro or dyadic view of the self.

Constructionism calls upon many layers of meaning making: history, culture, language, family patterns, social status, all of the "constructs" of a person's experience. In psychology, such a perspective demands that the level of discourse be deepened. It depends that the therapist uncover these constructs by listening carefully and understanding the client's story. The story itself is rooted in the larger cultural frame. Jerome Bruner takes a stance similar to Vygotsky's in saying that knowledge is "indefinable save in a culturally based system of notation" (21) and that through this cultural base, "meaning achieves a form that is public and communal rather than private and autistic" (33). In essence, making meaning is inherently a social process. Frames of reference become dialectical rather than static.

Postmodernism stretches these notions even further as "truth" itself comes into question. It offers a rich medium with which to examine notions about how psychology contributes to oppression. Nancy Fraser and Linda J. Nicholson point out how a postmodern perspective can be fertile ground for social criticism and provide room for political involvement. "A modern conception must give way to a new 'postmodern' one in which criticism floats free of any universalist theoretical ground. No longer anchored philosophically, the very shape or character of social criticism changes; it becomes more pragmatic, ad hoc, contextual, and local" (21). They call for a feminist postmodernism where theories respect different sociocultural and historical matrices, suggesting that such theory would resemble "a tapestry composed of threads of many different hues rather than one woven in a single color" (35).

This manner of questioning truth and placing it in context is a critical concept in the discussion of oppression. Psychological theory has historically made universal claims about the notion of the self. Universal claims in a postmodern light burst into multiversal ideas; the self under a postmodern lens broadens to a self in context, and meaning is made from these multiversal contexts. Such a concept challenges many existing psychological theories.

Postmodernism undoubtedly opens the door to a more egalitarian approach to psychology, but there are some elements of context that are not often spoken of: the economic and the political. Yes, one could argue that they are inherently included when one explores the constructions that contribute to one's meaning structure. But I would argue that usually they are not considered unless they are named; they are not considered unless they are directly addressed as an important element of one's constructions, a specific thread in the tapestry. Perhaps one of the reasons that they are not usually considered directly is that they are bound up in the very system that stratifies and oppresses people; they are related to power and control. If there is anything a dominant group fears losing, it is power and control. Psychologists, as discussed earlier, decidedly belong to the dominant group in society—the middle and upper classes.

This is where feminist theory strengthens postmodernism. No matter how carefully and respectfully one listens to the narratives of an oppressed person, it is possible to miss the stories of their oppression; it is even more likely that the receiver of the story will not decipher any mention of the oppressor. People in subordinate positions often believe the myths of the dominant group and see themselves as inherently inferior. Even if the oppressed person is able to speak of their oppression, their narrative can often be heard as irresponsibility, as being unable to accept their role in their position, as "displaced anger," as "projection," or as a characterological problem.

As Kenneth J. Gergen points out, "Words are not mirror-like reflections of reality, but expressions of group convention" (119). He also points out that words do not come with "labels" and that they are subject to the interpretation of the listener. Here I would share George W. Albee's caution that "each person entering a human service profession, should begin by examining her or his underlying assumptions about the human condition" (31).

The feminist paradigm cautions us to be aware of and sensitive to the misuse of power and control. The feminist stance is a political one. Jane Flax, in pointing out the shortcomings in French postmodern feminism, indicates:

A problem with thinking about (or only in terms of) texts, signs, or signification is that they tend to take on a life of their own or become the world, as the claim that nothing exists outside of a text. . . . Such an approach obscures the projection of its own activity onto the world and denies the existence of the variety of concrete social practices that enter into and are reflected in the constitution of language itself. . . . This lack of attention to concrete social relations (including the distribution of power) results, as in Lacan's work, in the obscuring of relations of domination. (47)

Flax points out here one of the limitations of the narrator's story and the importance of the listener's probing the story deeply with an eye to its political and economic components. Not to do so could leave the person in a structure of meaning that is limited, in effect leaving them blinded by their oppression. Donald E. Polkinghorne describes narrative as "a scheme by means of which human beings give meaning to their experience of temporality and personal actions" (11). This narrative scheme is pervasively affected by the broader macrostructures of society, politics, and culture that affect how one creates meaning out of experience.

Clearly, my own background has sensitized me to the issues of social class. The path of my educational journey has been quite long. Obtaining a bachelor's degree took fifteen years. Though I could do well in the classes, my successes were always accompanied by a fear of being found out, the sense that people like me did not belong in college. The values I was brought up with told me that hard work was important; sitting and reading seemed almost decadent, as though I were wasting time. There were many times when I asked myself, "Who do you think you are, going to school like this?" I felt like an impostor. It was not until my experience at the University of Massachusetts-Boston that I could even begin to think that going to school was a reasonable thing for me to do. My educational pursuits gained momentum after that, propelling me on to a master's degree and six years later to a doctorate. Like most events in one's life, this educational journey has been fraught with fulfilling accomplishments and very painful losses.

It is only through my studies and my increased understanding of marginalized populations that I have been able to come full circle and integrate the changes in my own life. There was a time when I had to take the cloak of my education on and off frequently, always trying to fit in. It is only in the last few years that I can leave it on all the time and still be myself; it is only in the last few years that I can truly accept and speak of my own history. For now, I truly understand the pervasive effects of being marginalized. I realize that my own pretense was an effort to fit into the dominant discourse when I felt I needed to.

I think that those of us who have experienced the oppression of being marginalized and have worked our way through the educational system to be able to engage in the dominant discourse have a responsibility to illuminate the effects of class oppression. It is important that we all, in our own teaching and professional work, speak to this issue and work toward helping others understand how broader social forces affect people's lives. I have had the immense good fortune to be in settings where there were true educators, guides who knew how to collaborate with students and peers and to help people learn and grow, to find their own voices. To these guides I am extremely grateful. I only hope I can follow their example in a manner that allows me to empower people to work through marginalization to develop new narratives of personal agency.

WORKS CITED

Albee, George W. "Opposition to Prevention and a New Creedal Oath." *The Scientist Practitioner,* 1, no. 4 (December 1991).

Assiter, Alison. "Autonomy and Pornography." In *Feminist Perspectives in Philosophy,* ed. Morwenna Griffiths and Margaret Whitford. Bloomington: Indiana University Press, 1988. 58–71.

Bateson, Mary C. *Composing a Life: Life as a Work in Progress—The Improvisations of Five Extraordinary Women.* New York: Penguin Books, 1990.

Bowles, Samuel, and Herbert Gintis. *Schooling in Capitalist America: Educational Reform and the Contradictions of Economic Life.* New York: Basic Books, 1976.

Bruner, Jerome. *Acts of Meaning.* Cambridge, Mass.: Harvard University Press, 1990.

DeMott, Benjamin. "America's Dirty Little Secret: Class." *Boston Globe* 25 Nov. 1990: A25–A26.

Ehrenreich, Barbara. *Fear of Falling: The Inner Life of the Middle Class.* New York: Pantheon, 1989.

Flax, Jane. "Postmodernism and Gender Relations in Feminist Theory." In *Feminism/Postmodernism,* ed. Linda J. Nicholson. New York: Routledge, 1990. 39–62.

Fraser, Nancy, and Linda J. Nicholson. "Social Criticism without Philosophy: An Encounter between Feminism and Postmodernism." In *Feminism/Postmodernism,* ed. L. J. Nicholson. New York: Routledge, 1990. 19–38.

Freire, Paulo. *Pedagogy of the Oppressed.* New York: Continuum, 1973.

Gergen, Kenneth J. *The Saturated Self: Dilemmas of Identity in Contemporary Life.* New York: Basic Books, 1991.

Jones, Enrico. "Social Class and Psychotherapy: A Critical Review of Research." *Psychiatry* 37 (1974): 307–19.

Miller, Jean Baker. *Towards a New Psychology of Women.* Boston: Beacon Press, 1976.

Polkinghorne, Donald E. *Narrative Knowing and the Human Sciences.* New York: State University of New York Press, 1988.

Rubin, Lillian B. *Worlds of Pain: Life in the Working-Class Family.* New York: Basic Books, 1976.

Sarason, Seymour B. *Psychology Misdirected.* New York: Free Press, 1981.

Simonson, Rick, and Scott Walker, eds. *Multi-Cultural Literacy: Opening the American Mind.* Graywolf Annual Five. St. Paul, Minn.: Graywolf Press, 1988.

23

Working It Out: Values, Perspectives, and Autobiography

John Sumser

My first academic position was as a lecturer in philosophy, one of the hordes of itinerant academics paid by the class and denied the luxury of tenured job security. I had an office that I decorated with pictures from a book of Japanese joinery, elegant wooden joints carved to serve precise structural purposes. A good structural joint in this tradition did not require nails, Wilhold glue, screws, bolts, or any other deus ex machina of poor design. A good piece of joinery allowed a structure to be built that was capable of holding itself together.

I taught logic and critical thinking and told students that their arguments had to be like the pictures in my office. Their ideas had to be put together in such a way that each part added to the strength of the whole and that the beauty of the finished product would lie not in extraneous decoration but in the functional simplicity of the structure. Rationality as craftsmanship.

My father was a craftsman. He was a precision grinder who made crude blocks of steel into incredibly precise pieces of machinery. "One molecule of oil," he used to tell us as he demonstrated the precise way one piece would fit into another. "That is what the tolerance is." My father died from breathing the molecules of lightweight machine oil and minute particles of steel that permeate the atmosphere of a machine shop. He died before he saw those bits of steel fashioned into the weapons used by his three oldest sons as they rotated sequentially through Vietnam. Died before they began using the GI Bill to go through college.

For years my father kept tucked away in his dresser a piece of finely crafted steel wrapped in gauze. It was a thick, jagged piece of grayish steel about an inch and a half across with grooves carved into one side. German craftsmen, probably not too different from my father, had made the bomb of which it was a part and also the airplane that had delivered it to northern Italy, where it was dropped and exploded, ripping through my father's body and ending his stint as an infantryman.

I thought of those pieces of machinery that my father had brought home when I looked at the pictures of the Japanese joinery and when I heard or read a very good philosopher make a very good argument—a quiet, steel-cold snick as the final piece of the argument slipped into place.

I know that this notion that form follows function would be classified as a modernist ideal. And while it would best serve my argument to tie this kind of thinking strongly to the modernist period in American history, I can't ignore that the pictures on my office walls originated in traditional Japan and that the value of simplicity in philosophy was perhaps best formulated in the fourteenth century by William of Ockham. So while I will be attributing much of what I believe are working-class characteristics to modernist values, I believe that historical changes in values are not concerned with the creation of new values so much as with the waxing and waning of existing values.

I grew up in a working-class section of suburban Los Angeles. My father was a machinist and my mother worked in a sewing factory making fashionable undergarments. When my father died, my mother went to school to be a licensed vocational nurse. She had been a nurse in the Women's Army Corps in the Second World War and met my father in an Army hospital in Tennessee when he returned from Europe with the piece of German machinecraft in his leg. Later she married another machinist.

It is not simply that my parents were working class and that I am claiming that status as part of my inheritance. I have been working class and I have been poor (which are increasingly related but still distinct qualities). Before becoming an academic, I supported myself for many years working in factories, in clerical jobs, in menial labor. I have cleaned toilets and guarded gravel pits and worked in factories assembling television sets and lawn edgers. One of my brothers and I lived in a condemned hotel for winos a half-step above homelessness while earning our undergraduate degrees. Later we moved to a hovel in which we would take turns sleeping on the bed. Another of my brothers, now a history professor, is a certified motorcycle mechanic and an experienced machinist. My youngest brother is a carpenter and my oldest brother is a bartender. Among the five of us we have two doctorates, three master's degrees, four bachelor's degrees, and two high school diplomas. All of us put ourselves through school.

In spite of being a sociologist, I think that the impact of a working-class background on an intellectual or academic is not reducible to standard social class variables. To a certain extent, this may be because my father was a skilled laborer and, as such, made enough money to have a house in suburbia and a new car every four or five years. A wide range of people lived in my neighborhood, from skilled workers to television actors to engineers. My present neighborhood has about the same makeup, if you substitute university professors for movie actors, and my children will never be considered to have working-class backgrounds. I think the key to the impact of working-class backgrounds on intellectuals is located not in the idea of class but in the idea of working.

What it means to work is contained in the contrast between John Locke's labor theory of value and Marx's exchange theory of value. Locke argued (for the capitalists, against the nobility) that the value of a thing was determined by the amount of labor required to transform raw materials into a finished product. Marx, in contrast, argued that the value of a thing was determined by the market and was independent of a thing's labor value. This more empirical definition allowed for profit, whereas Locke's did not.

The labor theory of value is a modernist value, tied to production and rationality. The problem identified by many of the modernist critics, including Marx, was that the rationalist system of production was distorted by the desire for profit. The exchange theory is very much a postmodern theory. It is postmodern in the sense that it allows for a concept of value that is continuously shifting, unrelated to any objective conditions and beyond any moral judgment.

In order to make this jump to exchange theory as postmodern, it has to be cut loose from its critical origin. When exchange theory was defined in direct contrast to labor theory, then, because it was a contrast between a sociologically descriptive term and a moral term, it was apparent that exchange theory described an immoral system. If exchange theory is separated from its contrast to labor theory, then it is just a sociological description—accurate or useful but having nothing to do with morality.

I think that working-class people (including working-class intellectuals) see work in terms of the labor theory. Work, then, is about the energy required to transform some raw material—realizing, of course, that frequently one person's raw material is another's finished product. When I assembled television sets, for example, the raw materials for my final assembly were all the finished products of the other departments. And sometimes the transformation is simply of this-material-here to this-material-there, as in coal mining and warehouse work. Non-working-class people see work in terms of exchange theory because their work requires either no raw materials or no transformation of raw materials. It is not pure happenstance that exchange theory is no longer the name for a theory of value but for a theory of communication based on a model of salesmanship.

As a result of this, I think working-class intellectuals see things in much more concrete terms than do non-working-class intellectuals. This does not mean (necessarily) that they are more "applied" than "theoretical." It means that they share Alfred North Whitehead's conviction that thinking about the world must begin and end at some concrete place.

I remember going to an art exhibit in the Legion of Honor museum in San Francisco in the mid-1970s and seeing a sculpture of an automotive-type thing. It looked like a race car minus the body and was constructed of gleaming chrome tubing and machinery and looked like the very essence of the mechanical ideal. Except that it didn't run. It bothered me that they didn't just steam clean the nearest Buick and haul it into the museum. If the point of the sculpture was to say something about machinery and cars and American culture, then surely the Buick would be superior to the nonfunctional car-like thing.

The problem, of course, is that Buicks (like Mercedes, Yugos, and Edsels) are made by working-class people rather than by artistic intellectual types. They are designed by engineers ("mechanics of the middle class," as Robert Zussman put it), and engineers personify the modernist value system, just as artists personify the postmodernist sensibility. Since automobiles could be said to symbolize American culture/decadence/decline, then car sculptures symbolize these symbols and the emphasis shifts from the actual production of culture to the recognition of the meaning of things. What is important is what is abstract.

Much of my current work is related to ideas developed in postmodernist theory. Postmodernism is the metaphysics of white-collar workers. Since "How to Do Things with Words" is no longer simply the title of a book of analytic philosophy but a description of the US economy, a worldview had to be articulated that could make sense of the world of word processing and leveraged buy-outs. As Marxism would lead one to expect, both modernism and postmodernism support and define the dominant economic systems; but modernism supported industrialism, and postmodernism supports the service economy.

Far too often, postmodernism is portrayed as developing because of the internal logical flaws of modernism (an argument, by the way, that would have a great deal of difficulty in accounting for the longevity of the major religions), rather than as resulting from the replacement of one sector of society with another. Postmodern theorists live in a world that has the qualities that postmodern theorizing describes: lack or weakness of objective standards or values, proliferation of occupationally specific worldviews, lack of certainty, and a deluge of words as the never-finished product. This social world is vastly different from the world of modernism with its interchangeability of parts, its objective machine-like certainty, its demand for a unified worldview.

Think about that great bogeyman of postmodern times, the logical positivist. As a metaphysical and epistemological position, logical positivism is tied to the material world and to the labor theory of value. It is a worker's ideology based in the transformation of material goods: the only differences are measurable differences, the meaning of a thing is its use, beauty is related to function, statements that cannot be empirically tested are vacuous. When I first met my stepfather, he told me that he was a machinist, "but not like your father." My father had been a great machinist, my stepfather said, and he knew this because of my father's reputation, his tools, and the examples of his work. I tried to downplay this huge gulf in quality, but my stepfather would have none of it. "By the end of the day," he told me, "I have produced a lot of scrap."

Scrap. The key to machine work is tolerances. Every part has a tolerance—the allowable margin of error. The higher the quality of the piece, the lower the tolerance. A piece that is ground to measurements outside tolerance is scrap, junk, garbage, wasted steel. And there is no ambiguity. A leadman or foreman checks a piece with a micrometer and it is either a finished product or it is scrap. There is no room for postmodern dickering here, no way to claim that the piece of steel is a polysemic text open to infinite evaluations and interpretations. The tested part must fit with another part that is being produced thousands of miles away to be shipped to a third site for assembly. It is not—it cannot be—one thing to you and another to me.

This is an extremely social view, and it is not surprising that one of the main threads of modernism was utopian thought. What is good for you is good for me; therefore, (enlightened, rational) self-interest is the epitome of sociability. Think of Kant's "unsocial sociability" or Adam Smith's "invisible hand," both of which saw private actions leading to social betterment in spite of the intentions of the people involved; actions informed by universal, rationalist values would lead inevitably to a more efficient and more just society. The modernist system could only be destroyed, its proponents believed, by irrational interference, generally portrayed as either provincial or religious bigotry or the desire for profit. The modernist insistence on objective standards allowed for the progressive belief that the basis for the social good was meritocracy and open competition.

But what is the white-collar equivalent of scrap? White-collar scrap is not produced by comparing a thing to an objective standard. The labor theory of value is not at work here, so we cannot say, for instance, that a memo falls outside the tolerance for inclusion in the class of memos. White-collar work is based in the exchange theory of value, so a memo (or any other product) is successful if it serves a profitable function in a communication process.

A good example of this is a bluff in a game of poker. The cards you hold are only as good as the pot you win. After being bluffed, you cannot claim that your hand was objectively better and therefore the money was "really" yours. (With a labor theory of poker, all hands would be dealt straight up.) It doesn't matter, then, if a report or a memo is better prepared in terms of research or writing or because it is more accurate or because it is true. A memo either works or it doesn't and that is based on, as the postmodernists would say, extratextual considerations such as the perceptions of those involved, the political ramifications of a situation, or the significance of any action for the various people involved.

One of the main differences between modernist and postmodernist views was first illustrated when the sociologist Max Weber claimed that even that most modernist creation, the machine, had a meaning that was ascertainable only through an examination of social structure and social processes. In this view, the pieces of machinery that my father brought home could no longer be defined in terms of how they functioned in the context of the whole machine. This structural sense of meaning as being contained by or within the meaningful object has been replaced by a view of meaning that is "poststructural," with meaning defined in terms of consequences, significance, and individual idiosyncrasy. The meaning of a seatbelt in a car is governmental interference, and the meaning of Japanese microchips is the failure of the Western socioeconomic system. Or at least that's what they *mean* to me and so that's what they *are* to me.

This is a tremendous shift away from the materialistic views of modernism. No longer is the meaning of a thing its use. Instead the nature of a thing is its meaning. And then the world dissolves into "intersubjectivity" and "texts" and, eventually, into an atomized conception of life with religion as the only way out. Once trapped, one can only be saved by a leap of faith. And I find myself adrift in this boundless world of white-collar thought, of intersubjective relativity, and remember my brother and me standing in front of shoe repair shops and hanging around the old man down the street who had six worn-out Hudson Hornets on his front lawn (much to everyone's embarrassment), thinking that being able to make shoes or repair an automobile were the things that moved one from being a child to adulthood. These men were in control of their environment. They took broken things and fixed them. They crafted finished pieces out of raw material. I remember the power I felt as a teenager in being able to use a hot patch on a punctured inner tube, and I remember the time as a young man I first rode the conveyor belt high over the factory floor to balance precariously and right a boxed television that had jammed against a support beam. I remember repairing a truck in Vietnam and having a Vietnamese man take a fumbling brush out of my hand and show me how to create the bead of paint required for painting the serial number on a jeep. I remember sitting in the dirt with two local men in the high northern plains of Afghanistan and working out how to create a dam that would divert water from an irrigation canal into the compound of one of the men. And, I remember sitting in silence with a disembarked busload of people as we watched the two drivers work in knowledgeable silence repairing the drive shaft that had marooned us in the middle of the mountains of central Afghanistan. I remember rebuilding the engine in my VW and replacing every known part on a series of British sports cars. And I remember, not too long ago, changing the heating element in my water heater and feeling absurdly proud of myself.

The characters in the old modern novels by writers such as Dos Passos, London, and others seemed very much keyed into this kind of working-class metaphysics. These characters always seemed in control of their physical environment—able to make and repair things—and yet their social world was controlled by those who manipulated symbols. This control and lack of control was a central theme in the novels of the twenties and thirties. In one of John Dos Passos's novels, a man absolutely at the end of his rope is told by his woman friend that he could go get a job as a logger, that it would at least be honest work, and he responds that he would just be cutting down trees to turn them into paper to be used to produce the *New York Times*. Like the proponents of modernism, these novelists seemed to believe that if we could get back to the ground level of material production we could have a spiritual life that was worthwhile.

It seems to me that we have gone full circle and that postmodernism looks very much like premodernism. If the intellectual opponents of postmodernism are positivism and universalism, then the major opponent of modernism was religion, and yet the men and women who move from non-working-class backgrounds through college and into academics have created a life that looks very much like the priesthood.

I was raised as a Catholic and for a while my mother was active in the church. Whenever she had to shake hands with the pastor of our church she would come home and tell us, with a visible shudder, that the priest had soft hands "like a fat old woman." She did not understand how anyone who was not old, especially a man, could have soft hands. "He's never *worked*," she would tell us, shaking her head that such people were allowed out in public. Implicit in her criticism was that such people had little business telling us how to live. I wonder that about academics. One of my acquaintances works in the sociology of labor and yet was supported through his doctorate by his parents and, with the exception of a summer job or two, has never worked to support himself as an independent, nonstudent adult.

It seems to me that there was a relatively brief period, never of course completely realized, in which the elective affinity of intellectual and economic life worked together to produce an ideal of human beings as essentially the same and of the world as objectively present and that this allowed for the ideas of equality and democracy. This equality and objectivity were based in the dominance of the mechanical model. Modernist philosophy is always based in mechanical models (such as billiard-ball models of cause and effect and clockwork metaphysics), and it is this mechanical model that comes to mind when we think of the working class. With the mechanical model comes the belief that the world is controllable, that if you look and think carefully you will be able to figure out how a thing works. This puts us all on a roughly equal footing because knowledge is not secret and is not private.

To a certain extent it was true that things could be figured out. To look at a Japanese joint is to see the forces that impinge on it and to understand why it was constructed as it was. When we were kids, my brothers and I rummaged through the alleys looking for discarded objects to take apart. A broken clock was a real treasure because it could be disassembled and its secrets revealed. The new digital clocks are somewhat more obliging in that they fall apart rapidly and easily, but their doing so provides no satisfaction. There is nothing inside of digital watches. Looking at and thinking carefully about a digital watch will tell you nothing. Compared with mechanical watches, digital watches are material versions of Gertrude Stein's Oakland: There is no there, there.

The move from the working class into intellectual life is like the move from analog to digital watches. You can no longer watch me and know what I am doing. I am no longer stamping rubber tires onto plastic wheels, something I did for over a year (almost six wheels per minute, seven hours a day five days a week for fourteen months equals roughly 750,000 wheels). You certainly can't watch me and know if I am doing my current work well or if I am producing a soft version of scrap.

I feel like I have changed sides in some very important game and that the values that drove me to play in the first place are no longer compatible with my role. I became an intellectual because I wanted a craftsman's brain and a craftman's world, I wanted clarity and certainty. At a recent convention, I was sitting with a few friends and acquaintances in a restaurant in Chicago. We were all sociologists who studied mass communication and culture, and I asked the woman next to me what her recently published book was about. She described it to me, and I told her that I was amazed by her description. She replied that she, too, was surprised that she could so neatly summarize her book. I didn't say it, but what I had found amazing was that in spite of our similar interests and comparable educations, I had absolutely no idea what she was talking about. I should have asked her if she had ever heard of Japanese joinery.

I have the good fortune to teach in a nonelite university system, which means that most of the students and a good many of the faculty do not come from privileged backgrounds. Unfortunately, the role of higher education seems to be to convert people away from productive lives and into basically parasitic occupations. And this, in turn, serves the needs of an economy in which labor is seen as an unfortunate by-product of the serious business of making money and collecting status awards. I think it is built into our educational system that the people who are involved in the labor economy are those who aren't good enough for the exchange economy: only losers are materially productive.

The end result of this is an extremely uncreative society, full of bickering intellectuals, self-centered noncitizens, and ego-maniacal relativists, that lacks the ability to establish the ground from which this consumer-ridden, nonsocial society can be criticized. Intellectuals have thrown in their lot with the affluent class, with what John Kenneth Galbraith calls the contented class, and are scrambling like mad to develop a left and right wing of white-collar thought as if that would indicate they were still serving a creative function. I can think of no greater indicator of the usefulness of Gramsci's idea of hegemony than the fact that intellectuals shifted to postmodernist values at the same time that American corporations shifted labor overseas and America became a service (or "servants") economy.

Like most people teaching at the college level, I find the passivity of students incredibly alarming and I think that at least some of the blame for this should be placed on an educational system that shies away from modernist values. I think the postmodern, white-collar viewpoint I have been describing pretends to be radical but cannot be radical in any social or political sense because in its most coherent form it cannot conceive of a social or cultural entity bigger than one individual at one moment in time. In its effort to undermine the assumption of universality that supported modern industrialism, it now lends support to individualist consumer capitalism and to the exchange theory of value.

It is difficult for me to tell to what extent my attitudes are based in an intellectual nostalgia for the modernist values that shaped my philosophical education or in the values and sentiments that I assumed and developed as a child and young man in working-class America. The modernist production-oriented metaphysics and epistemology fit my experience and yet do not fit my current position in society. The greatest conflict occurs when I am unable to join hands with colleagues who are critical of the impact of consumer capitalism on American culture and on the political system because my whole approach to analysis is seen as conservative because of my modernist assumptions.

So I think periodically about the photographs of the Japanese joinery and of the bits of machinery my father would bring home and realize that this is baggage—valued baggage—that I will never lose. A few years back I was on Governor Cuomo's Task Force on Bias Violence and at the same time taught a class at New York University. I remember getting to class early one evening, and I stood by the window looking down at Washington Square Park in Greenwich Village, and I had a sense of vertigo when I thought about how far it was from that window to the factory where I assembled the 750,000 plastic wheels. I do not want to lose the connection I have to my past. I do not want to forget that the person who worked in that factory and the person I am now are the same.

Part Four | Awayward Mobility

24

The Work of Professing (A Letter to Home)

Michael Schwalbe

Nearly all of his working life my father has been an electrician. He has sometimes done wiring jobs on the side, but mostly he has worked for large employers and received an hourly wage. For seven years he worked a second job at night as a truck driver hauling slag for a foundry. Before she married, my mother was a secretary for a food wholesaler. She went back into the paid labor force after the youngest of five children was grown. After several years of factory work assembling garage door openers, she took a job as a nurse's aide in a veterans' retirement home. My mother and father are in their early sixties and still working.

Because I grew up in it and still visit it twice a year, I know the world in which my parents live and work. But they have no similar knowledge of, nor even access to, my world, which is distant to them both geographically and socially. Despite my reports over the years, my world, the world of the university, remains largely a mystery to them. This means that I too remain in part a mystery to them, for it is in the university and through academic work that I have grown up these past twenty years and become who I am.

What I think would help to bridge the gulf that my awayward mobility has put between my parents and me is an account, set down in one piece, of my work and the place in which I do it. This chapter is such an account, in the form of a letter to my parents. It is not a real letter, of course, since it is also a public statement. This allows it to speak to more than one set of parents, if anyone would care to use it that way. I also want to address readers whose backgrounds and experiences may be similar to mine, as I presume will be the case for many readers of this book. I take pleasure in imagining that this audience will be able to appreciate my ambivalence about being in this fine place so far from home.

Dear Mom and Dad,

I'm not sure how it was that I decided to go to college. Uncle Fred went to college, and I wanted to be like him. That was part of it. Another part was being defined as "smart" in school and falling in with kids who expected to go to college. I also hoped that college would be a way to avoid ending up in a job where I'd have a boss in my face all the time. If nothing else came of it, I thought college would be a way to postpone that day.

I originally intended to go into biology or zoology but got talked into majoring in paper science instead. I'd never heard of paper science before a college recruiter told me about it. He'd seen all the math and chemistry on my high school transcript and zeroed in on me. He told me that paper science graduates typically have half a dozen job offers to pick from, with starting salaries (in 1974) around $14,000. I was sold. Here was just what I'd hoped college would provide: a sure route to a good job, like the posters on the buses promised.

Paper science was supposed to be a natural for me with my math and science background. But it wasn't long before going to my math and chemistry classes felt like going to a bad job. I just wasn't interested in the stuff anymore and, in a context fraught with distractions, I wasn't doing very well, either. Halfway through my second semester I knew that I either had to find a better reason to stay in paper science or find something else to study. A six-month internship in a paper mill the following fall convinced me that I had to find something else.

In looking for something else, I studied accounting, economics, psychology, and sociology. The sociology course, which was about crime, really clicked for me. It helped me understand why some kids in the old neighborhood—kids who never did anything worse than I did—had gotten in trouble, stayed in trouble, and were having tough lives while I was having fun in college. This was the first course I'd ever taken that gave me insight into my own life.

Sociology hooked me for other reasons, too. I was primed for it. Six years in a repressive German Lutheran grade school, four years on the debate team in high school, a desire to stand out for knowing the right answers, Dad's discipline at home, and a strong, if not sophisticated, sense of justice all predisposed me to choose a major that equipped me to detect bullshit and to challenge authority.

It wasn't easy to tell you that I was going to major in sociology. Paper science made sense: Whatever it was, you studied it and got a white-collar job in a paper mill. But sociology? I could barely explain what it was, let alone what kind of job it might lead to. Nor did it seem adequate to say that I wanted to study it simply because it interested me. So I suppose I said something about sociology being the "scientific" (to make it sound legitimate) study of society and about it leading to all kinds of job opportunities. I didn't know what I was talking about. I just didn't want you to think I was wasting my time.

If you thought my choice was foolish, you were kind enough not to say so. I think you were more perplexed than anything else. I remember feeling strange when I sensed this. I could see it was the start of moving away from you. It wasn't that I knew then where sociology would lead me. It was seeing how innocently unaware you were of the world I'd entered.

Even though I worried that my choice of a new major would disappoint you, it was exciting to make that choice on my own. Since I was paying my own way (with some help from the government), I figured that I could study whatever I liked. I also figured that I could make a living somehow since I had mechanical skills and had always been able to get good summer jobs. So even if I didn't know where sociology would lead, I was sure of one thing: I didn't have to major in a dreary but marketable field to survive.

Thinking this way set me on a new path. Instead of trying just to get through my classes, I tried to get as much out of them as possible. Finding a perspective from which to make sense of things—or at least from which to look at them—made everything more interesting. Grades were never again an issue. (I would have graduated with honors if not for that botched first year.) My confidence and energy rose, too. Over the next few years I got involved with student government, with the student activities board, and with the campus newspaper. I also got to know my profs.

Standing out in my classes and getting to know my professors had a big effect on me. The recognition and attention boosted my confidence even more. But there was more to it. For the first time since catechism class I felt appreciated for what I'd learned through reading. What was even better was that here I felt appreciated for the unauthorized knowledge I'd somehow acquired. Unlike my hapless grade school teachers and harried high school teachers, these professors *liked* to talk about things that weren't covered in the text.

Looking back, I can see that it also mattered that these were older men appreciating me for skills and knowledge that weren't worth much at home. I guess I also felt that the skills I had acquired at home—how to hunt and fish and how to build and fix things—never equaled those of the other men in the family. One time when I bragged that I knew how to run any machine in his shop, Uncle Carl said, "You wouldn't amount to a pimple on the ass of a good machinist." He was right. I couldn't wire a house, either.

Even though I began to feel accepted by my professors, it was still clear that I was coming from somewhere else. Once when I was talking to a professor in his office, another professor leaned in the doorway and said, "I just heard a new excuse for missing an exam. A student said he couldn't come in today because he had to move a trailer house." The professor to whom I was talking laughed and replied, "That's one I haven't heard before. I guess it tells you you're really at a blue-collar college." Part of me liked being privy to this exchange. I took it to mean I was being treated as an insider. But I also sympathized with the student. It made sense to me that you might have to miss an exam to move a trailer house. What was funny about that?

It wasn't until sometime in my fourth year that it occurred to me that I could be a professor myself. It happened one day as I crossed paths with two of my profs and said hello. In that moment it struck me that they were regular people, and I thought, "I'll bet I could do what they do." The thought shook me. That was the first time it dawned on me, after three and a half years of college, that I was within reach of a life I'd never thought possible.

It wasn't that I immediately wanted to be a professor; that still seemed far-fetched. But I let the idea stew, and I began to think about my other options. Journalism was the only thing I could come up with. I'd already done well with my newspaper writing and freelancing for some outdoor magazines. And the idea of being a writer had romantic appeal. But I knew that to make a living I'd have to find a job as a reporter, and those jobs were scarce.

My professors encouraged me to go to graduate school. When I asked how I was supposed to afford it, they told me that any decent school would waive tuition and give me a half-time job of some kind. This sounded like a better deal than earning low wages writing about city council meetings.

Sociology had also become important to me as a way to keep opening my mind. I felt that it had saved me from my own ignorance and prejudices. And though my sense of mastery was laughably premature, I felt I understood sociology well enough to use it to figure out almost anything about how the world worked. In this way, it was a source of power not just to figure things out but to make myself grow. I also wanted more of the fun of talking about sociology with like-minded people. I wanted even more intense intellectual experiences of the kind that had opened my mind and eyes as an undergraduate. That's what I expected to get in graduate school: more of the freedom, ideas, and fellowship I'd enjoyed as an undergraduate, only better.

This account of my motives makes it sound as if I'd already become hungry for an intellectual life. Not exactly. Another big part of choosing graduate school was wanting to avoid getting pinned down in a real job. I simply wasn't ready to give up the freedom I'd gotten used to during five years in college. I also wanted to get out of Wisconsin and see another part of the country. And I wasn't necessarily fixed on getting a Ph.D., either. I thought I'd keep up my writing on the side while I got a master's degree and decide what to do after that.

If college was largely unknown territory for our family, graduate school was another world entirely. At that time we didn't even have the words or images available to us to allow me to explain what graduate school was or why I wanted to go. But I felt that, as with majoring in sociology, you were generally supportive of my decision, even if you understood it only as "what I wanted to do." You seemed to have some kind of quiet faith that things would work out for me—maybe more faith than I had.

I still have two small gifts you gave me when I graduated from college and you knew I was going to graduate school in the fall. One is a plastic pen holder that bears the quotation: "There is no one road to success. There are as many as there are men willing to build them." I figured this meant you approved of my taking whatever route would get me where I wanted to go. The other gift was a trivet with a picture of an owl saying, "It's what you learn *after* you know it all that counts." I saw this as your way of reminding me not to confuse fancy degrees with wisdom. Both messages I took as blessings.

Graduate school was as intense as I'd hoped, if not in all the ways I had hoped. I spent so much time reading sociology, talking about it, and doing my work as a research assistant that I never had time to do any writing on the side. I was absorbed in what I was doing and was mostly satisfied with the situation. But one thing bothered me: many of the faculty seemed to care more about building their careers than about doing sociology to understand, let alone change, society. I was disheartened to discover this. I had assumed that what my undergraduate professors did with sociology—which was to debunk a lot of the pernicious nonsense their students believed—was the point of the whole enterprise. I hadn't yet learned to distinguish between sociology as an intellectual pursuit and the pursuit of an academic career as a sociologist. These are two different things that call for different skills and inclinations.

So it bothered me to see status seeking as the motive behind doing sociology, which seemed to me to betray what sociology was about. Fortunately, some of my fellow graduate students felt the same way I did and we supported each other. If this hadn't been the case, I probably would have quit in disgust. I also stayed because I found a few profs who shared my view that when sociology was done right, it was critical of unjust social arrangements and illegitimate authority.

Graduate school was scary at first because I didn't know how I'd measure up against my fellow students, who I assumed would all be top notch. I worried, too, because I had gotten an assistantship only after I drove two thousand miles and showed up on the department's doorstep. I supposed that all those other folks who'd gotten assistantships right away were better than me. My fears were unfounded, as I learned once the work began, and prior grades and test scores didn't matter. I saw some alleged hot shots crash and burn in one semester.

From this I learned a lesson about academic credentials: they often promise goods that can't be delivered, but they're still valuable commodities in themselves. They can be traded for jobs, access to powerful people, and for chances to display one's work. This became clear as I began to grasp the importance of having degrees from the right places.

I knew that some colleges were more famous than others, but I didn't realize how important institutional prestige is to academics. Nor did I know how this affects people's careers. I had assumed that once you got a Ph.D., regardless of where it came from, what mattered most was the quality of the work you did, as far as getting a job and being recognized for your work were concerned. Later I realized how much the academic obsession with status and prestige can distort perceptions of quality.

I mention this because it shows the naïveté I brought to graduate school. I didn't know what kind of system I was getting into, so I couldn't anticipate the consequences of my choices. By the time I found myself heading for an academic career and thinking that I wanted one, I realized there were places that wouldn't hire me because of where I'd gone to graduate school. At one time I considered changing schools and going somewhere more prestigious. But I couldn't see paying again the price of moving and establishing my credibility with another group of professors who were likely to be more snobbish.

Maybe my undergraduate professors should have advised me better. Then again, they didn't send many students on to graduate school and, despite my enthusiasm, they probably had doubts about my commitment to an academic career. When one of my undergraduate professors suggested that I apply to the University of California at Berkeley, I said, "That's in San Francisco, isn't it? I think I want to be closer to good trout fishing." That's how I was thinking at the time.

Most people who get Ph.D.'s and pursue academic careers get hired right away as professors. Many of my present colleagues went from being graduate students one semester to being professors the next. Things didn't happen that way for me. I left graduate school before my dissertation was done so I could maintain a personal relationship. I did manage to finish my dissertation on schedule (in 1984), but I wasn't free to take any job that came along. Being in a relationship meant that unless I found a job that offered us both a better situation, it would have been pointless and unfair to take it. So I took what I could get locally. These were my years as a part-time lecturer.

During those years I taught classes like a regular professor, but I taught on a course-by-course basis. The jobs were always temporary. I was more like hired help than a real part of the departments or universities where I taught. I was looking for a tenure-track (i.e., permanent, full-time) job but having no luck. Jobs for sociologists were scarce in the early-to-mid eighties, and there were probably two hundred applicants for each opening. Even so, *some* people were getting jobs, and I thought I should have been one of them since I already had a good publication record for a new Ph.D.

You could probably tell that was an unhappy time for me. The bleak job scene strained the relationship and created more unhappiness. One good thing about those years was that I had time to write. I revised my dissertation and published it as a book. I also published a bunch of articles, as new Ph.D.'s are supposed to do to show their "scholarly promise." I thought that my productivity was promising a lot and that I'd get a real job soon.

When that didn't happen, I started to get a little crazy. I began to obsess about publishing *one more article* that would put me over some magical line and cause interview offers to pour in. As a sociologist, I should have known better. But after all the years of school and hard work, I had to believe I could control my fate. Writing more was the only honest thing I could think of to do.

The reasons why I wasn't getting interviews are complicated. I didn't realize what was going on until years later when I watched the hiring process from the inside. I saw how any odd bit of information in a job candidate's file—anything out of the ordinary that couldn't readily be accounted for—made the candidate suspect. No doubt I was suspect because I'd left my graduate department early (trouble?), because I wrote about a variety of things (is he serious about any of them?), and because I had a good publication record (there must be a problem or someone would have snapped him up by now). If I'd known how I was being perceived, if I'd known how important appearances and networks are in this world, I could have been more strategic in my self-presentation and might have had better luck sooner.

In any case, after four years of applying for academic jobs, I was ready to say the hell with it. I liked teaching and writing and wanted to keep doing these things, but I didn't want to keep hanging on with no security, wondering if I'd have a job from one term to the next, feeling like a marginal person. By the fall of 1986 I'd decided that if nothing came through that season, I'd look for something nonacademic.

The academic job market was better that year. There were more jobs advertised and more jobs that fit my research and teaching interests. So I was hopeful, despite the previous three unproductive seasons. In January of 1987 I was ready to quit looking for an academic job when I got an offer to interview for the job I'm in now. Much to my surprise, I got two more interview offers in quick succession. This was more action than I'd seen in the previous three years. Things were looking brighter, even if I didn't yet have a job.

The folks here obviously thought I looked good on paper, but they too had suspicions. Before I came for my interview, one of the search committee members called to talk about the place and how I might fit in. Toward the end of the conversation, he said, "I know this is a rude thing to ask, but some people are wondering why, with your publication record, you don't have a job already. What can I say to put them at ease?"

This question tells you a lot about academia. It tells you that fitting in socially can be more important than being a good scholar and teacher. It also tells you how insiders can be blind to what it's like to be on the outside. For years I'd been trying to get a job in a tight market by building my credentials; I thought this was the right thing to do. But now the burden was on me to explain why, with my fine credentials, I didn't have a job! The explanation that made everything okay was that my marriage had ended and now I was applying widely for jobs and was willing to move to take a permanent position.

That same year there were two jobs open near home. I didn't apply for one of them, even though it fit me well, because it was at a school that I saw as "too small." As much as I wanted to be closer to home geographically, I was pulled away by the same concerns for academic prestige that were so distasteful to me only a few years before. It would have felt like failure to take a job at a school where there was no graduate program, too much teaching, and where some kids missed exams because they had to move trailer houses.

The other job was a post-doc (a temporary research position). I applied for it and actually received an offer, which I would have taken if I hadn't gotten the job here. I never told you about the job at the small college or about the post-doc because I thought you wouldn't understand why I chose not to pursue them. I always sensed that you expected me eventually to move back near home, and I didn't want to say why I'd passed up my chances. Holding out for higher status was a motive I wouldn't have been comfortable trying to explain or justify. I'm still not.

As it turned out, the interview here (in early 1987) went well. I liked the place and the people, and the people liked me. I got the job and for six years have been a full-time professor. The job isn't really permanent yet. This year I'm being evaluated (yet again) and considered for tenure. Let me digress a bit and explain what this means. Simply put, tenure is lifetime job security. To get it you have to pass muster after a six-year probationary period. In principle, you are judged on the quantity and quality of your research, the quality of your teaching, and your service to the university.

The way it's usually done is that a group of already tenured faculty members reviews your record and makes a yes-or-no recommendation to the department. The department then makes its recommendation to the dean, who makes a recommendation to the provost, who makes a recommendation to the chancellor, who makes a recommendation to the board of trustees. You can be turned down anywhere along the way—right off the bat at the department level or down the line by the muckety-mucks. The recommendation from the department is the first big hurdle. The dean is the second. If the dean says yes, the higher-ups usually rubber-stamp the decision.

The idea behind tenure isn't that you work hard or kiss ass for six years and then coast for the rest of your life. The idea, and I know this sounds pretentious, is that the pursuit of truth requires that professors be free to go wherever that pursuit leads them, even if it means adopting unpopular positions. So tenure is supposed to ensure that professors don't avoid seeking or speaking the truth for fear of losing their jobs. Of course, people who adopt too many unpopular positions can be weeded out before tenure. You can see why fitting in is so important. Professors and administrators don't want to have an irritating person around for many years.

Some people think tenure makes professors lazy and complacent. Maybe that's true in some cases, but on the whole I think tenure is a good thing. Job security doesn't guarantee that anyone will find the truth or even know where to look for it. But it does make a person freer to say what he or she thinks. It seems clear, too, that job *insecurity* is what keeps many people from saying what they think. And I think it hurts us all when people are afraid to speak their minds. By the way, tenure is not supposed to protect professors who fail to do their jobs; they can still be fired if they screw up badly enough. The problem is that there's a lot of rigmarole involved in getting rid of someone with tenure, so it's rarely done.

As I said, I'm up for tenure this year. Although I know better than to expect justice, I don't expect any problems, either. I've written and published more than most folks around here and I've worked hard as a teacher. Any complaints about me will probably stem from my inability to suffer fools lightly. (I'm still trying to cultivate more patience with my students and colleagues than Dad sometimes showed with me.) In any case, if all goes well I will finally have a secure job and a promotion in title from assistant to associate professor.

If I am denied tenure I can stay one more year while I look for another job. That's how the system works. It's civilized even when it gives you the boot. Right now I don't know what I'll do if for some reason I don't get tenure. The prospect of telling you, as I near forty and after so many years of school and academic work, that I was being fired is too painful to consider. I'll have to keep writing this as if everything will be okay. Maybe your quiet faith will prove to be warranted.

I set out to tell you about my work as a professor. Now that you know how I got here, I think an account of my work and what it means to me will make more sense. First you need to know a few things about the place where I work.

I'm in a state-supported research university that offers bachelor's degrees in eighty-nine fields, master's degrees in eighty fields, and Ph.D.'s in fifty-one fields. We have about eighteen thousand undergraduates and nearly five thousand graduate students. By comparison, there were about ten thousand students altogether at my undergraduate college, which offered bachelor's degrees in most of the usual fields but master's degrees in only a few. Being a professor in a place like this is different from being a professor in a four-year college. If I were at a smaller college that offered only bachelor's degrees, I'd spend more time teaching and much less time doing research.

Professors here are expected to spend a lot of time doing research, publishing the results, and training graduate students to do the same things. The idea is that in a research university we're supposed to find out new things as well as teach the old stuff. Professors are also expected to bring in money from outside sources to pay for their research. Teaching undergraduates still takes up a lot of most professors' time, even at a place like this. But since the rewards (raises, promotions, prestige) are greater for bringing in grant money and for publishing articles than for teaching, many professors put the greater share of their time and energy into research. I'll confess that this is my tendency, too.

It isn't that I dislike teaching. In fact, I like it very much; some of my greatest feelings of satisfaction come from teaching. Nor is it simply that I put more effort into research and writing because the payoffs are better. The situation is more complicated. For me, the greater appeal of research and writing has to do with what it's like to teach in a place like this. Here's a parable I made up to give you a sense of what it's like.

Imagine that while learning the practical skills of life a young man discovers a subject that fascinates him. It could be philosophy, physics, sociology, or whatever. If he could, he would be happy to spend all his days reading and writing about this subject. This seems like an impossible dream since he also needs to earn a living, which the young man has always expected to involve long hours of tiring work at whatever tasks his boss sets for him. But then the dream seems to come true when the young man finds an employer who will pay him to study the subject he loves.

The prospective employer says, "I will pay you to read and write about what most interests you, but you must also teach what you learn." The young man says, "Of course. I would be happy to teach others about the subject I love and what I learn. Do I get to choose my apprentice?" The employer says, "You might at some time get an apprentice, whom you may or may not get to choose. More often, you will have hundreds of students whom you do not get to choose and whom you will see for only a few months." The dream job now appears to have some rough edges.

"Hundreds of students!" says the young man. "How can I teach under such conditions?" But then, considering his options, he says, "All right, I suppose the situation can be handled if compromises are made." The employer says, "Yes, you will have to make compromises, though you should pretend that you are not doing so. And there is one more thing. Many of your students will not care at all about what you have to teach. Some will even dislike it. Knowing this, do you still want the job?" For the chance to study what he is most interested in and seeing no better way to make a living, the young man says yes.

Well, I said yes, and one reason I put more energy into my research and writing is that I would still rather read and write about what fascinates me than force-feed this stuff to students who are more concerned with degrees and jobs than with sociology. I understand my students' concerns with degrees and jobs: I began college with the same concerns. But then I made a risky choice to do what my heart said was right, and I guess I expect them to be willing to do the same. When students tell me they're majoring in a field they don't really like but that they think will get them a job, I get angry at them for their weakness and at the system that forces them to make such an alienating choice.

Even knowing the pressures they are responding to, it is still hard to stomach their indifference. It still feels like an insult when students don't find sociology as fascinating as I do. When I face this indifference, I think that either they're too dumb to be worth my efforts, or I'm no good at what I'm doing. Both thoughts are painful.

On the other hand, when students are tuned in and I can see that they're "getting it," then teaching is more fun than sitting alone writing. On days when teaching goes well, I think that I'd like to do more of it, maybe teach three courses a semester at a four-year college, a place where I could teach smaller classes and get to know my students better. But on days when I don't see the lights coming on or when I see students spacing out or when I see some sign that all this energy going into teaching isn't appreciated, then I feel like burying myself in research. At least I know that something will come of it.

Maybe that's also part of why I'm more drawn to research than teaching: I need to see a tangible product in order to believe I'm doing real work. You might never have said this in as many words, but somehow I learned that real work is done with the back and hands and results in things you can see and touch and use. Being a paper pusher in the front office meant getting away with doing nothing productive. As a teacher I'm a notch below paper pusher since most of what I do is talk. At least if I write a paper I can heft it. I can see that something exists where nothing existed before. And if I write lots of papers, I can see lines add up on my vita. All this is evidence of my ability to produce, which I also somehow learned is an important measure of a person's worth.

But what do I have to show for my work as a teacher of sociology? The immediate results are things students say or write. I know that other good things might happen in the long run; lives might be changed, even in cases where students appear indifferent. But this isn't like being able to eat vegetables from your garden or drive a car you've just fixed. It occurs to me now that telling you about my work is only part of what I want to do here. I also feel a need to convince you that I really do work, even if my work is different from yours and what I produce can't always be seen or touched or used.

I'll start with teaching since, as I said, this is where the relationship between effort and result is so uncertain. I usually teach two classes a semester (which means anywhere from fifty to one hundred fifty students altogether); each class meets for three hours a week. Sometimes people outside the university think this means I spend six hours a week teaching. That's not so. I spend anywhere from thirty minutes to three hours preparing for each hour of class time. It depends on what I'm doing. If I'm presenting new material, then I have to reread it and prepare lecture notes. If it's old material and no revising is necessary, then preparation takes much less time.

There's of course more to teaching than preparing to speak in class. I also have to create exams and evaluate the answers my students write. My exams usually call for essay answers, so I generate more work for myself than if I used multiple-choice exams, which can be graded by computer. I use essay exams because they let me see how much students understand. They also give me more openings for commenting on students' work.

Sometimes I have my students keep journals, which I read and comment on periodically. If I have fifty students who are keeping journals, it can take a lot of time to read them, even if I do it only twice a semester. In my graduate classes the students have to write papers, which I also read and comment on. I've never figured out how much time it takes to do all this because then I'd be tempted to calculate how much I earn per hour, and I really don't want to know.

There's more to it still. Between classes I meet with students. Sometimes I do what you'd expect: explain grades or give extra help with assignments. Other times it gets stickier. Students who come to my office for help often end up telling sad stories about messed up families, romances gone awry, overly demanding jobs. It's often hard to figure out how to help them get on with their course work and yet respond with humane concern for their troubles. If a student is in really bad shape, I'll urge a visit to the counseling center. More often I just listen and ask questions that they haven't asked themselves. Even this can be draining.

Teaching graduate students is different from teaching undergraduates (although the graduate students also tell sad stories). Graduate students are supposedly ready to devote years of their lives to studying sociology, so they're more serious and willing to do more and harder work. Graduate classes are kept small (usually fewer than twenty students), so the interaction is more intimate. This beats the hell out of teaching one hundred or more undergraduates in a theater-sized lecture hall. We also work closely with graduate students who help us with our own research and teaching. This is more like a true apprenticeship arrangement.

Professors teach in different ways, though mostly commonly by lecturing. This means profs fill up class time by doing most of the talking. A good lecture is supposed to be like a clear, informative, stimulating article read out loud. Lecturing works well if you just have a lot of information to get across. But I don't do it much because I remember hating long lectures when I was a student and because I think there are better methods. So in my classes I usually present for twenty or thirty minutes and then pose problems for students to work on in small groups. I try to find ways to put them on track to finding answers for themselves instead of telling them what they should know.

In some ways this makes teaching more tiring because I have to watch carefully to make sure things unfold productively. As you might imagine, it's easy for discussion to lapse into bullshitting, especially if students haven't done their assigned reading before class. So opening the class up for discussion also means creating more chances for things to go wrong. Writing everything out ahead of time and delivering a monologue would be less risky and less tiring. I think that's why many professors do it. It helps them maintain control.

It might surprise you that my work as a teacher isn't seriously evaluated. Students fill out rating forms at the end of each semester, but that's about it. No one pays much attention to the results of what I do as a teacher, at least not in terms of what students learn. On the other hand, if a professor is badly disorganized, gives tests that are seen as grossly unfair, or is abusive to students, word gets around and he or she will eventually be called on it. Truly bad teaching is hard to hide. What's much easier to hide is ineffective teaching since it can be packaged to seem more substantial, like putting candy bars in a box of breakfast cereal.

If there's a good side to this, it's the freedom it provides. As long as I don't freak out my students too badly, I can teach any way I want. As long as I can argue that doing things a certain way is effective and ethical, then I can do it. All professors want this freedom. No one wants anyone else second-guessing what they do in the classroom. Even people who teach the same courses might not agree on which books, ideas, and assignments are the best. Another reason professors insist on freedom in the classroom is that it's compensation for our lack of control over larger matters.

Most of my students seem to like how I teach, although I get along better with some than with others. The students with whom I get along best are the ones who are either really bright and unconventional (you might even say weird) or only average but highly motivated. I do well with these people. They want to think and learn things, and I try extra hard to make sure they do. Maybe I lean toward the unconventional students, and they lean toward me, because we sense that we are outsiders in a way. Maybe I get along with the average-but-hard-working kids because they sense my respect for their efforts to learn and develop themselves, as I tried to do.

The students I have trouble with are the average and indifferent, some of whom resent my expectation that they think and work hard. The problem isn't just that I want them to do more than they want to do. It's that I expect them to see the work (reading, writing, thinking, speaking) as serious and worth doing well. When they don't take it seriously, it digs at my insecurities about how real and worthwhile this work is. It bothers me almost as much when students work hard for the wrong reasons. If students are motivated only by the desire for high grades, then this, too, says that they see little value in sociology itself. If there's a subset of these kids who *really* bother me, it's those who think that a good life is assured for them whether they try to learn anything in college or not. These are the kids whose parents buy them cars and cellular phones for graduation presents. There just isn't much I can do for most of them since these kids have few reasons to think critically about how our society works. They're too comfortable to see any problems worth studying.

It might seem strange to say that kids come to college and then resist learning. I think it's pretty strange, too, but it's not all that mysterious. As I said, some of the kids from privileged backgrounds don't see any need to go out of their way to learn anything, at least not about sociology. And a lot of other kids would be working if decent jobs were available. What many of these kids want is to get a degree, get a job that pays better than flipping burgers, and buy things they think will make them happy. Professors with their damn courses, reading assignments, tests, and term papers just stand in the way.

Sociology can evoke another kind of resistance. In sociology courses the beliefs that students bring with them to college are often challenged. For example, I teach a course called Social Problems, which examines the causes and consequences of racism and sexism in our society. The clear moral message is that racism and sexism are bad because they damage people. You can guess what happens when students come to my class full of racist and sexist attitudes they acquired back home. Some conflict is inevitable and even desirable—the kids need to have their thinking disturbed—but not all of them like it. It's as if they expect to get through college without being upset by anything they learn. These are the ones who are bothered because I take it as part of my job to upset them.

I sometimes imagine that the conservative kids in my classes, the ones coming from working-class, small-town backgrounds, are like you were forty years ago. I wonder if we would have clashed if we had met as teacher and students. I wonder if you would have been as upset by what I teach as some of my students are today. I suppose so. As I recall, you went from supporting George Wallace in 1968 to Jesse Jackson in 1984. That's quite a change. Imagine a teacher trying to push you to make that kind of change in one semester.

It might sound like I try to convert students to sociology as if it were a religion. Maybe there is some evangelical fervor left over in me from grade school days. I really do believe in the value of a sociological point of view (in this sense I do "profess"), and I think the world would be a better place if everyone could adopt this point of view. But as a teacher, I don't want true believers. All I want are students willing to let themselves be affected by the facts and ideas I offer. Obviously, I hope they'll be affected for the better. I hope they'll be able to make better sense of the world and of their place in it and to be more responsible people. Beyond that, I have to trust that their sense of justice will tell them what is the right thing to do.

I know this sounds grandiose. But it tells you something about how I approach teaching, which is with the grand aims of shaping minds and transforming lives. Maybe this sets me up to fail most of the time since I can't possibly affect all of my students the way my professors affected me. Many things beyond my control have to be just right for that to happen, but I've seen it happen a few times, and knowing that it can and will happen again keeps me going.

Research is the other big part of my work life. I'd like to think that my research and writing will also affect people for the better. Hoping to have some effect keeps me going in this part of my work life as well. The work itself is also a source of motivation.

Part of the enjoyment comes from finding out what nobody knew before. I've studied how people's work affects their thoughts and feelings about themselves, the ways in which parents' behavior affects the self-esteem of their teenage children, the ways in which people's work affects their health, how women and men derive self-esteem in different ways, and what kinds of attitudes are associated with willingness to discriminate against people with AIDS. In each case I could say that I found out something new, and I was happy to put this new information into print under my name.

But the main satisfaction was and is more in the doing than in the discovering. I like the process of coming up with a question and figuring out a way to answer it. This involves reading other people's work and thinking, What's next? What else is there to find out about this stuff? What would be interesting to know that no one knows yet? You can always think of trivial answers to these questions; there's always some itsy bit of information you can go after. The trick is to think of what's worth the effort to find out. You also have to be realistic. There might be something that everyone is aching to know, but if there's no way to get a good answer, you're stuck.

I enjoy the challenge of figuring out how to find a good answer. A lot of this work goes on in my head or in conversations with colleagues or in notebooks. It's like seeing a need for a new gadget, then designing and building it in your imagination or on paper. If the thing is something you need or others will buy, then you might go ahead and build it. It's the same thing with research. You might imagine lots of possibilities before you settle on a project that's both doable and worth doing.

Research is satisfying because it is craft work. You have to imagine the product, figure out how to make it, and then go through dozens of steps to bring it into being. Each step has to be done just right in order to end up with something useful and respectable. Think of Grampa building a cabinet and all the things he had to do to make sure it turned out right. And as in any kind of craft work, unexpected problems arise. This means you get stumped occasionally and have to learn new skills. It also means that the final product reflects the energy and skill you put into it.

Not all of my scholarly work involves studying things firsthand. Sometimes I write articles in which I try to analyze some aspect of social life. For example, I've written about whether it's possible for competition to be non-destructive, about how the kind of work people do makes them more or less empathic, about why our students can't write, about how inequality affects moral reasoning, and about whether it's possible to know more about ourselves than we can say. In each case, I was building on or playing off arguments made by other writers. This is part of what makes an essay a piece of scholarship instead of just a long editorial. Doing this right—making the argument clear and tight and connecting it to what others have said—takes time and care.

My work involves a lot of writing. In addition to articles and book chapters, I write book reviews, grant proposals, comments on other people's work, memos, letters, and field notes. The comments, memos, and letters I do whenever there's time. The stuff that's really important to me I work on in the morning, when I feel freshest. Every morning when I'm not teaching I spend two to three hours writing at home in my study. This might not seem like much, but it's about the best I can do. My head goes dry after three hours staring into a computer screen. Besides, on a good day, three hours might yield five usable pages. That's not bad. Even one usable page a day would amount to a book a year.

On bad days, writing can be agonizing. It goes slowly and nothing sounds right. (To use the cabinet metaphor again, the corners aren't square, the joints are loose, and the drawers won't close.) Once I started the morning with five pages of a manuscript I had begun the previous day. Three hours later I was down to two pages. That's how it goes sometimes. What I really enjoy, though, is finishing something. Even if I sometimes hate writing, I love having written (as the writer Dorothy Parker said).

Before an article is finished it goes through umpteen revisions. *Umpteen* is the right word since I don't know how many drafts I do. If every bit of tinkering counts as revising, then a paper might be revised a hundred times before it appears in print. If only full drafts count, then I'd say I go through a dozen or so revisions. Few nonwriters appreciate this process. They seem to believe that articles either come out right the first time or they don't. Students often operate on this mistaken belief and thus produce junk (usually at the last minute before a deadline). When they learn how to do drafts and revise, they also learn that their professors aren't so smart.

For me, writing is an important part of the work of professing. It doesn't do much good to study something if you can't tell others what you've found. You have to be able to describe and explain complex things in writing. This is a hard craft to master (though it certainly doesn't require a Ph.D., which appears to be a liability in many cases). Even after much instruction and years of practice, I still struggle to write well. I feel like a perpetual beginner.

Writing isn't the same as publishing, and it is publishing that I'm expected to do; the manuscripts that stay in my desk drawer don't count. So I have to know not just how to write but how to get my writing into print in the right places. This is supposed to happen like so: I write a draft of a paper and ask colleagues to comment on it and help me improve it; after I've done the best job I can, I send the paper to a journal editor who sends it to several (two to four) anonymous reviewers for evaluation; the reviewers send their comments to the editor, who decides whether to accept the paper as it is, to ask me to revise and resubmit it, or to reject it; the editor sends me his or her decision, along with the reviewers' comments, and then the ball's back in my court. If the paper's rejected I can try a different journal. If the editor is willing to consider a revision, I can make the asked-for changes and resubmit. If it's accepted as it is, which happens rarely, then I might do some more tinkering, but I'm pretty much home free. As you might imagine, there's room in this process for bad things to happen.

The idea behind the process is that anonymous peer review produces objective evaluations of scholarly work, the best of which then gets into print. In reality it doesn't always happen that way. One problem is that an editor can kill a paper by sending it to reviewers who are likely to be extremely critical. Or an editor can do the opposite—maybe as a favor for a friend or for a big shot in the discipline—and send the paper to reviewers who will probably like it. Another problem is that editors often get back mixed reviews; one reviewer will like a paper, another will hate it, and another will feel so-so. The editor must then decide whether to reject the paper or ask for a revision. Here again the decision is subjective. A person who's a friend of the editor or a big shot in the discipline might get a second chance, whereas a person who's unknown will get rejected.

The reviewers in this process aren't supposed to know who the author is, and the author is not supposed to know who the reviewers are. On the one hand, this is good because it means that a paper is more likely to be judged on its merits than on the popularity of its author. On the other hand, the anonymity allows reviewers to take potshots they don't have to defend. If a reviewer doesn't like something about a paper, she or he can recommend that it not be published, and the author doesn't get a chance to respond to the criticism before the editor makes a decision. So it's wise to anticipate and preempt as many criticisms as you can.

Now you know why academic writing is often so dull. When you have to please two out of three reviewers and an editor, you're less likely to stick your neck out and say something that might anger or excite people. You're better off being bland and tentative—that is, better off if you want to get published in mainstream journals, not if you want to stimulate people or develop yourself as a writer.

Expectations about how much professors have to publish vary from place to place. In my department, people are supposed to publish two articles a year. But this is a loose expectation that some people never meet and others routinely exceed. You might think (or hope) that professors would care more about quality than quantity and some do, of course. But in a bureaucracy, quantity is emphasized because it's easier to assess than quality; tallying the number of articles, book chapters, reviews, and books a person has written is much simpler than actually reading and judging the stuff.

Turf defense also comes into play. Professors tend to get highly specialized, and they don't like it when people outside their areas of expertise judge their work. So, as with teaching, everyone sort of respects everyone else's freedom. It's as if professors in the same department agree not to scrutinize each other's work too closely, provided that the work is published in respectable places (like those boring, high-status journals I mentioned). Of course, if you're doing work that is unpopular or that some people find threatening, then you might be in for a lot of critical scrutiny.

With all this said about writing, I've almost forgotten to say that I also spend a lot of time reading. The pleasure I took in reading played a big part in getting me here. From as far back as I can remember I loved to read. (Thank you for teaching me!) I remember as a kid going to the branch public library and delighting in finding books about all kinds of amazing things, especially after I abandoned the children's section. I think I also took some delight in unnerving the librarians with my choices of books.

Although I don't have time these days to read everything I'd like to, this is still a great job for a reader. In an average day, I spend four to five hours reading *something*. The problem is that much of what I have to read can be hard to choke down, especially student papers, official memos, and journal articles. This is why I try to save at least an hour at the end of each day to read the best writing I can find. My faith in the value of intellectual work requires a daily dose of good writing. This would be impossible to get from sociology alone.

As much as I'm dedicated to a sociological way of seeing the world, it's less important to me that I do sociology than it is that I am part of a community whose members work with ideas. This community isn't limited to the university; it includes anyone who reads and writes with the aim of using ideas to make sense of what's going on in the world. And while some folks might say that intellectual work is its own reward, I think of it as a practical necessity. Everything we do (including wiring houses and caring for sick people) depends on ideas. We are effective or incompetent, happy or miserable, just or unjust, depending on the ideas we create, embrace, and act on. My job is trying to understand how all this is so in hopes that what I say and write will make people feel better, think more clearly, or act more responsibly. That's what it boils down to.

Another part of my work life is serving on committees. Most of the decisions made in an academic department are made in part or whole by committees. So we have committees to decide what courses students have to take, who gets into the graduate program, what kind of computers to buy, who we are going to hire when we have a job to fill, which books and journals to tell the library to buy, how to divide the photocopying money every year, and so on. People are sometimes elected, sometimes appointed to these committees. Some committees have a lot of work to do and might meet once a week throughout the year; others are less busy and might meet only once a semester.

Even though professors have a lot of say about how things are done in a university, this isn't a democracy. Few committees make binding decisions. Administrators can overturn just about anything a committee might do. Crafty administrators can also ensure the results they want by loading com- mittes with their toadies. A lot of this sort of game playing goes on in a university. Some professors enjoy it. They prefer committee work and being involved in bureaucratic intrigues to being teachers and researchers. After a while, these folks get promoted to being deans and provosts.

If you sense a bad attitude here, you're right. I see administrators who are, or were, lousy teachers and scholars get ahead (so to speak) because they are good at politicking or brown nosing. My bad attitude stems in part from a belief that it's unfair for people who aren't very good to earn more than those of us who slug it out in the trenches. It also stems from feeling that I had to struggle to get where I am on the basis of my merits (although being a white male helped), while a lot of administrators came from privileged backgrounds and just smooth-talked their way up. My attitude is also linked to lingering suspicions that the paper pushers in the front office don't do real work.

In thinking about committee work and administrators, it occurs to me that there's a way in which my work is so different from yours that I almost forgot to mention it: I don't have a boss. No one sets me to work at a task and supervises me. Within reason, I can usually teach the courses I want to teach and, as I said before, within those courses I can pretty much do what I want. I also pick my own research projects. Nobody tells me what to study. Of course, tabs are kept on my productivity, and the ratings my students give me are looked at to see if I'm upsetting them too much. Even so, the freedom in this job is wonderful. It's still close to having that wish-come-true job in the parable I told before.

Every time I've thought about leaving academia, it's the freedom I have here that pulls me back. Sometimes I feel guilty about this freedom—for instance, when I see the people who clean my office building or when I'm out for a run in the middle of the day and see workers building houses or roads or when I'm home for Christmas and you have only one day off during the entire holiday period. Do I deserve it so much better? Oh, I could justify my privileges. That's part of what you learn to do in college. But I'd rather make a case that the autonomy and control I enjoy shouldn't be privileges for a few but rights for everyone.

At one place where I taught most of the faculty had degrees from Ivy League schools (Harvard, Yale, Princeton, etc.). One time the conversation in the mailroom turned to sailing in the Mediterranean. I had nothing to say. For a moment I felt ashamed of my deficient background. But then I felt angry at the casual presumption of class privilege that I was witnessing. And though it wasn't intentional, I also resented being excluded for not having the expensive knowledge and experiences necessary to participate as an equal. This one episode is like academia as a whole. Acquiring what's necessary to participate as an equal *is* expensive. But some people begin with enough resources to pay the price with no pain at all. Those of us who pay dearly, and perhaps can never buy all that we need, may always have mixed feelings about our purchase.

Professors don't talk much about these matters, perhaps because they threaten the belief in achievement based on merit. We all have a stake in this belief, which is reinforced by the system we've come through to get here. Most schooling teaches the advantages of selfishness, and some people learn better than others. I'm not exempt from this. I didn't get here by spending my time organizing study groups for less adept students. If I'm different, it's only because I refuse to make peace with an economic system, of which the university is a part, that keeps us competing with each other for crumbs while the big shots keep most of the pie for themselves.

I hope I haven't led you to think that most academics are selfish, snobbish, or pompous. Many of my colleagues are thoughtful, gentle, smart, concerned with justice in the world, and fun to be around. And in this place, which is not the Ivy League, about a fourth of my colleagues in sociology come from working-class backgrounds. Most of them share my contempt for academic elitism, overpaid administrators, and lazy students from privileged backgrounds. Not being the only stranger in paradise makes it easier to be here.

You might not have been able to teach me how to deal gracefully with the pompous asses that do abound in academia or give me the experiences and knowledge that are valued here, but you did teach me to be self-reliant, and because of this I have been able to do well in this world where rewards come for being able to devise and carry out projects of one's own. You also instilled in me other good habits: to see a job through till it's done, to pay attention to details, to stand up for my point of view, to be curious (even at the risk of trouble). These too have helped me in this world. What you didn't give me you simply didn't have to give.

It seems strange, after all these pages, to think of telling you about my work as if it were separate from the rest of my life. There is no boundary. I'm working all the time. This doesn't mean I never do anything for the sheer mindless fun of it. It means that the way I see the world, the way I take it in and think about it, is part of my work. I'm always trying to see how people's thoughts and feelings and behaviors are shaped by the circumstances of their lives. I'm always trying to see how the things that people think and feel and do in everyday life keep our society going as it is or change it. This is what a sociologist thinks about. Thinking this way is part of who I am.

It's important, too, that I live with a sociologist. As you'd expect, we spend a lot of time talking about sociology. We talk about our research, the books and articles we read, projects we'd like to do, our departments and colleagues, and the discipline as a whole. We read and comment on each other's writing. But this isn't like being unable to get away from shop talk. Our shops, in a sense, are in our heads, so whatever we talk about is colored by our shared sociological view of things. Again, thinking this way and talking about the world sociologically are matters of being who we are.

I enjoy this life. I'm not split between an unfree world of working for someone else and a separate home world where I can do what I want. Sure, there's some scut work to do in this job, things I'd rather not do. But this is small stuff, and it's rarely dirty or dangerous. So even if students, reviewers, editors, colleagues, and administrators are sometimes a pain, I never feel like my work weighs down on me from outside my skin. I could say that my work is as much a matter of how I live as it is a matter of things I do as a professor.

This essay is both a piece of work and a piece of my life. Writing about how my personal history is connected to the way our society is organized is doing a kind of sociology. A famous sociologist (C. Wright Mills) said this is an important thing to do, this mucking around at the place where biography and society meet. The idea is that understanding one's self requires looking carefully at the ground out of which it grew. That's what I'm still trying to do: understand what my roots are sunk into. Sociology lets me make a living doing this. It could be that all my studies of other people are partly just a roundabout way to know myself better.

One of the losses I've felt in moving to this world is being unable to share my work with you. Oh, I've shown you some of the end results. But I've always wanted you to understand more about the process, about what the everyday doing of this work of professing means to me. That's what I've tried to convey in this letter. Having you read it in draft form and showing you the comments of the editors already have helped you see into the process. It's also opened up new conversations for us. If it does the same for others, it will serve its purpose. Opening up conversations that help people understand each other is what professors are supposed to do.

Considering where else I might have ended up, I'd have to say that I'm glad to be here, even though it is a long way from home. Maybe someday people won't need to travel so far to make a living without going to work tired and coming home tireder. I'll do the best I can to hurry that day along. In the meantime, you should know that I'm thankful for your help in getting here and in seeing what needs to be done.

Love,

Mike

Afterword

C. L. Barney Dews

During my Ph.D. preliminary oral exam, I was accused of intellectual dishonesty. A member of my committee said that my responses sounded like I was saying what the committee wanted to hear rather than what I truly felt. She said my responses lacked conviction. She was right. The only way I can be intellectual is dishonestly. Being intellectual is not part of my nature. I was regurgitating to my committee what I had learned they wanted to hear. I was saying what I had learned I was supposed to say in these situations. Graduate school hadn't really changed the way I think; it had only made me, although obviously not too convincingly, appear to think a certain way.

Nothing in my southern rural working-class (white-trash) background prepared me to think genuinely and with conviction about scholarly topics. I was in that conference room to be examined on what I had learned in graduate school, but I was called dishonest when I displayed what I had learned. Yet there was no natural way for me to deal with the questions of a preliminary exam.

My working-class way of knowing, my working-class epistemology, had failed me. There is no situation within working-class experience analogous to the preliminary exam. My background taught me that thinking or talking for the sake of thinking or talking is show-boating, a waste of time in a world where time clocks matter. My previous life experience hadn't trained me for the kind of thinking or knowing I was expected to display, so I relied on the more recently constructed and much less comfortable way of thinking I had learned in college and graduate school. I was caught between thinking and feeling, knowing and experiencing. Yes, I was being dishonest if I was expected to feel the answers as if they were organic within me. I will never be fluent in the language of the academy. It will always be at best a reluctantly learned second language.

I had set myself up for the confrontation in my prelims by having previously shown my working-class self to this professor. A year earlier I wrote a paper for her titled "Gender Tragedies: East Texas Cockfighting and *Hamlet*." In this paper I used a significant aspect of my white-trash background, weekends spent at cockfighting derbies, to interrogate traditional notions of gender construction in *Hamlet*. This paper was my first attempt to integrate my background with my foreground, to reconcile the conflicting voices within me and to use an insight from my life in a scholarly paper.

I had shown this professor "my hand." When she saw me performing in my prelims, she knew that it was just that, a performance. I wasn't being dishonest with integrity. I was a working-class boy trying to pass myself off as a scholar. In many ways this book is like my graduate school act; it's a working-class book masquerading as a traditional scholarly work.

When Carolyn and I first talked about this project and imagined the sorts of essays that people might contribute to a collection written by academics from the working class, we envisioned, more or less, traditional scholarly essays that included unique insights rooted in a working-class background, such as my seminar paper on cockfighting and *Hamlet*. We made up a few titles for the kinds of essays we imagined. My favorite was "That's *Doctor* Coal Miner's Daughter to You: Discipline in the Postmodern Classroom." Another had to do with white-trash cooking and the literary cuisine of *Babette's Feast*. In short, we imagined contributors drawing upon their working-class experiences to interrogate a scholarly topic. This wasn't the case with the real essays that started coming in, which were mostly auto-biographical and didn't resemble traditional scholarly essays. It was as though we had given our contributors a long-awaited opportunity to write about *themselves* and they responded with a gush of life stories.

Their response pointed out to us two significant things: that there are in fact many professionals in higher education from working-class backgrounds, and that these academicians are desperate to talk about their lives. Almost all of the over one hundred submissions we received for this collection were straightforward chronological stories of people's lives, with no explicit theorization and no use of a working-class background as a tool for investigation. We couldn't resist this powerful autobiographical gesture. To be honest, I would have preferred this autobiographical stance from the beginning, but the scholar-censor inside told me that no publisher would be interested in these autobiographical essays and that such essays wouldn't be seen as scholarly by critics and non-working-class colleagues. We would have preferred to ask for these autobiographical stories in the beginning, but we were constrained by a belief, which the institution quite thoroughly instilled in us, that the stories of our lives are subjective, inappropriate, and unprofessional. We thought that to justify telling our stories they had to be wrapped in a theoretical package, that they had to be presented within a recognizable scholarly frame. Resisting the institutional demand for just such justifications was in fact what many of our contributors were writing about in their essays. Many wrote about the pain caused by constantly trying to fit into an academic mold, which demeans those with working-class backgrounds. By forcing the stories of our lives to do scholarly service within a theoretical, critical, or analytical framework, we perpetuate the denial of our working-class selves. We realized that we did not want to be complicit in the institutional practice that has always erased our stories. It was apparent that our contributors did not want to write yet another theoretical, critical, analytical essay. They wanted to break their silence, to come out of the class closet. Having interpreted our call for papers as an opportunity, they had to tell their stories. These stories do not have to be yet again subordinate to a more righteous academic aim. Their stories should be and are enough. Their lives are enough.

What perhaps made this book unique and attractive to contributors was that it provided the space finally to talk about what it is like to be in the academy *and* from a working-class background. Also significant was that these working-class stories were solicited for publication within an academic setting—in a book to be published by a university press, destined for consumption by other members of the academy.

The essays here confront the academy's "don't ask, don't tell" policy regarding class. The disclosure, the coming out as working-class academics, is a necessarily autobiographical act and also a revolutionary one. These essays are revolutionary not in that the authors are working class but in that the authors admit to being working class in their essays. My life story is not a threat to the elite university until I tell it. As long as I don't talk about it, it's okay and the academy can go on pretending that it is classless. Breaking this silence is in part why this project feels so satisfying. We have taken the stories, the self-narratives, of people from the working class who have for various reasons ended up in the academy, and then told their stories from within the academy. We are telling tales out of school. These stories describe what it's like to face the erasure that the academy attempts to impose on those whom it accepts within its ranks but then asks to forget their past, to deny their stories.

If we had forced our original agenda onto these essays, if we had insisted on editing them into something they were not, or if we had continued to search for essays like those we originally had in mind and ignored those pouring in, this book would have looked like I did in my preliminary exam. The disingenuousness of the essays would have been obvious but not acknowledged. We would have been using an academic voice to tell a working-class story. Imagine the absurdity of William F. Buckley reading aloud from Studs Terkel's *Working*.

Although academics from the working class may never find a true home in either world, telling our stories helps at times to reconcile some of the painful ambivalence. I long to write and read scholarly essays that sound like my sister when she's talking—my sister who lives in a trailer house a few miles from my parents' house and continues to talk the way I used to talk, the way I often wish I still did, the way that feels honest. Unfortunately, I can't get rid of the contamination of the academy. I can't put the genie back in the bottle. I find myself using words like *hegemony* against my will. I just can't shake it. So what happens is that I shift back and forth between these styles (I sure didn't know what "style" was until college, if I really do know now). I vacillate (college word) back and forth (that's pretty comfortable) between my old way of talkin' (very comfortable) and the new discourse of the academy (academic language again,). If I take a few deep breaths, then type as fast as I can, I outrun the academic censor and write something my sister *and* a colleague might understand. But if I go too slowly, I end up thinking too much and my sister gets lost. That's my new goal: not to leave my sister behind, because when I leave her behind I leave myself, my family, and other working-class people behind.

The issue of academic versus working-class language made my editorial work on this collection particularly difficult. I don't like to play the role of gatekeeper, applying editorial standards implicated in the shaming of working-class people in the academy. Many times I resisted correcting syntactical errors because I felt that in doing so I was representing the institution and its prescriptive practices that the essay's author was railing against. These contributors were not just sending us scholarly papers we could argue over; they entrusted us with personal disclosures that represented a tremendous risk for them. A few of our contributors expressed great concern over the reactions their families might have if they ever saw the essays in this book. They were afraid of shaming their families by telling family secrets, especially secrets from within the class closet.

This book, like my tenuous "style," attempts to bridge the space between two worlds and at times finds itself in a linguistic and social chasm. There are two audiences for this book, and neither will understand it entirely. It speaks to two audiences but in the language of neither. I do not want to glamorize my working-class past and give the impression that I feel completely at home there either. The difficulty in using my more natural voice in my academic writing is mirrored by the difficulty I have in talking with members of my family about things beyond the current weather and how other family members are doing. The "liberalization" I underwent in college has turned politics and religion into subjects better left untouched. This book is fated, like its contributors, to exist in two worlds and not to be fully at home in either. It finds itself in the good part of town but still appears to be from the wrong side of the tracks.

About the Contributors

LAUREL JOHNSON BLACK has been a babysitter, waitress, maid, housekeeping supervisor, carpenter's assistant, blueberry picker, deli manager, newspaper carrier, cashier, traveling salesperson, nurses' aide, and admissions counselor. Presently, she is an assistant professor of English at St. John Fisher College in Rochester, New York, where she coordinates the writing program and works with the Writing Center. Her research interests lie in gender, language, and assessment. Her essay was written while she was a graduate student at Miami University in Oxford, Ohio.

MARY CAPPELLO teaches courses in American literature, creative writing, gender, and interdisciplinary studies at the University of Rhode Island. She has published poetry and literary criticism and is currently writing a book about the conditions of encounter and trespass in nineteenth-century American texts and contemporary cultural studies. "Useful Knowledge" was supported by a faculty development summer grant from the URI Council for Research.

JULIE A. CHARLIP is a visiting instructor of Latin American history at Whitman College in Walla Walla, Washington. A doctoral candidate in history at the University of California, Los Angeles, she specializes in nineteenth- and twentieth-century Nicaragua. Her current work examines changes in land tenure and financing arrangements that accompanied the introduction of the coffee economy in Nicaragua. She has also been an award-winning journalist.

RENNY CHRISTOPHER grew up in San Martin, California. She has worked as a typesetter, printing press operator, horse trainer, stable hand, carpenter, and teacher. She has a Ph.D. in American literature from the University of California, Santa Cruz, and is currently a lecturer at San Jose State University. She has published poetry and fiction in addition to academic work.

CARLOS LEE BARNEY DEWS received his Ph.D. in English from the University of Minnesota in 1994. His dissertation is an edition of the unfinished autobiographical writings of Carson McCullers. His essay "Gender Tragedies: East Texas Cockfighting and *Hamlet*," appeared in the February 1994 issue of the *Journal of Men's Studies*. He is an assistant professor of American literature at the University of West Florida.

STEPHEN GARGER is chairperson of the Education Department at Trinity College, Burlington, Vermont. He grew up within walking distance of the Polo Grounds and Yankee Stadium.

HEATHER J. HICKS is a student in Duke University's graduate English program. Her specialization is nineteenth- and twentieth-century American literature with particular emphasis on postmodern fiction, Southern literature, and the intersection of literature and technology. Her dissertation addresses the nexus of technology, gender, and the shifting status of the "writer" in late twentieth-century American fiction.

MILAN KOVACOVIC is an associate professor of French language and literature at the University of Minnesota, Duluth, where he has taught since 1974. He is the recipient of awards from the Minnesota State Arts Board, the Arrowhead Regional Arts Council, and the Lake Superior Contemporary Writers Series for various chapters of a bilingual social autobiography entitled in its English version *A Singular Education*.

DWIGHT LANG is a professor of sociology at Madonna University, Livonia, Michigan. He has published in a number of journals, including *Sociological Inquiry* and the *American Journal of Education*. He is currently principal investigator on a National Science Foundation-sponsored grant examining public attitudes toward science and technology.

NANCY LAPAGLIA is a professor in the Humanities Department at Daley College, one of the City Colleges of Chicago. Her doctorate is from Northern Illinois University, and she has received several NEH grants. She researches two-year colleges and is a supporter of feminist organizations. She lives on the South Side of Chicago.

CAROLYN LESTE LAW is a doctoral candidate in the Department of English at the University of Minnesota, where she teaches in the Program in Composition and Communication. She is an associate editor of *Hurricane Alice: A Feminist Quarterly*. Her research interests are in literary modernism and expatriation.

JENNIFER LAWLER is currently completing her dissertation, "Representations of Exile in Medieval Literature," at the University of Kansas. She teaches in the English Department at Neosho County Community College-Ottawa (Kansas). She is a writer/partner in Rainmaker Productions, a group devoted to creating and developing movie-length scripts.

NATON LESLIE worked at a variety of jobs while pursuing a B.A. in English at Youngstown State University and an M.A. and Ph.D. in creative writing from Ohio University. His poetry and fiction have appeared in *Alaska Quarterly Review, California Quarterly,* the *Chariton Review, Cimarron Review, Denver Quarterly, Indiana Review, Ironwood,* the *Massachusetts Review, Mid-American Review, Prairie Schooner, Puerto del Sol,* the *Texas Review,* and a dozen other journals. Twice nominated for Pushcart Awards, he received a grant for poetry from the National Endowment for the Arts in 1993. He is an assistant professor of English at Siena College in Loudonville, New York.

GEORGE T. MARTIN, JR., received a B.A. in English and Russian literature from Vanderbilt University, an M.A. in social service administration and a Ph.D. in sociology from the University of Chicago. He is a professor of sociology at Montclair State University in New Jersey. His most recent book is *The Ecology of the Automobile* (Black Rose Books, 1993).

RAYMOND A. MAZUREK was born in Chicago but grew up in Lawrence, Massachusetts, the child of several generations of factory workers who had immigrated from Poland. Finishing high school when financial aid was plentiful, he received a B.A. from Colby College in 1974 and a Ph.D. from Purdue in 1980. He has taught at Purdue, Southern Illinois, and a Penn State branch campus in Reading, where he is currently employed.

WILSON J. MOSES is professor of history at Pennsylvania State University. His publications include *The Golden Age of Black Nationalism, Black Messiahs and Uncle Toms, Alexander Crummell,* and *The Wings of Ethiopia.* His articles have appeared in the *Western Journal of Black Studies, Phylon,* the *Journal of Negro History,* and *American Literature.*

SHARON O'DAIR is an associate professor of English at the University of Alabama. She has published essays on Shakespeare, the uses of social science in literary criticism, and the issue of class in literary study and in the profession. She is working on a book tentatively titled *Bottom Lines: Class, Culture, Critics.*

CHRISTINE OVERALL is professor of philosophy at Queen's University, Kingston, Ontario, where she teaches courses in feminist theory and in applied ethics. She is the author of *Ethics and Human Reproduction: A Feminist Analysis* (Allen and Unwin, 1987) and *Human Reproduction: Principles, Practices, Policies* (Oxford University Press, 1993), and the co-editor of *Feminist Perspectives: Philosophical Essays on Method and Morals* (University of Toronto Press, 1988) and *Perspectives on AIDS: Ethical and Social Issues* (Oxford University Press, 1991).

IRVIN PECKHAM, a former high school English teacher, is now an assistant professor of English at the University of Nebraska at Omaha, where he directs the writing program. He has published essays in *English Journal* and *Composition Research/Freshman English News.* His research interest is in the sociology of genres.

ROSA MARÍA PEGUEROS is an assistant professor of history and women's studies at the University of Rhode Island specializing in modern Latin American history, particularly women's history.

WILLIAM A. PELZ is an academic historian in the Social Sciences Program at DePaul University, specializing in European and comparative labor history. He has written several books and numerous scholarly articles.

DONNA BURNS PHILLIPS is an associate professor of English and the director of the Writing across the Curriculum Program at Cleveland State University.

DEBORAH PIPER is a licensed marriage and family therapist who teaches in the Liberal Studies Program at Lesley Graduate School in Cambridge, Massachusetts, and is in private practice. She holds a doctorate in clinical psychology from Antioch/New England; much of her clinical work has focused on working with women.

MICHAEL SCHWALBE grew up on the south side of Milwaukee. He went to St. Lucas Evangelical Lutheran Grade School, Boys' Technical High School, the University of Wisconsin at Stevens Point, and Washington State University. He has taught at San Bernardino Valley College, Cal State San Bernardino, the University of California at Riverside, and North Carolina State University, where he is now an associate professor of sociology.

JOHN SUMSER was born in Pennsylvania and raised in California. He has advanced degrees in philosophy and sociology and is currently an associate professor in the Department of Communication Studies at California State University, Stanislaus. His primary interests are in mass media and the sociology of knowledge.

GLORIA D. WARREN has a B.S. in nutrition from Michigan State University. She has worked in community-based organizations and the public health sector providing education services to families in the areas of parenting, health, and nutrition. Warren is currently a doctoral candidate in family and parent education at the University of Minnesota, where she is project leader for the Graduate Student Coalition for Women of Color.